First light of the new Millennium on the West Coast of Ireland,
Old Head, Louisburgh, Co. Mayo: 8.15 a.m. 01-01-00.
Photograph – Liam Lyons.

ACKNOWLEDGEMENTS

We are grateful to the following for their enthusiastic support and encouragement throughout this project: Minister Séamus Brennan, the staff in the Millennium Office: Richard Holland, Jerry Kelleher, Eoin O'Leary, Kathlyn Butler, Nicola Carey, Sinéad Somers, Rita Byrne, Marguerite Harkin, Catherine O'Brien, Neil Carron and John Coleman; the members of the National Millennium Committee; our goods friends in the Chief Whips section; Alice Kearney, David Spencer, Mary Browne, Cathy Bruton, Frank Lahiffe, Aileen Treanor, Kim Byrne, Suzanne Hand, Sharon Keely, Gabriel Bradley, Margaret O'Brien, Michael Keane, Bobby Holland, Kevin Casey, Dympna Lyons, Ann Ormond, Bernie Maguire, Tom Collins, Peter O'Grady. The staff in the Department of the Taoiseach, in particular Eileen Dolan, Ashley Lowrey, Nick Reddy, Brendan Ward, Martin Fraser, all in Reception and Security, Finance, Personnel, Management Services and Government Information Services. And Margaret Cosgrave for the many comforting cups of coffee.

To each and every one of the project promoters, managers, co-ordinators, committees and workers, a special word of thanks is due for facilitating the production of this book. We are deeply indebted to the generous response from all those who were asked to write individual contributions. The chronicling in words and photographs of the hundreds of Millennium projects featured in this book would not have been possible without the enthusiastic involvement of organisations and communities countrywide who submitted illustrations and information. We have endeavoured to include the maximum number of these contributions and regret that it was not possible to include all of them. We wish to thank the following who were generous in contributing photographs: Laurie Campbell, Liam Lyons, Maxwell Photography, Domnick Walsh, John Eagle, Kenneth O'Halloran, Fennell Photography, MacInnes Photography, Dave Meehan Photography, Mick Quinn Photography, Bryan O'Brien, Don MacMonagle, Kieran Corrigan, John McElroy, Tony O'Connell, Ken Finegan, Clive Wasson, Frank Miller, Liam Burke Press 22, Christy Lawless, John Power, John Donohoe, Raymonde Standún, Patrick Cotter, Brendan Fogarty, BSK Photo Library, Brian Brennan, Independent Newspapers, Liam Mulcahy, Group Photographic Manager, Independent Newspapers, Peter Thursfield and Dermot O'Shea, Photographic Department, *The Irish Times*; Margaret Mary O'Mahony, RTÉ Archives; Cóilín MacLochlainn (*Releafing Ireland* magazine); In relation to specific projects featured we wish to thank: John McLoughlin, Gerry Egan, Breda Keena, Michael Carey and Michael Doyle (The People's Millennium Forests); Jim Kelly, Brenda Moriarty, Sinead O'Donoghue amd Ruth McManus (AIB); Declan McCulloch, Dorothy Barry, Kevin Dowling & Ruth Dowling (River Liffey Boardwalk); Tamsin Young & Tom Shiel (The Irish Landmark Trust) ; Ciara Boylan & Liam O'Dwyer (Children's Hour); Jay and Sandra Fox (Last Light, Florida); The National Gallery, Eugene Keane, John Harrison & Associates & Country House publishers (*Battle of the Boyne*);

Bríd McElligott, Deputy Jimmy Deenihan & Greg Ryan (Lartigue Monorail): Rosemary Yore, Susan Campbell & Turlough McKevitt (Ledwidge Cottage); Ciana Campbell & Dermot McMahon (The Scattering); Ciara Higgins (R.I.A.M. Millennium Concerts), Laura Mahoney (Genetic History of Ireland); Don Hall (Birr Castle Millennium Gardens); Christy Boylan, Leslie Moore & Fr. Edward O'Keeffe (Seismograph House); Robert Matthews M.C.D., John Butterly, Brona Cusack & Dennehy P.R. (New Year's Eve Celebrations); Neil Whoriskey (Millennium Coin); Pauline McAlyster & Willie Kealy (Veronica Guerin Memorial); Michael Forde, Rose Morris, Ultan Cowley, P.J. Leyden & Patrick Marmion (Irish World Heritage Centre); Mary Hopkins P.R. & Ray Shanahan (S.H.A.R.E. Centre), Miriam Nolan (Barretstown Gang Camp), Seamus Shields (Gascoigne House), Dorothy Gray (Bank of Ireland Millennium Scholars Trust); Peter Feeney (RTÉ "100 Years"); Ann Mulrooney, Mary Phelan and Deputy John McGuinness (Missing Persons Sculpture); Paul O'Hare (The Samaritans), Christine Buckley & Carmel McDonnell Byrne (Victims of Abuse Groves); Mary Nolan (Irish Wheelchair Association), Rose McGowan & Stuart Kenny (St. Vincent de Paul Society), Celine Curtin & Joe Saunders (Cinemobile); Geraldine Kearney (Gaiety Theatre); Marguerite Cappock & Jessica O'Donnell (Francis Bacon Studio); Area Development Management Ltd. (Millennium Recognition Awards), Vybika Dykman (Wicklow Film Trail); Eddie Breen & Paddy Power (Waterford Millennium Plaza); Lorcan O'Toole & John Marsh (Golden Eagles); Ronnie Devlin & Pat Macken (GreenTown 2000); John McEllin & Stephen Clancy (Dawn Oak 2000); Dr. Noel Kissane and Catherine Fahy, The National Library, and John P. Kelly (Write Here Write Now); Tommy Dunne (LarCon Centre), Kathryn Meghen (Sacred Places Exhibition), Brendan MacHale and Vincent Kenny (Missionary Film Archive), Johnny Groden & Breda Hyland (Murrisk Millennium Peace Park), Ben Maile, Canon Trevor Sullivan, Maolsheachlainn Ó Caollaí & Liam Furlong (Battle of Aughrim), Shay Byrne (Skyreach 2000), Brian Hosford (Millbank Theatre), Bord Failte & Michael Kennedy (Cavan-Leitrim Railway), Noel O'Connell (Donegal Hospice), Liam Reid (Bell of Inchmore), Frank Buckley (Sports Against Racism Ireland), Ian Wilson (Inishowen Maritime Museum).

The designers, Roomthree, merit our special gratitude for their extra enthusiasm and involvement.

Finally, a very special personal word of thanks and appreciation to Mary, Kathleen and Thomas Rowley for their support, understanding and, especially, patience, and Myles McWeeney too, for his patience, support and sustenance.

– Tom Rowley & Laurie Cearr *May 2002*

Contents

Foreword
An Taoiseach Bertie Ahern

One of my most abiding memories of the Millennium is of the afternoon of New Year's Eve, 1999, when the people gathered throughout Ireland to light candles and witness the last light of the 20th century and of the second Millennium. Standing on stage at the Millennium Eve Concert in Dublin's Merrion Square, I had the honour of lighting my candle from the Omagh Beacon, a flame of hope and inspiration born out of the terrible tragedy one year before in the County Tyrone town.

As the natural light slowly faded to dusk I looked out over a sea of thousands of flickering candles and realised that at that moment Millennium Candles were being lit in every corner of Ireland, in homes, churches, on streets, at crossroads, on beaches, within caring institutions, on islands and, indeed, wherever people gathered. It was a ceremony of great emotion and symbolism that reflected our strong Christian tradition and close community spirit.

In many ways the Last Light Ceremony encapsulated Ireland's approach to the Millennium, as we reached beyond the celebrations to invite everyone everywhere to participate in marking this momentous benchmark in a meaningful and memorable way.

The National Millennium Committee deserves our full gratitude for delivering such an imaginative and inclusive programme of projects and events. The flagship projects have sown the seeds for lasting legacies for generations to enjoy and the hundreds of other innovative projects will be of enduring benefit for many decades to come.

D'éist Coiste na Mílaoise go géar le muintir na hÉireann agus tríd a gcuid oibre bhí fhios acu go cruinn, creidim, céard a bhi ag teastáíl ó ollmhór na ndaoine. Smaoinigh siad, mar chloch mhíle stairiúil agus mar cheiliúradh Críostaí go raibh an Mhílaois ró-thábhachtach le giorrú i gcúpla nóiméad ar an dá thaobh de mheánoíche Chinnbhliana na Mílaoise. Shínigh clár na Mílaoise go dtí gach cearn den tír agus chlúdaigh sé gach duine de ghach aoisghrúpa agus de gach cúlra. Bhí sé go fírinneach mar Mhílaois na nDaoine.

I wish to thank the Chairman of the Committee, Minister Séamus Brennan, and the members of the Committee for their vision and commitment. The staff of the Millennium Office contributed enormously through their enthusiasm and hard work. I wish to pay tribute to those who in whatever capacity and wherever in Ireland, contributed to the success of the Millennium, not least the 34 local authority Millennium Officers.

This book gives a comprehensive account of how the Millennium was marked in Ireland. It is an important document of record and its pages offer a revealing insight into our growing maturity as a country at this landmark time in history. The people of Ireland are living through an extraordinary period of transformation, which has no precedent in our history. The population is growing fast and will probably reach four million within the next decade.

But we must have a caring society as well as an expanding and prosperous one. We must strive to further improve the standard of living and quality of life for all our citizens, with special regard for the excluded. Failure to do so would be to diminish the contributions of those whose energies and sacrifices helped shape the modern, vibrant Ireland we have today.

It is my most earnest hope as we take our first tentative steps into this new Millennium that the new understanding on this island will bring that long cherished, permanent peace and that it in turn will act as a beacon to other countries and communities searching for a peaceful future for their peoples.

Let us stride confidently into this new Millennium and embrace the challenges and opportunities it will offer us and the generations to come.

[signature]

– Bertie Ahern T.D.

Right At 4.15 p.m. on the 31 December, 1999, on stage at the Millennium Concert in Merrion Square, the Taoiseach, Bertie Ahern T.D., lit symbolic candles held by members of the armed, emergency and public services, specially chosen to represent the *family* of Ireland. Photograph – Frank Fennell Photography.

We Did It Our Way

Séamus Brennan *Chairman, National Millennium Committee*

From an objective point of view, nothing much was going to distinguish 31 December 1999, from any other late December day. All over the world, the sun would rise and set at its appointed time. Depending on the latitude, it would be warm or cold, the skies clear or cloudy, and it might rain or remain clear. But for millions upon millions of people worldwide, 31 December 1999, marked a once-in-a-lifetime experience, the passage from one century to another, the transition from the second to the third Millennium. For Irish people, given our Christian heritage, the day had a particular resonance.

As a generation we have had the unique experience of witnessing this remarkable transition in time. When you consider that a Millennium occurs only once in every forty generations you begin to get some inkling of how momentous an event it was as a global celebration.

We are privileged to be the generation fortunate enough to have witnessed this historic benchmark. The challenge to us as a nation was to commemorate it in a way that was fitting and memorable.

Ireland responded in a way that I feel emphasised our growing maturity as a nation. It was a core belief of the National Millennium Committee that we should not condense the Millennium into just parties and fireworks for a few minutes either side of midnight on New Year's Eve, 1999. To do so would have diluted its historical and spiritual significance. Nor did we try to encapsulate the significance of the Millennium through a single monument or edifice, to the exclusion of the thousands of proposals and suggestions that the Committee received.

One of the first decisions taken by the Committee was that the Millennium in Ireland should be marked in ways that were lasting, visionary, involved as many communities as possible and reflected the deep belief that this was essentially a Christian celebration. In other words, a Millennium for the people that sought to reach into every home and involve everyone everywhere. This, I feel, was achieved in ways that surpassed our most ambitious aspirations.

Having examined closely many thousands of proposals, the Millennium Committee eventually undertook to give realistic and practical support to almost 2,500 projects. These projects spread the length and breadth of the country, and embraced all strands of Ireland's social, cultural and economic heritage, ensuring that the unique Millennium milestone will be remembered well into the future. Some of the projects were very ambitious, and at least two touched every single household in the nation. The unique Last Light ceremony which involved the delivery of a special candle and a commemorative scroll to 1.28 million homes. This ceremony more than anything else captured the symbolism of the Millennium as the entire nation bore witness to the last sunset of the thousand year cycle. Later in the year these same homes received another special scroll. This one detailed the location of the native Irish tree planted in the family's name in one of 14 different People's Millennium Forests throughout the four provinces. Each tree will make a valuable contribution to what is the largest project ever undertaken to restore our precious native woodlands.

Other projects are altering and enhancing the fabric of our major cities. Dublin's Liffey Boardwalk is maximising the full amenity value of the River Liffey. Bridges are symbolic of spanning divides and uniting peoples. New Millennium bridges in Cork, Galway and Carlow will further enhance those places, while the permanent illumination of the prominent bridges in most cities will change their night-time face forever. In Limerick, one of the city's favourite landmarks, Tait's Clock in Baker Place, is being transformed.

The Christian celebration is represented in hundreds of projects, perhaps most symbolically in the illumination of scores of churches of every denomination in parishes up and down the country which have, in every sense, become beacons in the night.

Ón gcéad lá bhí orainn cothromaíocht a fháil idir an Mhílaois mar cheiliúradh Críostaí agus na fleánna a bhriseann amach go cinniúnach, tráth go sroichtear féile chomh hollmhór agus chomh stairiúil sin. Cuireann sé an-áthas orm ach go háirithe, gur i lár an bhfuadair agus an tnúth a ginneadh trén Mhílaois go raibh traidisiún bródúil na hÉireann mar náisiún Críostaí aitheanta agus athneartaithe.

Recognition was a theme central to the work of the Millennium Committee. What better way to mark a nation's progress at such an historic time than to recognise in a tangible way such projects as the Irish World Heritage Centre in Manchester and those whose energy and sacrifices, whether at home or as exiles, helped shape the modern, vibrant Ireland of today.

Other projects are attempting to repair the damage of the past and improve the environment. Future generations will, I feel, have reason to be thankful that Ireland looked beyond fireworks and parties when finalising this generation's Millennium response as they walk in the cool shade of a People's Forest, take time for reflection at the Croagh Patrick Peace Park, visit beautiful, rugged headlands to see the restored lighthouse properties or watch a majestic Golden Eagle soaring in the sky for the first time in a century.

But perhaps of even greater importance is the fact that a great many of Ireland's Millennium projects reached right into the very heart of score upon score of our smaller communities. Thanks to the Millennium Recognition Awards and the Millennium Events Awards, well over 2,000 different events and projects were identified by the 34 County Millennium Officers. It didn't matter that projects ranged from the ambitious, as in providing sheltered housing and day-care facilities for the elderly in a community, to the small-scale, such as developing a garden in a village – what counted was the energy, dedication and commitment of the community promoting the scheme.

I wish to express my sincere gratitude to each member of the National Millennium Committee. They gave selflessly of their time and it is thanks to their enthusiasm and dedication we have such an innovative programme of lasting Millennium projects. A committee faced with such a daunting challenge can only function effectively if it has the support of a committed and hard-working support team. The Millennium Office responded to the challenge and worked tirelessly, often under extreme pressure, to ensure that the programme devised was turned into reality.

The Millennium Officers in each county deserve our gratitude. They were the people in touch with what was happening locally and their contribution was central to the overall success of the Millennium. A special word of thanks is due to organisations and people the length and breadth of Ireland for recognising its significance and responding with initiatives that will continue to enrich their communities.

This book outlines the story of the Millennium in Ireland. Through descriptions of projects, photographs and incisive observations from contributors, it builds into a comprehensive record of a unique event. Perhaps most important of all, it charts how, what began for many as a much hyped opportunity for parties and champagne, evolved into a sensitive celebration at national level that truly was the People's Millennium. The editors, Tom Rowley and Laurie Cearr, are to be complimented on compiling such a compelling and readable account of our Millennium.

Beidh iombualadh na hÉireann nuair a mharcálu an Mhílaois le sonrú i gcathracha, i mbailte agus i sráidbhailte go ceann i bhfad. Agus i bhForaoisí Mílaoise na nDaoine creidim go bhfuil tionscnamh sainiúil ag Éirinn nuair a smaoiníonn tú go bhféadfadh na crainn atá ag fás anois, nó a sliocht, a bheith ina seasamh ag deireadh na Mílaoise seo.

I feel Ireland's response to the Millennium is something we can all be proud of because, above all else, we had the confidence to do it our way.

Séamus Brennan

– Séamus Brennan T.D.
Chairman, National Millennium Committee

01 Flagship Projects

Flagship Projects

> The Millennium in Ireland was about people, and the desire to include the whole population in the commemoration and marking of this historic event. The celebration year began with the Last Light Ceremony and the special Millennium Candles, symbols of light, hope and peace, being delivered to 1.28 million households in the country as enduring gifts; it ended with native broadleaf trees being planted in the name of every household in the country. These trees represent strength, growth and regeneration and will be permanent reminders of the Millennium pledge to help rescue and restore our vanishing native woodlands.

The **Last Light Ceremony** and **The People's Millennium Forests** were just two of six special "flagship" projects selected by the National Millennium Committee. The six were designated flagship undertakings because they touched the lives of a broader community than some of the other popular initiatives supported by the Committee, and because they had a special resonance for us as a people and a nation.

Bhí na crainnte riamh anall mar chuid buanseasmhach de thírdhreach, oidhreacht agus béaloideas na hÉireann, ar feadh na mílte bliain. Ár bhforaoiseanna agus ár dtailte coille dúchasacha a bhí íontach tráth dá raibh, faraor, tá siad ag dul i léig de réir a chéile agus anois i mórán cásanna níl ach fuilligh fágtha. Tá tionscnamh Foraois- eanna Mílaoise na nDaoine ag tosnú ar an tarrtháil agus ar athchóiriú na bhforaoiseanna dúchasacha.

Tá an fhreagarthacht orainne agus ar na glúinte atá le teacht, iad a chaomhnú agus leanacht leis an athchóiriú

ins na blianta agus na céadta atá romhainn amach. Mar a scríobhann an Dr. John Feehan in áit eile sa leabhair seo; "We need the vision to plant for a future where trees become again the measure of the land."

The Children's Hour, for instance, showed once again how Irish people have always responded with generosity and unselfishness to help others less fortunate. The initiative, conceived by the Irish Youth Foundation, asked workers to contribute one hour's pay to help under-privileged children. Thousands upon thousands of workers, realising that our children are our future, rowed in behind the concept to the tune of €2,539,476 (IR£2million), a sum matched by the National Millennium Committee. The money will help a number of nationally prominent organisations dedicated to helping socially and educationally deprived Irish youngsters achieve their full potential.

The Millennium has given us all the opportunity to reflect on our sometimes unhappy and tortuous history and how, as we embark on a new century, our leaders have the

opportunity to forge a lasting peace. With this in mind, the Millennium Committee supported the move to take the site of the **Battle of the Boyne** into state ownership and dedicate it to peace and understanding between the two traditions on this island.

Another flagship project that extends to all parts of the island is **The Irish Landmark Trust** undertaking to restore five historic lightkeeper's cottages. Ireland has a rich maritime heritage, but, with the automation of the lighthouses that saved thousands of mariners' lives over the centuries, the associated buildings where lightkeepers lived while carrying out their essential duties, no matter how foul the weather, are in danger of crumbling away and being forgotten. The project extends from Galley Head in Co. Cork to Black Head in Co. Antrim and incorporates the preservation of the flora and fauna on these wild promontories.

Dublin's River Liffey is the focus of the sixth flagship project. Unlike many European cities built on a river, Dublin has never had a city-centre recreation area alongside the Liffey until now. **The Liffey Boardwalk**, an elegant structure suspended over the river, has been a popular success with both citizens and tourists, and a magnetic attraction for workers on their lunch hour.

Opposite Page Native broadleaf woodland. Photograph – Aileen O'Sullivan.

The People's Millennium Forests

> The People's Millennium Forests will stand as a testament that this generation cared about our natural heritage and aspired to undo some of the damage inflicted on it over previous Millennia. The planting of a native Irish tree in the name of every household in the country and sending each household their own personalised certificate will foster a sense of responsibility and ownership that can only be of enormous benefit in the long-term protection and enhancement of our environment.

Fifteen hundred acres of native Irish woodlands have been designated as The People's Millennium Forests in which 1.2 million trees have been planted, one for every household in the country. The undertaking includes a number of forests which have been extended and the restoration of existing native woodlands under threat of extinction.

Signs at each of the forests will clearly indicate the number and location of the household trees. The native trees now growing are oak (sessile and pedunculate), ash, birch, alder, hazel, yew and Scots pine. The forests will grow and mature in harmony with nature but it is in the decades to come that we will see the full benefits of this visionary initiative.

One can only imagine the magic of these rejuvenated forests during seasonal rambles: great oaks forming a natural canopy, the dappled sunlight seeping through the branches and all around a carpet of bluebells and moss upholstered rocks. This very ambitious €6,348,690 (IR£5 million) project is sponsored by the National Millennium Committee, AIB and the Forest Service.

It is being managed by Coillte in partnership with the Woodlands of Ireland Group and has the strong support of environmental organisations.

It is the strong belief of all those involved in the project that the planting of the new trees, combined with conservation of existing forests and the education of the next generation about the value of our native forests, will leave a valuable and lasting legacy for future generations.

Above all it will show that this generation cared about our natural heritage. Future generations will look back to the year 2000 as the year when a positive statement was acted upon, signifying the development and rehabilitation of our native woodlands for the benefit of us all.

Right Map showing the location of the forests in which the trees for each household are planted and the nearest towns to these forests.

Opposite Page A mature native woodland scene.

Photograph – Wild Ireland Magazine.

the people's millennium forests

sponsored by

2000 IRELAND   AIB

- Derrygorry
- Sligo
- Monaghan
- Cullentra
- Tourmakeady Wood
- Tourmakeady
- Portlick
- Athlone
- Loughrea
- Rosturra
- Derrygill
- Lacca
- Ballygannon
- Mountrath
- Rathdrum
- Shelten
- Choill an Fhaltaigh
- Kilkenny
- Cahir
- Camolin Park
- Enniscorthy
- Glengarra
- Killarney
- Mucross
- Killgarvan
- Rossacroo-na-loo

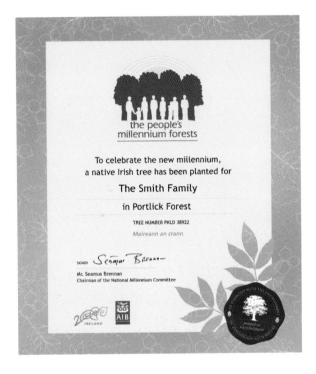

Lochlann Quinn

> Millennium Committee Favourites

For me the most important project was **The People's Millennium Forests**. Different strands of the idea came in from about five different sources. When we on the Millennium Committee assembled it together we realised the costs were going to be substantial, so I got AIB to come in along with us. The bank's involvement, along with that of Coillte, was what put the deal together. There are three things about it that make it my favourite. The first is that trees are likely to last a very long time, so it is a permanent monument to the Millennium event.

Secondly, trees are the sort of thing we should be planting to improve our environment. Thirdly, I thought it was a lovely idea to allocate a specific tree to every household in the country. It made the concept personal and inclusive. I was really surprised at the number of people who have literally stopped me in the street and thanked me, saying it was such a nice idea.

I was also very taken by the scheme that restored a number of disused lighthouse properties around the coastline, including two in Northern Ireland. This was a project initiated by Nick Robinson and the idea was to turn these landmarks into places to which people could come and stay, giving the properties a new lease of life and purpose in these days of satellite navigation.

I was impressed too by the project in Waterford that utilised a pontoon to create an open-air theatre and concert area. Waterford has a real waterfront and lives along the edge of the harbour more than any other city in Ireland that I know of. This ambitious project now makes the quays even more the focus of the city's community life.

– Lochlann Quinn *Chairman AIB Group and Member of the National Millennium Committee*

Right Only the best will do. The selection of the best acorns for The People's Millennium Forests at Coillte Nursery, Aughrim, Co. Wicklow.

Éamon de Buitléar.

Hundreds of thousands of acorns have been planted as part of The People's Millennium Forests project. In years to come these forests will provide wonderful habitats for the many plants and animals which choose to live in our magic woodlands.

– Éamon de Buitléar

(Extract from *"Magic Woodlands",* an information video on The People's Millennium Forests which was distributed to schools.)

Photograph – RTÉ Archive Stills Collection.

John McLoughlin in Rossacroo-Na-Loo Wood, Co. Kerry.

> A Personal Note

Since I began working with The People's Millennium Forests Project I have often been asked: "How long do native trees live for?" I say to people the question we ought to ask is "How long do forests live for?" A tree's natural environment is the forest and provided there is no major climatic change or human intervention, forests continue to renew themselves. Our problem is that today we have only remnants of our native woods. How do we manage to create a native forest again? The People's Millennium Forests Project provided the answer. So we collected native tree seeds in the autumns of 1999 and 2000, sowed them in poly-tunnels and planted them out in the forests in late 2000 and 2001. We planted more than 1.2 million trees in the Republic and 200,000 at two sites in Northern Ireland. Deer, rabbits, hares, goats and domestic animals are a menace when trying to regenerate

a forest or to plant a new one and so the newly planted trees had to be fenced against grazing animals. The planting of more than 1.4 million trees was a very big task and it didn't end there. There are other elements to the project – a mobile exhibition visiting shows and large towns and a schools outreach programme with three officers visiting primary schools.

The nicest part of the project was the interaction with the public, in particular the hundreds of queries about the household certificate. People who did not receive a certificate rang the office looking for one; some people could not understand why we were not sending them the tree directly and others did not want the tree sent as they had no space for it. Then there was the chaos of relationships, one woman who had lost her husband got married again but wanted her maiden name included with her other two names, and we did it. We also had to deal with people who wished to see the tree immediately, advising them to wait until the trees were a little stronger. All in all it was a wonderful experience and 99.9% of callers went off happy – not a bad result!

Today we know a lot about woodland dynamics and with this knowledge we can protect and enhance our native woodlands. What we have created with The People's Millennium Forests will survive into the next Millennium and will bring joy to many generations. Now to answer the question – woodlands live forever!

– John McLoughlin *Project Manager*
The People's Millennium Forests

> Millennium Committee Favourites

Patricia O'Donovan

My favourite Millennium project was **The People's Millennium Forests**. It is the one I feel represents most accurately the approach of the National Millennium Committee, which was to leave some long-lasting benefits for future generations rather than splashing out and spending all the resources on some big party events. I think that this project had broad appeal across all sections of Irish society. There is a growing awareness of the importance of the environment and the contribution that our native Irish trees make to it, as they fit so harmoniously into our landscape. The project also reinforces the message that protecting the environment requires long-term commitment and that investment is needed now for the future.

What made the project so wonderful was that it was all-inclusive. Every household the length and breadth of the country benefited from the event, including people who did not fit the standard definition of a household.

– Patricia O'Donovan *Former Deputy Secretary ICTU and Member of The National Millennium Committee*

Opposite Page From little acorns … the Millennium trees growing at the Coillte Nursery, Aughrim, Co. Wicklow, in May 2000 as eight-year-old Laura Byrne shows a sample of the acorns used.

Dr. John Feehan

> The Spirit of Trees

When the first people arrived in Ireland, nine thousand years ago or so, it was not yet an island, and had scarcely recovered from the long ages during which it lay in the grip of snow and ice. The woodlands, which are the natural vegetation cover for our part of the world, had not yet established themselves. Only gradually did the trees return to Ireland's furthermost north-western outpost: willow, birch and pine at first, the dominant trees of colder climes, and then, later, oak and elm, alder and hazel, and, finally, ash. As succeeding species of colonising trees joined those that had already arrived, Irish society was undergoing its own progression through the ages of stone and bronze and iron. Irish society, in other words, evolved with the woods themselves, advancing and retreating as new technology made fresh progress possible, or the setback of climatic decline or war threw it into reverse. The main cultures of this island grew up in the company of trees. They provided us with most of what we needed for building and farming and food for ourselves and our animals. And, on a deeper level, they provided security and pleasure. The cultural landscape has always been a landscape where people grew up with trees and woods. We are genetically programmed to spend our lives among trees. Our spirit declines in their absence.

The period following the collapse of the Gaelic economy in the 16th century saw the extinction of the woodlands that at one time surrounded and embraced every townland. As the population soared in the 18th and into the 19th centuries, trees disappeared from the Irish landscape, which became treeless to an extent we could hardly credit today were it not for the numerous accounts left by travellers.

The century upon which we have just closed the door saw an improvement, at least in the sense that the percentage of tree cover began to increase, but these were mostly regimented alien conifers. Only in recent decades have new policies rekindled the hope that Ireland can regain its lost woodlands. The measure of that recovery is not simply the total area under elm, oak, ash, pine, willow, hazel and other native trees which have a special claim upon the landscape because they made it their own without our help; it must also be the extent to which trees and woods become again part of our lives, and especially the lives of our young, from whose everyday experience they have largely been absent for so long.

Today, we are trying to restore the richness of trees to our experience because a world without woods is a world without healing for the human spirit. They are part of what we are. Groves have stood at the edge of mystery in the human psyche from the dawn of human awareness. In the past everybody knew trees by their names. Today, children know every star of television, cinema, the pop charts and sport, but no trees: yet anonymous trees people their dreams, and will people the dreams of their own children even if the last woods have vanished from the earth.

In our time we are discovering the values of woods and trees in new ways, and seeking to preserve them as the great repositories of biodiversity, and because of a newly awakened awareness of the many different ways in which they are important to our welfare. More than ever do we need to learn to treasure the few old woods we have left as the sacred places they have always been for the human soul, and especially to nurture new woods where we can fall in love again with trees.

We need the vision to plant for a future where trees become again the measure of the land, and for a future that reaches even beyond this Millennium, for a yew tree can live for a thousand years. And the great hope of The People's Millennium Forests is that such an Ireland, where trees and substantial woods frame every view, can and will once again be ours.

– Dr. John Feehan *Department of Environmental Resource Management, University College Dublin*

Anything that makes the general public more aware of their environment, and more interested in protecting it, must be beneficial. Planting a tree for every household is a fine gesture.

Editorial *The Irish Times, 8 November, 2000*

Left Collecting the seed. **1** The saplings appear. **2** John Bardon caring for the young trees at Coillte Nursery, Aughrim, Co. Wicklow. **3** The O'Leary Family from Killarney, Co. Kerry, are first to receive the household tree certificate from the Taoiseach, Bertie Ahern.

In early Ireland there was a saying that expresses the belief that nothing living was older or more venerable than the ancient yews, the centuries of whose lives had grown to Millennia in forests which today whisper only in relics of placenames from Newry to Youghal to County Mayo.

They are the measure of the land:

Trí cúaille fáil, cú…
Trí cú, each…
Trí eich, duine…
Trí daoine, iolar…
Trí iolair, bradán…
Trí bradáin, iubhair…
Trí iubhair, eitre…
Trí eitreacha ó thús an domhain go deireadh an domhain.

The lives of three wattles (hurdles used to fill a gap in a hedge) equals the life of one hound

The lives of three hounds is the lifetime of one horse

The lives of three horses is the lifetime of one human being

Three human generations pass in the lifetime of an eagle

A salmon's life lasts for three generations of eagles

The life of a single yew tree is as long as three generations of salmons

Nothing that lives is older than a yew

Only a ridge on the land survives three generations of yews

And the duration of three ridges is all the time from the beginning of the world to its end.

– Dr. John Feehan

> A Personal Note

Mick Lally in Tourmakeady Wood

I was born and reared about a half a mile from Tourmakeady Wood in a place called *Doire an Mhíanaigh* – *Doire*, being an oak-wood; a common Irish place-name, and *Míanach* meaning well-bred and strong. So, *Doire an Mhíanaigh* probably means the good oak-wood. The place-name has been anglicised and is now generally referred to as Derryveeney.

When I was growing up in the fifties, Tourmakeady was the local centre of commerce and social activity. It had the church – two, in fact – the main shop and pub, the post-office, the dance-hall, and also the school. To get to any of these amenities from Derryveeney involved a journey of nearly three miles by road; but by taking the short-cut through "the wood", the journey was shortened considerably.

At a time when cycling or walking was the usual mode of transport, this short-cut was of great importance. It didn't matter that there was another which was probably shorter, the short-cut through the wood was the one that mattered and much more exciting. It was full of mystery and strangeness, and afforded all sorts of possibilities for fun and imaginative adventure.

It was also full of danger and our parents were always warning us to keep out of it. The river running through it was very deep and treacherous in places and God knows what would happen if someone fell in.

And then there was the waterfall. Now this indeed was a dangerous place where serious injury might occur. The terrain was very hilly and uneven and full of tree stumps, roots, fallen branches, rocks and stones, and the narrow footpath ran directly beside a sheer drop to the bottom of the waterfall some 20 or 30 yards below. It drew us youngsters like magnets with its array of opportunities for daring and devilment and all manner of bravery and bravado.

Apart from its exotic pleasures and unfulfilled dangers, the wood also provided benefits of a more mundane nature - firewood. Wet summers often meant that turf or peat, our main source of heat, was scarce, and the wood provided the shortfall. She was rarely found wanting. At times like this my father would bring me along to help cut some branches or indeed, on many occasions, to cut down some fine tall trees. We would go into the wood armed with a good sharp hatchet and crosscut (a long two-handled saw), and cut down whatever tree my father picked out. In hindsight I think he was more ecologically minded than he realised, as generally he would pick a tree "that would fall in the next storm anyway!" From him, I learned the names of the various trees – oak, beech, birch, spruce, ash, larch, sycamore and indeed many more.

Over the years I've seen the wood change. In the mid fifties it was completely laid bare, the native and the semi-native trees were cut down, sawn into planks and sold off. It was then replanted with evergreen conifers which altered the look and atmosphere of the wood. More recently, these in turn have been cut down and sold off for various purposes. It is now being re-planted with the more familiar broadleaf native trees which in time will restore its original look and atmosphere.

Well, the river still runs interminably, bringing waters down from the streams and rivers of the nearby hills and mountains. The waterfall still cascades, sometimes in raging torrents, other times with an amazing passivity as if it were almost at a standstill. It is now the backdrop to almost every wedding picture in the locality and this is only fitting. All woods are romantic and Tourmakeady Wood is no different. Over the decades romantic trysts were not unknown in its environs. It is commonly held that Éamonn de Valera and Sinéad (Ní Fhlanagáin) would sojourn there when Sinéad was teaching at the nearby Irish language Coláiste Chonnacht.

Tourmakeady is now a People's Millennium wood; a far cry from its early days when, as the private property of the local landlord, any incursion by local peasantry was at best, discouraged, if not actually forbidden. *G' maire sí buan!*

– Mick Lally *Actor*

Opposite Page In time The People's Millennium Forests will grow into mature native woodlands like this one where flora and fauna will thrive with the trees. Photograph – Mike Hartwell.

Last Light Ceremony

> For most of New Year's Eve, 1999, fog and cloud shrouded Dursey Head in Co. Cork, the place where the sun would set on Ireland for the last time in the 20th century and the second Millennium. Then suddenly, as the last minutes of daylight ticked away, the fog lifted and the clouds parted, revealing a spectacular sight as the dazzling orange ball of sun sank towards the distant horizon.

This vivid and striking scene was a fitting climax to the most symbolic, sensitive and emotive of Millennium events in Ireland, the Last Light Ceremony.

While most countries were happy to concentrate solely on spectacular fireworks and non-stop parties, Ireland used this simple ceremony to involve everyone, irrespective of age, location, health or belief, in a moving farewell to the old Millennium and a light-filled welcome to the new.

In the weeks leading up to the event, a Millennium Candle and scroll, gifts from the National Millennium Committee, had been sent for delivery to more than 1.2 million households in the country. The candle was to be lit as the sun sank for the last time on the second Millennium, while all those who shared in the unique moment were encouraged to sign the scroll.

Shortly after 4 p.m., the natural light began gradually to fade. Daylight slowly melted into the greyness of dusk and as the minutes slipped by dusk gave way to darkness. Across Ireland, in cities, towns, villages and at crossroads,

candles flickered in a national wave of nostalgia mixed with celebration and anticipation.

At Áras an Uachtaráin, President Mary McAleese led a live television ceremony to celebrate the lighting of the first candle. At 4.15 p.m. the Taoiseach, Bertie Ahern, before a crowd of 25,000 in Merrion Square, lit his candle from the Omagh Flame, itself a symbol of hoped born out of terrible tragedy. He quoted Kerry writer Bryan McMahon: "Mention the word candlelight and a host of memories – sacred, romantic, nostalgic, sentimental, dramatic, joyous and sorrowful – bombard the mind."

And then, right across Ireland, people joined their families and friends, either privately or in specially organised community events, to light their Millennium Candles. Everywhere there was a strong sense of spirituality, of mysticism as the flame was passed from candle to candle. Families that might otherwise be scattered on New Year's Eve remained together so that they could be part of this special ceremony.

Ireland's important international role as a peacekeeper abroad meant that some who wished to be home on this special day could not be. But they were not forgotten. In the Lebanon, a special overseas enactment of the Last Light Ceremony was held at twilight in Tor-on, a 900-year-old Crusader Castle in the village of Tibnin, headquarters of the Irish Battalion. Irish people living abroad also joined in the ceremony, many using Millennium Candles sent to them by close relatives.

Anecdotal evidence collected since clearly shows the Last Light Ceremony had a profound effect right across the country. It united communities, repaired differences, created magical memories and generally evoked a sense of peace and hope. Most remember it as a simple, moving and beautiful occasion that was unique to Ireland.

Above The Millennium Candle and Last Light in Florida.
Opposite Page The Millennium Candle, symbolising light, hope and peace.

>Millennium Committee Favourites

Very early in the life of the National Millennium Committee we had to make two major decisions. The first one was to reject the idea of spending the entire €41,901,356 (IR£33 million) allocation on one major landmark statement; the second was to reject the idea of having the biggest party Ireland had ever seen. I was always against the idea of a big party, but I must say I did like the idea of a landmark statement, and I had my own idea. I wanted to create, in Dublin Bay, the world's tallest fountain jet of water.

In retrospect I'm very pleased with the route we took. Ireland celebrated the Millennium on a very human, Christian and personal level, from the symbolic **Last Light Ceremony** on New Year's Eve to The People's Millennium Forests. Every household in the country has been involved in some way, so our celebrations have been very inclusive and binding for the nation as a whole, much more so than any other country I know of.

I thought the Millennium Candle was a wonderful idea. Everywhere I go, in almost every house I visit, people point to the candle on the mantelpiece and show me the scroll that came with it, signed by all the members of their family who were with them on New Year's Eve, 1999. It's like an heirloom. I'm proud of what the Committee did and I'm very proud, too, that we as a people had the maturity and the confidence to do it our way.

– Séamus Brennan *T.D. Minister for State to the Taoiseach, Government Chief Whip and Chairman of the National Millennium Committee*

At Dursey Head in West Cork, the Last Light faded. Ireland watched a spectacular orange sun sink into the Atlantic, catching its breath at the picture postcard beauty of the scene. That moment of noble stillness was worth any amount of Millennium millions.

– Miriam Lord *Irish Independent*

Above This photograph, taken from RTÉ television coverage at Dursey Head, captures the unique image of the sun sinking on Ireland for the last time in the 20th century and the second Millennium.

Centre Mrs. Sarah Seawright, then 102 years old, helped Minister Brennan at the national launch of the Last Light Ceremony.

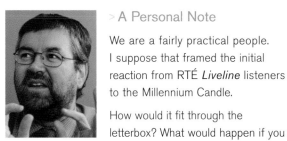

Joe Duffy

> A Personal Note

We are a fairly practical people. I suppose that framed the initial reaction from RTÉ *Liveline* listeners to the Millennium Candle.

How would it fit through the letterbox? What would happen if you were not at home? What about the postal staff lugging these lumps of wax over their already strained shoulders? Would the candles be made in Ireland?

Practical questions from a Viking nation, who invented the spade, got used to calling a spade a spade and using it as such. We thought the candle was a bad idea, but wondered how we would get it anyway. Maybe it had a practical use after all. But of course at the end of the day the little candle was much bigger than that. It transcended, it glowed without even being ignited.

Because, like all great ideas, the Millennium Candle lit people's imagination. And magnificently, on New Year's Eve it wasn't the dawn that captured people, it was the dusk!

Remember it was the sun that dominated the last ten days of the 20th century — beginning on 22 December with the glorious uplift of the sun rising at Newgrange through the 5,000-year-old lintel to illuminate the central chamber. This was witnessed by unprecedented numbers live on national television showing what a wonderful imaginative impractical people we were after all — long before the Vikings ever slung a spade over their shoulders …

And Newgrange worked — just like it did 5,000 years ago — no Y-2K bug there!! I think it set the scene for the success of the simple Millennium Candle.

Here we were on the western edge of Western Europe where the sun would slice the Atlantic for the last time and we could all participate. The small candle became a big idea. On New Year's Day, *Liveline* was the first live programme on RTÉ for the new Millennium and what did our listeners want to talk about?

The Millennium Candle.
How it was such a brilliant idea.
How it lit the spot.
Simple ideas work with imagination.
One match and the candle worked.
One imagination and it lived, straddling two Millennia.

– Joe Duffy *Broadcaster*

Above Joining in the Last Light Ceremony.

When Time began to rant and rage
The measure of her flying feet
Made Ireland's heart begin to beat;
And Time bade all his candles flare
To light a measure here and there;

– W.B. Yeats *"To Ireland in the Coming Times"*

Above A gift to every household ... the Millennium Candle, scroll and presentation box.

Opposite Page 4.41 p.m. 31 December, 1999, at Dursey Head, Co. Cork. As the sun sets for the last time in the second Millennium, Mrs Maud Lewis, Church of Ireland Deacon, Castletownbere and Fr. Liam Comer, Parish Priest, light the Millennium Candle. Uilleann piper, Brendan Ring, from Bonane, plays "An Aisling Geal".

> Millennium Committee Favourites

From a personal point of view I have to admit that *The Children's Book* project was *primus inter pares*, the first among equals, for me. It was a real privilege to conceive something and be able to follow it through to a successful conclusion. It gave me a great thrill to watch it grow all the way from just an idea to a physical reality that will still be around in a thousand years from now, held in the archives of the National Library in Dublin.

The book is really beautiful, 23 exquisitely bound volumes of hand-written manuscripts from schoolchildren around the country, about their own lives. Their words are unmediated and unedited by any adults, so it is a snapshot of Ireland as it was on 12 May, 1999. Most of the children wrote for someone reading their words a thousand years from now, so they were telling their descendants exactly what it was like to be alive in 1999. One hundred thousand contributions were received and one was chosen, at random, from each class of each school that submitted entries. The book contains about 2,500 individual essays. It was a huge but enormously satisfying project and entailed an enormous amount of effort, particularly on the part of teachers.

I also thought that the idea of re-introducing the Golden Eagle to Donegal was wonderfully imaginative and important.

Of the many other projects, one that captured my imagination was the **Last Light Ceremony** on New Year's Eve, 1999. I thought it captured to perfection what our take on the Millennium celebrations was all about. I thought it was deeply significant on a number of levels, emotional and spiritual. The candles, as a universal symbol of light, brought an awe-inspiring, contemplative dimension to the ceremony. I think it made people stop and think for a moment about where we, as a people, had come from and where we were going.

–Deirdre Purcell *Author and Member of the National Millennium Committee*

> Letter to the Irish Times

14 January, 2000

Sir, - Asked to speak at the Nollaig na mBan dinner in a Vancouver hotel, I concluded my remarks by describing the candle ceremony at sunset on New Year's Eve in homes throughout Ireland. I then lit my candle, which I had brought back with me from Dublin, and was about to take it back to my table when it was taken from my hands. It was not returned to me until it had been held, with some emotion, by every one of the 120 women in the room.

Mr Brennan, on behalf of the Irish women of Vancouver, thank you for your Millennium Candle.

- Yours, etc.,

– Mary Hatch *Irish Women's Network of British Columbia, Avenue Delta, Vancouver, Canada*

> A Personal Note

In the aftermath of the Omagh atrocity in August 1998, the people of Omagh received the perfect pick-me-up with the news that the United Kingdom Millennium Celebrations were to be launched at an open-air concert in the Omagh Showgrounds. Months of meticulous planning culminated in a concert attended by 30,000 people, and by civic leaders from across Northern Ireland and the rest of the United Kingdom, and the ceremonial lighting of the Millennium Beacon from which all the other beacons across the UK were subsequently lit.

Then from the National Millennium Committee in Dublin another prestigious invitation arrived for myself as Chairman of Omagh District Council, together with my grandchildren, to extend the Beacon of Light to the greater part of Ireland, the 26 counties. This I readily accepted because, over a number of years, I had built up a strong relationship within the ploughing fraternity and, in later times, as a result of our unforgettable experiences in Omagh. Many people from the Republic, amongst them many notable and important personages, one of course being the Taoiseach, Bertie Ahern, had poured out their hearts to the grieving and injured families in messages and monetary terms.

Three of my grandchildren, Bethany, Hannah and Clive, accompanied me on what was to be an eventful trip to Dublin. Whatever the original plan had been for the handing over of a flame from Omagh, it was, I believe, quickly put to one side. Bethany, together with Hannah and Clive, was soon the centre of media attention, making the unforgettable presentation and leaving the Chairman of Omagh District Council very much in the background, something I approved of. Here we experienced the innocence of a child meeting the most powerful man in Southern Ireland, offering him the flame of light, which symbolised the drawing to a close of a past era and the beginning of a new Millennium with the simple belief in her heart that this was a man in whom she could place her trust. Likewise the humility of the Taoiseach graciously receiving it and publicly demonstrating that in receiving the gift, pledging a trust to be "your Guardian, not just for this year but the many more to come in your young and tender life."

Well, things did not stop there. Amid all the excitement of meals and sightseeing tours in Dublin I left my Chain of Office in a taxi. Panic had well and truly set in and there was nothing to be done except call in the Gardaí, all the time thinking the next morning's news headlines could be "Orangeman Mislays Council Chairman's Chain in Dublin!" The good news was that by 6.00am the Gardaí were back with everything accounted for. And, when we came down to our breakfast, the newspaper headlines were very different to what I had envisaged. Bethany, Hannah and Clive, together with the Taoiseach, looked out from the front page. Well, I think it is a story that will go down in the history books. Every time I see Bertie heading up a coming together of minds to move our situation forward that little bit further, I always reflect on the day and night spent in Dublin. They were without doubt two of the highlights of my term of office. It clearly demonstrated to the watching world that, in the face of horrific adversity, the people of Omagh had emerged a stronger and more united community and that those who, by their actions, sought to destroy the very fabric of our community had succeeded only in strengthening the resolve of the people of Omagh to build a better future for everyone.

– Councillor Allan Rainey *Chairman, Omagh District Council, 1999-2000*

Opposite Page Bethany Rainey, from Omagh, enjoying the media attention alongside the Taoiseach, Bertie Ahern, after he had lit her Millennium Candle from the Omagh Beacon. Photograph – Maxwells.

Left Councillor Allan Rainey, at the reception to welcome the Omagh Beacon to Dublin, with his grandchildren, Clive, Hannah and Bethany, and Minister Brennan.

River Liffey Boardwalk

> Almost every cosmopolitan city has its own promenade, a meeting place to relax and stroll, away from the bustle of traffic and the rush of crowds. Dublin now joins these cities with an amenity that has transformed the city centre area, maximising the recreational appeal of the famous River Liffey.

Millennium Committee Award €1,904,607 (IR£1.5 million)

The Liffey Boardwalk stretches one third of a mile along the North quays from O'Connell Bridge to Grattan (Capel St. Bridge. It is 4 metres (13 feet) wide and 560 metres (1,837 feet) in length and is accessible from four bridges – O'Connell, Ha'penny, Millennium Bridge and Grattan. The emphasis throughout is on relaxation, with benches at fixed intervals and permanent kiosks dispensing refreshments. The Boardwalk is illuminated by a state-of-the-art lighting system and protected on the riverside by a 1.15 metre high balustrade boundary.

David Norris

> ## A Personal Note

Long before the Millennium, when I was young in the 1950s, there was a song called "Under the Boardwalk". We all sang along although we didn't quite know what a boardwalk was. We associated it with the remote glamour of America, Atlantic City, and Venice Beach, California. Little did we think that one day

as part of our Millennial celebrations we too, in Dublin, would have our very own boardwalk. Dublin is spectacularly lucky in its setting with the mountains as a backdrop and a gently curving bay that stretches out to welcome visitors to the city, and our own unique river Anna Liffey, whose waters were reputed to be the single, most potent and magic ingredient of Guinness's stout. But the river itself was usually neglected, dirty, polluted and stinking to high heaven, especially at low tide.

Although it was celebrated in a series of Jack B. Yeats paintings of people waiting wearily on the quayside for a country bus or leaning hungrily over to watch the Liffey Swim, the river was usually held in affectionate contempt. In fact, until comparatively recently the city looked on the river as a fairly convenient sewer. Joyce in *Ulysses* makes fun of this when in the middle of all the obeisance and homage which greets the Vice-Regal cavalcade in the Wandering Rocks episode, the poor little Poddle River, bottled up and culverted away, emerges triumphantly from the quay wall under Tom Devan's "hanging out in fealty a tongue of liquid sewage" and blowing a raspberry at the Empire.

Up till the sixties, seventies and even the eighties, there was a certain bustle amid the decay on the quays. On the Bachelors' Walk side there was a proliferation of auctioneers; Tormey's, Scally's, Butler's, Balfe's, Cox's (who in my memory announced their auction with a hand bell) and Lawlor Briscoe's (now the Zanzibar), with up-market furnishing materials in the front and auctions at the back, while on the other side of the quays there were the book-shops beloved of Joyce. On our new boardwalk the signs are promising, spaces are allocated for booksellers so that, perhaps, the banks of the Liffey will become a haunt for "Le Bouqinistes", those little Parisian stallholders who sell books and paintings on the banks of the Seine. With the development of the boardwalk we are placing ourselves in a position to appreciate the advantages of our capital's river. Until now we have only had the various bridges, including the Ha'penny Bridge and the wonderful, modern pedestrian bridge, from which to let our eyes roam over the expanse of the river. And from these what wonderful sunsets can be seen; for it is not only Japanese tourists with their cameras who appreciate the very special light of Dublin. And it is very tempting. I have strolled on the boardwalk and I can testify that what looked initially a slightly daft idea is now a real success and well on the way to being adopted by Dubliners and tourists alike as one of the city's special treats.

– David Norris *Senator and Joycean Scholar*

Opposite Page The Liffey Boardwalk. Photograph – Gary Jordan.

> A Personal Note

We all know the words of the Dublin Saunter:

Dublin can be Heaven
With coffee at eleven
And a stroll down Stephen's Green
And …
Grafton Street's a wonderland
With magic in the air

I believe with the opening of the wonderful Liffey Boardwalk on the Northside of the river we now have a rival to the Dublin Saunter. I fully expect this riverside walk will become synonymous with Dublin and find its way into verse and song. Dublin Corporation is proud to have originated the concept of a boardwalk and to prove once again it has the vision and imagination to make our capital city one of the best in Europe. Generous funding from the National Millennium Committee ensured the boardwalk concept became a reality as a lasting legacy for Dublin of the Millennium.

The Millennium has seen some wonderful projects come to fruition; like the illumination of the Liffey bridges, the Millennium Bridge and the magnificently restored City Hall, which has received such wonderful acclaim. The City Architect, Jim Barrett, told me that his vision for the boardwalk was that it would draw the city together by removing the barrier that exists between the street and the river. I think that is a wonderful concept and I believe the boardwalk amply achieves this objective.

– Alderman Maurice Ahern
The Right Honourable Lord Mayor of Dublin, 2000-2001

> Millennium Committee Favourites

Paul McGuinness

There were so many projects that I really liked, but the ones that stand out in my mind were the lighting of the bridges along the Liffey and the **Liffey Boardwalk**. Dublin is one of the few capital cities in Europe which has not made a feature of the river running through it, as have London, Paris and Budapest, so these were very important.

I was also very taken by Waterford's Millennium Plaza project, which has transformed a derelict area of the bustling city quays into a really imaginative outdoor performance area and recreational space.

I was in complete agreement with the Committee's decision to spread the available money across the country as a whole and I was pleased that so many smaller events were assisted. It would have been a great mistake, I believe, to have opted for a single, overblown and grandiose project. Many people will have good memories of the Millennium year for the rest of their lives and many of the projects, both large and small, will benefit their communities for generations to come.

– Paul McGuinness *Manager of U2 and Member of National Millennium Committee*

Top Left "Dublin can be Heaven …" Minister Séamus Brennan and Alderman Maurice Ahern enjoying the sun on the boardwalk.

Left Capturing the moment.

Right Coffee at eleven – alfresco. Photograph – Irish Independent.

Pat Liddy

> A Personal Note

Great cities of the world have always celebrated momentous events or significant anniversaries in their history by the erection of such features as monuments, temples, statues, cathedrals of commerce, sporting arenas and grand boulevards.

These works were often intended as signals to its own population or to the outside world of a city's grandeur and power. In modern times there is a new awareness that cities are not just political, administrative and commercial hubs but places to be lived in and enjoyed. This reawakened enlightenment has led to the welcome culture of preserving the heritage of past generations while seeking new ways to further enhance the built and natural environments of urban centres.

Decaying for years, Dublin began its process of rejuvenation in the early 1980s, receiving a major boost in this activity during 1988, the year the city celebrated its original foundation. From this point forward, helped more recently in no small way by unprecedented economic growth, Dublin's streetscapes and large stock of heritage buildings and sites have been improved out of all recognition, a fact attested to by the vast increase in tourist numbers visiting the city.

It was obvious that the year 2000 would offer a particular opportunity to imaginatively supplement the ongoing improvements to the city. Thankfully the National Millennium Committee were not tempted to plunge all the resources which they allocated to Dublin into a single grandiose scheme that might prove ultimately pointless or

temporary. Instead, grants were allocated across many fronts, which included cultural and artistic ventures and community and social service projects, in addition to various civic improvements. To this writer, at least four undertakings in the latter category will have a consequence and a long-term benefit far outweighing their expenditures.

The new **Liffey Boardwalk**, opened in December 2000 and stretching from Grattan (Capel Street) Bridge to O'Connell Bridge, has successfully returned people's focus to the River Liffey, the waterway that spawned the very origins of Dublin.

Here, while sitting on a bench in warm sunshine or leaning across the rails, one can almost shut off the noise and bustle of the city and be restored by gazing at the gently flowing waters. An added side effect of the boardwalk is that the authorities will have to maintain the same waters in tip-top condition. City centre cultural and tourist facilities will also be uplifted when artists move onto their allocated spaces on the boardwalk to display and sell their paintings. When night falls the river is brought even closer into the life of the city with the illumination of the 13 bridges from Heuston Station to the East Link. Symbolising the optimism of the new Millennium, the winding river of green lights adds a distinctly Parisian feel to the city.

In this digital age there is no richer evocation of times past than the sound of church bells ringing in Dublin's former medieval quarter. The National Millennium Committee assisted the restoration and replacement of bells in several city churches but the largest project was the casting and hanging of seven new bells in the tower of Christ Church Cathedral. At midnight on 31 December, 1999, the crowds outside Christ Church, the traditional gathering point for welcoming the New Year, heard the glorious melodies rung

out by the cathedral's change-ringers on the world's largest peal of 19 fully rotating bronze bells.

Pavement cafés, so long thought impossible in our climate, have brought a new style of social interaction onto our city centre streets. This feeling of projecting and extending a building's internal activity onto the footpath has also been effectively accomplished in the case of the 130-year-old Gaiety Theatre. Partly funded by the National Millennium Committee, the elegant new canopy, contemporary yet Victorian in character, and the widened plaza in front of the Gaiety, have created a space which gives a heightened sense of occasion when passing or entering the theatre.

These achievements give Dublin a simple yet dignified grandeur, which might have been denied to us had the expenditure of even hundreds of millions of pounds been spent unwisely. If imitation is the highest form of flattery, then I would expect to hear of many other cities around the world taking a leaf from the book of the National Millennium Committee.

– Pat Liddy *Author*

Right When night falls the River Liffey is brought even closer to the life of the city with the illumination of the 13 bridges, including the famous Halfpenny Bridge (and the inviting Liffey Boardwalk running alongside). The winding river of green light sweeping past the boardwalk adds a distinctly Parisian feel to the city.

Photograph – Dave Meehan Photography.

The Childrens' Hour

> The Children's Hour was the largest fundraising initiative of the Millennium. It gave the people of Ireland an opportunity to show, in a practical way, their concern for those less well off and for the marginalised in society at the turn of a century and a Millennium. More importantly the Children's Hour appeal brought a nation's attention to the fact that young people are our most precious resource but, sadly, often the most vulnerable in society.

Millennium Committee Award €2,539,476 (IR£2 million)

The Children's Hour, an initiative of the Irish Youth Foundation supported by the National Millennium Committee, encouraged the Irish workforce to give one hour of their pay to help children's causes.

This appeal directly raised €2,539,476 (IR£2 million) and this was matched with a donation from the Millennium Committee. The total fund of €5,078,952 (IR£4 million) is now being dispersed to help more than one hundred organisations involved in supporting, promoting and educating young people.

The monies raised are being shared equally between the National Children's Trust, the Irish Youth Foundation and five other designated charities – Barnardos, Focus Ireland, Temple Street Children's Hospital, the National Youth Federation and the Irish Children's Museum.

The aim of *the National Children's Trust* is to alleviate the effects on children of social and educational disadvantage and to attack the root cause of such deprivation. The Trust seeks donations from a wide range of donors but it will concentrate on building endowment funds so as to create a permanent stream of income to support its work.

The Irish Youth Foundation is an independent charitable trust, the first of its kind in Ireland dedicated exclusively to meeting the needs of the less advantaged and the major problems they face, such as educational disadvantage, poverty, homelessness and substance abuse.

The Children's Hospital, Temple Street, is using the funding to secure urgently needed equipment, to improve accommodation and to appoint a specialist pain nurse in a new pain prevention training programme.

Barnardos, an independent voluntary childcare organisation, will develop an anti-bias approach to working with children in Dublin; facilitate increased access to computers and information technology for children and young people in Galway and provide new supports for children and their families in Carlow.

The National Youth Federation is, in partnership with locally based youth services, building a youth café in Killarney; refurbishing youth premises in Athlone; equipping a mobile unit with multimedia technologies in Galway and constructing a purpose-built youth centre in Waterford.

Focus Ireland works with young homeless people. It will use the funds for the development of "foyer" type accommodation for 40 to 60 young people. This concept is based on good quality accommodation and also incorporates training, job skills and help with finding employment in a friendly and supportive environment.

The Irish Children's Museum intends developing a museum, which will be a place for children and their parents to experience the magic and wonder of the world around them.

Above Canoeing with the Irish Youth Federation.
Right The Millions Mount …

> Millennium Committee Favourites

Because of my two little kids, Jack and Marie, anything to do with children is very important to me. When the opportunity came for the Millennium Committee to get involved with the Barretstown Gang Camp, the centre for seriously ill children set up in 1994 by Paul Newman, I was behind it all the way. I'd been down there a couple of times even before the Committee got involved, and it's a fantastic place; the children who are there have been through so much, yet you should see the smiles on their faces when they're there. They've suffered so much pain but being at the Camp helps them forget it all for a while. It's magic and it makes me feel proud that we were able to help it in a small way. We helped fund a special cottage there that allows parents to come and stay for a while with their kids. You'd want to see it; it's really great.

We were also involved in **Children's Hour**, the Irish Youth Foundation's scheme that gave people the opportunity to donate their final hour's wages in 1999 to children's organisations. Children's Hour raised over €2,539,476 (IR£2 million) and we were able to match it with another €2,539,476 (IR£2million).

It was an honour to be involved and to be able to help in a small way to make life a little better for some children. Children are our future and if we don't look after them we won't have one.

— Ronan Keating *Singer/Entertainer and Member of the National Millennium Committee*

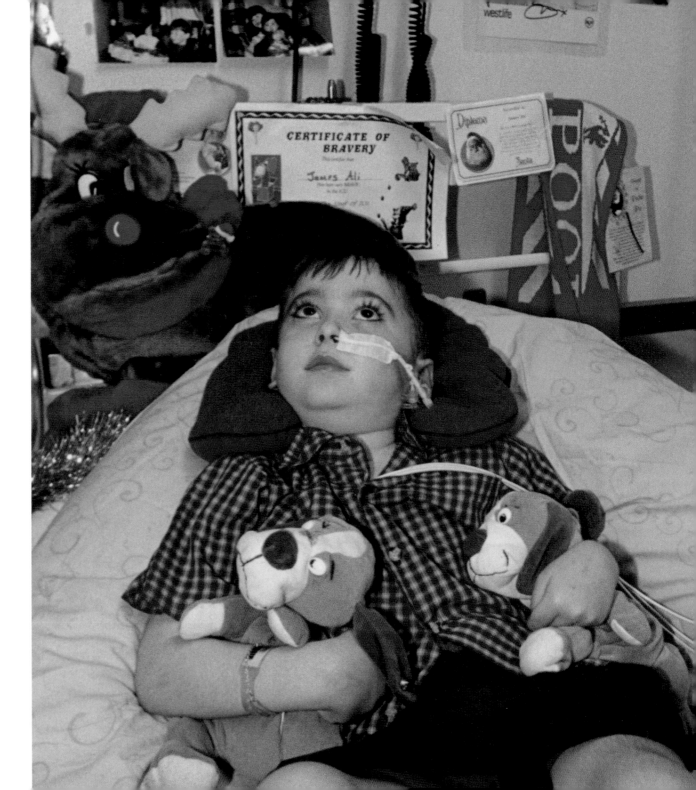

Helen Cosgrove

> A Personal Note

Top Flat is situated on the top floor of The Children's Hospital. This extremely busy 36-bed ward is divided into two areas – Medical and Surgical.

Many children who arrive in the Accident & Emergency Department of the hospital and have to be admitted, end up staying in Top Flat and there is rarely a spare bed. It caters for a huge range of ages – from babies of only six months to teenagers of 14 years and some even older with special needs such as those with Cerebral Palsy or Retts Syndrome, an inherent neurological disorder not easily detected.

Our Medical Unit treats children with a large variety of medical conditions, especially in the areas of respiratory, dermatology and neurology, in addition to dealing with infection control. The Surgical Unit treats children following surgery.

The equipment, purchased with the Children's Hour donation has made a huge difference to the young patients and the staff of Top Flat. The equipment includes:

Three Cardiac Monitors: The three isolation cubicles cater for very ill patients with infectious diseases, including Meningococcal Meningitis, who require very close monitoring. Because of the infection, equipment cannot be moved from one cubicle to another. It is a great medical advantage that one monitor is now available at all times, ensuring that Top Flat more easily adheres to the strict infection control guidelines.

Three Oxygen Saturation Monitors: These measure or test the respiratory efficiency of the children. Importantly, the procedure is non-invasive and is particularly suitable for those children suffering from asthma, cystic fibrosis and bronchoilitis. These mobile units can be used from patient to patient.

PA System: As Top Flat covers a very large area with a number of different cubicles, the new PA has allowed for more efficient communication between staff, children, parents and visitors. An added advantage is that music can be played through the system, creating a nice, relaxing atmosphere.

Thanks to the donation from Children's Hour we have been able to improve the service that Top Flat offers to the children in its care.

– Helen Cosgrove *The Children's Hospital, Temple Street, Dublin*

Left Seven-year-old James Ghazouani is cared for in The Children's Hospital Temple Street, surrounded by his favourite toys and a certificate of bravery. Photograph – Maxwells.

Right The appointment, with support from the Children's Hour fund, of a Pain Nurse Specialist has allowed The Children's Hospital, Temple Street, to establish a pain prevention programme which raises awareness of the methods used and the techniques involved in alleviating and preventing pain in children. This letter, from 11-year-old Brian McQuillan, explains the difference this service makes to children.

9/10/00

Hi, My name is Brian. I am 11 years old. I am in 5th class. I live in Castleblayney Co. Monaghan. When I was 6 I was having pains all night. I went to temple st and Dr Hennessy told me I had Arthritis. I have been on medication for four years, firstly steroids and then metotrexote tablets. The tablets were upsetting my stomach which made me feel sick and weak a lot of the time - sometimes this made me feel sad. Instead of taking the tablets Dr. Hennesey put me on an Injection which my Doctor at home would give me every tuesday. Because I improved so much I was able to stop taking the steroids and this made me very happy. Since the summer of this year I have been taught by nurse Norma O' Keefe how to give myself the injection of Metotrexote. This means I don't have to go to my own Doctor and I have more time to spend playing and doing things I enjoy. At first I was frightened and worried about injecting myself but now I've got used to it and it's not so bad at all!

Brian Mc Quillan.

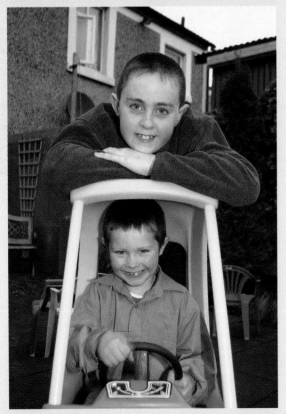

> A Personal Note

Focus Ireland is a national organisation, founded in 1985 to prevent, alleviate and eliminate homelessness. Since 1991 we have been endeavouring to establish the European Foyer system of assisting young adults living out of home or homeless.

This concept is based on good quality accommodation and incorporates training, job skills and help with finding employment in a friendly and supportive environment.

Focus Ireland's own perspective was initially based on our work with young people out of home or homeless. We quickly realised they should not be seen as a group apart from the mainstream experience of young people who are endeavouring to make the transition from their family home to more independent living.

Most north European countries have housing provisions, which enable young adults to make this transition. In France, for example, there are over 450 Foyers providing accommodation for more than 100,000 young people each year. We visited Foyers in France and Germany and participated in exchange visits for young people. We also networked with other organisations to promote the Foyer proposal.

This has been a slow and arduous process for a variety of reasons, including the fact that Foyers are a new form of housing provision for young people. During 1999/2000 Focus Ireland and the Mount Street Club (established in the 1930s to assist men who were unemployed) came together to discuss common interests.

These discussions have created the possibility of their site in Fenian Street – a prime location in inner city Dublin – being made available to us to develop as a Foyer.

Our initial design would accommodate 50 young people and have facilities to enable training, and incorporate a restaurant and a nursery which would be open to both residents and people living or working in the area. The awarding of €330,131 (IR£260,000) from the Children's Hour Millennium Fund is significant in making this project possible.

Thus, in the new Millennium, an identified need, a new idea and a sympathetic response combine to offer opportunity and hope to young people struggling to make the transition to independence.

– Justin O'Brien *Head of Housing Division, Focus Ireland*

Top Left Sister Stanislaus Kennedy of Focus Ireland with members of the Irish soccer squad at the launch of the "Focus on Home" initiative. Photograph – David Maher/SPORTFILE.

Left Enjoying themselves at the opening of the Barnardos Family Support project in Carlow were Tommy Bolger and Danny Thompson.

Opposite Page Smiles all round from Michaela Byrne, Jessica Holden and Anne Marie Thompson at the opening of the Barnardos Family Support project in Carlow. Photograph – Tony Maher.

Barnardos, the independent voluntary childcare organisation, is developing an anti-bias approach to working with children (Dublin), facilitating increased access to computers and information technology for children and young people (Galway) and providing new supports for children and families (Carlow). The Barnardos Family Support project in Askea Lawns, Carlow, provides after-school groups and a free drop-in information service for parents on all issues relating to children and childcare.

1

2

3

> A Personal Note

Bill Cullen

It all began with a small paragraph in a British Sunday newspaper. I was reading the *Mail on Sunday* when I came across a brief mention that employees of Marks and Spencer in the UK were prepared to donate one hour's pay for disadvantaged children as part of a new Millennium goodwill fundraising event. I immediately thought that this would be a unique and simple way of asking the workers of Ireland to support the disadvantaged young people who still exist despite the prosperity of the Celtic Tiger.

As a guy who grew up in inner city Dublin in the 1940s and 50s I knew well how easy it was for poverty and deprivation to continue from one generation to the next. Indeed, in 1956 I wrote more than 700 applications for job vacancies in the evening newspapers. I got absolutely no response due to the no-go area I lived in at that time. And while the Ireland of the Celtic Tiger has come a long way in education and in prosperity, it is still a fact that we have very many young people who have a bleak future ahead. Indeed, the new prosperity has only served to heighten the difference between the "haves" and the "have nots" and the poor are often even more deprived and marginalised than they have been in the past.

As Chairman of the Irish Youth Foundation, the motto of which is "No Achievement without Opportunity", I was determined to make Children's Hour a watershed for fundraising in Ireland. With the help of Marks and Spencer

in Ireland we formed a fundraising committee. Through the enthusiastic work of this group, the media responded with sponsored marketing support, enabling us to spread the word the length and breadth of the country.

The idea gathered momentum and eventually at the end of the year came the final tally, which showed that amid all the Millennium hype the workers of Ireland had not forgotten those less well off. They contributed €2,539,476 (IR£2 million) to Children's Hour. Through the efforts of Séamus Brennan and the Millennium Committee this amount was matched by government money. First came €1,269,738 (IR£1 million) from the Millennium Committee itself and then, on their recommendation, a further €1,269,738 (IR£1 million) from Charlie McCreevy, Minister for Finance.

And so, less than two years after I read that paragraph in the newspaper, the dream had become a reality. We had a total fund of €5,078,952 (IR£4 million) to disburse around the 32 counties of Ireland to youth projects supporting and helping young people in need.

The idea of contributing one hour's pay to help our vulnerable young people is so simple and so appealing to workers that in the year 2000 we received another €177,763 (IR£140,000). So with that kind of enthusiasm we have decided to make Children's Hour an annual event.

– Bill Cullen *Chairman, Children's Hour*

Left Taking part in a variety of Irish Youth Foundation projects.
Right Building for the future … Millennium Committee awards €1.65 million (IR£1.3 million) to the National Children's Trust.

The Irish Landmark Trust

> The National Millennium Committee has recognised Ireland's proud tradition in seafaring through support for an initiative to rescue and restore historic lightkeeper's houses, North and South.

Millennium Committee Award €634,869 (IR£500,000)

Having lived in a lighthouse
On a bare rock
Surrounded by sea
For most of my life
And now retired;

The thing I remember
Is dense fog clearing
At the turn of high tide;
And the stars coming out
Like primroses in the sky

– D. J. O Sullivan
Lighthouse Keeper (on his retirement)

Our rugged coastline evokes warm feelings. Like the poet John Masefield, we are invariably lured to land's end on our wild Atlantic shores where we turn our back on civilisation, stare at nothing but the "lonely sea and sky".

Lighthouses, of course, are an essential part of this invigorating panorama, noble in bearing, beautiful to look at. Spanning centuries – even Millennia – they are an essential part of our rich maritime heritage.

Tradition tells us that the unique lifestyle of the lightkeepers has existed in Ireland since the establishment of Hook Head in the 5th century. The succeeding centuries have seen the 'spreading of the light' to dozens of rocky headlands. Those reliable, flashing beacons have saved countless lives. As the hands of time turn inexorably, all of Ireland's 86 plus lighthouses are now fully automated. The houses where the keepers slept and ate are now largely empty, awaiting an uncertain future.

The award to the The Irish Landmark Trust is to restore lighthouse properties at five locations – Galley Head, Co. Cork; Cromwell Point, Co. Kerry; Loop Head, Co. Clare; Black Head, Co. Antrim; and St. John's Point, Co. Down, and it's not just a case of bricks, mortar and paintwork. Not only will actual buildings be preserved but the flora and fauna of entire headlands will also be secured for future generations. The Irish Landmark Trust is an all-Ireland charitable organisation founded in 1992 to rescue worthwhile buildings from neglect.

The acquisition and refurbishment of these key lighthouse properties assures access for future generations to buildings which are fundamental to Ireland's rich maritime history. The historical importance of the selected lighthouses is beyond doubt. The buildings – potent reminders of our seafaring culture – when restored, will be fully accessible to the public, both as holiday homes and through open days, and the revenue generated used for ongoing maintenance.

Their restoration is also vital because of the opportunities they will provide for future generations to experience the sea and coastline at its rawest, down by the serrated shoreline, where the seagulls soar and the wild spume flies.

There is something magical about the lone lantern lighting up the furthest reaches; just when you thought you had reached the last place on earth and there is a beam of light.

– John Eagle *Photographer*

Opposite Page – Black Head lighthouse, Co. Antrim, has been perched on the north shore of the entrance to Belfast Lough since 1901. Located on a beautiful headland, the granite building allows stunning views onto the Irish Sea. The light from Black Head would have guided countless seafarers, perhaps most notably those sailing on the huge vessels constructed in the nearby Belfast shipyards in the earlier part of this century.

Photograph – Christopher Hill.

Peter Barry

>Millennium Committee Favourites

The **Lighthousekeepers' Cottages** restoration was an outstanding project. We're an island nation, so the first thing you see when you sail towards our shores is almost always a lighthouse. In fact, I'm sorry we didn't restore more of them. The People's Millennium Forests project was also a wonderful undertaking. It's going to be there for a long time, it's spread all over the country so its impact is huge and every single family has an involvement. Trees are very symbolic things; you plant them and they grow and outlive you, so they are an important gift to the future generations of our country.

I think the most difficult decision we had to make was made early in the life of the Committee. We had to decide whether to go for a single, massive Eiffel Tower-style project, probably sited in Dublin as the capital city, to mark the transition from one Millennium to the next or to spread the finite amount of money available throughout the community in a meaningful way. On reflection I do think the approach we settled on was the right one. It's great that so many communities were able to improve their environment, whether it was by painting the community hall, replacing a bell in a church tower or just installing a couple of benches in a park. It was each community that decided how they were going to mark the Millennium.

– Peter Barry *Former Government Minister and Member of the National Millennium Committee*

1 St. John's Point, Co. Down, is an area steeped in history and legend. The lighthouse was built in 1844. It was along this stretch of coastline that the ill-fated Titanic conducted her sea trials in the earlier part of the last century.

2 Cromwell Point, Valentia Island, Co. Kerry, is captivating and picturesque territory. The lightkeepers' houses at this lovely spot have traditionally been a base for lighthouse families while the keepers were assigned to even more remote locations.

3 There has been a lighthouse at **Loop Head, Co. Clare**, since 1670, reflecting the importance of the peninsula as a navigation point on the busy River Shannon. The first beacon was primitive by today's standards. It consisted of a brazier, a metal container with burning coal, atop the lightkeepers' cottage.

Opposite Page – Galley Head, Co. Cork, was built in 1875 and is situated on a lofty headland. It's an inviting, inspiring place whose history is embroidered further by the colourful tale in the 1860s of a 30 foot sea serpent which inspired author Ray Bradbury when he wrote his tale of a sea monster who fell in love with the lighthouse foghorn.

Photography – John Eagle.

THE IRISH LANDMARK TRUST

Nicholas Robinson at the restored Wicklow Head Lighthouse.

> A Personal Note

The basic philosophy of The Irish Landmark Trust is simple – to acquire, by gift or nominal lease, buildings of architectural and cultural significance, and raise the once-off capital necessary to restore them. These are buildings that, because of their age, location, size or method of construction, are difficult to adapt for contemporary, everyday use. They are, however, perfectly suited to short-let holiday use, for which these constraints become positive attractions to those wishing to escape briefly to a historic building with character and charm. With the revenue generated by holiday lettings, each property can be sustained into the future.

The restoration of lightkeepers' houses is an ambitious undertaking. The Commissioners of Irish Lights generously made lightkeepers' houses at five majestic locations around the island of Ireland – North and South – available for sensitive restoration.

The Millennium Committee award allows this exceptional opportunity to be grasped and, with our technical expertise

and proven record in the management of similar restoration projects, we look forward to a successful completion to this worthy heritage programme.

The project ensures that the lightkeeper's life can be experienced in a tangible way and it also protects public access to the five headlands and their flora and fauna by keeping them in the public domain. This is an important principle in the face of the diminishing amount of Irish coastline that is still available to the public.

The powerful symbolism of these enduring headland properties which have guided our island's shipping over the centuries – a light was first established in Ireland in the 5th century – adds to their appropriateness as a Millennium project.

– Nicholas Robinson *President, The Irish Landmark Trust*

> A Personal Note

Bill Long

From 1989 to 1993, I spent long spells living in the Baily Lighthouse – built on a tip of rock near the Nose of Howth on the northern shore of Dublin Bay – researching and writing *Bright Light, White Water*, the story of Irish lighthouses and their people, published in 1993. I did not visit The Baily again until March of 1997, when the light was automated and demanned – the last light on our coasts to become another *Mary Celeste*, "still lit, but in a sense abandoned and drifting in the dark". A few of us gathered there on a clear and sunny morning, as guests of the Commissioners of

Irish Lights, to mark the end of an epoch. There followed a sincere attempt to create a festive spirit at what was really a wake. RTÉ had live interviews on morning radio. Howth and Dunlaoghaire lifeboats cruised close to the rock, saluting us with their sirens. Lighthouse families – Crowleys, Murphys, Butlers, Sullivans, and many others – recalled the "old days". "Banjo" Barney McKenna, perched on a rock below a cliff, a-gaggle with raucous gulls, playing **"The Sailor on the Rock"** and cheering us all with his sad music. But, after all the jollity, as with an American Wake, a cloud of melancholy descended on us all, with the realisation that no one would ever live here again. No lightkeeper would tend the light and watch the sea. And, slowly, quietly, in little knots, we drifted shame-facedly away, and the last keepers left the lighthouse forever.

As our children and our grand-children ask us now about the origins and uses of the old Martello towers on our coasts, so, future generations of children will ask their elders about these strange buildings called lighthouses. What exactly were they? What were they used for? How did they function? And hopefully in that future time the wonderful work of the Trust, assisted in this instance by the National Millennium Committee, will be there to tell them something of the "lighthouse story" and of the lives of those who lived and worked in them.

– Bill Long Author *Bright Light, White Water*

Opposite Page April 2002. Inside the newly refurbished Galley Head light-keepers' house. Photography - John Eagle.

Battle of the Boyne Site

> The Battle of the Boyne, the biggest battle fought on Irish soil, shaped the nature of Ireland, politically, for the following 300 years.

A new era dedicated to fostering a greater understanding of the historic site in the context of reconciliation and mutual understanding has now begun with the purchase by the state of more than 500 acres of the battle site at Oldbridge, between Drogheda and Slane. This site will be dedicated to promoting the message of peace and reconciliation on the entire island

The Battle of the Boyne was fought on July 1, 1690. The opposing armies of King William III (Netherlands) and King James II faced each other across a six mile battle-field in an Irish battle with strong European implications. The wider battle site extends from Rosnaree in the West, two miles from Donore, to Drybridge in the East, on the outskirts of

Drogheda. The battles of the Boyne and Aughrim were both part of William's campaign against the mainly Catholic forces of James II in 1690-91 for the throne of England. In turn, these events in Ireland were an extension of the war of the Grand Alliance fought against Louis XIV of France in much of continental Europe.

An interdepartmental committee has been examining the development of the location and the appropriate approach to ensure a fair and balanced interpretation of the battle itself and the subsequent ramifications for history.

The National Millennium Committee assisted in the purchase of the site and is contributing to the cost of Phase One of the development which includes improved access to the site, comprehensive signage and a guide service and summer presentation programme. Further significant development of the site will include more public accessibility and the provision of information on the battle's military, political and cultural significance, in its own time and since.

Left A replica of a six pound Saker field-cannon, of English origin, which would have been used at the Battle of the Boyne. The cannon will be displayed at the battle site as part of a presentation for the 2002 tourist season.

Right The Battle of the Boyne by Jan Wych (c.1640-1702). Reproduced with permission of the National Gallery of Ireland.

Following Pages Information panels at the battle site.

> The Bend of the Boyne

Below the village of Slane in Co. Meath and above the port and town of Drogheda, the river Boyne takes a dramatic loop, encompassing an elongated ridge on whose summit stand the great Stone Age passage-tomb cemeteries of Knowth, Dowth and Newgrange. Today this area is known as the Bend of the Boyne, in former times it was called Brugh na Bóinne. Its rich fertile soils and south-facing slopes are set in the most accessible, low-lying part of Ireland, close to the Irish Sea and with river access westwards to the Atlantic, a geographical province that stretches all the way from Norway to Brittany and Spain. Brugh na Bóinne is where the great Stone Age tomb-building tradition of Atlantic Europe reached its zenith. It is where legend says the foundations of Irish Christianity were laid, and is the home of the earliest of our great Cistercian monasteries at Mellifont. It was beside the Boyne that one of the most important battles in Irish history was fought. Almost every period of our past has left conspicuous traces in this remarkable land.

- From *The Bend of the Boyne* by Geraldine Stout
(Published by Country House in association with the National Museum of Ireland)

The Battle of the Boyne
Cath na Bóinne

King William's Camp, Tullyallen
Campa an Rí Liam, Tulaigh Álainn

King William's army set up their camp on the high ground north of the Boyne behind the village of Tullyallen.

The encampment of 36,000 men, with their accompanying baggage, stores, hospital, camp followers, wagons and thousands of horses, occupied a very large area. Both armies positioned artillery near the river, and there was an exchange of fire in which William, while on reconnaissance, suffered a mild flesh wound.

There was no further action, the day being a Monday 'on which the King never undertakes anything of importance'.

At 6.00am the following morning, a force of 10,000 men under Count Meinhard Schomberg and Lieutenant General James Douglas marched through the rising mist in a flanking movement towards Slane to attack the Jacobite left wing. About three hours later, with drums beating, the Williamite infantry marched down the slope to the stretch of the Boyne east of Oldbridge.

Ghlac arm an Rí Liam seilbh ar shuíomh ar thalamh ard ar an taobh thuaidh den Bhóinn ar chúl shráidbhaile Thulaigh Álainn.

Bhí campa 36,000 fear, a gcuid bagáiste agus stór, ospidéal, comhluintir, vaigíní agus na mílte capall scaipthe thar limistéar mór. Shocraigh an dá arm gunnaí móra gar don abhainn, scaoil siad roiseanna lena chéile agus goineadh an Rí Liam, a bhí ar taiscealaíocht, go héadrom sa bhfeoil i gceann de na heachtraí lámhaigh sin.

Tharla gurbh é an Luan é, 'lá nach dtugann an rí faoi aon rud tábhachtach,' ní dhearnadh aon rud eile.

Ag 6.00 r.n. an mhaidin dár gcionn, mháirseáil 10,000 fear faoi cheannas an Chúnta Meinhard Schomberg agus an Leifteanant-ghinearál James Douglas i ngluaiseacht chliathánach i dtreo Bhaile Shláine, trí cheo a bhí ag ardú, d'fhonn sciathán clé arm Shéamais a ionsaí. Tuairim is trí huaire an chloig ina dhiaidh sin, agus drumaí á mbualadh, mháirseáil coisithe Liam síos an fánán go dtí an chuid sin den Bhóinn taobh thoir den Seandroichead.

King William III

Map legend:
1. Williamite flanking movement
2. Jacobite response
3. William's forces cross the Boyne
4. Jacobite retreat to Duleek

WILLIAMITE CAMP
TULLYALLEN
Oldbridge
Drybridge
Main Battle Site — DROGHEDA
JACOBITE CAMP
To SLANE
RIVER BOYNE
ROUGHGRANGE
DULEEK

Dúchas The Heritage Service

Boyne Valley

Text by the Military History Society of Ireland

30 June/1 July 1690

The Battle of the Boyne

Caṫ na Bóinne

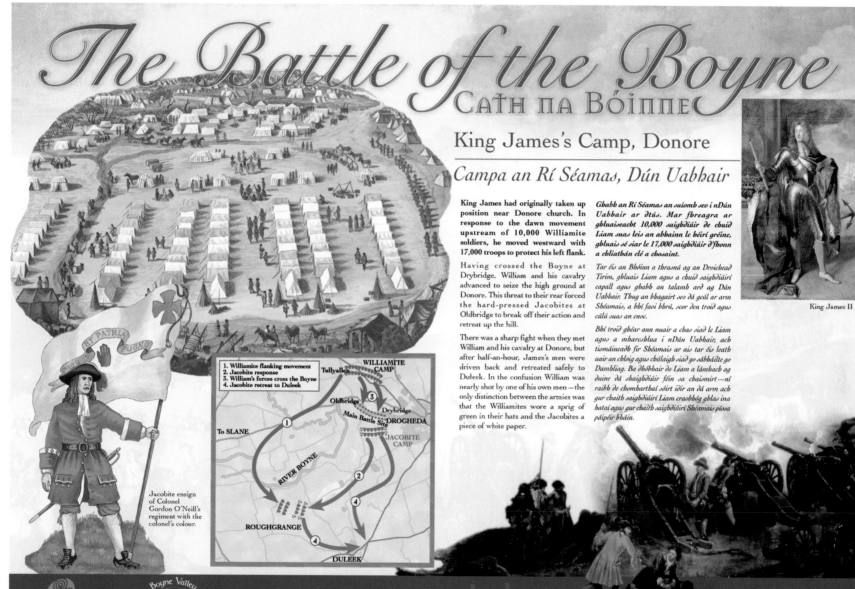

King James's Camp, Donore

Campa an Rí Séamas, Dún Uabhair

King James had originally taken up position near Donore church. In response to the dawn movement upstream of 10,000 Williamite soldiers, he moved westward with 17,000 troops to protect his left flank.

Having crossed the Boyne at Drybridge, William and his cavalry advanced to seize the high ground at Donore. This threat to their rear forced the hard-pressed Jacobites at Oldbridge to break off their action and retreat up the hill.

There was a sharp fight when they met William and his cavalry at Donore, but after half-an-hour, James's men were driven back and retreated safely to Duleek. In the confusion William was nearly shot by one of his own men —the only distinction between the armies was that the Williamites wore a sprig of green in their hats and the Jacobites a piece of white paper.

Ghabh an Rí Séamas an suíomh seo i nDún Uabhair ar dtús. Mar fhreagra ar ghluaiseacht 10,000 saighdiúir de chuid Liam suas leis an abhainn le béirí gréine, ghluais sé siar le 17,000 saighdiúir d'fhonn a chliathán clé a chosaint.

Tar éis an Bhóinn a thrasnú ag an Droichead Tirim, ghluais Liam agus a chuid saighdiúirí capall agus ghabh an talamh ard ag Dún Uabhair. Thug an bhagairt seo dá gcúl ar arm Shéamais, a bhí faoi bhrú, scor den troid agus cúlú suas an cnoc.

Bhí troid ghéar ann nuair a chas siad le Liam agus a mharcshlua i nDún Uabhair, ach tiománeadh fir Shéamais ar ais tar éis leath uair an chloig agus chúlaigh siad go sábháilte go Damhliag. Ba bhóbhair do Liam a lámhach ag duine dá shaighdiúir féin sa chaismirt—ní raibh de chomharthaí sóirt idir an dá arm ach gur chaith saighdiúirí Liam craobhóg ghlas ina hataí agus gur chaith saighdiúirí Shéamais píosa páipéir bháin.

King James II

Jacobite ensign of Colonel Gordon O'Neill's regiment with the colonel's colour.

Map legend:
1. Williamite flanking movement
2. Jacobite response
3. William's forces cross the Boyne
4. Jacobite retreat to Duleek

WILLIAMITE CAMP
Tullyallen
Oldbridge
Drybridge
Main Battle Site
DROGHEDA
JACOBITE CAMP
To SLANE
RIVER BOYNE
ROUGHGRANGE
DULEEK

1 July 1690 12.15 pm

02 Millennium Miscellany

A Dream of Newgrange
Seamus Heaney

Qual è colui che sognando vede,
che dopo 'l sogno la passione impressa
rimane, e l'altro a la mente non riede,

cotal son io …
      Dante, *Paradiso*, Canto XXXIII

Like somebody who sees things when he's dreaming
And after the dream lives with the aftermath
Of what he felt, no other trace remaining,

So I live now, for what I saw departs
And is almost lost, although a distilled sweetness
Still drops from it into my inner heart.

It is the same with snow the sun releases,
The same as when in wind, the hurried leaves
Swirl round your ankles and the shaking hedges

That had flopped their catkin cuff-lace and green sleeves
Are sleet-whipped bare. Dawn light began stealing
Through the cold universe to County Meath,

Over weirs where Boyne water, fulgent, darkling,
Turns its thick axle, over the rick-sized stones
Millennia-deep in their own unmoving

And unmoved alignment. And now the planet turns
Earth-brow and templed earth, the crowd grows still
In the wired-off precinct of the burial mounds,

Flight 104 from New York audible
As it descends on schedule into Dublin,
Boyne Valley Centre Car Park already full,

Waiting for seedling light on roof and windscreen.
And as *in illo tempore* people marked
The king's gold dagger when he plunged it in

To the hilt in unsown ground, to start the work
Of the world again, to speed the plough
And plant the riddled grain, we watch through murk

And overboiling cloud for the milted glow
Of sunrise, for an eastern dazzle
To send first light like share-shine in a furrow

Steadily deeper, farther available,
Creeping along the floor of the passage grave
To backstone and capstone, to hold its candle

To the world inside the astronomic cave.

With gratitude to Seamus Heaney
Published with the permission of The Irish Times.

Right The Millennium winter solstice at Newgrange, Co. Meath, 22 December, 1999, as a shaft of sunlight penetrates the ancient passageway.

Photograph – Bryan O'Brien (used courtesy of *The Irish Times*).

Oireachtas Millennium Session

> On 16 December, 1999, following a suggestion from the National Millennium Committee, both Houses of the Oireachtas met in an historic Joint Session as a special acknowledgement of the Millennium and of its significance as a benchmark in our civilisation. The President, Mary McAleese, accepted an invitation to address the Joint Houses. The Taoiseach, Mr. Bertie Ahern T.D. delivered an address as did the Tánaiste, Ms. Mary Harney T.D. There were also contributions from the leaders of the opposition political parties.

The following are extracts from the addresses of President McAleese and Mr. Ahern:

Extracts from the address by the President of Ireland, Mary McAleese, to the Joint Houses of the Oireachtas.

> "Ní mhaireann glún den ghinealach a chuaigh romhainn siar go hÁdhamh; mise féin ní feasach mé an liom an lá amárach. Is cuí agus is tairbheach dúinn, agus muid ar chuspa ócáide móire, súil a chaitheamh siar ar a bhfuil caite agus caillte, ar a bhfuil déanta agus thart. Murach sin is beag a bheadh foghlamtha againn mar chine. Ach ní miste dúinn fosta aghaidh a thabhairt ar an todhchaí; agus, murab ionann is an manach bocht tinneallach, is cóir dúinn é a dhéanamh go hurrúsach, lán dóchais agus dánachta, lán mórtais agus cinnteachta, muid múnlaithe ag a bhfuil imithe ach gan a bheith faoi chuing ag an stair."

> Decisions

"The decisions we make now and in the years ahead, the values which imbue those decisions and the use we make of today's opportunities, these will give our future its shape and its depth. They will determine the kind of Ireland we hand on to future generations for while, thankfully, we have come a long way, we still have a distance to travel before our star stops over an Ireland where the shadows have lifted for all our people. The choices are ours. Will the old iniquities and inequalities lurk beneath the veneer? Will idealism be dulled by selfish materialism, shrill begrudgery and apathy or will we bequeath to our children a land of peace, prosperity, equal opportunity and respect for difference?"

> Gratitude

"We owe a debt of gratitude too to those who left this island. Some went as missionaries or as volunteers in health care and education, some went simply in search of adventure. Most emigrants, however, left reluctantly, driven out by hardship and lack of opportunity in circumstances no different from those which bring refugees from other parts of the world to our shores today. These were not the celebrated Wild Geese or political refugees of previous centuries. They were poor men and women who ploughed very lonely furrows in strange lands. It was our emigrants who globalised the name of Ireland. They brought our culture with them, refreshed and enriched it with the new energy it absorbed from the varied cultures into which they transplanted it. Many of them kept faith with our island's destiny through the generations. They gave us that huge multicultural Irish family now proudly celebrated and acknowledged in the new Article 2 of the Constitution."

> Success

"Today, where the name of Ireland is spoken, the word success is very close behind. We really have taken our place among the nations of the world. Part of our success we undoubtedly owe to our membership of the European Union. Part of our success we owe to ourselves, to the spirit of enterprise, of partnership and common purpose among our people, to the genius and initiative which was unlocked by widening educational opportunity, to the visionary leadership and public endeavour which together pushed Ireland into a new gear."

> Benefits

"Along with the manifest benefits of success have come new challenges. We are the first generation to have the eradication of poverty within our grasp, the first generation to experience Ireland as a land of fresh starts and new opportunity for people from other cultures. We are the first generation to be seriously tested on the bona fides of our legendary hospitality, our *Céad Míle Fáilte*. We are the first generation for centuries to have the opportunity to build and consolidate a lasting peace between this island's two traditions. And so, as the shadows lift, the world looks very different. The world is very different."

> Friends

"Today's Ireland is a first world country but with a third world memory, a memory to keep us humble, to remind us of the fragility of it all, a memory to remind us that too many people across the world waken up each day to lives of sheer terror and dread. They too need dreamers to imagine a day when their shadows will lift. They too need friends to help make those dreams happen. We have a long and proud history of being just such a friend, a champion of the poor, the oppressed, the ignored and the neglected. And for all our success, we have them too on our own doorstep."

> Love

"This century has created many incredible images and stories from holocaust to moon landing, from women's suffrage to the world wide web, but one recent image struck me as powerfully symbolic at this jubilee time. It was the picture on the front page of an Irish newspaper of an unborn child's tiny hand reaching out from the womb and wrapping itself around the finger of the surgeon who was operating to save its life. Another moving nativity, another reminder of how much we need each other, how much we have to offer each other. We have had all the lessons we could ever need in hatred, in neglect and in hurt. We know deeply that human beings need to be respected and loved, that we blossom in giving and in receiving love and that its withholding, its absence, shrivels us."

Right The President, Mary McAleese, addressing the Joint Houses. Photograph – Michael Quinn Photography.

**Extracts from address by The Taoiseach,
Mr. Bertie Ahern T.D.**

> *"A Thríonóid ag atá an chumhacht an mbeidh an dream
seo ar deoraíocht nó an mbeidh an t-athaoibhneas againn.*
Those lines were forced out of the pain and the despair of
a people defeated after the Flight of the Earls, people from
whom government of their affairs had been torn away. However,
in that last line of the verse, one can detect the indomitable
hope of the Irish nation, the expectation that a bright new
era of freedom and prosperity could yet dawn, the expectation
of a second flowering, a second period of happiness."

> Optimism

"There is hope, optimism and self-confidence among our
people in place of the doubts, and often despair of earlier
years. As we approach the Millennium, so many new
possibilities are opening up before us. However, we have
to recognise that progress in solving old problems will
often reveal new ones. The management of prosperity
brings with it great responsibility. We need to ensure that
our society adapts to rapid change in a harmonious,
cohesive and inclusive manner, and that we do not leave
behind any section of our population."

> Credit

"Creating a viable independence did not come easily or
quickly, but great credit is due to the first generation of
nation builders who set up institutions to serve all the people
impartially and with integrity, Éamon de Valera, Michael
Collins, W.T. Cosgrave and Seán Lemass. I also pay tribute
to the vital contribution of the labour movement founded
by James Connolly and Jim Larkin. My party, Fianna Fáil

played an important role in completing our independence,
in giving us our Constitution and in the early economic and
social development of the country. All parties should be
generous in the credit they are prepared to give to the
contribution in good faith of their political opponents."

> Peace

"We have now only begun a new journey as we set out to
work with an inclusive system of government in Northern
Ireland. Devolved government there, reflecting the special
needs of a divided society, will be conducted on a
partnership basis. A prosperous and violence-free Ireland,
where people can work together on everyday economic
and social issues, notwithstanding deep-seated and unresolved
political differences, represents a huge advance. It is difficult
to think of any other development which is more vital to
our country's future than stable and permanent peace."

> Progress

"Our democracy and our national progress rests on, and
has been greatly strengthened by, the participation of
women at home, in the workplace, in voluntary bodies and
in political, social and cultural life. This century has seen
historic and welcome advances in equal participation by
women. Much more remains to be done to promote equality
of opportunity for women in formal decision making
structures, be they in politics, the public service, trade
unions or business life."

> Opportunity

"In the 20th century, Ireland was put back on the map as a
country in its own right. It has been, in many ways, a long,
hard journey to where we are today. The opportunity facing

us now is, in a relatively short space of time, to go out in
front, setting no limits to the onward march of a nation while
catching up in areas where we are still behind."

"President John F. Kennedy addressed the Oireachtas 36
years ago. In his final remarks on 28 June, 1963, he made
an appeal to the House thus:

*Great powers have their responsibilities and
their burdens, but the smaller nations must fulfil
their obligations as well … My friends, Ireland's
hour has come. You have something to give to the
world, and that is a future of peace with freedom.*

President Kennedy's remarks ring truer with each passing
day. His words echo with great faith in the Irish people, in
our destiny to be a nation which plays its full and active
part in international political and economic affairs."

Right An historic moment as senior members of both Houses of the
Oireachtas are photographed with the President, Mary McAleese, prior
to her address. Back left to right; Dr. Rory O'Hanlon, Leas-Cheann Comhairle,
Dáil Éireann, Deputy Trevor Sargent, The Green Party, Deputy Ruairi Quinn,
Leader of The Labour Party, Deputy Mary Harney, Tánaiste and Leader
of The Progressive Democrats Party, Deputy Bertie Ahern, An Taoiseach,
Deputy John Bruton, Leader of Fine Gael Party, Senator Liam T. Cosgrave,
Leas-Chathaoirleach, Seanad Éireann, Mr. Martin McAleese. Front:
Deputy Séamus Pattison, Ceann Comhairle, Dáil Éireann, President
McAleese, Senator Brian Mullooly, Chathaoirleach, Seanad Éireann.

Photograph – Michael Quinn Photography.

An Síol ag Borradh

Micheál Ó Muircheartaigh

Tá sé tráthúil bheith ag féachaint siar agus ar aghaidh faid atá deireadh Mílaoíse amháin agus tús chinn eile beo beathaithe san aigne go fóill.Is tréimhse ana fhada é 1,000 bliain agus cé gur do réir a chéile a théann athraithe i gcion ar phobail tá na mílte cor curtha de ag an saol soisialach i rith an ama sin. Is beag athrú atá tagtha ar ghnéithne aiceanta na tíre – tá Corrán Tuathail isteach agus amach mar a bhí sé sa bhliain 1,000 A.D. – tá drompla na talún ar fud na hÉireann glas ar an mórgcóir díreach mar a bhí agus i bhfocla Paul Robeson "old man river, she just keeps rollin' along".

Ag an am úd Gaeilge amháin a bhí ag pobal na tíre agus is cosúil go raibh fíor sprid na Criostaiochta go doimhin i gcroíthe na ndaoine. Bhuel, is mór le rá é go bhfuil an Ghaeilge agus an Chríostaíocht fós linn míle bliain níos deanaí in ainneoin tionchar na n-athraithe go léir.

Ar bhealach is cruthu é go bhfuil fiúntas ag baint leo agus dar liom is tuar dóchais é go mbeidh siad ann agus níos treise sa bhliain 3,000 A.D. Is spéisiúil an t-ábhar é ceist na Gaillge. Is fuirist liosta a chur le chéile de's na cúiseanna ba bhun leis an meath in úsáid na teangan idir 1000 A.D. agus 2000 – athraithe ar nósanna na ndaoine a bhí i gcumhacht idir cléir agus tuath – an Muirthéacht Tionsclaíoch agus forbairt trádála – gluaiseacht daoine go bailte agus cathracha – méadú ar an líon daoine ag dul ar imirce éigeantach – agus tuiscint go raibh buntaistí móra ag an mBéarla mar theanga cumarsáide go mórmhór acu síud go raibh orthu dul thar lear ar thóir oibre.

Ní gádh cur leis mar ní mór glacadh leis an scéal mar atá sé. Ní chreidim go bhfuil aon bhaol ann anois go dtiochfaidh a thuilleadh laghdú ar an líon daoine a bheidh ag labhairt na Gaeilge.

Bhí an baol sin ann tráth ach béidir gur ins an scór bliain a lean an Gorta a cuireadh síol a chuir ar chumas glúnta eile gnéithe de chultúr a bhí dúchasach ag an bpointe sin a chaomhnú agus cur leo faoi thionchar nósanna ó'n iasacht. Béidir gur le cúrsaí spoirt a thosnaigh sé agus go raibh baint ag an Rialtas I Londain leis an síol a chur i dtalamh.

Cuireadh an t-Act a chuir cosc ar chluichíocht de short ar bith seachas "Archery" d'eagrú ar ceal uair éigin c 1850. Tús a bhí anseo le forbairt bríomhar sa chultúr áirithe sin agus is dá bharr a tháinig leithéidí an Irish Rugby Football Union, I.F.A. an tSacair, G.A.A. na gCluichí Gaelacha, G.U.I. an Ghailf agus go leor cumainn eile ag plé le lúthchleasaíocht agus caitheamh aimsire mar Leadóg, Cricket &rl.

Bhí pobail á n-eagrú do'n gcéad uair do nithe nár bhain go díreach le polaitíocht nó cogaíocht agus níorbh ionad go raibh gnéithe eile seachas spórt á gcur san áireamh – Gaeilge, Ceol, Rince agus mar sin de.

Sea, tháinig na h-eagraíochtaí a chuir réimeas an chaomhnaithe sa tsiúl agus anois breis agus céad bliainníos faide anonn an bóthar sé mo thuairm go bhfuil muintir na h-Éireann gafa ag an bhfealsúnacht go bhfuil sé tábhachtach go mairfeadh goch aon ghné de chultúir na tíre. Maidir leis an nGaeilge is I gcomhthéasc eile a bheidh sé le sonrú-ré an Dá-Theangachas agus go luath ré an Trí-Theangachas.

Is teangacha forbartha agus luachmhara iad Béarla, Fraincís, Spáinnis, Gearmánais, Seapánais agus go leor eile agus is ar chomhchéim leo uilig a shamhlaím toghcaí na Gaeilge. Sé an fís atá agam ná go dtiochfaidh an t-am go mbeidh céatadán árd de phobal ne tíre líofa agus I dtaithí ar Ghaeilge agus Béarla a labhairt go rialta agus go mbeidh cumas maith acu freisin I dteangacha eile do réir mar is toil leo. Tá an t-atmasféar i gceart faoi láthair chun gabháil sa treo sin anois. Tá comharthaí agus gníomjaíocht a léiríonn go bhfuil an Rialras sásta níos mó airgid ná riamh a chaitheamh ar chursaí "cultúrtha".

Má's mall is mithid agus is suntasach gur mór é suim an phobail óig sa chlaonadh breise i leith cultúir agus na timp-eallachta. Sa tsaol atá romhainn tiocfaidh "an t-seachtain oibre Trí Lá" agus dá bharr breis ama ag daoine le caitheamh ar aidhmeanna eile.

Gan amhras is chun leas na Gaeilge a cheidh an córas nua agus ná dearmadaimis go bhfuil saineolaithe ag tuar anois go mbeidh faid saoil de thart ar 130 bliain ag na leanaí atá á saolú sa Mhílaois iontach seo. Ní bheidh bac ná cáin ar bith ar Gaeilge a labhairt ná ní gádh go gcosnódh sé airgead ach oiread. Tá Mílaois an Chultúir ag eirí in áirde – cé'n fáth nach mbeimis "Lán-dóchais agus grá" mar a bhí Raifteirí an File thart ar 200 bliain ó shin.

– Mícheál Ó Muircheartaigh

2000 Ireland – Logo Designer

The challenge of creating Ireland's official Millennium symbol was given to students studying art and design in third level institutions, North and South. The now very familiar Millennium logo emerged as the winning design in a competition organised by the National Millennium Committee.

The winning design was by Dubliner Paul Donnelly, then a 3rd year design student at the Dublin Institute of Technology, Mountjoy Square. It has established itself as the enduring symbol of the Millennium in Ireland and has been featured extensively on commemorative plaques, souvenirs, books, jewellery, flags, banners, advertisements, promotional material, and even bricks used in the building of houses in 2000. Paul was awarded €2,539 (£2,000) for winning the competition and his college received €3,809 (£3,000). The eleven other finalists each received €634 (£500).

Paul said his design sought to convey a sense of celebration. "It encapsulated several strands of ideas, combining Celtic spirals and fireworks which make up the numerals of 2000 in a very vigorous and spirited way. I feel it achieved a very good balance between the informal script style and the formal typography. The colour elements convey freshness and newness. I always felt one of the real strengths of the design would be its wide and youthful appeal. Having had the honour of designing Ireland's symbol for this unique celebration has been a thrilling experience."

Left Logo designer Paul Donnelly. **Above** Students shortlisted in the Millennium Logo Competition display their designs."

Behind the Scenes

Tom Rowley

Been there, done that and I have the T-shirt to prove it. Looking back now I'm inclined to believe the T-shirt should have carried that much used slogan "You don't have to be crazy to work here ... but it helps."

So just what was it like to be one of those at the centre of organising Ireland's Millennium? I think it can best be appreciated if you compare the experience to taking a trip on one of those death-defying, stomach churning, rollercoaster amusement rides. It was 1999 and Millennium mania was gripping the world. The Millennium Bug threatened computer chaos, the race was on to find the best locations in the world to fly to for the dawning of the new Millennium and everyone, from barmen to baby-sitters, was talking of charging a fortune to work on the big night.

In the midst of all this hype the National Millennium Committee set about the daunting task of deciding how best Ireland could mark and celebrate the Millennium. The first six months were taken up with slowly climbing the approach to the summit. The submissions, proposals and ideas poured in, the structure of the planned events began to evolve and an outline of how the year would end started to take shape. The final six months of '99 were the white knuckle ride down the steep slope at jaw stretching speed towards a New Year's Eve in a thousand. There was no stopping, no getting off and no turning back. It was a case of holding tight and getting there. In the end it was all a memorable cocktail of anticipation, excitement, exhaustion, achievement and, above all, satisfaction. In many ways the real satisfaction came later, after that famous Millennium night, when there was time to relax and take in what had been achieved. Around the world when the last of the fireworks fizzled out and the hangovers receded, people were left to ponder "is that all there is?" In Ireland a whole array of projects and events were there to fill that vacuum and to make sure the Millennium was not just a one night wonder.

I suppose the Millennium really all began with candles. One of the first decisions of the Millennium Committee was to make a gift of a Millennium Candle to every household in the country. It may well end with trees. Sometime before the end of this Millennium the last of the 1.2 million native species planted will probably groan from age and slowly topple over. But it won't really end there. Every year each one of the trees will have scattered the woods with seedlings that will produce even more trees. They in turn will grow and repeat the process. So you could say Ireland's distinctive marking of the Millennium will still be visible in more than a thousand years. All in all not a bad little legacy to leave.

Candles can be symbols of hope. They evoke wonderfully happy as well as sad memories. Now the truth is they can also be the bane of one's life when you are trying to send one to every household in the country. The Kerry writer Bryan McMahon wrote "Mention the word candlelight and a host of memories – sacred, romantic, nostalgic, sentimental, dramatic, joyous and sorrowful bombard the mind". Mention candles to me now and a thousand memories of a different kind come to mind.

I particularly remember an afternoon around the middle of 1999. A few of us from the Millennium Office were seated in the office of the Committee chairman, Minister Séamus Brennan. Now Séamus Brennan is a patient man. He has been years at the cutting edge of politics, through the ebb and flow of elections and the drama of the formation of governments and their untimely end. But even the most patient of people have a point beyond which the steady advice, the reassuring demeanor will not stretch. Instinctively I knew we were reaching that point. The table in the Minister's private office is oval-shaped and of polished hardwood. Normally it is used for meetings involving small groups. It is here he meets with the Whips from the other parties and, individually or as a group, with the Independent T.Ds.

On this particular day it had another purpose. It looked for all the world like a table in a crèche after the children had finished art class. It was covered with candles of every size and shape. The large beeswax alongside the traditional penny candle, formidable church candles looking down on stubby red candles, candles with the Millennium logo glued on and others featuring everything from Amnesty International to Brendan Behan and his fellow Irish writers.

Right No, this is not Ronan Keating fronting his new band, The Millennium Movers. It is Ronan at the Barretstown Gang Camp, Co. Kildare, with Laurie Cearr, Tom Rowley and Minister Séamus Brennan. Photograph – Maxwells.

For weeks before Laurie Cearr, the Marketing and Projects Manager, who was central to the whole project, could be seen like a modern day Florence Nightingale, "the Lady of the Candles", roaming the corridors of Government Buildings with an array of candles. Everyone was canvassed for their view on what candle should be chosen as the national gift for the Millennium. Now, around the Minister's table, it was decision time. The full Millennium Committee were meeting the following day and a final recommendation would have to be made to them. The discussion had been going on for a good half hour when the Minister's patience grew decidedly thin.

"Listen, I'm supposed to be in the middle of keeping the government of the country going. I'm not supposed to be sitting here for hours talking about wax and wicks and the size of bloody candles. Now let's make a decision and go with it." Inside five minutes the candle size and that of the scroll to accompany it was chosen. The candle selected was stout enough to be safe when set upright and large enough to make a decent gift. If we chose a candle that, when packaged, would fit through the standard letter box it would have been an insignificant item, a penny candle size that would merit little attention. It would also be a real danger if children came across the package inside the door and tried to light the wick, not to mention the fall-out for all the dogs unable to resist the smell of beeswax. Instead the sturdy candle would be hand delivered by An Post which would add to the sense of occasion. And that, as they say, should have been that. But then along came the listeners to Joe Duffy's *Liveline* and the *Pat Kenny Show* who could not contain themselves at the great joke about the Millennium Candles that would not fit through letterboxes.

To this day I still don't know how the rumour started but putting the record straight was a long and infuriating business. The Minister, other members of the Committee, Laurie and myself explained until we were blue in the face that they were never supposed to go through letter boxes. Pat Kenny himself told me he loved the candle idea but all the rumpus about it was good radio and that was his job. It was only when people began receiving their candles and realised it was a thoughtful and enduring gift that the so called "joke" quietly vanished.

The Millennium Candle did feature again on *Liveline*. This time it was New Year's Day 2000, the first day of the new Millennium, when caller after caller talked of how the candle and the whole emotion and symbolism of the Last Light Ceremony had the night before been the highlight of the Millennium for them. As the gift of the candle to every house-hold had originally been my idea, I sat back and relished the moment. Hardly had the candle wax been cleared from the Minister's desk than it was covered again, this time with bunches of healthy oak saplings. And so began the quest to plant a tree in the name of every household in the country and to post a certificate to each telling them where their individual tree was located. Along the way we did have the odd call from people wondering how we were going to fit the oak saplings through letter boxes. Phew!

A Big Idea … Séamus Brennan suggested a fountain in Dublin Bay. Not just any fountain but one that would rival for size and impact famous fountains in Geneva (460ft) and Jeddah (753ft). It would emit a powerful jet of water several hundred into the air that would in turn cascade with dramatic force. During the day, the fountain would be a landmark right in the middle of Dublin Bay, visible from O'Connell Bridge and from both sides of the bay. At night it would become an even more impressive spectacle with floodlighting to enhance its gushing, dazzling impact. A considerable amount of time went into researching the feasibility of the plan, everything from shipping lanes, silting and tidal influences, to wind velocity and water power were looked at in consultation with the Port Authority. In the end it came down to size and location. Yes, the fountain could be installed but only if it was located well out in the Bay. Put it closer in and problems arose, particularly when the wind blew. If water is shooting hundreds of feet up then when the wind hits it the fall-out will splatter a wide area. Passing ships could expect an occasional water-laden slash and residents of Ringsend or Clontarf might be soaked whenever they ventured outside their front doors, depending on the prevailing winds. A great idea but unfortunately it sunk, literally, under the weight of technical and practical advice!

Political Push … To Kerry in June 2000 to announce funding for one of the most intriguing projects, the restoration of a section of the Lartigue Monorail in Listowel. The day served to show that the best laid plans of a press officer can quickly go awry. The event was split into three separate ceremonies, a sod turning in one place, speeches in another and the main photocall at the farm of Mick Barry in Lisselton where he had lovingly reconstructed a carriage from the old Lartigue and set it on a section of the original raised track.

The photo opportunities were great. Senator Maurice Hayes, whose grandfather worked on the original Lartigue, Minister Brennan and Mick chatting as they leaned out the window of the first class carriage. I was already visualising the photograph on page one of the local papers. It was a natural for it.

And then things went a little, forgive the pun, off the rails. Getting to Mick's house had taken us up narrow stone wall lined side roads and onto a grassy field. Now, as the Minister prepared to leave, the wheels on the ministerial car spun, the mud flew but the car was going nowhere. So what was the main photograph in the following week's papers? Yes, you've guessed it. Politicians, press officer and all assembled looking red-faced, and not just from embarrassment, as they pushed the car towards the road.

Left Paul Newman obviously paying close attention to my suggestions on how he might improve his screen performances. Laurie Cearr is having more success. Paul had called to thank the Millennium Committee for supporting his Barretstown Gang Camp. Photograph – Maxwells.

Poet, Singer and Eagles … There are many other memories. Seamus Heaney calling to offer his advice on the verse to be used on the scroll accompanying the Millennium Candle. A genial man with great warm hands the size of shovels, he modestly steered us away from using a verse of his own in favour of lines from a W.B. Yeats poem. Ronan Keating calling me out of the blue just days before New Year's Eve to say he would be back in Ireland and available to perform at the big concert in Merrion Square on Millennium night if we needed him. If we what! Remember this was at a time when performers of his stature were demanding small fortunes to perform live on that night. In the end he appeared – money was never mentioned – on stage a number of times to the delight of the thousands attending and the vast television audiences in Ireland and abroad. A quiet spoken man from the Salvation Army Hostel calling to ask for Millennium Candles so that he and others using the facility over the Millennium could take part in the Last Lights ceremony. Families battling through horrendous storms and floods in November 2000 to be the first households from their native counties to receive the Millennium Trees certificates from the Taoiseach. The thrill of being in Glenveagh National Park on the day the first wild Golden Eagles returned to Ireland in almost a century. A tray of Irish coffees emerging from Campbell's pub at the foot of Croagh Patrick on the day we opened the Murrisk Millennium Peace Park. And that was at 11 o'clock in the morning! I could go on and on.

Unusual to Whacky … Of course there were plenty of the ideas and proposals that can be collectively tagged "unusual, original and downright whacky". There was the artist who wanted to put on an exhibition during the Millennium year tracing the history of ladies undergarments, i.e. knickers. The general ideal was to have them strung out on display along Dublin's Ha'penny Bridge. Even more intriguing was the offer to have a facility that would allow enthusiasts to donate an item on the spot for public display. Equally original was the formula to help the people of Ireland exorcise themselves of bad memories and experiences. The idea was simple. Build two Viking boats, anchor them for a few weeks along the quays in Dublin and encourage people to dump on board confessional tapes, home videos, notes, books, clothes, in fact anything that rid them of past demons. On Millennium Eve, the boats would sail out into the middle of Dublin Bay and be ceremonially burned. And with them, as the charred remains sank beneath the waves, would go all the bad memories. Well, that was the theory at least. Then there was the suggestion that the All-Ireland Hurling Final should be staged in Croke Park on New Year's Day, 2000, and turned into a day-long celebration of Ireland, its people, culture and sport. The entrance gates to Croke Park, enthused the proposer, should be thrown open and everyone allowed in free. Not one, as you will appreciate, that the G.A.A. warmed to.

Spinning Away … The Millennium Office is now winding down. Soon we will all go our separate ways. Deep down I still have a picture in my mind that is akin to the television advertisement a few years back for Carlsberg lager in which the complaints department is in an office where obviously nobody has worked for years and cobwebs cling to everything, presumably because there are no complaints from customers. When the phone does ring and is answered by a curious passer-by it is a wrong number. In my mind's eye, I see an empty office at the end of a long corridor, somewhere in Government Buildings. It is sometime in the future. An official passing hears the phone ringing and steps into a dust-covered room. The conversation that follows goes something like this.

Caller Hello, yes, you see it's about the Millennium Candle.

Official The Millennium Candle, but that was years ago, back in 1999, I think.

Caller Well, yes, I know that. But you see the problem is that I never got my candle. All my neighbours got theirs and they still light them every New Year's Eve. They say it brings back great memories for them. I'm sure the postman delivered mine but for whatever reason it went walkabout from my doorstep. Now there is a family up the road that have more than one but I'm not saying anything more about that, if you get my drift.

Official But this is 2015. It's 15, 16 years since the candle was sent out.

Caller I know and I suppose I've left it a bit late, but can you send me my candle anyway? Oh, and while you are at it, can you arrange a bus or a lift of some kind so I can visit my tree in the forest? It should be fairly big by now.

Official Ahem, leave it with me, I'll see what I can do. I think I have a number somewhere for a Tom Rowley who used to work here years ago. He's your man.

It has been some spin on the Millennium rollercoaster. Thanks for the memories. And, as Séamus Brennan is prone to say when asked about the whole experience "I'm definitely not doing this job next Millennium."

– Tom Rowley *Press Officer*

Right Getting close, but not too close, to a wild Golden Eagle chick on its arrival in Co. Donegal. It remains safe and secure in the care of project leader Lorcan O'Toole with John Marsh of the Irish Raptor Study Group in the background. Photograph – Clive Wasson.

Top Right Political push needed during sticky moment at Lartigue Railway launch in Kerry. Photograph – Don MacMonagle.

Right The Collins Family, who in November 2000 battled through storms and floods to reach Dublin when chosen to be the first family from Co. Cavan to receive the Millennium Tree certificate at a ceremony in Government Buildings.

Millennium Memories

Laurie Cearr

For almost half a decade people all over the world had been thinking about the significance of a new Millennium and wondering how to mark it. When I joined the government's Millennium Office in June 1999 it still seemed like a date in the dim and distant future. Little did I know that I was boarding an express train that was running full tilt at the buffers of 31/12/1999.

The Press Officer, Tom Rowley, had been at the helm since the beginning, and I came on board as Marketing and Projects Manager on secondment from RTÉ. I had previously been closely involved in a number of major projects with a national dimension, such as the Papal visit, a brace or two of Dublin City Marathons, the launch of 2FM and Dublin International Piano Competitions. Where was the mystery? Just apply the formula and everything would go smoothly. It would be fairly routine, an extension of the day job.

Let me tell you a little secret. When it comes to Millennium celebrations there are no formulae. Once I was aboard the rollercoaster ride that the Millennium celebrations became in those last adrenalin-charged six months, all the conventional rules went out the window and I learned it truly is a once in a lifetime experience. What was needed was dedication, a touch of fearlessness, the tenacity of a bulldog and an unpuncturable sense of humour. Oh yes, and loads of staying power. Twenty-four seven? That was what wimps did. It was only in the last few frantic months, when the Millennium

celebrations programme was accelerating at breakneck speed towards that once-in-a-lifetime shift from one millennium to another, that it dawned on us just how big a task we had taken on.

What was truly exciting was just how much was happening. It wasn't just about the big headline-grabbing projects like the Millennium Candle or the New Year's Eve celebrations in Merrion Square in Dublin or The People's Millennium Forests. I suddenly found myself immersed, body and soul, in literally dozens upon dozens of exciting schemes and projects that had been dreamed up by committees and communities the length and breadth of the country.

Some were hugely ambitious, others were of much smaller scale but nevertheless just as meaningful to the communities from which they had emanated. I was completely taken by the enthusiasm with which villagers and townsfolk every-where had seized upon this extraordinary date in all our lifetimes to do something that would, in some important and lasting way, mark this significant moment. It could be something as unusual as sending live goats to East Africa or as modest as erecting a park bench in the village square; whatever it was, it was important to the community involved.

The government-appointed National Millennium Committee examined literally thousands of submissions and decided on the level of financial support those given the green light would receive. Apart from the guiding hand of the Civil Service's Richard Holland, himself a member of the NMC, who, with Kathlyn Butler co-ordinated the projects, and

admin. assistant Nicola Carey, it was really just two of us: Tom Rowley and myself, to make it all happen and tell the world about it.

The first meeting with the Committee was an eye-opener. It was chaired by one of the most unflappable people I have ever met – the inscrutable Séamus Brennan. As Chairman of the Committee he certainly didn't have it all his own way. With such strong and diverse individuals on board, decisions were not easily or quickly taken and, unless there was a majority, a project just did not make it.

One project that did get the thumbs up though, was Tom Rowley's idea of the Last Light and the candle for every household in the country. It was the first task I was assigned. Not too difficult – a few telephone calls, a couple of meetings and the whole thing would be sorted out. It didn't work quite like that. First off, there was the culture shock of the Civil Service tendering process.

The contract for the supply of the candles had to be put out to tender in Europe. Then there were the weeks and weeks of reducing (with me trying to add another inch) the size of the candle. More weekly summits with An Post (who at the time felt the candles could not be delivered to every householder in time), Rehab who packed the 1.28 million candles and scrolls and, of course, Rathbornes, whose representative Justin Kneeshaw's personal and profess-ional input went that extra mile. Then what would we do with the surplus? An Post had nowhere to store them. Little did we know!

the new millennium

1 Mrs. Rita Duffy, Co. Waterford's oldest lady receiving her Commemorative Millennium Silver. **2** Co. Waterford's first born Millennium baby Muireann Walsh pictured with her parents Martina & Paul, and sisters Chloe & Aoife.
3 Listowel Millennium baby Michaela Lauren with her parents Caroline O'Connor and Kevin Barry
4 Dursey Island cable car.

I have to admit that at times during those weeks I thought "when Tom Rowley has a good idea, he should keep it to himself". But I'm nothing if not tenacious, and, somehow, between us all, we got it done. And wasn't it a nice (not so little) candle? The envy of many a foreigner, indeed.

Throughout all this, hundreds more projects were still being processed and assessed. Arrangements, down to the finest detail, were being made for Millennium Eve. Dunsink Observatory advised on the precise location of the last light in Ireland; where the sun would sink for the final time in the 20th century. That Dunsink said Dursey Head in West Cork was the spot led to my finding a little bit of heaven here in Ireland and two of my own birth-family namesakes, no relation to me or to each other – Tadgh O'Sullivan from the Allihies Co-Op, and local school teacher, John L. Sullivan, a fount of local lore and wisdom.

To find the exact point, John L. arranged a memorable trip to Dursey Island for me, travelling by cable car and sharing the rickety, swaying cabin 100 feet or more above a rushing swell, with a load of concrete blocks for an island farmer. I was petrified with fear the whole way, and I am not known for long silences. However, my Dursey Island visit was just about worth the terror.

The spot selected locally for the Last Light celebration with the best vantage point was simple and unspoiled. I hoped no one would try to "improve" it, to make it showbizzy or artificial. I hoped they would do it their way – and they did. The people of Alihillies left it to nature, which didn't let them down on the day.

It would have seemed that little could top the stirring experience of the Last Light Ceremony with the Taoiseach and more than 25,000 people in Merrion Square in Dublin. But we hadn't allowed for the magic of Dursey.

At lunchtime on Millennium Eve, I learned that the weather there was abysmal, but I felt compelled to see the televised ceremony, which happened 15 minutes after the celebrations in Dublin. I watched, entranced, as the clouds parted and the sun appeared, fleetingly lighting up the sky as an almost perfect orange sun slid into the Atlantic Ocean for the last time in the second Millennium. What can we say? Dursey delivered a spectacular moment for worldwide television from Ireland!

But, of course, Ireland's celebrations weren't all about Millennium Eve. Almost 2,000 special events took place in the 34 Local Authority regions, funded through the Millennium Events Awards scheme, and administered by a dedicated resident Millennium Officer. Many of these people took on the task in addition to their regular duties. Through almost daily contact, I came to know several of the officers and was hugely impressed by the enthusiasm and dedication for even the smallest affair in their own bailiwicks. These Awards allowed locals to organise their own special marking of the historical high point without the constraints of bureaucracy and they did so with alacrity, greatly encouraged by the officers who got right out there into the community with help and encouragement. To my mind, the Millennium Officers are the unsung heroes and heroines of the Millennium.

Ireland's recent prosperity and wealth has brought its own complexities including, some might think, the loss of our sense of neighbourliness and community. We needn't worry. It is still there in abundance in the towns and villages of Ireland. I witnessed it at first hand on my many visits to various projects. Everyone was eager to be involved and to participate, without the unnecessary frills that so often take over to the detriment of the enterprise/venture.

Of the press launches and photo-calls; how do you capture the atmosphere, how do you make them interesting and appealing for the photographers? Children always work and as they were often the subjects or beneficiaries, why not include them? The young pupils of the Montessori Education Centre in North Great George's Street were always the willing victims – impish, outgoing, confident, always polite and charming. Any parent or teacher would be proud. They augur well for our future. We are grateful to them and their teachers for their frequent willing co-operation. A chance encounter with the 102-year-old Mrs. Sarah Seawright provided an ideal focus for the national launch of the Last Light Ceremony. Indeed, I was privileged to meet a number of special Irish citizens during 2000. Some at the dawning and others in the twilight of their years – Millennium babies and centenarians who were singled out for special tributes in their momentous year.

It was an enormous honour to be involved in the engine room of this monumental and historic event. I thank the Chairman, Minister Séamus Brennan, and the members of the National Millennium Committee for that honour. Thanks also to RTÉ Director-General Bob Collins for facilitating my secondment. Above all my gratitude to my partner in the great Millennium adventure, a master of diplomacy and compromise, the serene Tom Rowley.

– Laurie Cearr *Marketing & Projects Manager*

1 Sharing the Last Light. **2** The "Willing Victims" from The Montessori Education Centre, North Great George's Street, Dublin. **3** Mrs. Sarah Seawright launching the Last Light with Minister Séamus Brennan.

03 Arts, Music, Culture

Arts, Music, Culture

> Ireland has long enjoyed the reputation of a country that nourishes and supports culture and the arts. This proud heritage was very much enhanced by the many artistic projects throughout the country supported by the National Millennium Committee. The breadth and scope of these events ranged from the intimate event to the bigger national affair.

One of the most ambitious and imaginative of all these projects was the relocation of Irish-born artist **Francis Bacon's London Studio** to a specially prepared site in the Hugh Lane Municipal Gallery of Modern Art in Dublin. Bacon, regarded as one of the greatest painters of the 20th century, was born in Dublin in 1909 and moved to London in his mid-teens. When he died in 1992, he left a spectacularly chaotic studio, but the more than 8,000 items it contained were painstakingly documented and carefully removed from Reece Mews and replaced in exactly their original positions in Dublin by the Municipal Gallery's team of skilled art archaeologists.

Two of Ireland's best-known theatres received major funding, in both cases to undertake major structural works. The landmark **Cork Opera House** has expanded its seating to 1,600 and now boasts a stunning new glass frontage, while the **Gaiety Theatre** in Dublin has also had a handsome facelift. The Gaiety's frontage has been restored to its original Victorian splendour, and a splendid new plaza area has been built for the enjoyment of patrons and passers-by alike.

Music was a central part of many community Millennium celebrations. For instance, St. Eunan's Cathedral in Letterkenny was the venue for a special performance of **Haydn's Oratorio, The Creation**, performed by choirs from all over Co. Donegal and the County Donegal Senior Youth Orchestra.

The place of classical music in Irish affections was underlined by a number of awards. They included contributions towards the Irish round of the **Millennium AXA Dublin International Piano Competition**, the restoration of the **Church Organ** in Daniel O'Connell's Cahirciveen Church and a **Grand Piano** in Ennis in Co. Clare. There was also funding for a series of **Millennium Concerts at the National Gallery of Ireland**, which allowed students of the Royal Irish Academy of Music to play in public on the same stage as their teachers, internationally recognised soloists such as John O'Conor and Hugh Tinney. Subventions were also agreed for the **O'Carolan International Harp Festival** in Keadue, Co. Roscommon, and the inaugural **Bray Jazz 2000**, a festival featuring many of Ireland's top jazz musicians and visiting international guest artists. But the Millennium Committee also helped fund schemes to purchase instruments for community bands, including the **City of Waterford Brass** and the **CJ Kickham Brass and Reed Band** in Tipperary

town, thus ensuring a continuing musical heritage well into the new century.

Film is probably the one art form that is quintessentially of the 20th century. County Wicklow, where Ardmore Studios are situated, is possibly the most filmed county in Ireland, its stunning scenery having been the backdrop to movies as varied in theme and time as Mel Gibson's *Braveheart*, the World War I flying epic *The Blue Max* and *Spice World*, which featured late 90s teen idols, the Spice Girls. With the help of a Millennium Award, a **Wicklow Film Trail** has been established which allows cinema enthusiasts and tourists to visit the more important film locations and learn about the movies made there through specially prepared on-site storyboards.

Another highly innovative film-based Millennium project is the **Cinemobile.** This is the first all-Ireland travelling cinema, an articulated truck that expands to three times its width to reveal a state-of-the-art 100 seater enclosed auditorium which brings feature films, documentaries and educational films for schools to towns and villages around the country which have no local access to the world of cinema.

Thosnaigh an Cinemobile amach ar chamchuairt i mí Aibreán 2000 faoi ardmheas agus ceiliúradh an Phobail. Beidh an fheithicil seo ar chamchuairt ar feadh 48 seachtainí gach bliain, le trí léiriú in aghaidh an lae, de réimse leathan scannáin Éireannacha agus idirnáisiúnta ag gach ionaid. Trén duais ó Choiste Náisiúnta na Mílaoise dob'fhéidir íoc as ceannacht agus soláthrú treallamh na feithicle agus na costaisí cuí a ghlanadh, leis an tionscnamh a chur ar chamchuairt. I measc na bpairtnéiri sa tionscnamh seo tá

Institiúd Scannánaíochta na hÉireann, Bord Scannán na hÉireann, RTÉ, ESAT, Fusion, B.S.L. agus na Comhairlí Ealaíona sa Phoblacht agus i dTuaisceart Éireann.

Less well-received critically, but nevertheless popular with the audiences that attended its performances in the RDS in Dublin and watched it on RTÉ television, was **Messiah XXI For A New Millennium**, Frank McNamara's very modern interpretation of Handel's masterwork which was first performed in Dublin's Fishamble Street in 1743. The production was partially funded by the Committee and featured Gladys Knight, Chaka Khan, Roger Daltrey and Jeffrey Osborne.

A number of entertaining and original theatrical events were also supported. These included Kilkenny's Barnstorm Theatre's **River Through Time** travelling pageant, which opened in the ruins of Kells Priory on the banks of King's River. Another event, **Over the Bridge**, a community arts project celebrating the culture and history of Ringsend, which straddles the Dodder River in Dublin, evoked events as different as Oliver Cromwell's visit in 1649 to the considerably less disruptive concert by Bill Haley and the Comets in the Regal Cinema in the 1950s.

Left R.I.A.M. Millennium Concerts at the National Gallery of Ireland.

Cinemobile

> The Cinemobile will visit towns and villages throughout the 32 counties, bringing the magic of the silver screen to communities that have no local access to the world of cinema. The vehicle will be on the road for 48 weeks each year, with three daily screenings including a range of Irish and international releases. There is a strong educational element which supports the school curriculum.

Millennium Committee Award €674,230 (IR£531,000)

> A Personal Note

I first saw the Cinemobile in action on a lonely lay-by somewhere in Co. Louth. It was on loan from France then and Lelia Doolan had organised a little tour to see how it all worked. They showed *Guiltrip* that night and I was impressed with the quality of the facilities – not just the sound and vision of the film itself, but also the comfort and space afforded the audience.

Gerry Stembridge

So when Lelia Doolan told me she was trying to raise money to provide the country with its own permanent Cinemobile, I was happy to give it my wholehearted support. I would be proud to have any film of mine aboard this particular truck. It is, I think, a sign of remarkable vision and understanding that the National Millennium Committee saw the present and future possibilities for small communities in Ireland to have this facility passing their way. It provided the funds to realise the dream. I haven't the capacity to describe the Cinemobile in a technical way, but in my head this ungainly looking truck combines the romance of the old travelling circus, or theatre fit-ups, with the required technology and comfort for viewing modern movies.

I could not imagine a small community that would not get excited at the prospect of an annual or biannual festival of film brought to their nearest lay-by or parking spot, no matter if there is a big town with a multiplex only 25 miles away and Mum and Dad occasionally bring the kids to see a Disney, or manage a night off themselves once a month to catch the latest Tom Cruise. This is different. For one night each year people in tiny communities can feel part of an elite club. The cinema has come to them, and at each screening a hundred or so privileged souls can snuggle up in cosy comfort and lose themselves in their chosen film. For kids particularly, it will be a wonderful romantic introduction to cinema going. They will see the Cinemobile pull out of town and yearn for the day of its return.

I was, and am, genuinely excited by this extraordinary piece of machinery. It should be travelling the byroads of Ireland permanently for it will bring only joy, and delight, and passionate discussion wherever it parks itself and unfolds its magic.

– Gerry Stembridge *Writer/Director*

"It is vital that cinema is brought to as many people as possible, not just in cities but right across the country in towns and villages. Watching a film on the big screen in the company of others is an experience which television can never match. Children, especially, should be able to experience the magic of the movies and what better way than in a moving cinema that comes right to your road."

– Gabriel Byrne *Actor*

The travelling cinema rolls in … transformation from truck to cinema! The articulated truck hydraulically unfolds to three times its width to become a comfortable 100-seater auditorium with wheelchair access. Ireland's first travelling cinema took to the roads in April 2000, opening its doors to a large audience, waiting for a unique experience. Film stills, courtesy of the Irish Film Board.

> A Personal Note

There was film-making in Ireland long before there was Irish film. Those images that flooded our consciousness were of fiery, red-haired Mary Kate Danaher, heroic Seán Thornton, the bullying farmer, the wed-able widow, those wily Irish fellows, Barry Fitzgerald, Bing Crosby and Arthur Shields – and all the rest who made up a world that was not real but real enough for a night out – more droll, more tragic, more extravagant – peopled by the odd man out, the cripple, the aching lovers and all those shadows of ourselves.

There were queues for the cinema as long as the street, immense anterooms of expectation, hormonal agitation and chat. And then there was Irish television and, not so long after, more and more Irish film-makers staying at home and making up their own stories for the screen. It takes a bit of getting used to – that it's not just those experts from Hollywood or Elstree but a bunch of native nobodies standing up and telling our tales with their version of the hero, the fool, the knave, the steadfast mother, the fiery flapper and so on – the whole damn cast.

In 1945, there were 50 cinemas in Dublin, in Belfast, etc. Theatre groups toured; travelling companies brought variety and film shows. Today, there are fewer cinemas with more and more screens, in fewer places; more and more television channels. Our dream for the Cinemobile is that it will travel the country, wooing fresh generations of cinemagoers to scenes of suffering and wonder.

Bhí scannáin á ndéanamh in Éirinn sula raibh scannáin Éireannacha á ndéanamh. B'iad na híomhánna a bhíodh ag líonadh ár n-aigne ná cinn den bhean rua fíochmhar, Khate Danaher, an laoch Seán Thornton, an feirmeoir brúidiúil, an bhaintreach so-phósta, na rógairí Gael – Barry Fitzgerald, Bing Crosby agus Arthur Shields – agus iad sin eile ar fad a bhí i saol nach raibh fíor ach fós a bhí sách fíor le oíche amuigh a chaitheamh leis – saol a bhí níos greannmhara, níos tragóidí níos áibhéilí – saol ina raibh an cadhan aonair, an cláiríneach, na leannáin chráite, agus na scáilí eile sin ar fad dúinn féin.

Bhíodh scuainí fad na sráide lasmuigh de na pictiúrlanna, ionaid ollmhóra tnúthánacha, na hormóin ag bíogadh, agus cabaireacht.

Ansin tháinig Teilifís Éireann agus go gearr ina dhiaidh sin thosaigh níos mó agus níos mó de lucht déanta scannán na hÉireann ag fanacht sa mbaile, ag cumadh a gcuid scéalta féin don scáileán. Tógann sé tamall dul i dtaithí ar an smaoineamh sin – nach hiad na saineolaithe ó Hollywood nó Elstree amháin atá ann, ach go bhfuil grúpa de dhaoine dúchasacha anaithnid ag aithris a gcuid eachtraí féin lena leagan féin den laoch, den chneámhaire, den mháthair stuama, den ainnir fhíochmhar, agus mar sin de – an fhoireann iomlán le chéile.

I 1945 bhí leathchéad pictiúrlann i mBaile Átha Cliath, i mBéal Feirste, srl. Bhíodh grúpaí drámaíochta ag taisteal; thagadh comhlachtaí taistil le seónna geamaireachta agus scannáin. Inniu, tá níos lú pictiúrlanna ann, ach níos mó scáileáin iontu, agus iad níos scoite óna chéile ná riamh; ach tá i bhfad níos mó cainéal teilifíse ar fáil.

Is í an aisling atá againne don Cinemobile ná go rachaidh sé ó cheann ceann na tíre ag mealladh glúnta úra de lucht féachana chuig radharcanna anró agus ionta.

– Lelia Doolan *Chairperson, Cinemobile*

Richard Holland

> Millennium Committee Favourites

What strikes me most is the sheer range of the projects the Committee were involved in, from ambitious large-scale structural undertakings such as the Irish World Heritage Centre in Manchester, right down to the simple planting of a tree by a primary school. I don't think it was the original intention to have a huge number of schemes, but in the final analysis I'm pleased it happened this way because it was representative of how the Irish people wanted to mark the Millennium.

I think the concept of the travelling cinema, **The Cinemobile**, is great. We live in a highly technological age, and for most children today, entertainment is packaged in DVDs, videos, CDs and CD-ROMs played in our living rooms or on our PCs. But I think there is something magical about going into a darkened space and sharing a wonderful experience with a lot of other people as reality is suspended for 90 minutes or so. This will now be available once or twice a year for children and adults alike who don't live anywhere near cinemas.

I was very taken by the Liffey Boardwalk and in particular how it changes the perspective of the Liffey, east to west, rather than the old way of seeing the city as north and south.

Glendalough 2000 is also very impressive. I love the idea of the five small "cillíns" they've built, little rooms of retreat where people of all religions or none can seek respite from day-to-day living and spend some time in contemplation amongst some of the most beautiful scenery in Ireland.

– Richard Holland *Secretary National Millennium Committee, 1999-2001*

Right Dermot Healy in *I Could Read The Sky*
Still courtesy of the Irish Film Board.

Gaiety

> The façade of Dublin's oldest theatre has been restored to its former Victorian splendour as part of a major restoration and conservation project. The theatre, which first opened in 1871, has since then provided a huge range of entertainment from pantomime to grand opera for generations of Irish audiences.

Millennium Committee Award €634,869 (IR£500,000)

Maureen Potter

> A Personal Note

C'mon, Christy, we're going down town. No, we're not going shopping. I'm skint. No, I haven't got a credit card. My American Excess card was stolen. Your father never reported it because the fellow who stole it was spending less than me.

We're going to see the new front in the Gaiety Theatre. All spruced up for the new Aluminium. I know it's the Millennium, Christy, but the Aluminium is easier to say. The Old Lady of South King Street is shining there like your granny when she puts her teeth in. How old is she? About 130. No, not your Gran, the Gaiety, and there she is in all her glory like she was all those years ago.

Your Gran used bring me to the Gaiety. To plays, musicals, pantos, operas, the lot. We used to climb up to the Gods because there you were nearer to God than the rich people

in the Dress Circle. The rich people. You know, Christy, when they have bingo in Foxrock they don't shout, "house"; they call out "bungalow". God be with the days when we went to bingo in Gardiner Street. They used call out the numbers in Latin so as the Protestants couldn't win. The Jesuits said it wasn't very ecumenical but it was very economical.

But what about the Gaiety? When I went there first, Maureen Potter was a child performer. And that's not today nor yesterday. Now *she* must be 125. Your Gran loved d'Operas. I remember one opera and the huge big woman singer was supposed to be sick. Yet she was singing away. She was supposed to have a wasting disease. If we had waited for her to waste away, we would have missed Christmas. She let a screech out of her and died. This little tenor fellow was supposed to carry her off the stage. He tried to lift her off the bed and the sweat was pouring off him. He lifted one of her arms and a fellow sitting near us shouted out, "Take what you have and come back for the rest." Gran was raging and hit him with her bag of bull's eyes.

Ah, them were days, Christy, them were days. Of course, I'll bring you to the Gaiety some night. Your home ecker? We'll let you off that night. Tell the teacher a boy's education is not complete until he's been to the Gaiety.

– Maureen Potter *Actress*

Above The Panto at the Gaiety. Photograph – Tom Lawlor.
Right The Gaiety Theatre's restored Victorian façade. Photograph – Jonathan Hessian

> A Personal Note

The Gaiety Theatre has been part of Dublin's rich cultural life for the past 130 years. The award from the National Millennium Committee enabled the Gaiety to restore the façade of the theatre to its original Victorian splendour, with a new glass and steel canopy of the period. Dublin Corporation's redevelopment of the South King Street area provided the Gaiety with a new plaza in front. The provision of the plaza and completion of the Millennium restoration work enhances the experience for the public attending performances and the passers-by.

John Costigan

This generous award is the first grant in the theatre's history, and is the first phase of the major redevelopment programme. This phased programme of works will provide the public and theatre production companies with improved facilities. In public areas, new seating will be provided with improved leg room as well as provision for air conditioning and improved bar and front of house facilities. In the stage area, it is planned to improve the facilities, including increased flying capacity and orchestral and artist accommodation.

The overall result of this redevelopment will ensure the Gaiety's future as a major part of Dublin's cultural life, with the ability to programme a wider repertoire of work in comfortable, elegant surroundings.

– John Costigan *Director*

Cork Opera House

> The Cork Opera House, a venue synonymous with entertainment in the city for almost 150 years, underwent a complete transformation for the Millennium. The ambitious Millennium project saw the Opera House acquire a splendid new glass frontage while its public floor space doubled and audience capacity increased to 1,600. Outside, the new Millennium Plaza further enhances Ireland's only purpose-built opera house. The completed development and refurbishment programme will ensure that the Opera House continues to be a major cultural, artistic and recreational focal point in the lives of all Cork people and visitors to the city.

Millennium Committee Award €571,382 (IR£450,000)

Kathleen Lynch

> A Personal Note

The plan to transform the Cork Opera House was like trying to repaint the Mona Lisa. No one could ever say she was the most beautiful of women but, just like our Opera House, which itself was not the most attractive, she was a beloved jewel. The people of Cork were used to this historic and original but plain building and so were not too well-disposed to changing it. Let's be honest, we all knew they wouldn't easily forget if we made a mistake. However, undeterred and with very little money but a firm belief in our great design and a team that believed implicitly that it could be done, we braced ourselves and got on with the job. I believe the end result justified the heart-stopping moments and the meetings where the only views expressed were doubts.

We have, in my humble opinion, transformed an ugly duckling into what can only be described as a flagship of light, a beacon for the future, which sits in its rightful place on the River Lee.

– Councillor Kathleen Lynch *Director, Cork Opera House*

Above Cork Opera House, before …
Right After the transformation. Photograph – Michael McSweeney.

Eithne Healy

Being a theatre person, I can say from the heart that I'm particularly pleased that the National Millennium Committee was able to help both the Gaiety Theatre in Dublin and the Cork Opera House. In both cases, awards from the Committee allowed the building of splendid new façades.

The Gaiety Theatre occupies a special place in many people's hearts. It was probably their first theatrical experience – being brought to Christmas pantomimes there. As a privately owned theatre, not in receipt of any subsidy, it exists on a knife-edge all the time, so the Millennium money meant a great deal. Frequently a large capital grant can act as a spur and I believe that the Gaiety's owners are planning ambitious refurbishment of the theatre's interior, this is brilliant. **The Cork Opera House** is the main theatre in the country's second city and an important part of the social fabric and deserves to be supported equally.

In general, I do think the Arts and the Environment are important and I think both were well looked after in the Millennium year. Notable projects such as The People's Millennium Forests made big headlines but a good deal of the money distributed by the Committee to local authorities around the country will have filtered down to community arts projects of all kinds.

– Eithne Healy, *Chairman of the Abbey Theatre Board and Member of the National Millennium Committee*

Francis Bacon Studio

> Francis Bacon's London studio has been faithfully reconstructed in the Hugh Lane Municipal Gallery in Dublin. Already established as one of the most exciting visual arts attractions in Europe, this unique treasure has been made possible with a significant award from the National Millennium Committee.

Millennium Committee Award €380,921 (IR£300,000)

> A Passionate Accumulation of Traces ...

I still remember my astonishment in 1947, standing before a painting by Francis Bacon in London. Its subject was merely a herringbone tweed overcoat slung over an invisible support and topped by a man's hat. In spite of human absence, it emanated an ominous presence, which greatly impressed me. Since that moment I have considered Francis Bacon to be as significant in our time as any artist during the last century.

Louis le Brocquy

Knowing Francis gave me a further insight into his painting, still widely misunderstood as to its nature and inner motivation. I personally owe him much for his constant encouragement and support. He had strong ideas, but remained open to new ones. In his last letter to me, which lay unanswered on my desk when I learned of his death in Madrid, he remarked: "At the Saatchi Collection there is a very interesting installation by a young man called Damien Hirst entitled 'A Thousand Years'. It is of a calf's head in one compartment and in the second part they breed flies which swarm around the cow's head it really works."

Francis Bacon infused the very texture of his feelings – and indeed of his life – into his work. For this reason alone the installation of his marvellously disordered studio in Dublin's Hugh Lane Municipal Gallery of Modern Art is of the utmost interest, for in it we can witness a passionate accumulation of traces, vestiges not only of his ways of working, but of the ideas and images that moved him to work.

This spectacular mess, meticulously rearranged and filed in its explanatory database will, I believe, reveal much in the research of Bacon's work by students in Ireland and throughout the world.

And what would Francis himself think of all this? No one can answer. But I imagine he might be wryly amused and possibly pleased that his well-loved Reece Mews studio had somehow survived on its own, ironically making its way full circle to Ireland.

– Louis le Brocquy *Artist*

Above Portrait of Bacon on display in studio.
Right The Reece Mews studio reconstructed.

LarCon Centre

> The LarCon Centre in Liberty Hall will be a major cultural and performance amenity in the heart of Dublin City. It is being developed by SIPTU as a Millennium project and will replace the Connolly Auditorium meeting venue. The LarCon Centre will be a venue for the people of Dublin to enjoy art, leisure and creative and community activity and entertainment. The centre has been named jointly after James Larkin and James Connolly, the founding fathers of the Irish Trade Union movement.

Millennium Committee Award €317,434 (IR£250,000)

Bertie Ahern T.D.

> A Personal Note

The new LarCon Centre will be a fitting Millennium tribute to the valuable role the labour movement has played in the evolution and growth of modern Ireland. It will be a living monument to the men and women who have contributed at national and local level to the development of Irish industrial life. The centre is also a meaningful and lasting way of saluting the work, memory and sacrifice of two of the giants of the labour movement, James Larkin and James Connolly.

Liberty Hall has, for the best part of a century, played a central role in the development of Irish life. In 1913 Liberty Hall served as a centre of the Dublin Lock-Out, providing a meeting place and frugal relief to the strikers. In 1916 the Proclamation of the Irish Republic was printed in Liberty Hall and it was from there also that James Connolly marched the Citizen Army to the G.P.O.

The new Liberty Hall continues to play a central role in the lives of Irish workers, and this is why it is the ideal location in which to celebrate, at the start of a new Millennium, their progress in a manner that all workers can be proud of.

The LarCon Centre will be many things to many people. It will be a multi-cultural venue, offering a public facility to celebrate our tradition, culture and art; a facility where community groups, young performers and artists can practice their talents, and a venue supporting inner-city groups struggling to beat the scourge of drug abuse.

Most of all the centre will be a lasting tribute to the courage, tenacity and vision of Irish workers.

– Bertie Ahern T.D.

Ruairí Quinn T.D.

> A Personal Note

My first memory of the then Conference Hall was the substantial concrete structure that held up the roof. As an architectural student in UCD, I was attending my first Labour Party Conference there in 1967. The excitement of the event was compounded by the sense of modernism that the structure represented.

Brendan Corish presided over the modernisation of the Labour Party in the 1960s, straddling the influx of radical young students and the caution of some of the rural deputies, along with the re-affiliation of the two big unions – ITGWU and WUI, and the arrival of Conor Cruise-O'Brien, David Thornley and Justin Keating. Corish had an innate kindness along with his inner strength. He made a habit of moving around the Conference Hall talking to delegates or sitting down with groups during the debates.

Towards the end of the Conference I was sitting on the balcony, Corish asked me to propose a vote of thanks to the Chairman at the close of Conference. It was an honour, one of Corish's ways of integrating the young and the old. I was critical of the way in which some aspects of the Conference had been dealt with and, while I appreciated his honour, I could not propose the vote of thanks. It was a cheeky thing to do. He laughed and thanked me for my frankness. He clearly did not disagree with me.

Brendan Halligan, General Secretary, had organised a large photograph of Brendan Corish as a backdrop on the stage. The task of erecting it was given to me. A problem arose when the staff at the entrance to Liberty Hall heard that a photograph of the Labour Party leader was being erected. They were reluctant to allow that unless James Connolly was put up. Then, political balance demanded Jim Larkin would also have to be on the stage! After various telephone calls from Liberty Hall to Labour Party head office, two suitable portraits of the founding fathers of the Irish Labour Trade Union movement were found and erected on stage.

Liberty Hall, with its Conference Centre, now the LarCon Theatre, has been the centre of so much political activity during my lifetime that I regard it as a political home from home.

–Ruairí Quinn T.D. *Leader of the Labour Party*

Above The LarCon Theatre preparing for the overhaul.

Messiah XXI For a New Millennium

> **MESSIAH XXI For a New Millennium** was a modern arrangement by Irish musician Frank McNamara of Handel's choral masterpiece. The original was first performed in Dublin in 1742 and the new version was premiered in the city in December 1999 and televised by RTÉ. Its strong Christian message and historic links to Ireland combined to offer a production that was original and challenging.

Millennium Committee Award €888,816 (IR£700,000)

MESSIAH XXI has to date been broadcast in Australia, Brazil, Canada, Cyprus, Ireland, Japan, Latin America, the Philippines, Portugal and the USA. The international distributors estimate that a worldwide audience, to date, of some 40-60 million people, has seen this unique Irish contribution to the international Millennium celebrations.

– John Kearns *Director, Messiah XXI Productions Limited*

> A Personal Note

When the idea of staging a major entertainment event for the Millennium was first mooted, a wide range of ideas were considered. Other countries were staging spectaculars, ranging from large rock gigs with pyrotechnic displays to pageant type trips through the history of time. How should we uniquely mark this key moment in a creative and meaningful way, which would have special relevance to this country? The answer lay in the real meaning of the Millennium itself – the 2000th anniversary of the birth of Christ. Allied to this was the fortunate historical fact that the greatest musical telling of the life of Christ, Handel's *Messiah*, had its first performance in this country in 1742.

The idea was born: to re-tell that musical tale of Handel's, in an adaptation representative of the musical style of the 20th century. With the support of the churches, RTÉ, commercial sponsors and the backing of the National Millennium Committee, the task began. Frank McNamara,

one of Ireland's foremost arrangers, undertook the large-scale musical adaptation and a cast of international performers was assembled. Gladys Knight, Chaka Khan, Roger Daltrey, Jeffrey Osborne, The Visual Ministry Gospel Choir and the Irish Philharmonic Orchestra & Chorus performed the work. The script was written by Irish playwright, Frank McGuinness and narrated by Irish American film-star, Aidan Quinn. Celebrated international director, Bill Cosel, filmed the event for international TV release.

The event was staged at the RDS to standing ovations and the popular acclaim of those in attendance. Some of the newspaper critics had a different response. However, I feel that one authoritative Arts Editor reflected the views of many when writing, "We have a history of formal, private belief and we are in such shocked retreat from a Catholic system of values which we think has failed us that a religious message, emotionally delivered, is bound to have a rough time in the media."

Above Gladys Knight with members of the cast in the live performance at the RDS. Photograph – MacInnes Photography.

The Wicklow Film Trail

> The Wicklow Film Trail is Ireland's first location trail for cinema enthusiasts and tourists. It links the locations used for top box office films for cinema and television and provides the opportunity to walk in the footsteps of screen stars such as Sean Connery, Mel Gibson, Liam Neeson, Pierce Brosnan, Jane Seymour and Mia Farrow.

Millenium Committee Award €31,743 (IR£25,000)

> A Personal Note

Morgan O'Sullivan

Wicklow has been the cornerstone of the Irish film industry for many years. One of its principal attractions for film makers is its proximity to Ardmore Studios, the nation's largest film-making facility. Wicklow and the studios have welcomed major film-makers such as Francis Ford Coppola, making a small movie called *Dementia 13* on Ardmore's smallest sound stage in the early sixties, and Mel Gibson utilising the studios together with the Coronation plantation and plains of Kildare for the epic film *Braveheart*.

The majority of the expert crews live in Wicklow or close to it. Ardmore is ideally placed for film-makers as it is close to both rural and urban environments. In many of the period productions I have been associated with, such as *Braveheart*, *Moll Flanders*, *David Copperfield* and, more recently, *The Count of Monte Cristo*, we were able to draw on the great estates of Wicklow, among them Powerscourt. The landscape and villages can be adapted as other European locales. I remember us transforming Enniskerry into a small French village. Distinguished artists such as Matthew M. Conaughey, Morgan Freeman, Peter Ustinov, Jane Seymour and others have remarked on the graciousness and hospitality of Wicklow and Ireland in general.

To this day, long-lasting friendships have developed between visitors and crews. Some of them have come and settled, enriching the community and industry. To begin the new Millennium, County Wicklow played host to the largest and most expensive film ever made, *Reign of Fire*. Above Glendalough at Wicklow Way, a medieval village, the centrepiece of this production, was built. It was the largest motion picture structure ever to be built in this country and a great example of the environmental and local authorities working side by side and helping in the development of an industry that has profound economic and creative benefits for all of Ireland. I look forward to the Film Trail bringing the magic of Wicklow and the film world to an even greater audience.

– Morgan O'Sullivan *World 2000 Entertainment Limited*

Above Filming in Wicklow.
1 The dramatic man-made set for the futuristic film *Reign of Fire*.
2 Scene from *The Nephew* starring Pierce Brosnan.
3 Jane Seymour "taking five" at the launch of the Wicklow Film Trail.

Millennium Snapshots

> If music, culture and the arts are the heart of any nation, then Ireland proved this case in the Millennium year with thousands of events the length and breadth of the country, with the help of the National Millennium Committee funding. Some of them were caught on camera. Here is a selection:

1 > Wexford Arts Centre - Every Little Peace

Wexford Arts Centre marked their Millennium Community Arts Programme with a day-long celebration of peace, and the creation of a Peace Mural in the form of a giant jigsaw. Entitled "Every Little Peace", the mural was fashioned by the people of the twin villages of Rosslare Harbour and Kilrane. It is now on permanent display at the foot-passengers' entrance to Rosslare Europort.

2 > Wexford Arts Centre – Self Portrait

Community Artist Anne Heffernan worked with the Árd Aoibhinn Centre for people with special needs in the creation of a unique self-portrait mural. The mural, which was created by clients of the centre such as John Power (above) from Wexford Town, now hangs in the Foyer at Árd Aoibhinn and will be featured in Wexford Art Centre's Millennium Book.

3 > AXA Dublin International Piano Competition

The AXA Dublin International Piano Competition, which takes place every three years, provides Irish musicians with an opportunity to compete on their home ground with the best of their peers from all over the world. Pictured at the launch of the Irish Qualifying Round which was funded by the National Millennium Committee are John O'Neill, Chief Executive AXA Ireland, Síle de Valera T.D., Minister for Arts, Gaeltacht, Heritage and The Islands and John O'Conor, Pianist and Artistic Director of the Competition.

4 > Clare Music Makers

The Millennium Award provided the Clare Music Makers Parents' Association in Ennis with the unique opportunity to purchase a concert grand piano. Local ownership of the piano will facilitate public concerts and recitals and offer opportunities for advanced music students.

5 > Millbank Theatre

The Millbank Theatre, Rush, Co. Dublin, is owned by the Rush Dramatic Society, one of the oldest amateur groups

3

4

5

6

7

8

in Ireland. Millbank Project 2000 is intended to transform the purpose-built theatre into a modern state-of-the-art venue for the performance of dramatic arts. Photograph is from a production of *Of Mice and Men* by John Steinbeck.

6 > Waterford Brass Band

The purchase of new instruments has enabled the Waterford Brass Band to increase its membership. As well as starting a class for new young beginners, for the first time in the history of the band, there is a class for adults who want to discover the joys of music by playing a brass instrument.

7 > Bray Jazz Festival

Bray Jazz 2000 was inaugurated in the Millennium year with the support of the National Millennium Committee and other sponsorship supporters. The festival featured more than 15 concerts and recitals, with headline shows taking place in a specially created concert club venue at Bray's Ardmore Film Studios.

The festival weekend featured the top names in Irish jazz as well as a number of visiting international guest artists. These included Claire Martin, British Jazz Singer of the Year, with her Big Band, The Ray Gelato Giants and an 18-piece orchestra, Night in Havana.

Free public recitals were staged each evening at the Town Hall with artists such as distinguished Irish guitarist Louis Stewart, while a jazz pub-trail brought music to almost a dozen other venues in the town over the weekend.

Thanks to the great success of the inaugural Bray Jazz Festival, the event was staged once again in 2001, with artists from New York, Cuba, Sierra Leone and the UK.

8 > C.J. Kickham Band

The C.J. Kickham Brass and Reed Band in Tipperary used their award to replace instruments, some of which were up to 50 years old.

9 > Caherciveen Celtic Music Festival, Kerry

10 > Donaghmoyne Youth Band, Monaghan

11 > Donegal Choral Society
In the performance of Haydn's choral masterpiece
The Creation.

12 > Dublin Chamber of Commerce
Distinguished international composer/pianist Philip Martin
was commissioned by Dublin Chamber of Commerce to
write a celebratory piece for the Millennium entitled *Dublin
– A Celebration.*

13 > O'Carolan International Harp Festival
The special Millennium Year O'Carolan International Harp
Festival was opened by President Mary McAleese in the
charming village of Keadue, Co. Roscommon. This annual
ten-day celebration of Irish music and culture features
traditional music concerts, sessions and workshops. The
International Harp Competition is named after the
celebrated harper Turlough O'Carolan.

14 > River Through Time
Kilkenny's Barnstorm Theatre Company's *River Through*

Time included the Ballad of Rory Roe, a Millennium open-
air theatre spectacle celebrating Co. Kilkenny's heritage
and its people.

15 > St. Mary's Arts Group
St. Mary's Arts Group, Limerick, created opportunities for
community participation in street theatre and costume-
making and design.

16 > Samhain 2000
The Beg Borrow and Steal Theatre Company, Dublin,
organised the Samhain Parade to celebrate this ancient
Celtic festival in carnival style.

15

16

17

18

19

20

21

17 > Smashing Times

One thousand years of Ringsend's history was at the core of a Smashing Times Theatre Company presentation.

18 > Members of The Tipperary Millennium Orchestra

A new golden age of music has dawned for Co. Tipperary with the launch of a 60-member Youth Orchestra. The orchestra made its debut before an audience of 300 guests in the restored 13th century Old St. Mary's Church, Clonmel in November 2000.

19 > Leitrim Millennium Choir

Church choirs from Carrick-on-Shannon, Mohill and Longford joined forces to form the Leitrim Millennium Choir. This combined choir of over 100 voices performed a series of concerts to full houses and were subsequently invited to New York for four performances including one at St. Patrick's Cathedral.

20 > Yeats Summer School

Sligo Millennium Events Awards … the Yeats Summer School.

21 > New Composition

Lumen Christie, a choral symphony, was composed by Philip Carty to celebrate Ireland in the new Millennium.

The National Millennium Committee was pleased to support Philip's musical expression of Ireland's social and economic success, our willingness to accept diverse cultures and faiths and our passion for peace. The symphony was premiered at the National Concert Hall, Dublin, by the Orchestra of St. Cecilia, The Lassus Scholars and Piccolo Lasso Choirs under the direction of Colin Block.

04 Environment

Environment

> Over the past thousand years the environment, that most precious of the Earth's resources, has suffered enormously. An event of the magnitude of the Millennium brought into sharp focus the responsibility on all of us to play our part in passing on to the generations to come an environment that is healthier, cleaner and, in every sense, greener.

This aspiration was reflected again and again in the type of projects submitted to the Millennium Committee for consideration with well over a quarter of all submissions related in some way to a desire to protect and enhance the environment. These ranged from large-scale tree planting programmes and major new amenities in cities, to the reintroduction, after a century, of one of the world's most majestic birds, and a plethora of improvement initiatives at village level.

In addition to flagship projects like **The People's Millennium Forests** and the **River Liffey Boardwalk** (see Flagships), scores of other initiatives are being undertaken that will help undo some of the damage of the past, as well as altering and enhancing the fabric of our major cities. Each of the cities has benefited. In the case of Cork and Galway the main emphasis is on bridges and their symbolism of spanning divides. An award of €634,869 (IR£500,000) has been made for the new **Millennium Footbridge in Cork** crossing the River Lee between Cornmarket Street and Pope's Quay. The design is for an attractive steel structure with two symmetrical arches and a timber deck.

Galway's Millennium Footbridge will be equally striking in design. It will be constructed at a high profile location immediately upstream of the Salmon Weir and will use the piers and abutments of the old Galway to Clifden Railway Line as supports for the modern structure. **Waterford's Millennium Plaza** breathes new life into the once obsolete Clyde Wharf part of the city, transforming it into an outdoor performance area and recreational amenity space with facilities for music and theatre events. There is a strong maritime theme, from the sail-like tensile canopy to the detailing of seats, lights and railings. One of Limerick's favourite landmarks, **Tait's Clock in Baker Place**, is also being transformed into a modern plaza using a high-tech glass based structure. It is being designed as a tribute to Co. Louth-born Peter Rice, one of the world's great glass technologists, whose work until now has been little known in his native country.

Light symbolises hope and that is the theme that runs through the extensive **illumination of prominent bridges in Dublin, Cork** and **Limerick**. Millennium funding of more than €1,269,738 (IR£1 million) is changing forever the night-time face of the cities. In Dublin, the **"Liffey of Lights"** scheme illuminates 13 bridges over three miles of the river. Outside of the cities, many towns and villages have responded with attractive, innovative projects. **Carlow's Millennium Bridge** over the river Barrow opens up direct access for the 3,000 plus residents of Graiguecullen Village. **Town Parks in Athlone and Roscommon** will further enhance amenity facilities there.

Two projects in particular captured the spirit of the Millennium: The entire population of the town of **Balla, Co. Mayo,** stole a march on the rest of the world when in the first seconds of the year 2000 they began planting 2,000 Irish oak trees in the town park. The feat has earned them widespread admiration and a special acknowledgement from the Guinness Book of Records.

And what could be more appropriate at the start of a new Millennium than to reintroduce to Ireland a majestic species of bird, the **Golden Eagle** that was forced to extinction almost one hundred years ago. The eagles, for centuries symbols of strength and freedom, have returned to Donegal as part of a carefully managed conservation programme which is receiving generous support from the Millennium Committee. The reintroduction of such a magnificent species will capture people's imagination and is another significant way to celebrate, at the start of a new Millennium, Ireland's growing awareness of just how precious and fragile our environment is.

Taispeánann go leor logainmneacha Gaelacha cé chomh comónta is a bhí na hiolair órga tráth dá raibh. An t-ainm

Ghaleach aba chomónta ná Iolar, cé go raibh roinnt éagsúlachta eile ann ar nós illar nó ulra. Ainmníodh roinnt mhaith áiteanna ar fud na hÉireann i ndiaidh Iolair ar nós, Meenanillar, Co. Dhún na nGall agus Gleann na nIolar i gCo. Chiarraí. Tá móitífeanna Iolar le feiscint ar roinnt croiseanna chloiche luath-Cheilteacha. Léiríonn na líníochtaí ar imeall Leabhair Cheanannais ón ochtú aois, íomhánna de Iolair.

Bhí an t-athrú leanúnach ar bhailte agus ar shráidbhailte na hÉireann trí fheabhsaithe timpeallachta i gcroílár **Green Town 2000**, tionscnamh ardcháil Gradam na Mílaoise. Bhí an tionscnamh seo in a chomórtas mór náisiúnta a thug deis do Choistí Tidy Towns ar fud na hÉireann an Mhílaois a shonrú trí thionscnaimh a fhorbairt a chuir go mór len a limistéar agus a chothaigh níos mó aithne ar agus eolas faoin timpeallacht. Fuarthas 259 iontrálacha san iomlán de thionscnaimh éagsúla. Ina measc san bhí forbairt samhlaíoch de thalamh pháirce; áíseanna; oibreacha athchóirithe/oidhreachta agus tionscnaimh bainistíocht drámhuíoll/athchúrsáil.

Bhuaigh Leithghlinn an Droichid, Co. Ceatharlach, an gradam iomlán de €25,394 (£20,000) agus dealbh chréumha a choimisiúnú go speisialta le Páirc Mhílaoise a fhorbairt. D'fhág an comórtas in a dhiaidh meascán mór de thionscnaimh ar fud na tíre a rachaidh chun leasa na glúine seo agus na glúinte atá le teacht.

Right A male Golden Eagle arriving at the eyrie with food for a chick. The eyries, built mainly from sticks, are usually located on ledges of cliffs or crags.

Photograph – Laurie Campbell.

Waterford Millennium Plaza

> The William Vincent Wallace Plaza transforms the historic but once obsolete Clyde Wharf area of Waterford City. It creates a spectacular outdoor performance arena and recreational amenity space. The design of all elements has a strong maritime theme, including a sail-like tensile canopy. The overall intent is to make the Plaza visually interesting, even during inclement weather and to maintain open views down the river. The performance area is protected by a tent structure backed by strongly coloured elements that simulate Viking shields and maritime flags.

Millennium Committee Award €1.079 million (IR£850,000)

A sculpture, tall and slender in design, is an elegant counterpoint to the nearby Reginald's Tower and incorporates a small camera that transmits live images of the quays worldwide. The sculpture is set on a raised steel base and rotates slowly, while the natural rhythm of the tides constantly changes views and shadows.

A timber boardwalk goes right around the external perimeter of the wharf to the existing marina. Seating and lighting has been provided along the the boardwalk.

The Millennium Plaza is named to honour the Waterford-born composer William Vincent Wallace (1812-1865) whose work, *Maritana*, was the most popular opera of the 19th century. It was performed all over the world including La Scala, Milan.

Alderman Davy Daniels

> A Personal Note

The Waterford Millennium Plaza has quickly become one of the most striking and beautiful features of the city. As a resident of Waterford all my life, I cannot recall a project which has transformed the city so spectacularly. The citizens of Waterford share this view and I have received more compliments and congratulations on this particular project than on anything previously under-taken in the city. Every time I look around the Plaza I feel a tremendous pride, especially when I recall the old derelict warehouse, which it replaced. One of the most striking features, in my view, is the way the City Architect totally captured the maritime feeling, which is exactly in keeping with its riverside setting, with a marina alongside. The sculpture at the "bow" is quickly becoming a landmark for

Waterford, almost rivalling Reginald's Tower, and standing out as a symbol of Waterford's bright future.

In my view, the two features in the design which signify Waterford's progress, are the Waterford Crystal at the base of the sculpture and the Internet link. This provides a model of the co-operation which exists in Waterford between the public and the private sector.

I would like to extend my appreciation to all involved, particularly the National Millennium Committee and its Chairman, Séamus Brennan, my fellow councillors and former mayors who were involved since the outset, none more so than Minister Martin Cullen, the City Architect and the people of Waterford who have fully supported the project. I know they will enjoy long summer evenings of music and dance at this fine facility.

– Alderman Davy Daniels *Mayor of Waterford, 2000-2001*

Above The derelict Clyde Wharf.

Right Now transformed into the Waterford Millennium Plaza.

Brian (Barry) Murphy

> Millennium Committee Favourites

I feel it is important to make a distinction between the excitement of the actual happenings in the Millennium year and the legacy that the year has left to future generations.

In the actual year, I thought the fireworks in Dublin were pure excitement and delight. It was a quite stunning display and a wonderful night out. I really enjoyed the sight of so many people enjoying themselves. The buzz around town was just terrific afterwards. The whole thing was absolute magic.

In terms of a legacy for the future, my favourite is **Waterford's Millennium Plaza**. It really is a most striking construction, one of the best new public spaces I've seen. It came to us on the Millennium Committee as just a two-dimensional outline idea, and to see it realised so beautifully is absolutely astonishing. It has an incredible lasting quality to it, and is a real extension of the city that will be used and appreciated by the people of Waterford for the foreseeable future.

– Brian (Barry) Murphy *Chairman*
Commissioners of Public Works, Member of National Millennium Committee

Golden Eagles

> The Golden Eagle, one of the world's most magnificent birds of prey, has returned to Irish skies. Almost a century after the species was driven to extinction – the last breeding pair was found in North Mayo in 1912 – the birds are once again flying free. Under an ambitious Millennium initiative, eagle chicks are being brought from Scotland and released into the wild in Glenveagh National Park, Co Donegal. The first birds arrived in June 2001 as part of a strategy that will see up to 75 birds released over five years to re-establish a viable breeding population there. By 2010 it is envisaged that up to eight pairs of Golden Eagles, great symbols of strength and freedom, will be breeding in the county.

Millennium Committee Award €63,486 (IR£50,000)

Derek Mooney

> A Personal Note

I'm delighted to see that the plan to reintroduce Golden Eagles to Donegal is doing so well. Recently I travelled along with my colleague Richard Collins, to Glenveagh National Park to meet Lorcan O'Toole, project manager. We were there to record the final chapter for a radio documentary about the first year of the reintroduction programme.

We had a great day, I even got to see my first Golden Eagle in flight. It was a spectacular sight and a great thrill to see Golden Eagles once again in Ireland. It was a moment I will never forget. Lorcan's honesty and frankness when discussing the pros and cons of this project impressed me greatly. He told us of his disappointment that one of the six chicks had perished but that he was hopeful the others would make it. Lorcan now must carry a huge weight on his shoulders and I think anything we, as broadcasters and nature lovers can do to help him, must be done, to ensure this venture is a success.

I remember well my first visit along with author and naturalist Don Conroy to see the ospreys' nest at the Royal Society for the Protection of Birds (RSPB) visitors' centre at Loch Garten in Scotland. I was like a 12-year-old with a new bike, only I wasn't 12, I was in my mid-twenties, old enough to realise the significance of what had been achieved there. What a great blessing it is when a species is brought back from the brink of extinction. One feels that a great wrong has been put right. We in Ireland have exterminated our eagles so what could be more fitting at the beginning of the third Millennium than to restore the Golden Eagle to its rightful place.

Glenveagh National Park is the perfect habitat for this magnificent bird and, make no mistake about it, this is a golden opportunity for Donegal and the people who live there. Every year thousands of people make the journey to the osprey nest site in Scotland, generating millions of pounds for the local economy. I have no doubt that the prospect of seeing this top predator soaring over the Derryveagh and Blue Stack Mountains will attract birdwatchers and naturalists from far and wide.

– Derek Mooney *Producer and Presenter*
"Mooney Goes Wild" RTE Radio 1

Above Project Manager Lorcan O'Toole monitoring the progress of the young Golden Eagles.

Right The Golden Eagles acquire their golden head and nape when they reach maturity after four to five years. Photography – Laurie Campbell.

> A Personal Note

As I scaled the side of the glen to reach a neighbouring corrie the wind picked up and the mist and fine rain quickly descended. The vegetation thinned out as I climbed. By the time I reached the ridge the wind was blowing a gale. I had to lean forward and stagger into the wind to make headway. My kagool was tightly strapped about my eyes as I picked my steps across the rock-strewn plateau. Visibility was less than ten feet as the sea mist was sucked relentlessly into the glen I had just left. Suddenly a dark shadow passed nearby, low over the ground. The shadow wound around me and then broke through the veil of mist and revealed itself as a Golden Eagle. It effortlessly circled me several times, tilting its wings and finger-like primaries, as it slipped in and out of the clouds. How comfortable it seemed in these extreme elements. This was the eagle's domain.

In 1992, I spent six months surveying Golden Eagles from Ben Nevis to Glencoe. Of all my special Highland memories, I vividly recall that afternoon searching for signs of Golden Eagles in a remote glen. Golden Eagles were once ripped from the Irish landscape by human actions. Imagine Golden Eagles reappearing through the mists above the Twelve Pins, Carrantuohill and the hills of Donegal.

In June 2001, after years of planning and lobbying by the dozen members of the Project Steering Group and finally overcoming real concerns over the Foot and Mouth situation, we arrived in Glenveagh National Park with our first Golden Eagles. What a relief! Everyone who has seen the Golden Eagles in Glenveagh has noted how they bring the rugged landscape to life. The eagles look so natural and at home above the hills of Donegal. Recently I saw a Golden Eagle weave and sheer through the gusts swirling around Errigal's ridges. We know these same updraughts around Errigal have buoyed eagles for Millennia, before humans intervened. And as I admired this latest spectacle from the newly improved mountain road, it was clear that our real goal is to marry the needs of local people and an awareness and protection for the vulnerable wildlife and landscape that surround these communities. Feelings of satisfaction and relief were quickly followed by an ardent hope that our society will follow a more sustainable road in the future.

– Lorcan O'Toole *Manager, The Irish Golden Eagle Project*

Left The eagles have landed! Lorcan O'Toole with one of the young eagles collected from the wild in Scotland and taken to Co. Donegal in June 2001.

Above Feeding time in the eyrie.

Right A Golden Eagle chick in the eyrie.

Photography – Laurie Campbell.

GreenTown 2000

> The ongoing transformation of Ireland's towns and villages through environmental improvments was at the core of GreenTown 2000, a prestigious Millennium Awards initiative. The GreenTown 2000 scheme, with a prize fund of €190,462 (IR£150,000), sponsored by the National Millennium Committee, was a major national competition that gave Tidy Towns Committees all over Ireland the opportunity to mark the Millennium by developing projects that enhanced their area and promoted greater awareness of the environment.

In all, 259 entries were received, with a variety of projects including the imaginative development of parklands, amenities, heritage/restoration works and recycling/waste management initiatives. Leighlinbridge, Co. Carlow, won the overall award of €25,395 (IR£20,000) and a specially commissioned bronze sculpture for the development of a Millennium Park. Awards ranging from €635 (IR£500) to €12,697 (IR£10,000) were made to 70 projects.

Noel Dempsey T.D.

> A Personal Note

When I was asked for an idea to celebrate the Millennium, two points immediately struck me. Firstly, we should use this as an opportunity to showcase sustainable development in a way that people could readily identify with and relate to. And secondly, we should make sure that the local communities could choose their own manner of celebration. These two notions were enshrined in the GreenTown 2000 competition. In terms of

sustainability, the competition has left behind an extraordinary range of projects right around the country – projects that bring joy, that add to the lives of the people who use them, and, most importantly, that will serve the current and future generations. Rather than marking the stroke of midnight, they mark progress and the continuum between the Millennia. And the execution of the projects brought communities, individuals, local agencies and local businesses together in an effort to scoop one of the many prizes. So, in the very best sense, these projects represent the efforts of the local communities to mark the Millennium in their own way.

I thank the National Millennium Committee for their kind sponsorship of GreenTown 2000 and each of the 259 communities who entered. Everybody has benefited from this competition, not just the winners or those who participated in projects, but everyone who enjoys these projects, now and into the future.

– Noel Dempsey *T.D.*
Minister for the Environment and Local Government

Above Children at play on the Greystones, Co. Wicklow, Millennium Walkway, another of the award winning projects.

Opposite Page Leighlinbridge won the overall GreenTown 2000 award for their development of a Millennium Park, which was described by the adjudicators as a "summary in stone of peace, harmony and friendship". It comprises of a series of miniature gardens dedicated to the themes of peace, harmony and happiness. The gardens are linked by gravel paths and illuminated by old-world street lighting.

GreenTown 2000 Winners

OVERALL WINNER

LEIGHLIN BRIDGE, CO. CARLOW. A MILLENNIUM PARK, COMPRISING INDIVIDUAL GARDEN SPACES AND ALL-SEASON PLANTING.
€25,412.96 AND BRONZE SCULPTURE.

REGIONAL WINNERS

CASTLEBAR, CO. MAYO. THE DEVELOPMENT AND ENHANCEMENT OF LOUGH LANNAGH PARK, INVOLVING PLANTING AND PATHWAY CONSTRUCTION.
€12,706.48 AND BRONZE PLAQUE.

COOLANEY, CO. SLIGO. THE DEVELOPMENT OF A DERELICT SITE INTO AN AMENITY/MILLENNIUM PARK.
€12,706.48 AND BRONZE PLAQUE.

EMLY, CO. TIPPERARY. THE DEVELOPMENT OF A FOUR SEASONS' PARK.
€12,706.48 AND BRONZE PLAQUE.

ENNIS, CO. CLARE. SUBSTANTIAL UPGRADING OF EXISTING PARK, INCORPORATING SCULPTURED WATER FEATURE.
€12,706.48 AND BRONZE PLAQUE.

LUSK, CO. DUBLIN. THE RENOVATION AND ENHANCEMENT OF "JOE'S BRIDGE", A LOCAL LANDMARK, INCORPORATING TREE AND SHRUB PLANTING.
€12,706.48 AND BRONZE PLAQUE.

NEWTOWNCASHEL, CO. LONGFORD. THE DEVELOPMENT OF AN AMENITY/SCULPTURE PARK, ON THE SITE OF A DISUSED QUARRY.
€12,706.48 AND BRONZE PLAQUE.

RATHBARRY, CO. CORK. THE RESTORATION OF THE SPRIGGING SCHOOL, AN HISTORICAL LOCAL LANDMARK, AS WELL AS THE RESTORATION OF "THE LAKE WALK".
€12,706.48 AND BRONZE PLAQUE.

SPECIAL RECYCLING AWARD

CLARE ISLAND, CO. MAYO. INSTALLATION AND MANAGEMENT OF RECYCLING FACILITY.
€1,270.65 AND CRYSTAL TROPHY.

Full list of winners available on www.2000ireland.ie

Bridges of Light

> Light can transform the ordinary and make the merely interesting visually spectacular. By investing more than €1.269m (£1 million) in the permanent illumination of prominent bridges in Dublin, Cork and Limerick, the National Millennium Committee has helped to transform the night faces of these cities. Central areas are now bathed in a warm after-dark glow that highlights the architecture and status of the bridges. The lighting reflects on the waters of the rivers Liffey, Lee and Shannon, creating a sparkling, glistening effect.

The "Liffey of Lights" scheme illuminated 13 bridges over three miles of Dublin's River Liffey, from Seán Heuston Bridge to the East Link Toll Bridge. Green light illuminates the underside of the structures and arches. The body of each bridge is lit by wall-anchored projectors emitting warm colours of light and interesting artistic features on some of the bridges are highlighted even more by spotlights.

Cork is famous for its many bridges – it has, we are told, even more than London – and the great variety of their designs. The lighting on several bridges takes advantage of the architectural qualities while others have been transformed into lighting sculptures.

Limerick City is in many ways defined by its rivers, the Shannon and the Abbey, and the bridges that span them are among the city's most dramatic features. The illumination of Sarsfield Bridge, which was inspired by the Pont de Neuilly in Paris, brings this famous landmark even closer to the life of the city.

1 Limerick **2-4** Cork **Opposite Page** Dublin's Liffey of Lights.

Millennium Bridges

> In the new Millennium the cities of Dublin, Cork and Galway, as well as Carlow town, will benefit from the building of new pedestrian bridges. These modern structures will improve access to and from busy central locations in each case, while at the same time taking the pedestrian closer to recreational amenities.

1 > Dublin Bridge

Dublin's Millennium Bridge was a project undertaken by Míle Átha Cliath, Dublin's Millennium Partnership. The purpose of this pedestrian bridge is to open a new route between Temple Bar and the Mary Street/Jervis Street shopping district and to relieve congestion on the nearby Halfpenny Bridge. The commission for the design of the bridge was the outcome of an international competition promoted by Dublin Corporation.

2 > Carlow Bridge

Carlow's Millennium Bridge will be a functional and practical facility as well as a landmark feature in the town. Located beside the River Barrow Track, it links Cox's Lane on the east bank to the Millennium Park and Children's playground at Graiguecullen on the west bank. Graiguecullen is a village situated within the administrative area of Carlow Urban District Council, yet half of its population of more than 3,000 actually live across the county boundary in Laois. The bridge will encourage greater interaction between the communities on both sides and strengthen the cultural and social life of the area.

3 > Cork Bridge

Cork City is sometimes referred to as the "Venice of the South" because of its array of bridges of all sizes and descriptions. Now, with the help of funding from the National Millennium Committee, the city is to have another attractive bridge. The new Millennium Footbridge will span the River Lee between Cornmarket Street and Pope's Quay. The bridge was designed to look well in daylight and at night-time and will incorporate a lighting scheme.

4 > Galway Millennium Bridge

Galway City's Millennium Bridge over the River Corrib is spectacular in design and will be an instantly recognisable landmark structure in an already high profile location. The footbridge will be located upstream of the famous Salmon Weir and will use the piers and abutments of the old Galway to Clifden Railway Line as supports for the modern structure. The line operated between the years 1894 and 1935. The bridge will be a natural extension of the existing riverside walkways and will provide a direct link between University College Galway and the city centre by a much shorter, scenic route.

1 Dublin. 2 Carlow. 3 Cork. **Right** Galway.

Dawn Oak 2000

The town of Balla, Co. Mayo, made a powerful statement of hope and renewal at the start of the new Millennium through a combination of highly original projects, hard work, persistence and an unquenchable community spirit. Unique amongst them was Dawn Oak 2000 which brought more than 600 men, women and children to the local Town Park to plant 2,000 Irish oak trees, starting on the stroke of midnight, New Year's Eve, 1999.

Millennium Committee Award €75,803 (IR£59,700)

> A Personal Note

The fuss of the Millennium is over, life has returned to normal and the trees are growing. The memories will always be with us. Our great tree planting event – 2,000 oaks to mark the beginning of the new century, a new Millennium – and to replace in some way the devastation caused by storms in recent years.

The event took months of careful planning, hard work and serious commitment. A big boost was the allocation of National Millennium Committee funds for the Dawn Oak 2000 project. Part of the plan was to create a world record to have the first trees to be planted in the year 2000. An ambitious project for Balla, a small town in middle Mayo, but great credit to the Town Park Committee, they succeeded and achieved their goal with style.

The night was magical. Dry, calm and not even cold. Following the piper and the beat of the Ancient Balla Drum, we proceeded to the planting site. The preparation had been carefully organised so all we, the public, had to do was follow directions and plant our little sapling. After a roll of the drum at exactly midnight, the planting started and, before we knew it, the job was done. Two thousand trees planted and everybody was happy as they exchanged New Year greetings.

It was great, everybody was invited and all were welcome. They came, young and not so young. Entire families and children were catered for. How many of the faces would see the following year? As on any New Year's Eve we thought about the future, thanked God for being there and able to enjoy a memorable night in our own little town, knowing too, that however long we live, we can't hope to see the oak trees grow to maturity, but please God, future generations will enjoy the Dawn Oak 2000 forest, the dream of Balla Town Park.

– Emer McEllin *Resident, Balla*

Top The first tree was planted by Balla's oldest citizen, Mattie Larkin (93), assisted by his grand-nephew, John Larkin (14), a pupil of Saint Joseph's School for the Blind in Dublin.

Above Balla residents John C. McEllin, Noel Lyons and John Dempsey monitoring the progress of the oak trees. Photograph – Ken Wright.

Tait Monument, Baker Place

> The Tait Clock in Baker Place, one of Limerick's favourite landmarks, is central to the plans to transform an area of the city in need of attention.The existing paving will be replaced by a rectangular plaza surfaced in a high-tech, frameless structural glass. By day it will reflect the Tait monument, by night below-surface lighting will give a subtle glow to the entire square.

Millennium Committee Award €380,921 (IR£300,000)

> A Personal Note

I'm someone who believes in the future, but I really think that late 18th century Ireland would have been a great place to spend the Millennium and here's the reason why. In Ireland, we're still inclined to second-guess things and spend a lot of time worrying about being second-guessed. When I worked as an architect in America, if my ideas failed to excite people I was out of work.

Here, above all other concerns, the architect must design things that nobody could possibly trip over no matter how drunk they happened to be. And there's a limit to the excitement designs are expected to provoke.

So when I was asked to come up with a treatment for Baker Place in Limerick, I started with eliminating the tripping hazards. After that, I tried to identify the level of public outrage I could possibly bear and set out to work within those parameters. At first glance it seemed like a boring project but in the end I found inspiration in history.

Baker Place is a little square in the middle of Newtown Pery, the Georgian part of Limerick. Edmond Sexton Pery created Newtown Pery in 1769. Pery was a politician – three times Speaker of the Irish House of Commons and an opponent of the Act of Union – and in between he built himself a brand new city outside the walls of Limerick, a mile long and a half mile wide. When he needed inspiration for laying out his new town, he disregarded the pompous squares of Dublin and London and looked instead at the humble and democratic gridiron that was then popular in revolutionary America.

This was because Sexton Pery was himself a radical, a free thinker and a liberal. Positive, progressive, energetic, often wilful, above all else Pery was always to his own self true. I returned to my drawing board, this time motivated to design something that Sexton Pery might have respected and suddenly things were a lot less boring.

– Gary Miley *Project Architect*

Above Transforming the Tait Clock and Baker Place.

Millennium Snapshots

1

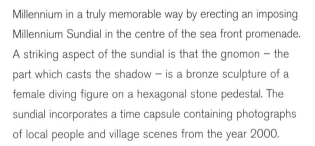

2

Throughout the country, communities, voluntary organisations, schools and individuals responded to the Millennium with a wide and diverse variety of initiatives which were supported by the National Millennium Committee. Here we feature a selection:

1 > Athlone Town Park

The historic town of Athlone, made famous by the deeds of Sergeant Costume and as the home of the great tenor, John Count McCormack, has experienced unprecedented growth over recent years.

The new vibrant Athlone, however, was deficient in terms of a central recreational park. This has now been redressed with the development of the Millennium Park, made possible by an award of €126,973 (IR£100,000) from the National Millennium Committee.

The Millennium Park is a long-time dream come true for Athlone, benefiting the tourist and the local resident. Plans include a tree-lined crushed stone boulevard, stone benches, recessed ground lighting and a children's playground. Visitors will enjoy a relaxed environment as they observe the natural beauty and wildlife of the Shannon, the river traffic easing through the Lock Gates and the dominance on the landscape of Athlone Castle, the Town Bridge and St. Peter's

Church. The Park encapsulates the recreational needs of all age groups, from the elderly to the children, and will be a haven for the weary worker seeking a peaceful retreat during the lunchtime break

2 > Batterstown Village

A Millennium Recognition Award added impetus to the already highly motivated Batterstown Community Association in Co. Meath to mark the Millennium by erecting a garden sculpture and water feature. The village subsequently won the Super Valu Best Endeavour Award in the National Tidy Towns competition

3 > Beagh Rural Development

Millennium stones, such as this one, have been erected by Beagh Rural Development Association in the village of Shanaglish, Gort, Co. Galway, to commemorate cultural sites in the parish.

4 > Blackrock Millennium Sun Dial

The Co. Louth seaside village of Blackrock marked the

Millennium in a truly memorable way by erecting an imposing Millennium Sundial in the centre of the sea front promenade. A striking aspect of the sundial is that the gnomon – the part which casts the shadow – is a bronze sculpture of a female diving figure on a hexagonal stone pedestal. The sundial incorporates a time capsule containing photographs of local people and village scenes from the year 2000.

5 > Stanhope Green Sanctuary Garden, Dublin

The Stanhope Green Sanctuary Garden transformed a derelict site beside the Sanctuary into an area of beauty and reflection.

6 > Leghowney Community Group

The Leghowney Millennium activities in the Co. Donegal village promoted rural interdenominational relationships, bringing the youth and senior citizens of the area together to celebrate. One symbolic gesture was a souvenir presentation to each family in the locality. Another was the

unveiling of a commemorative stone on New Year's Day 2000. This ceremony was attended by local clergy, politicians and a large gathering from the area.

7 > Roscommon Town Park

The Roscommon Town Park will provide the County Town with an attractive amenity area that will also double as a central meeting place for local people and visitors.

The Park is being sensitively developed on an area around the town's historic 13th century Norman castle, within a few hundred yards of the town centre. The completed park will create a new public access to Roscommon Castle, play and picnic areas, water and arts features and landscaped gardens.

8 > Tallaght Plaza

South Dublin County Council is undertaking a major overhaul of Tallaght as a new European-style city. The newly named Millennium Square is part of that ongoing development, and will create a lively residential and commercial town centre with apartments, an hotel, restaurants, bars, retail outlets and car parking.

The Council has commissioned the internationally renowned artist, Eilis O'Connell, to create a centrepiece for Millennium Square. The National Millennium Committee supported the project with an award of €101,579 (£80,000). Eilis got inspiration from the circulation of people in such places and the way in which they claim ownership of them. The work, entitled "The Appetites of Gravity", and made of robust, durable and timeless materials is in two parts, each with opposing purposes, one to defy gravity, the other to acknowledge it. One reaches to the sky, the other sprawls across the ground and the artist intends that the juxtaposition of the vertical and horizontal will balance the sense of space in the Square.

9 > Dublin Seal Sanctuary

Brigid, the Millennium seal, was released at Cullenstown Strand, Co. Wexford, in April 2000. She was the 100th seal to be rescued, rehabilitated and released by the Irish Seal Sanctuary. The National Millennium Committee contributed the funding required for the rescue, care and release of Brigid.

10 > Baltimore Sundial

The Millennium Sundial was erected in the village of Baltimore, Co. Cork, to mark Ireland's passage into the new Millennium. The sundial is positioned in a prominent location visible to all in the centre of Baltimore, adjacent to the main street, overlooking the harbour, the children's play green, and Sherkin Island beyond.

05 Youth

Youth

> One of Ireland's greatest national resources is its youth. It is they who will inherit this country during much of the first century of the new Millennium. What could be more fitting in the marking of the Millennium, than to focus particular attention on our children and young people.

The creation of brighter horizons for young people was identified as a priority very early on by the Millennium Committee. The Committee took the view that one of the best ways to channel funds into a long and lasting legacy was to invest in those in whose hands the future lies. Throughout the Millennium programme, many initiatives were dedicated specifically to the care, protection and promotion of children and teenagers.

The Children's Hour national appeal raised more than €5,078,952 (IR£4 million), half of which came through the National Millennium Committee, and which is now being distributed to over one hundred children's causes. Its success is detailed elsewhere (see **Flagships**). Scores of other initiatives and projects focussed on celebrating our youth, investing in their future, gaining insights into their hopes and fears and encouraging participation in sport and social activities.

Write Here Write Now – *The Millennium Book* was a highly original idea, unique to Ireland. Students in 5th Class primary schools and Transition Year in secondary schools were asked to share their thoughts about their lives and the world around them as they experienced it on one particular day in 1999. The result is an attractively bound

book in 23 volumes that provides a fascinating snapshot of contemporary Irish life through the 2,200 original submissions. Equally fascinating is *Ireland's Millennia*, **RTÉ's CD-ROM** and **website** celebrating Irish people, history and culture over the centuries. The Millennium Committee's sponsorship allowed for the CD-ROM to be distributed free to every school and library in the country so as to create an educational and archival legacy.

An chuid sainiúil den CD-Rom agus den suíomhlíon isea an úsáid forleathan tríd is tríd de shliochtanna fuaime agus fístéipeanna ó chartlann RTÉ. Tugann na sliochtanna seo, mórchuid daoibh nach bhfacthas ná nár chualathas leis na blianta, spléachadh agus léargas dúinn ar na doine agus ar na cúrsaí lárnach do fhorás Éire na Nuaoise. Chomh maith leis sin, taispeánann siad nóiméid glórmhaire ag ócáidí móra spóirt agus sóisíalta.

Tá trí rannóg chomhcheangailte san "Ireland's Millennia", gach ceann daoibh ag soláthrú eolais ar chultúr agus ar oidhreacht na hÉireann ar bhealach údarásach, sainiúil agus ag an am gcéanna éascaí le tuiscint. Comhlánaíonn na rannóga – Daoine, Stair agus Áiteanna – a chéile agus tá comhcheangail eatarthu an bealach ar fad tríd.

Daoine, sin bunachar sonraí cuimsitheach ag soláthrú eolais ar os cionn 1,500 beathaisnéisi Gaeil. Stair, sin croinicí stairiúil na hÉireann ó aimsir réamhstairiúil go dtí 1966, agus Áiteanna, seo treoir trí 32 contae na hÉireann, a stair agus a dtíreolaíocht.

Active participation by young people was central to a number of the projects supported as exemplified in **World Youth Day 2000**. To fully appreciate the extent and enthusiasm of the Irish participation in this great event in Rome one would need to have been at Dublin Airport as the airlift of the 2,000 young pilgrims got underway. It was a scene of vibrant colour and excitement, as they set off, many of them sporting our own identifying colours, to join more than two million other young people from all over the world.

Equally exciting are the **National Community Games Finals** at Mosney. The Games provide a wonderful opportunity for young people to take part in sporting activities in a spirit of camaraderie and friendship. Of international significance was the **Millennium Gold Encounter**, an initiative of The President's Awards-Gaisce, which brought to Ireland 88 participants from 27 countries for a truly memorable cosmopolitan event.

The **Millennium Youth Centre** in the old Franciscan Friary building in Killarney, Co. Kerry, will be a national prototype centre for a new Millennium; increasing programmes, services and information dedicated to responding to the needs of all young people. **The Ark Cultural Centre** for children marked the Millennium in an innovative way with Committee support. Thousands of children visited the

ADESTE exhibition to see how the pictures of 12 Irish artists were inspired by the Nativity. Another later attraction at the Ark was a music theatre presentation, *The Fourth Wise Man*. The emphasis in the **Millennium Children's Park in Galway City** will be on relaxation, entertainment and fun. Children's music and drama will be performed in the natural amphitheatre and young and old alike will find it hard to resist trying their hand at model boating and fishing on the canal.

For decades **Scouting Ireland** has been assisting young people strive towards achieving their full potential. In the Millennium year its contribution was acknowledged through support for new sport and recreational facilities.

Hundreds of youth-centred projects at community level were supported all over the country, particularly through the Millennium Events Awards and the Millennium Recognition Awards. **The Mullingar Millennium Gym** is helping early school leavers to qualify as fitness instructors. In Co. Wexford the **Bunclody Playground** is an inviting new facility and in Cork the **Glen Neighbourhood Youth Project** has put the emphasis on skills, in and out of the water.

For originality and sheer daring it is hard to beat **Skyreach 2000**. Under this Youthreach project a group of early school leavers are, with strict professional supervision, building a two-seater aircraft from a pre-supplied kit, training six of the group to private pilot licence standard and eventually flying the plane.

Left Barretstown Gang Camp children at the spider web where challenge, success, discovery and reflection occur everyday.

Write Here Write Now

> *The Write Here Write Now Millennium Book* provides a fascinating snapshot of contemporary Irish life that will stand as a record for centuries. This highly original idea brought pen pictures from thousands of primary and secondary school students who described their own lives and the world around them on one day in 1999.

Millennium Committee Award €101,579 (IR£80,000)

> A Personal Note

It is only rarely that a finished product exactly reflects its original concept in the mind of its instigator, but *The Millennium Book* surpassed all imaginings. It is a new National Treasure, a resource for the future genealogist, folklorist and historian but, most of all, what has been captured in these 23 beautifully bound volumes is a pageant of hope, dreaming and love. The idea, conceived at the first

meeting of the National Millennium Committee and accepted with alacrity for full funding, was that on 12 May, 1999, students of Irish schools in 5th Class and Transition Year, having been prepared in advance by teachers, would hand write on a piece of special, longlife manuscript paper, their own, unedited version of their life stories, their impressions of the world, their vision of life in Ireland and what they would like to leave behind as their footprints on this Millennium.

The concept was taken up with enthusiasm throughout the country and, in the weeks following Millennium Book Day, more than a hundred thousand pages poured in, one page to be selected at random from each class envelope.

The students sent drawings of their houses, cats, dogs, trains, landscapes, spaceships, The Spice Girls, Westlife, their Mammies, Daddies, baby sisters and brothers, an enlarged planet and the Manchester United logo. Photographs too – of themselves, their First Communions, their local G.A.A. teams. We got a collage of current product wrappers, an Irish dancing medal, original songs.

The written pages are laced with idealism, sadness and private grief and are permeated with a sense of place, of parish and of nation. Some students wrote letters to descendants a thousand years hence to explain what life is like in Ireland now. Poignantly, some wrote of family separations and siblings' deaths. From special schools came communal drawings, sets of hand prints, a page in Braille.

The decision that entries would be unmediated and unedited contributed in no small way to the freshness and honesty of what we received. But what was most striking was the optimism and love. These young people see great futures for themselves. They love their homes, friends, pets, brothers, sisters, aunts, uncles and mentors. They think their teachers and schools are on their side. They want the best for the world and see that the best is possible.

And so, on 15 December, 1999, in the entrance hall of the National Library, I stood in front of Minister Séamus Brennan and our National Millennium Committee, our multitude of volunteers and committed teachers, our project committee drawn from ASTI, TUI, INTO, the Department of Education and Science, RTÉ and the National Library. In the presence of students, one representing each county, I gave *The Millennium Book* to our patron, President Mary McAleese, who entrusted it to the National Library.

It was one of the proudest days of my life.

– Deirdre Purcell *Author*

The Millennium Youth Centre, Killarney

> The Millennium Youth Centre in the old Franciscan Friary building in Killarney, Co. Kerry, will be a national prototype centre for a new Millennium, providing practical support, programmes, services and information for young people.

Millennium Committee Award €126.973 (IR£100,000)

Tim O'Donoghue

> A Personal Note

This visionary project began in 1995 when the Franciscan Order decided to donate their noviciate in Killarney to be developed for the benefit of the young people of the area.

The Franciscan Friars have been involved in Killarney for centuries, from the foundation of Muckross Abbey in 1448 to the present day Friary situated in the very heart of the town. The Friars have been guided by a strong vision and in their own words – "Our history has been one of constant change and adaptation, while remaining faithful to Killarney and the surrounding area."

This vision has guided them and the people of Killarney over the centuries through to the dawn of a new Millennium. The Franciscans donated the Friary building to the Kerry Diocesan Youth Service which currently provides a wide range of programmes and services responding to the social, recreational, educational and developmental needs of young people throughout Kerry.

In addition to being a national prototype, the centre will also be an international training ground for young people, facilitating second chance training and education programmes for socially and educationally disadvantaged young people. The centre will facilitate and promote exchange between Southern and Northern Ireland as well as international exchanges.

The project has been a magnificent achievement and will stand proudly as a tribute to the vision and determination of all those involved. The centre is a wonderful way for us to celebrate the advent of the new Millennium. The Friary has been a part of our town for 140 years as a place of learning, support and nurturing.

In the new Millennium it will continue this great tradition of welcome and support for all young people. It encapsulates the spirit of the Millennium in that we have taken the learning from the past and dedicated it to our vision for the future.

– Tim O'Donoghue *Development Manager*
National Youth Centre

1 The imposing front of the old Franciscan Friary. **2** The youth café area. **3** The entrance to the Millennium Youth Centre.

World Youth Day Rome, August 2000

> World Youth Day 2000 was a truly memorable expression of faith, devotion and caring from the millions of young people who converged on Rome that August. More than 2,000 from all over Ireland attended the largest youth event of the Millennium year 2000 AD. Two million young people, aged between 17 and 30, converged on Rome for the celebration. Catholic Youth Care organised for over 1,000 young people to fly from Dublin to attend the historic event. The National Millennium Committee assisted with the travel costs and presented the pilgrims with special mementoes.

Millennium Committee Award €12,697 (IR£10,000)

> A Personal Note

Andrew Greeley, the American priest psychologist, has said that contemporary young Irish people are like the pilgrim monks of old who left Ireland with only a haversack and their faith when they travelled throughout Europe. For World Youth Day in Rome thousands of young Irish people came to Rome as modern-day pilgrims. They met with young people from different parts of the world, all of whom were gathering to celebrate their faith with Pope John Paul II. Young people slept on floors provided by many local parishes; attended events and listened to bishops and cardinals speak to them about what it means to be a follower of Christ in today's world.

Cardinal Desmond Connell travelled from Dublin and received a huge welcome. Over two million young people assembled for the vigil with Pope John Paul. They heard the Pope tell them: "If you are what you should be, you can set the world on fire." Twenty-four-year-old Derek O'Byrne, from Waterford, said that he was "deeply challenged by the words of the Pope who, although aged over 80, still has something relevant to say to young people." Gemma Cullen, aged 25, who works with young people in a number of Dublin parishes, described the event as "one of the most amazing experiences ever".

Twenty-one-year-old Susan Mooney, from Blanchardstown, said: "It is not just about seeing the Pope. It is about being able to see that being a young Catholic can be fun and challenging. I only wish other young people back in Ireland were able to share this wonderful experience." The modern Irish monks still travel light and are setting the world on fire.

– Gerard Gallagher *Co-ordinator*
World Youth Day, Catholic Youth Care

Above The melting pot of youth ... Rome 2000.
Photography – John McElroy.

The Ark

> The Ark cultural centre for children in Dublin drew strongly on the birth of Christ when deciding how to mark the Millennium. Thousands of children came to the ADESTE exhibition to see how 12 Irish artists made pictures inspired by the Nativity. A year later the attraction was a music theatre presentation, *The Fourth Wise Man*.

Millennium Committee Award €63,486 (IR£50,000)

Martin Drury

> A Personal Note

Like all birthdays, this one deserved to be celebrated. And it was. Twice over!

At either end of the Millennium year, the Ark wanted to mark the defining, originating moment: the Nativity. And to mark it as a cultural centre for children should. A moment of promise in which a child is the central figure. A moment that has fed a whole tradition of Western art and drama. A moment that is a centrepiece of primary school experience whether that is making a crib or participating in the annual nativity play.

Thousands and thousands of children came to the Ark for the ADESTE exhibition to see how 12 Irish artists made pictures inspired by the Nativity. They found no sentimental babe in a manger, but a visualisation of tenderness and terror, of astral vastness and domestic intimacy. Later they walked through our extraordinary crib installation and then made their own 3-D version.

Twelve months later, another new piece made for children. This time it was a music theatre showing *The Fourth Wise Man*, drawing from the Russian Orthodox legend of that name. At the heart of it was the childish King Jack who had to learn that true wisdom is thinking with your heart as well as with your head. Off in the distance of Bethlehem, huge events were occurring, but in the cockpit of the Ark's stage, the children were engrossed by how Jack rescued the silent, sad-faced servant girl Maria and her baby from the soldiers of the cruel King Herod. Resonances of the story of 2000 years ago, of course, but sadly resonances of our contemporary political landscape too, in case anybody thought we were not dramatising a true story.

– Martin Drury *Founder and Director, The Ark, 1992-2001*

1 Ciaran McIntyre in the title role in *The Fourth Wise Man*.
2 Mal Whyte as "The Owl" in *The Fourth Wise Man*.

RTÉ CD-ROM for Schools

> *Ireland's Millennia* is a fascinating CD-ROM and website celebrating Irish people, their history and culture over the centuries. The National Millennium Committee's sponsorship allowed for the comprehensive CD-ROM to be distributed free to every school and library in the country to establish an educational and archival legacy.

Millennium Committee Award €190,460 (IR£150,000)

> A Personal Note

When Eugene Murray, whose responsibilities then included RTÉ's Internet Department – RTÉ Online – first came up with the idea of using the web as a vehicle to share some of the national broadcaster's vast archive of sound and moving pictures with the Irish people, many ideas where talked about. Finally it was decided that a small website with a brief outline of Ireland's history and a couple of hundred biographies of important Irish people, linked to short extracts from our archives, would be the way to go.

The idea took on a life of its own and evolved into *Ireland's Millennia*, an ambitious project to create a database of Irish cultural information available throughout the world on the Internet and free to every school in Ireland through a CD-ROM. With the generous support of the National Millennium Committee this idea is now a reality. The website/CD contains nearly 2,000 biographies of Irish people, living and dead; a comprehensive history of Ireland, based on the structure of the RTÉ television series *The Course of Irish History*, as well as a brief cultural guide to the 32 counties of Ireland.

The CD has been distributed to schools and the website (www.rte.ie/millennia) is in place. The number of biographies is growing steadily and existing entries are being updated daily as the achievements of Ireland's people continue to be recorded. While the website grows, the CD provides a marking point at the beginning of the new Millennium.

– Diarmuid de Paor *Site Producer, RTÉ*

An chuid sainiúil den CD-ROM agus den suíomhlíon isea an úsáid forleathan tríd is tríd de shliochtanna fuaime agus fístéipeanna ó chartlann RTÉ. Tugann na sliochtanna seo, mórchuid daoibh nach bhfacthas ná nár chualathas leis na blianta, spléachadh agus léargas dúinn ar na doine agus ar na cúrsái lárnach do fhorás Éire na Nuaoise. Chomh maith leis sin, taispeánann siad nóiméid glórmhaire ag ócáidí móra spóirt agus sóisíalta.

1 The cover of the 'Ireland's Millennia' CD-ROM.

2 A page from the database.

Millennium Gold Encounter

> Millennium Gold Encounter, an initiative of The President's Awards-Gaisce, with the support of the National Millennium Committee, brought to Ireland Eighty eight participants from 27 countries for a truly memorable and stimulating international occasion.

Millennium Committee Award €38,092 (IR£30,000)

> A Personal Note

The President's Awards-Gaisce is the national challenge award to young adults aged between 15 and 25. A similar programme exits in over 60 countries worldwide.

Corresponding with the build-up to the Millennium year, Gaisce won its bid to host the international Millennium Gold Encounter event in Ireland. Gold Encounter is held jointly with The Duke of Edinburgh's Award in Northern Ireland. Eighty eight participants from 27 nations, who were Gold Award Holders within their respective countries, participated in a 20 day conference and training exercise North and South of the border.

President McAleese and H.R.H. Prince Edward opened Millennium Gold Encounter in Dublin Castle. Minister Séamus Brennan, Chairman of the National Millennium Committee, which supported the event, represented the Government.

Participants came from countries as far away as The Ivory Coast, India, Jordan and South Africa. The first week of the conference was held at An Grianán in Termonfeckin, Co. Louth, and the third week at Gortatole, Co. Fermanagh.

The middle week, entitled "Grass Roots" was held right around the country. This was an opportunity for participants to meet young Irish people from The President's Awards-Gaisce, with their leaders and families. Here they had the opportunity to discuss the way of life for young people in Ireland, to hear of their hopes and fears for the future and for the young Irish in turn to hear the views of delegates from all over the world.

The Irish event was evaluated internationally as an outstanding success, some of the highlights being: leadership training, grassroots experience, North and South working together, public relations and communications, the youth forum and, of course, the Irish scenery.

–John T. Murphy *Director, Development*
The President's Award-Gaisce

1 President Mary McAleese and H.R.H. Prince Edward, the Earl of Wessex, with Mr. Martin McAleese and Sophie Rees Jones, the Countess of Wessex.

2 Participants in Millennium Gold Encounter.

3 President McAleese chatting with participants.

"There are two types of people; the 'Doers' and the 'Cynics'. You gold achievers are the 'Doers' and it is great to meet you."

– *President Mary McAleese in her address to the participants.*

Scouting Ireland

> Scouting Ireland (CSI) has embarked on an ambitious programme of upgrading and expanding sport and recreational facilities as part of its overall goal of assisting young people to achieve their full spiritual, intellectual, physical and cultural potential.

Millennium Committee Award €38,092 (IR£30,000)

The new facilities being developed include the construction of an artificial caving complex and a new timber frame chalet. The programme of upgrading and expanding sport and recreational facilities at CSI's national camp at Larch Hill, Tibradden, Dublin, will allow scouts to enjoy all the thrills and adventure of caving but in a safe environment

The 160 metres of inter-linked tunnels will afford the young people in the camp the opportunity to experience caving in a friendly, secure facility. The construction and fitting out of the timber chalet will provide indoor accommodation on site for an additional 24 persons.

Other projects planned as part of the upgrading programme include the construction of an indoor climbing wall and the provision of covered firing bays on the archery range that will allow for participants to take part in this growing sport all year round.

The improvements to the facilities will lead to an increased usage of the centre, which at present is mainly used by scouts at weekends. It can become an ideal centre for schools wishing to offer outdoor pursuits education as part of the

Transition Year programme. With the improved facilities, the centre can offer outdoor activity packages to school groups mid-week.

Children at Play

> Several communities selected the building of new children's parks and playgrounds, or the expansion of existing ones, as their way of marking the Millennium.

> Millennium Children's Park, Galway

The children's park on land near the centre of Galway has been designated as an area for family recreation. The gently contoured central green will be an ideal haven where families and children from two to twelve years can enjoy the fully equipped playground alongside. The broad, stone-paved canal walk will be an ideal setting for model boating and fishing. A striking timber and steel suspension bridge will link the park to other pathways and to a small amphitheatre where children's music and drama will be performed.

> Doonbeg, Co. Clare

Doonbeg Children's Playground in Co. Clare caters for toddlers from one to four years of age and offers a range of activities, including mini-football and basketball, on a safe playing arena. Funding for the playground was provided by the National Millennium Committee and Clare County Council.

> Bunclody Playground, Co. Wexford

Bunclody Swimming Pool Committee, Co. Wexford, is continuing forward and going from strength to strength with their playground for the children of the new Millennium.

1,2 & 3 Doonbeg, Co. Clare. **4** Bunclody. **5** Millennium Children's Park, Galway.

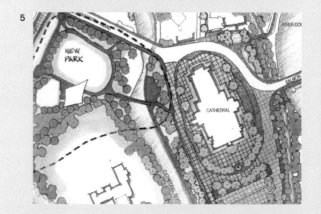

National Community Games

> Every year almost 500,000 young people across the country take part in the Community Games. The games introduce these people to the joys of sport and recreation and help them to develop in a healthy and balanced way.

The National Millennium Committee supported the National Finals in 1999, 2000 and 2001. Ronan Keating, singer/entertainer and member of the National Millennium Committee, himself a former participant, sent this message to the finalists.

"I have really great personal memories of the Community Games. I competed myself at national level on a number of occasions and was lucky enough to pick up a few medals along the way, which I still treasure. Remember you are not alone out there because you are competing as a team for your community. You know what they say "it's not about the winning, it's about the taking part."

Remember to enjoy the honour of competing in the Community Games and keep your head high whatever happens. I must admit I still miss standing at the starting line waiting for the crack of the gun with only one thing on my mind – oh no, I forgot to do my homework again! Only joking, of course. But seriously, at the end of the day, make sure you enjoy yourselves and be very proud."

Skyreach – Wicklow Working Together

> Skyreach – Wicklow Working Together is a captivating project, offering a group of early school leavers a once in a lifetime chance that could change their lives dramatically. The youngsters are undertaking the construction of a two-seater aircraft from a supplied kit in a local Youthreach project that is being strictly scrutinised and supervised.

Millennium Committee Award €35,235 (IR£27,750)

Already the 12 participating students have passed a compulsory aviation assessment for potential Aer Lingus and Air Corps pilots. While diligently working on Skyreach, the students have also managed to sit and pass the Leaving Certificate Examination.

In addition, six of the group will be trained to private licence standard. The culmination of the project will be the eventual flying of the plane by the trained pilots.

"The plan was to get a two-seater aeroplane kit. At the moment we have the tail section of the aeroplane built which in all took us 18 working hours. I have learned that it is important to be dedicated to this project because it is a lot of hard work and there are a lot of opportunities in this area when I complete the training required to obtain my pilot's licence."

– Linda Redmond *Ashford, Co. Wicklow*

"I think the aeroplane project was a brilliant idea. I am not sure if I would have expected to be doing something like this a few years ago. Now I am pleasantly surprised. I thought I handled the whole prospect of both flying in and taking the controls of a plane fairly well or at least as well as anyone could. Although I think I was buzzing too much to even notice fear."

– Jason Roche *Wicklow*

Millennium Snapshots

> In addition to the major youth-centred projects, there were also a variety of smaller but equally enduring endeavours by communities, schools and voluntary groups celebrating and supporting the nation's young people. This is a selection:

1 > Leitrim Book

The *Leitrim Book* is a unique collection of contributions from children in primary schools in the county, in which they write of their hopes, dreams and fears at the start of the new Millennium. The original book is on display in the County Library.

2 > Holy Cross School Sandford

Pupils and staff from Holy Cross School, Dundrum, Dublin, designed and planted a Millennium Garden in the school grounds as their way of marking the Millennium. The photograph shows pupils involved in the planting of trees and shrubs.

3 > Glen Neighbourhood Youth

The development of skills in water sport, teamwork and leadership is the Millennium project of Cork's Glen and District Neighbourhood Youth project.

4 > Mullingar Millennium Gym

The Millennium Gymnasium in Mullingar, Co. Westmeath, is a fully equipped state-of-the-art facility that provides early school leavers from disadvantaged backgrounds with the opportunity to qualify as fitness instructors. The Training Development Agency in Mullingar utilises the gym, offering a course in Sport and Fitness for those wishing to make a full-time career as trainers. The gym is available to all trainees in the agency, as well as to other groups in Mullingar who cater for young people.

5 > Laois Youth Group

Three hundred participants of all ages from all around the county are receiving ongoing tuition in the Laois School of Music. Older students are also being trained for orchestral playing.

6 > Forum for the Arts, Ballymun

Forum for the Arts in Ballymun, Dublin, aims to introduce the arts to children at a more sustainable level. With the Millennium Award the primary schools benefited from professional input through the medium of drama, instrumental, choral works and visual arts. Tá ceol agus drámaíocht tráidisiúnta caomhnaithe do na páistí i Bunscoil Bhaile Muna, buíochas le Dáil na hÉalaoin agus Coiste na Mílaoise.

06 Church, Christian

Church/Christian

> In an increasingly secularised world, as the year 2000 approached, it would have been all too easy to forget that the dawn of a new Millennium has strong religious connotations. For Christians it is not an arbitrary calendar date that is being celebrated, rather the anniversary of the birth of Jesus Christ, the Son of God.

The general consensus now is that in Ireland we managed to strike the right balance between the sacred and the profane in our celebrations of this unique occasion in all our lives. Many people, for instance, found the Last Light Ceremony with the special Millennium Candles profoundly spiritual, and as many again enjoyed the fireworks and special events arranged around the country for midnight on New Year's Eve, 1999.

What is very clear is that Ireland's proud tradition as a Christian nation was not overlooked; on the contrary, it was reinforced by dozens upon dozens of imaginative projects that reinforce our people's religious and spiritual commitment, their pride in their shared Christian heritage and their dedication to the search for peace and reconciliation on this island.

Large or small, these projects galvanised communities the length and breadth of the country. Among the most visible was the **Church Illumination** project involving scores of churches, Christian monuments and heritage sites through-out the countryside, and most audibly the restoration of

bells and bell towers in a number of churches. In Mayo, €317,435 (IR£250,000) was allocated to the **Millennium Peace Park** built on six acres in the shadow of Ireland's holy mountain, **Croagh Patrick**.

As the pace of modern life accelerates, many people find themselves stressed, and a number of Millennium initiatives have been undertaken to provide places of retreat. One such place is Glendalough in Co. Wicklow, one of the oldest and most important of Christian places of pilgrimage in Europe, and one of Ireland's busiest tourist destinations. Aided by the National Millennium Committee a project called **Glendalough 2000** has been developed and five small, simple, single houses of retreat, *cillíns*, built where people of all faiths can distance themselves from modern life for a spell.

The quest for solitude can be pursued also on the revitalised **Pilgrim Paths** around the country where we can walk the sacred routes of ancient pilgrims. The story of one of those pilgrims, St. Fin Barre, dating back to 606 AD, will be enshrined in the modern context in a new display centre at **St. Fin Barre's**,

the cathedral in Cork City named after the saint on the site of his original monastery.

Sometimes a dream can be almost a century in the making. Thanks to a sizeable award from the National Millennium Committee, the townspeople of **Ballyhaunis, Co. Mayo**, were able to make a long-held ambition a reality by completing St. Patrick's Church in time for New Year's Eve, 1999. When it had been built in 1903 there had been no money left to build a spire, but now, three generations later, a graceful steeple has been constructed, a potent symbol of community and Christian pride. But of course devotional symbols don't have to be as high-flying as Ballyhaunis' flèche, as the **Knock Area Development Association** proved with their pilgrimage town's unique, low hedge labyrinth. Such complex labyrinths were Celtic and mediaeval devotional tools that put pilgrims on the path to God, and this venture must be one of the more unusual helped by the National Millennium Committee.

Bhí "Sacred Places" ina thaispeántas mór tábhachtach ag ceiliúradh 2000 bliain de ailtireacht eaglasta ar oileán na hÉireann. Bhí an réimse ard-chaighdeánach de foirgnimh eaglasta i "Sacred Places" i a fhianaise don díogras agus do shamhlaíocht na ndaoine sin a dhearaigh agus a thóg iad. Bhí níos mó i gceist san taispeántas ná bailiúchán de íomhánna foirgnimh eaglasta, d'inis sé ár scéal maireachtála ar an oileán seo anuas an 2,000 bliain seo thart, ach go háirithe ag taispeáint forbairt ilghnéitheach sóisialta agus cultúrtha na hÉireann.

The Christian Message –
Light, Pilgrimage and Reconciliation

> The fundamental significance of the Millennium year was that it marked the 2000th anniversary of the birth of Jesus Christ. Our celebrations in Ireland centred on remembering our heritage of faith and on renewing our commitment to that faith. They focussed especially on the themes of light, pilgrimage and reconciliation.

On the wider level, church bodies in Ireland joined in the worldwide call for a reduction of the third world debt.

– Laurence Ryan *Bishop of Kildare and Leighlin*
Chairman, Jubilee Committee of the Irish Bishops Conference

Laurence Ryan

Light has a special Christian significance. The special Jubilee candles, which were lighting in churches and many homes, were symbols of Jesus Christ, the Light of the World. Parishes throughout the country had their own celebration of light to mark the beginning of the Millennium year. These celebrations displayed wonderful creativity and were deeply meaningful. They linked in too with the civil inauguration of the Millennium year and, in particular, with the National Millennium Committee's gift of a candle to every home in the state. Pilgrimages to sacred sites, ancient monastic settlements and holy wells took place in dioceses and parishes throughout the country. The National Millennium Committee supported a number of these pilgrimages, especially by floodlighting churches and monastic sites and by reopening major pilgrim routes. A particularly memorable occasion was Sunday, 21 May, 2000, which was designated by the Irish Bishops National Jubilee Committee as a National Day of Local Pilgrimage.

In dioceses and parishes throughout the country, people travelled as pilgrims to Christian sites of historical significance and joined in liturgical celebrations. It was an occasion rich in meaning, in that people celebrated the fact that the Christian faith was transmitted and kept alive in their own place. At the same time they were celebrating in unison with people in places all over the country.

Reconciliation, especially between the churches, featured in the Jubilee year celebrations. An ecumenical celebration to mark the inauguration of the Millennium year was held on 2 January, 2000, at the National Concert Hall. This was attended by the President and leading politicians as well as the leaders from the different Christian churches. Mr Séamus Brennan, Chairman, represented the National Millennium Committee, whose financial award had facilitated a live broadcast by RTÉ television. Special ecumenical celebrations were held at Pentecost and there was an ecumenical dimension to all the celebrations throughout the year with Christians of different churches travelling together in pilgrimage and joining in liturgical celebrations.

Above The stone-built Temple Mac Dara, Co. Galway. Photograph courtesy of Dúchas, the Heritage Service.

Pilgrim Paths

> The Pilgrim Paths initiative was the main Millennium project of The Heritage Council. It is the development and upgrading of a series of walks, based on medieval pilgrimage routes, to six sites.

Millennium Committee Award €63,486 (IR£50,000)

> A Personal Note

Pilgrimage was one of the great unifying and celebratory themes of the year 2000. On National Pilgrimage Day parish communities all over the country went on pilgrimage to holy places. Here in the Diocese of Kerry, all 54 parishes had a pilgrimage to a local holy place and people of all levels of faith and church involvement felt a sense of inclusion and a sense of going back to their roots.

All over the world the importance of pilgrimage in different faith traditions brings together the largest gatherings of people on this planet. It is estimated that a recent pilgrimage in India to the sacred waters of the Ganges brought over 70 million people together. One of the most sacred duties of the pious Muslim is to undertake a pilgrimage to Mecca.

Many of us in Ireland have grown up with pilgrimage, be it Knock, Lourdes, Medjugorje, Croagh Patrick or Ardmore. We have a great tradition of going on pilgrimage. The Heritage Council Pilgrim Paths project undertaken in partnership with local communities and public bodies seeks to revitalise the medieval pilgrim paths to some of our most important and sacred pilgrimage places. Many people like to walk the

"waymarked" trails around the country. Walking the pilgrim routes brings an added dimension, which fascinates and draws people in a very particular way. Like the pilgrims of old, taking these paths today brings the walker in the footsteps of countless numbers of people who have trod this path before. It brings us in contact with many different aspects of our heritage, man-made and natural. Those who have gone before us were full of hope and they nurtured dreams, carried petitions and shouldered burdens.

– Father Tomás Ó Caoimh

(Fr. Ó Caoimh is a priest of the Diocese of Kerry. He is a Member of The Heritage Council and chairs the Pilgrim Paths Working Group. He is also a Consultor to the Vatican's Pontifical Commission on Cultural Heritage.)

Opposite Page Walkers relax along St. Kevin's Way, the first of the six pilgrim paths to be restored. The path runs the 26 km from Hollywood to Glendalough through some of the most scenic countrywide in Co. Wicklow. It follows the original route taken by pilgrims visiting Glendalough which has been a place of pilgrimage and spiritual activity for one-and-a-half Millennia.

– Photograph by Frank Miller (used courtesy of *The Irish Times*)

The routes will be upgraded to the status of official "waymarked ways". Guidebooks are being drawn up for each route.

The routes included in the project are:

- **Cosán na Naomh**
  On the Dingle Peninsula, Co. Kerry.
- **Tóchar Phádraig**
  Ballintubber Abbey to Croagh Patrick, Co. Mayo.
- **St. Kevin's Way**
  From Hollywood to Glendalough, Co Wicklow.
- **Lough Derg**
  A route to the shore opposite Saint's Island, Co. Donegal.
- **St. Declan's Way**
  From Lismore to Ardmore, Co. Waterford.
- **Slí Mhór**
  Ballycumber/Leamonaghan to Clonmacnois, Co. Offaly.

Church Floodlighting

> The Christian symbolism of light and hope is emphasised with the illumination of churches and Christian heritage sites all over the country, which now stand out as welcoming beacons on the darkened landscapes.

1 St. Mary's, Carrick-on-Shannon. 2 Turlough Round Tower, Co. Mayo. 3 St. John's Church, Ballybunnion. 4 Sacred Heart Church, Monkstown, Cork.
5 St. Andrew's, Westland Row, Dublin. 6 St. Therese's, Mount Merrion, Dublin. 7 St. Thomas', Mount Merrion, Dublin.

5

6

7

Let the Bells Ring ...

> From the earliest times, bells have been associated with the secular and religious life of all civilised communities. Bells have played an integral part in social history, ringing to give the alarm in the case of invasion or fire or to proclaim the good news of births and marriages, and tolled to mark the passing of the dying.

Bells are still an important element in Irish life, pealing from the steeples of churches in cities, towns and villages through-out the country. It is believed that bells were introduced to Christian churches as far back as the end of the 4th century. It was only toward the end of the 8th century that bells were hung in buildings specially designed for them, buildings that eventually became belfries incorporated in the design of churches.

To mark the Millennium, the Committee assisted a range of church and community projects for the restoration, refurbishment and enhancement of bell towers and bells throughout the land. The following is a selection of thoughts from people closely involved with just a few of the projects:

> Christ Church

No musical sound in Ireland is so inclusive as the pealing of bells. When the National Millennium Committee contributed €25,395 (IR£20,000) to the cost of seven new bells for *Christ Church Cathedral*, the role of these famous bells in the life of Dublin and Ireland was publicly recognised. The glory of the world record achievement at Christ Church,

where 19 bells are now available for full-circle ringing, can be heard in the normal thrice weekly pealing and in the extra ringing at special times for the city and the country. Like a river in spate, from the top of the scales to the bottom, from rushing sweetness down to contrasting rich depths, such music has never before been heard in Ireland.

The Committee also contributed €63,487 (IR£50,000) to the restoration of the beautiful sound of the eight bells of the former St. George's Church in their new home in *Christ Church, Taney, Dundrum*, Dublin. *St. Peter's Church, Drogheda*, Co. Louth, received €50,790 (IR£40,000) for the restoration of its bells. The great octave of bells was regularly rung there as an expression of confidence in the future throughout the period of necessary closure of the church for restoration, following a fire in 1999.

– Leslie Taylor *Ringing Master, Christ Church Cathedral, Dublin*

> St. Peter's Church, Drogheda

St. Peter's Church of Ireland in Drogheda has been described as "probably the finest provincial Georgian church in Ireland". Sadly the church was the victim of an arson attack in May

1999. The Rector and parishioners determined that the opportunity presented by this mindless act of vandalism should not be missed, and so a conservation and restoration programme was put in place to, once again, make St. Peter's the centre of an active, worshipping community.

The church boasts a peal of eight bells in its magnificent tower and steeple. Thanks to a generous award from the Millennium Committee the bells, too, will be restored along with the rest of the church so that they may be rung regularly each week to call worshippers of all denominations in the town to prayer.

– Reverend Michael Graham *Rector*

> Bell of Inchmore, Lough Gowna, County Longford

Since 1932, the Tower Bell of Inchmore – a rare example of an early tower bell – remained unused and unseen in the belfry of St. Colmcille parish church.

Early tower bells are a rarity in Ireland and this is among the oldest known. The bell is said to have belonged to the monastery of Inchmore in Lough Gowna, an ancient site associated with St. Columcille and later an Augustinian house. It is believed the bell was used to call the monks to prayer.

The Bell of Inchmore is a cast bronze bell of early form, probably made in Italy or France in the 15th century. An inscription in Latin near the base has been partially deciphered: the word "magister" refers either to God or to a master bell-founder. In the 1840s the bell, which had been missing for many years, was recovered from the lake and hung in Dunbeggan (Aughnacliffe). It remained the only bell there until the great renovation of 1932 when the present bell was installed.

National Millennium Committee funding has facilitated its installation in the church. It also provided for a sophisticated security system so that the bell could remain on public display in the locality. The alternative would have been to remove the bell to the National Museum.

– Father Michael Reilly *P.P. Aughnacliffe*

From Left to Right St. Peter's Church; Bell of Inchmore; Leslie Taylor at Christ Church Dublin.

Following Page Schoolchildren celebrating the arrival of the seven new bells for Christ Church Cathedral.
Photograph – Maxwells.

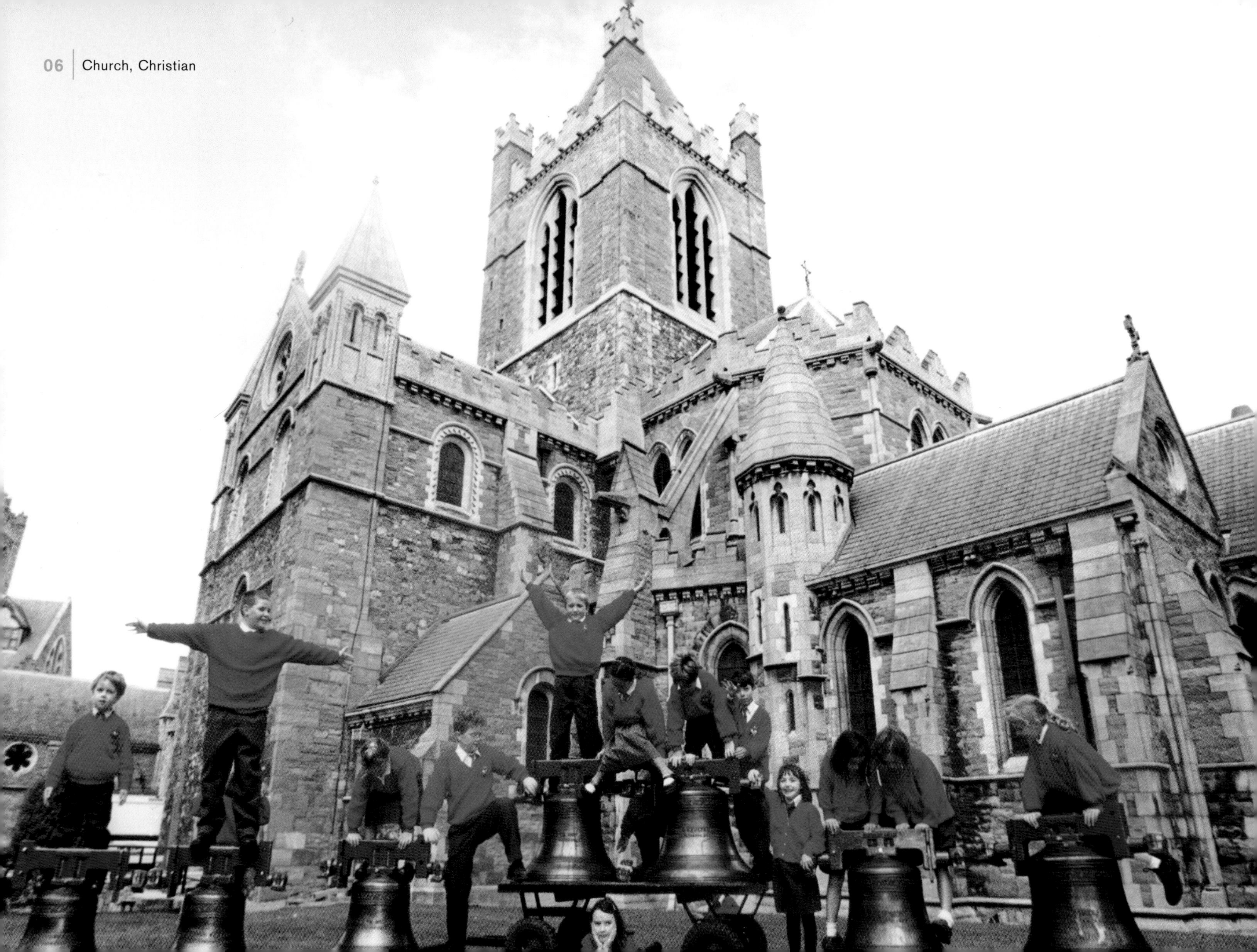

Christian Care for the Elderly

> I believe that one of the most important elements in social justice is the care of the elderly. Because of the great strides made by medical science, life expectancy continues to increase, which, of course, is something about which we should rejoice. However, the elderly continue to be vulnerable and it is the duty of all the citizens of this state to ensure that the greatest care is taken of them.

Walton N.F. Empey

Members of the Church of Ireland have been and are deeply involved in the provision of homes for the elderly. The diocese approved of the building in Dublin of a new state-of-the-art home, "Cowper Care" Gascoigne House, as a central element in its Millennium list of projects. The building of such a home is extremely costly. The generous award from the National Millennium Committee made a huge difference in bringing the project to a successful conclusion. It is now providing excellent care for the elderly. We are most grateful for the very generous contribution made to this project and also to other projects taken on by the diocese, which were not so costly.

One of these projects was the re-hanging of the historic bells of St. George's Church, which was closed some years ago. These beautiful bells had no home for many years until Taney Parish decided that it should provide a home for them. The parish knew that it was going to be a difficult

and costly operation but felt that it was a fitting project for the new Millennium. It demanded a great deal of skill and hard work to re-hang these old bells in their new home. It caused great joy, not only to the parishioners but also to the local community when, quite fittingly, the old bells rang in not only the New Year but also the new Millennium. We thank the Millennium Committee not only for their generosity in providing finance but also for their vision in seeing this as a fitting project.

– Walton N. F. Empey *Archbishop of Dublin*

1 Church of Ireland Deacon Maud Lewis and Fr. Liam Comer lighting the Millennium Candle at Dursey Head.

2 Archbishop Empey with Minister Séamus Brennan and Mr. Howard Kilroy at the opening of Gascoigne House residential home for the elderly in Dublin.

Murrisk Millennium Peace Park

> The Murrisk Millennium Peace Park at the foothills of Croagh Patrick, Co. Mayo, has been developed as an area of peace, reflection and rest for those who have completed the arduous Croagh Patrick climb. The Park will also have special meaning for the aged and people with disabilities and all those unable to make the demanding ascent. A permanent feature in the five-acre park is the National Famine Monument, a large bronze sculpture by John Behan, depicting a "coffin ship" with skeletal remains.

Millennium Committee Award €317,434 (IR£250,000)

Seán Staunton

> ## A Personal Note

Croagh Patrick stands citadel-like over the quaint and beautiful village of Murrisk, five miles from Westport. It has been a centre of pilgrimage for over 1,500 years, an oasis of peace in a magnificent landscape and a fount of spirituality for hundreds of thousands of pilgrims throughout the centuries.

The Murrisk Millennium Park, which has been so sensitively developed, recognises the mountain's spiritual and aesthetic significance and enriches the broad appeal of this world-class ancient landscape. It has the potential to be an outstanding park to mark 2000 years of Christian living.

From the aeons of time, Patrick's mountain has been the symbol of the human struggle, bearing the scars of famine and the footprints of life's journey. It has always been thought of as more than a mountain, comparable to a national icon with which all Christians can identify.

More than 100,000 pilgrims scale Croagh Patrick's paths annually, with up to 30,000 making the ascent on the last Sunday in July, the traditional national day of pilgrimage. The park will have special meaning for those unable to climb the mountain but who wish to have a pilgrim association with it.

The completed park was the culmination of the work of partnership of local and national interests, which included Murrisk Development Association, the National Millennium Committee, Mayo County Council and the Christian Churches. The Murrisk Millennium Peace Park adds greatly to Croagh Patrick's reputation as a place of peace, meditation, prayer and history.

– Seán Staunton *Editor, The Mayo News*

"And presently, from an eminence, I caught sight not only of a fine view, but of the most beautiful view I ever saw in the world."

– *The Irish Sketchbook 1842, William Makepeace Thackeray*

Above A unique moment, full of mystery, Croagh Patrick soaring 2,510 feet in communion with the clouds.

Right The Murrisk Millennium Peace Park with the National Famine Monument in the foreground and the backdrop of Clew Bay.

Photography by Liam Lyons

Glendalough Hermitage Retreat Centre

> Glendalough, Co. Wicklow, has been a place of pilgrimage and spiritual activity for one-and-a-half Millennia. One of the unique projects undertaken to mark the third Millennium was the addition of five *cillíns* or hermitages as solitary retreats for those wishing to take time out from the pressures of modern living. The hermitages were built as a response to the growing number of persons of all faiths who come to Glendalough seeking solitude, spiritual guidance and the opportunity for spiritual renewal through retreat and pilgrimage.

Millennium Committee Award €317,434 (IR£250,000)

Seán O'Toole

> ## A Personal Note

Glendalough (gleann dá locha) is one of the best known and loved early medieval Christian sites in Ireland. During its golden period, Glendalough was, for the whole of Europe, a centre of creative excellence. It achieved this pre-eminent position, not only through the extraordinary educational process initiated by that spiritual genius Caoimhín (St. Kevin) in the 6th century, but also through the "genius of place" which it so transparently possesses. Crowds of tourists and pilgrims daily testify to the special spirit of mysticism that the valley imparts.

I believe that in this age of new technology, which has again propelled Ireland into the creative forefront, Glendalough's mysticism and spiritual energy have a powerful role to play. Coming here, away from the noise and the tension of modern living, enables one to harmonise personal instincts with those of nature and the Divine.

"Glendalough 2000" endeavours to meet this need. Our project entitled *Suaimhneas Chaoimhín*, offers hospitable space for people who would like to get away from it all and be alone for a brief period.

Nestling snugly on the side of Brockagh Mountain close, to the old monastic site, these beautifully designed edifices will, please God, stand for centuries to come as an outstanding memorial to the great Jubilee year 2000 A.D.

This unique service for pilgrims was made possible by a very generous award from the National Millennium Committee. Míle Buíochas.

– Father Seán O'Toole *Chairman, Glendalough 2000*

Top His Eminence Cardinal Desmond Connell blessing the Hermitage Retreat Centre.

Above The interior of a *cillín* or hermitage.

St. Fin Barre's, Cork

> St. Fin Barre left the monastery he had founded at Gougán Barra, close to the source of the River Lee, in 606 AD and journeyed along the beautiful river's length until he came to its sluggish, marshy mouth, just before its waters flowed into the majestic expanse of Cork Harbour. Here, on rising ground just above the marsh (*Corcaigh* – Cork), he founded another monastery and brought both Christianity and learning to this wild, Viking-infested place. St. Fin Barre is regarded as being Cork's first bishop.

Millennium Committee Award €126,973 (IR£100,000)

> A Personal Note

The people of Cork hold the saint in great affection and many a son of the city bears his name – or its diminutive, Barry. The local hurling and football club is, of course, called after him and throughout the playing season Cork rings to the chant "Up de Barrs!" The surname Barry or Barra, also common in Cork, is Norman in origin and is something different altogether

In the middle of the 19th century a splendid new cathedral rose on the site of Fin Barre's monastery, the latest in a succession to be built there. The gleaming white limestone of the area of which it is built shows off the soaring design of William Burges, an English architect and medievalist, like a heavenly vision. Every detail of structure, furnishing and decoration displays Burges' extraordinary genius in what is regarded as his ecclesiastical masterpiece.

Modern-day pilgrims visit in increasing numbers to worship Burges, perhaps St. Fin Barre – maybe even God. But time and Cork's damp climate have taken their toll. Renovations and development to meet these needs became necessary. Now Burges' roof is intact once more, his stained glass glows safely in its lead supports and congregations are comfortably warm. Shortly, in a new display centre, modern pilgrims will learn of St. Fin Barre and Cork, here where it all began. We are grateful to the National Millennium Committee for its support.

– Michael Jackson *Deacon*

Right The landmark St. Fin Barre's Cathedral, Cork.

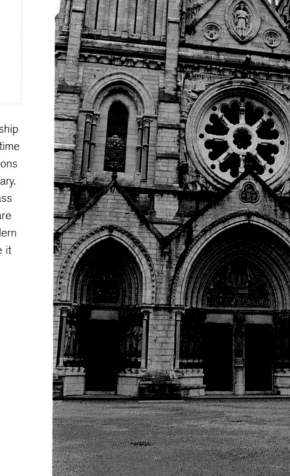

Mayo Millennium Spire

> The town of Ballyhaunis, Co. Mayo, waited the best part of a century to have St. Patrick's Church crowned with an imposing spire. The erection of the Millennium Spire completes an aspiration that dates from 1903. And it also gives the town a striking landmark which can be seen from a distance of several miles.

Millennium Committee Award €126,973 (IR£100,000)

> A Personal Note

The spire on St. Patrick's Church started off as a plan in 1903, it remained a dream for almost a hundred years and became a reality in 1999. At a special Mass on New Year's Eve, 1999, the people of Ballyhaunis saw that dream come true when the completed spire on their church was dedicated to the memory of those who had planned it a hundred years earlier. Now it rises gracefully over our church and, with flood-lighting at night, it seems to be keeping vigil over the sleeping town.

It is a distinct landmark and though there may have been sceptics, people are now proudly claiming that they can see it from their homes, even those a few miles away. Many will now say that they find it hard to visualise what the town and church looked like before the spire was completed.

From within the town and from a distance, its towering presence is as powerful a call to prayer as the church bell. School children are captivated by it and constantly enquire about its height. We are all proud to be part of the project,

which completed a dream that is now part of our history and folklore. There is tremendous pride in this visual and permanent symbol of what Ballyhaunis did to mark the new Millennium, and great satisfaction that the National Millennium Committee recognised the appropriateness of the project and supported it.

– Father Joe Cooney *P.P. Ballyhaunis, Co. Mayo*

Above St. Patrick's Church before it was crowned.

Right The Millennium Spire after the completion. Photograph – Henry Madden.

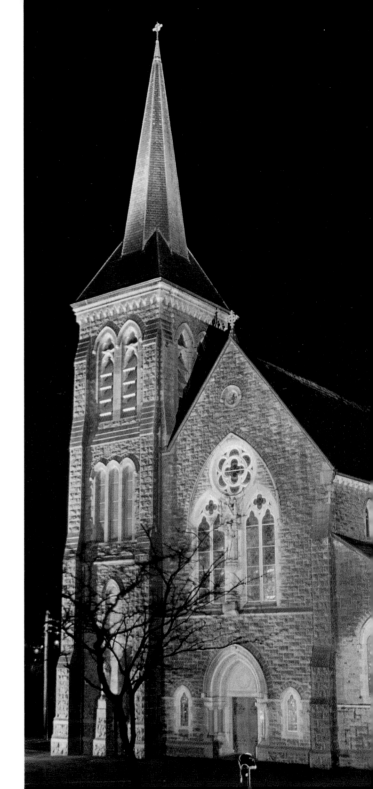

2000 Years of Church Architecture

> *Sacred Places* was a major exhibition tracing and celebrating 2,000 years of church architecture on the island of Ireland.

Millennium Committee Award €92,690 (IR£73,000)

The exhibition was developed jointly by the Royal Institute of the Architects of Ireland (R.I.A.I.) and the Royal Society of Ulster Architects (R.S.U.A.) to celebrate the shared tradition of Christian building on this island over the last two Millennia.

It was divided into six sections: Early Christian and Romanesque; Middle Ages; Reformation and Plantation; Age of Ascendancy; 19th Century and 20th Century.

The range of quality of the church buildings in *Sacred Places* was a testament to the commitment and imagination of those people who designed and built them. The exhibition contained photographs and drawings of some of the land-mark church buildings from each era and tradition, in the region of a hundred in all, tracing the evolution of Christian architecture in Ireland up to the present. However, the exhibition was more than a collection of images of church buildings; it told the story of how we lived on this island over the past 2,000 years, in particular showing Ireland's diverse social and cultural development.

Sacred Places also contained models and replica artefacts from some of the churches featured. In addition, a full-colour exhibition catalogue featured essays by the country's leading experts in this area, Professor Roger Stalley, Dr Paul Larmour and architect, Richard Hurley.

Above St. Michael's Church, Creeslough, Co. Donegal.

Right One of the *clocháns* situated many hundred feet above the waves on Skellig Michael.

Irish Missionary Film Archive

> The Irish Missionary Church has made a valuable contribution to both the spiritual and cultural development of many countries throughout the world. A priceless film collection telling their story is now being assembled.

The pioneering work around the world of Irish missionaries has been a source of pride and inspiration for decades. During the 20th century, missionaries played a significant role in the social, political, economic and cultural development of several countries, particularly in Africa, Asia and South America. Their contribution has been captured on an historic film collection, dating back to the 1930s, which had been dispersed among the archives of the societies of the Irish Missionary Union and was in danger of being damaged or lost forever. Throughout the 20th century, Irish missionaries commissioned or collaborated with the making of many professional films of their work overseas. Amateur film-makers also created valuable insights into the work of the missionaries and of the social conditions prevailing at that time in emerging countries. With support from the National Millennium Committee, the Millennium Missionary Film Project undertook the sourcing, collecting and cataloging of all the film material with the objective of creating a centralised home for the collection in the safekeeping of the National Film Archive in Dublin. To date more than a hundred films, professional and amateur, have been sourced. The films capture the work of the Irish missionaries in a variety of countries, including China, The Philippines, Japan,

Burma, Korea, Fiji, Peru, Chile, Hong Kong, Nigeria, Malawi, Zambia and Tanzania. The result is a collection that represents a rich cultural chapter in Ireland's international heritage.

Above Columban Fr. Philip Crosbie, who was imprisoned for three years during the Korean War, with a Korean wedding couple in 1958.

Right Irish Columban, Fr. Seán Dunne and a Korean translator on a boat from the Korean city of Mokpo in 1957 while filming the Gregory Peck narrated *Path to Glory*, an account of the suffering endured by Korean Catholics between 1790-1953.

Photography – Courtesy of Columban Missionaries.

Opposite Page Lay missionary Dr. Vincent Kenny, Director of the Volunteer Missionary Movement, addressing health care issues with a local community in the remote desert region of Turkana, North West Kenya, in 1998.

07 Celebrations

Celebrations — Millennium Eve

> From lunchtime onwards on New Year's Eve, 1999, a steady trickle of people began to converge on Merrion Square in Dublin. Their object was to get as close as possible to a huge stage that had been built outside Government Buildings. This stage was to be the focal point for a free four-hour special afternoon family-orientated concert whose centrepiece was going to be the Last Light Ceremony, Ireland's unique farewell to the final hours of the 20th century.

By 2.30 p.m., when the legendary *Kilfenora Ceilí Band* took to the stage and started playing some lively jigs, reels and hornpipes in their inimitable style, the trickle of people had turned into a flood. Throughout the next hour or so, as *Sharon Shannon* and her band, and then *Brian Kennedy*, played their sets, the crowd, mostly family groups with teenagers, excited boys and girls and even babies in strollers in tow, continued to grow, filling the square right down to Clare Street. By the time dusk approached and the Last Light Ceremony began it is estimated that more than 25,000 people were there, cheering to the echo every song of surprise guest artist *Ronan Keating*, a member of the National Millennium Committee.

As Ronan hushed the crowd with an unaccompanied "She Moved Thru' the Fair", the Taoiseach, Bertie Ahern T.D., slipped quietly onto the stage with selected members of the defence forces and the emergency services. At 4.20 p.m., as President McAleese lit the official Millennium Candle in Árás an Uachtaráin, the Taoiseach lit his candle with a flame that had been brought from the perpetual flame in Omagh, lighting in turn the candles of the defence, public and emergency

services personnel. While he was doing this the crowd in Merrion Square lit tapers that had been passed to them until the entire street became a sea of yellow, flickering light in the gathering darkness.

A few hours later Merrion Square was filling up again, this time for a 20,000 all-ticket pop concert featuring *Picture House*, Welsh pop sensation *David Gray, The Divine Comedy, The Afro Celt Sound System* and, at the count-down to midnight, the final minutes of the 20th century were hammered out on the thunderous *Millennium Drum*, the largest drum in the world, with the enthusiastic and hilarious participation of Galway's madcap *Macnas* troupe.

As midnight came and went, the city was filled with the sound of bells. At Christ Church, the traditional gathering point for welcoming the New Year, the crowds were treated to glorious melodies rung out by the cathedral's change-ringers on the world's largest peal of fully rotating bronze bells. Bell towers all across the nation joyously pealed in the new Millennium, but before they began their ringing there had been plenty of celebration in cities and towns the length and breadth of Ireland.

Above The world-famous Grucci family from Long Island in New York launched a spectacular fireworks display from a site on the South Wall in Dublin Bay. Simultaneously dazzling pyrotechnics were seen by tens of thousands of people from vantage points.

Opposite Page The crowds gathered in Merrion Square to join in the Last Light Ceremony.

Above Throughout the afternoon and into the night on Millennium Eve, 1999, thousands in Merrion Square were entertained by such notable international artists as **1** Donal Lunny and Sharon Shannon. **2** Ronan Keating and Brian Kennedy **3** Afro Celt Sound System **4** The Kilfinora Ceilí Band **5** David Gray and **6** The Divine Comedy. Hundreds of thousands more saw the broadcast on television.

Opposite Page The original Three Irish Tenors on stage.

Photography – Courtesy of M.C.D.

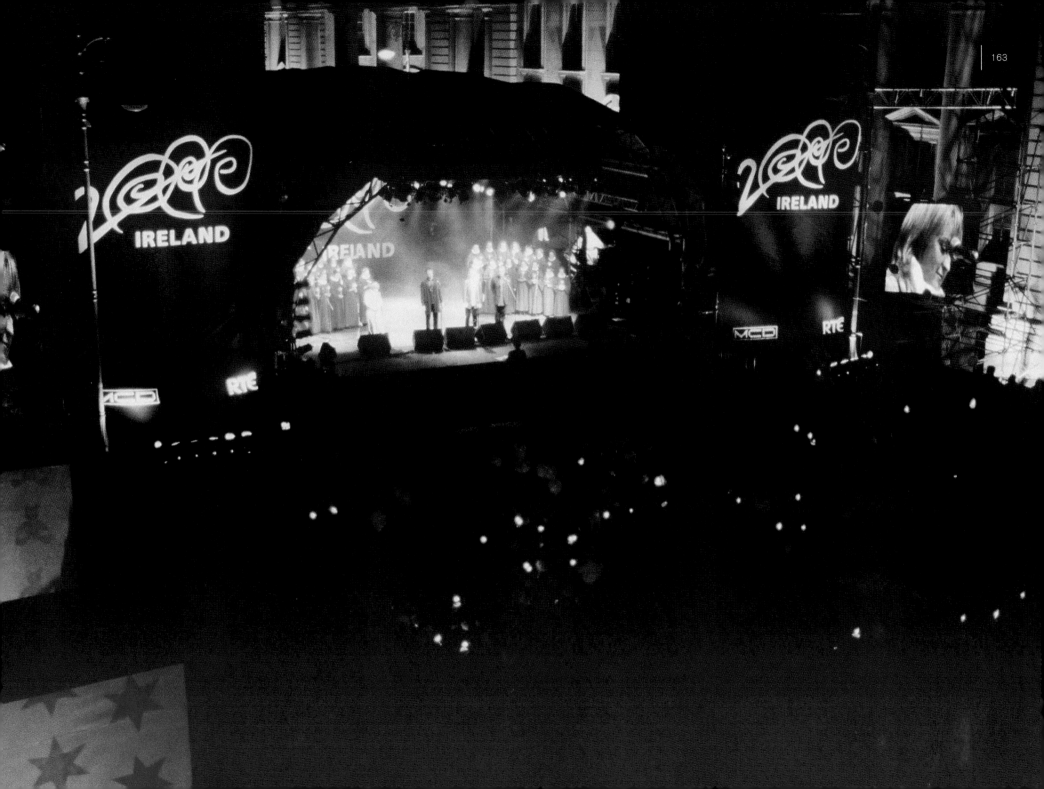

On an evening that remained generally benign, many celebrations were held outdoors. In **Cork City** the focus for many of the celebrations was the famous banks of the River Lee. Two thousand torches were distributed to schoolchildren for the procession of light along by the river. Many families brought along their Millennium Candles and joined in the festivities. Later in the evening the celebrations continued at the *Millennium Invitation Concert* in City Hall featuring an array of talent, including Cara O'Sullivan, Roger Creagh and the Cork Pops Orchestra. Cork erupted on the stroke of midnight when the "Last Call of the Millennium'" lit up the skies. Over three-and-a-half tonnes of fireworks were blasted 1,000 feet into the air in what was the city's biggest ever pyrotechnic display.

Waterford boasts one of the noblest quays in Europe and this was used to stunning effect for the Millennium celebrations. Celebrations began at 9.14 a.m. on New Year's Eve, signifying the year 914 when the Vikings first sailed up the Suir. A chronology of dates was drawn up giving a series of short entertaining commemorative events as Waterford's human Millennium clock passed through 1,000 years of history in just ten hours: marching bands with colourful majorettes; the Catholic and Church of Ireland cathedrals both hosted bands and choirs; city centre shopping areas staged performances from jazz to traditional to country to modern; Irish dancing, set dancing and just pure enjoyable dancing; the jive dancers and drummers and fire jugglers. The ruins of the former Franciscan Friary in Grey Friars, founded in 1240, were the venue for Waterford City's Last Light Ceremony. Then it was on to the the Gala Concert in the

famous Theatre Royal where names synonymous with entertainment in the city, including Val Doonican, Anna Manahan, the Clancy's and Jim Nolan to name just a few, created a unique and memorable night. And finally to "Quayfest" where 50,000 people gathered in a spirit of enjoyment and friendship to count down to the new Millennium. The fireworks display after midnight was the most spectacular ever seen in Waterford.

Galway's citizens enjoyed a free open-air concert in Eyre Square that was followed by the ceremonial lighting of a giant Millennium Candle, and later many of the city's children led Macnas on a parade through the streets that ended at a dazzling firework display.

In **Limerick**, the River Shannon became the stage for an ambitious light, laser and fireworks show that attracted more than 30,000 men, women and children.

Some of the celebrations were very different and unusual – at **Carlingford Lough**, for instance, the North and South of Ireland were momentarily united symbolically by a laser-generated "Bridge of Peace" projected into the night sky, while in **Enniscorthy** in Co. Wexford, peace was also the theme, with a flock of doves being released into the sky during an interdenominational service. In **Sligo** more than 2,000 people packed into the grounds of the 13th century Dominican monastery for a special medieval Last Light ceremony.

Mayo claimed a world record when the townsfolk of Balla managed to plant 2,000 oak saplings within ten minutes of the stroke of midnight, and earlier in the day hundreds of people had gathered at the foot of Croagh Patrick for a

special service as the sun set over the 365 islands of Clew Bay for the last time in the 20th century. A similar ceremony at **Dursey Head** at the extreme tip of the Beara peninsula, presided over by Agriculture Minister Joe Walsh, was brightened by a spectacular technicolour sunset that was televised all over the world. But wherever people celebrated this unique day in all our lives, and whatever the manner of their celebration, there is one thing certain – it will have been one of the most unforgettable days they have ever experienced.

Below Rudolph Giuliani, Mayor of New York, admires a rendition of the **Waterford Crystal Ball** which was lowered at the stroke of midnight, 1999, in Times Square, New York.

Right Macnas at the witching hour in Merrion Square.

Above Snapshots from Millennium Festivals around Ireland.

Right Ar Spraoí ag Waterford Spraoí. Photograph – Kenneth O'Halloran.

Millennium Festivals

> The Millennium Festivals project was one of the earliest to benefit from National Millennium Committee funding. The organisation's brief was to provide opportunities for Irish people to celebrate the Millennium while at the same time increasing Ireland's profile amongst potential visitors.

Millennium Committee Award €1,269,738 (£1 million)

> A Personal Note

Doireann Ní Bhriain

Two important decisions were taken at an early stage. The first was to work through the infrastructure of existing and successful Irish festivals, supporting them to programme additional celebratory events over a full year. The second was to start early so as to attract attention worldwide, hence the slogan "The Party Starts Here".

And it did start here, at Saint Patrick's Festival in Dublin in March 1999, when the extraordinary Skyfest set the Dublin skies ablaze. The party continued throughout 1999 at eight flagship festivals – Saint Patrick's, the Galway Arts Festival, Kilkenny Arts Festival, The Rose of Tralee, Fleadh Cheoil na hÉireann, Wexford Festival Opera, The Guinness Cork Jazz Festival and The Belfast Festival at Queens – and nine additional smaller festivals in Ennis, Sligo, Drogheda, Letterkenny, Waterford, Foynes, Clifden, Westport and Derry.

The events programmed at these festivals to mark the coming of the new Millennium were all free of charge and attracted huge audiences of all ages. There were extraordinary fireworks displays and wonderfully creative street theatre, walls of water, a bay illuminated by candles, pyrotechnics on land and on water, music and dancing in the streets. Thousands participated and millions watched.

At the centre of each of the 17 Millennium Festivals was the specially constructed Millennium Drum. Validated in 2000 by the Guinness Book of Records as the biggest drum in the world, it is now a tangible memento of a truly memorable year of celebrations.

– Doireann Ní Bhriain *Former General Manager*
Millennium Festivals Limited

Right Celebrations in Temple Bar, Dublin.

Opposite Page Macnas fireworks spectacular at Galway Arts Festival.

> Millennium Committee Favourites

Derek Keogh

While I liked and admired a lot of the Millennium undertakings, such as the Last Light Ceremony and The People's Millennium Forests projects, my special favourite was the **Millennium Festivals.**

Firstly, I liked the fact that it covered the whole island from Donegal, Derry and Belfast to Kerry, Cork, Waterford and Wexford. Our partner festivals ranged from big, powerful events that had a national impact, to small intimate ones that reflected their own local communities.

There was a lot of satisfaction, too, in seeing that we were adding something important to these festivals, bringing a special celebratory dimension and making them more accessible to everyone. We did it through open-air events, firework displays, street parades and lots of free entertainment. This worked for every festival, even those with very specialised themes. I am delighted that these new elements have been embraced by all of the festival organisers and will continue to be a major part of their festivals in the future.

But, most of all, there was the opportunity to experience some really special moments: watching one of the world's biggest fireworks displays at Saint Patrick's Festival in the company of several hundred thousand locals and visitors; seeing 2,000 candles gradually light up the rim of the darkened harbour in Clifden and, right on cue, the moon coming out from behind a cloud to complete the sequence (I swear it!); seeing and hearing the sometimes hilarious

wishes of the people of Kilkenny displayed against a giant water spray over the River Nore and sharing the nervous joy of young boys and girls bashing the world's biggest drum in Waterford and other places.

We shared these and many other touches of magic with people of all ages up and down the country and I know that we helped provide some very special Millennium memories.

It was a delight and a privilege to have been a part of it all.

– Derek Keogh *Former Chairman Millennium Festivals and Member of the National Millenium Committee*

Left and Above Scenes from celebrations in Waterford and Dublin.
Opposite Page Killorglin, Co. Kerry. Photograph – Kenneth O'Halloran.

Saint Patrick's Festival & Skyfest

> SkyFest 2000 was an exhilarating and memorable finale to the four-day Saint Patrick's Festival in March 2000. Spectacular volleys of fireworks thrilled the several hundred thousand spectators who lined the quays along the River Liffey for what was Ireland's biggest ever fireworks display.

Millennium Committee Award €165,065 (£130,000)

Marie Clare Sweeney

> A Personal Note

What effect did the involvement of the Millennium Committee, and the Millennium itself, have on Saint Patrick's Festival 2000? In a word, huge! And in many diverse ways. Rupert Murray, the artistic director, and I started work on Saint Patrick's Festival in November 1995, with a then daunting brief to change the way we celebrate our national holiday and create a major international festival within five years. The 2000 Festival was the fifth year and, indeed, it turned out to be our last in organising the event, as we had both decided to pass on the mantle to a new management team. What better time to exit than the Millennium year and what better way to stamp that benchmark that had been with us for five years?

A benchmark that meant the added personal drive to create the best festival yet for 2000, as well as striving to meet the expectations and anticipation of the thousands of people coming into Dublin city centre for an expanded festival as

part of the Millennium celebrations. In the end, over 5,000 performers and participants entertained over 1.36 million people on the streets. Four hundred thousand alone turned up for the extra-special Millennium Skyfest fireworks extravaganza on the Liffey quays and many millions more watched the event on TV and computer screens worldwide.

March 17 is like no other national day of celebration in the world and no other national day is celebrated so exuberantly throughout the world. The 2000 Millennium Saint Patrick's Festival held in Dublin was the best celebration of the Irish national holiday anywhere for the Millennium. That's not just my opinion but also the opinion of hundreds of thousands on the streets, and the testimony of millions watching on TV, listening on radio, keying in on the Internet, and reading about it.

Truly a celebration for the Irish and those who wish they were Irish, wherever they reside.

– Marie Clare Sweeney *Former Executive Director Saint Patrick's Festival, 1995-2000*

Above, Opposite Page and Following Pages Spectacular volleys of fireworks thrilled a vast crowd of excited spectators as 15 tonnes of fireworks were detonated at Dublin's Custom House Quay. Pyrotechnics synchronised more than 50,000 explosions at Ireland's biggest ever spectacle, Skyfest 2000.

Photography – Frank Fennell Photography.

08 Heritage

Heritage

A challenge when deciding how best to commemorate the Millennium was to find projects that celebrate the past while at the same time looking to the future. Ireland's past is captivatingly rich and varied. It is also a priceless heritage that is becoming increasingly vulnerable as the digital age and pace of life threaten to sweep away so much that we now take for granted.

That is why the Millennium afforded a timely opportunity to focus attention on facets of Irish life that are in danger of being forgotten, if not lost, forever, while at the same time encouraging the quest to discover more about our origins as a Celtic people.

The Millennium Committee supported dozens of projects that seek to preserve and protect our heritage. From restoring a unique railway in Co. Kerry to rebuilding in Dublin a seismograph that monitored earthquakes, the emphasis has been on renewal and revival as new life is breathed into endeavours that were once part of the everyday life of the country.

One had only to see how the nation became engrossed in the *100 Years* series on RTÉ each day of the year 2000 to understand our fascination with history, even relatively recent social, political and sporting events. This series each day gave a brief snapshot of events on that particular date in Ireland over the past hundred years using archival film, newspaper photographs and headlines and radio reports. The assured commentary of Brian Farrell led older viewers on a nostalgic memory trip, while giving the younger generations new insights into the birth of a nation.

Railways, particularly the old steam engines and carriages, hold a fascination for many people. Few come as unique as the **Lartigue Monorail** railway in Co. Kerry that ran between Listowel and Ballybunion from 1886 to 1924. During that time it attracted worldwide attention as the only working railway of its type to be found anywhere. It was unique because the engine and carriages were carried along a single raised track that ran through the centre of the train. Millennium funding is now helping to restore a section of track from Listowel and to revive the curiosity, excitement and bewilderment which the original Lartigue generated.

The restoration of a section of the **Cavan-Leitrim Railway** at Dromod is on a smaller scale to Lartigue but it is also an example of a community refusing to relinquish an important part of its heritage.

The same can be said of the people of **Mizen Head**, the most southwesterly point of Ireland. When the "light" at the signal station was made automatic in 1993, they refused to allow the "human link" with this historic warning point to be lost. Now with the help of Millennium funding a new visitor and interpretative centre has opened at the top of

the cliffs. All around the country there are other examples: the **Allihies Mining Museum** in West Cork rising from the remains of the greatest copper mining venture in 19th century Ireland; funding to add a planetarium at the **Inishown Maritime Museum** in Co. Donegal; €76,184 (IR£60,000) to renovate and convert the Martello Tower on **Bere Island**, Co. Cork; restoring the **Windmill in Elphin**, Co. Roscommon; commemorating heroine **Countess Markievich** in Sligo; designing the innovative new Clock Tower in **Stranorlar**, Co. Donegal; capturing the lives of Co. Clare people worldwide in **The Scattering** and returning **Woodstock Gardens**, Co. Kilkenny, and **Birr Castle Gardens** to much of their original beauty.

Ireland's first **National Field Study Centre** at Ballinafad, Co. Sligo, will actually reach into three Millennia. Built with support of €126,974 (IR£100,000) from the Millennium Committee, it will provide a range of specialist and holiday programmes on archaeology, geology, ornithology, flora/fauna, mythology and folklore, painting and drawing, photography and crafts. Those who come to use and enjoy the facility will be looking back through the past two Millennia as they search for and source identity to the archaeology of the region.

Tracing our origins is at the very core of an engrossing investigation being undertaken by the Royal Irish Academy. **Irish Origins** is an all-Ireland study of the origins and genetic relationships of the ancient prehistoric peoples of Ireland and their links with the ancient peoples of Europe, even with those of the Near East and North Africa.

On the 31 July, 1917, at Boezinge, near Ypres in Belgium, the poet Francis Ledwidge, from Slane, Co. Meath, was killed in World War I. Much of his poetry in its timelessness evokes the beauty of the rivers, fields, peoples and places of Meath and Louth. Later he wrote of war. In 1998 a monument was unveiled on the exact spot where he died. Now a replica of this monument, constructed in stone from Belgium, has been erected in the garden of the **Ledwidge Cottage Museum**, Slane.

*Bhí tionchar mór ag **Cath Eachroime** i 1691, ar thodhchaí mhíleata, shoisíalta agus eaglasta na hÉireann go ceann 300 bliain. Dob é an cath mór deiridh é a troideadh ar thalamh na hÉireann. Anois tá suíomh an chatha sin dírithe ar shíocháin agus ar athmhuintearas.*

All of these imaginative projects will endure for many years as a valuable resource for all those interested in Ireland and its heritage.

Left The Millennium Gardens, Birr Castle.

Lartigue Railway

> The Lartigue monorail railway in Co. Kerry ran between Listowel and Ballybunion from 1886 to 1924, a period during which it attracted worldwide attention because of its uniqueness amongst rail transport systems. It is now being restored as a heritage attraction.

Millennium Committee Award €222,204 (IR£175,000)

The Lartigue is believed to have been the only one of its type in the world, as efforts to replicate the system in Panissieres, France, had limited success. It was characterised by the steam engine and carriages running along a single rail through the centre of the locomotive that stood approximately 3ft off the ground.

The curiosity and excitement generated by the original Lartigue Monorail will be brought alive once again with the restoration of a section of track. A replica steam engine and carriages, with capacity for 40 passengers, will run along a 500-metre track from Listowel. Later, a monorail museum, incorporating an exhibition and interpretative centre, will be developed.

When the Lartigue is restored as a tourism and heritage attraction, this famous railway will have spanned three centuries, from its construction in the 1880s, through its unfortunate demise in the mid-1920s and now its restoration in the 21st century.

> A Personal Note

My first memory of travelling on the Lartigue Railway is 1922 when I was four years old. I was travelling with my Aunt Mai, my two sisters, baby Liam and a nurse to Ballybunion. I can still recall the frightening screech of the wheels of our carriage on the metal rails behind our backs.

My father lived over the shop in Listowel during the week and used to travel out to Ballybunion at weekends to join the family. We would all go to the station to meet him. Being an inquisitive four-year-old, I must have pestered him with questions concerning the Lartigue so much so, that on one occasion when we were walking he said:

"Jackie [Reidy], like a good man, will you show this young fellow how the engine works?"

Jackie took me up in his arms and into the cab.

"There now boy," he said. "Pull that lever", and I gave a heave to this black handle and with a CHUFF CHUFF the engine moved off to the end of the platform. Jackie stopped and handed me back to my father. So one of my claims to fame is that I drove the Lartigue!

The Civil War put paid to the railway's viability. In 1924 it became bankrupt and went into liquidation. At the auction of the company assets my father bought a sizeable portion of the site of the Listowel Station. The development he had in mind for it never materialised so I inherited the site, which has many remnants of the original track system. It was always my hope that some restoration of this legendary railway would miraculously come about, and when the National Millennium Committee offered very substantial support, I gladly handed over this site to the Lartigue Monorail Restoration Project.

– Jack McKenna *Listowel*

Above The unique Lartigue.
Right A fanfare welcome for the replica Lartigue locomotive in Listowel, March 2002. It was built by Alan Keef and Company at their works in Herefordshire, England. Photograph – Domnick Walsh.

> A Personal Note

When Minister Brennan was launching the Lartigue Restoration Project as a Millennium scheme, he and I were asked to pose for a photograph looking out the windows of what was grandly labelled a "First Class" carriage. This wooden box had been rescued by a local farmer, along with other bits of old railway stock and running-rail. It had been used for years as a hen house. The basic construction was still sound, and now mounted as part of the old trestled rail, it could even move a few yards.

We were celebrating the invention of a French engineer, Charles Francois Marie-Therese Lartigue, who had produced what had seemed to be the answer to the transport problem of North Kerry in the 1880s. I remember a much humbler, and much less grandly titled contributor to the enterprise, my maternal grandfather, Maurice Nugent, who had come to Listowel, a journeyman carpenter, to assist at the building of the railway and remained on the staff until it closed down.

As I examined the carriage the basic structure was still sound. The cladding, newly varnished, had withstood the ravages of time and the Atlantic gales. The mortice and tenon joints, the dovetails and the neatly spaced rows of nails, their heads countersunk in the timber, were all, possibly, the work of my grandfather over a century ago. He can be seen in many of the old photographs – a heavy set man with a grey beard and moustache and a bowler hat, carrying his tools in his joiner's creel.

My mother, who spent her childhood in a cottage in what might grandly be called the marshalling yard of the Lartigue Railway, left home at the age of 15 and finally ended up at the other end of Ireland. She fed our young imaginations with talk of this wondrous railway, the Lartigue, a miracle invention and contrivance requiring constant acts of heroism, and improvisation to keep it going.

It became a dragon, snorting fire through two flaming nostrils, with a single glowing eye, bearing down out of the dark, carrying revellers home from the races or early morning farmers to the fair. We heard of the train having to be balanced, two thin ladies to counter weigh one fat man, or the passengers having to get out to push, or the farmer borrowing a calf to get to Ballybunion with the other one he had bought and left with the unsolvable problem of sending only one back to Listowel.

I like to think that, thanks to the Lartigue, I was given an early lesson on the need for balance in life, and a sense of proportion of the importance of weighting both sides of an argument and of the values too of zany eccentricity and enthusiasm and a respect for the ridiculous.

– Senator Maurice Hayes

1 The original Lartigue steaming into Listowel.

2 Working on the turntable in Listowel.

3 Minister Brennan and Senator Maurice Hayes travel "First Class" in an old Lartigue carriage on Mick Barry's farm.

National Field Study Centre

> The National Field Study Centre at Ballinafad, County Sligo, provides a range of specialist holidays for those interested in a variety of heritage and nature pursuits. It is a residential facility offering a range of programmes in archaeology, geology, ornithology, flora/fauna, Irish folklore, local history, painting and photography.

Millennium Committee Award €126,973 (IR£100,000)

> A Personal Note

Below the Bricklieve and the Curlew mountains of South County Sligo and located on the shores of Lough Arrow lies the village of Ballinafad. This small village has in recent times seen intense activity, and the gradual emergence of a unique facility. Beside the Castle of Ballinafad a 20 bedroom residential centre has grown from a green field site into a unique facility dedicated to the pursuit of environmental education and heritage appreciation – the National Field Study Centre Ireland.

The centre offers a range of courses as diverse as the region's heritage and environment which it seeks to promote. Archaeology, mythology, botany, geology, arts and crafts are some of the courses on offer. Explore the megalithic complex of Carrowkeel, perched atop the Bricklieve mountains; wander the mythological battlefield of Moytura; learn from our expert tutors how prehistoric peoples approached life and death. You can study the Whooper Swan, Barnacle Goose, the Burnet Moth or the Purple Hairstreak butterfly,

Bee orchids, ferns, lichens; mountain, lake, woodland, coastal and peatland habitats. All from a centre conceived, designed and built to be comfortable, functional and yet complementary to the environment of which it has become an intricate part.

At the centre the aim is to provide an experience, whatever your field of interest, that will satisfy a thirst for knowledge in a relaxed and friendly manner. Unwind after a day of field study with the other participants in the restaurant or common rooms. Continue your studies in the lecture rooms, laboratories or library. Or perhaps join the others for a pint and the craic in the village. When your visit comes to an end the hope is that you will leave having enjoyed new friends, and with a fresh insight into what heritage and the environment can mean to you.

– Lauder Clarke *Director*

Top "Field study" for all ages.
Above The National Field Study Centre.

RTÉ 100 Years

> *100 Years* on RTÉ was a fascinating glimpse into the day-to-day events in Ireland in the 20th century. The programme, narrated by Brian Farrell, drew on archival newsreel footage, newspaper accounts and RTÉ's own film library to piece together events that made the news at home and abroad on the date in question.

> A Personal Note

100 Years was a short programme broadcast every day in the year 2000, looking back at events on that day in the last century, to remind people not only of the big historical events but also some of the smaller ones which reflected social conditions of the time and showed us warts and all.

So we had the Gaelic and Literary revivals at the turn of the century; the Easter Rising and the executions of the leaders; the first Dáil; the Treaty negotiations and the subsequent Civil War. We had the Eucharistic Congress and many other big religious gatherings and, later, the economic development of the Lemass era. There was the famous Lemass/O'Neill meeting, the Civil Rights movement in the North; the demand for change there; Bloody Sunday; and our entry into the EEC.

Northern politics played a large part over the last 25 years, with many bombing atrocities including the Abercorn, McGurk's Bar, Enniskillen and Omagh.

We also had tenements, civil unrest, strikes and lock-outs early in the century; the founding of the Abbey Theatre.

Later we had the last tram and the last working horse in Dublin. We had Noel Browne and the Mother and Child Scheme. In more recent times we had a teacher losing her job because she was living with a married man; the divorce referendum, the abortion question and the X Case. We had child abuse, both sexual and physical with clerical involvement in many cases, which shocked all the more because of the added betrayal of trust. And, of course, there was sport, from the G.A.A. to football and Italia '90, to our recent Olympic and rugby successes. And we ended with tribunals about political donations, planning scandals and contaminated blood products.

It may have been a mere two-and-a-half minutes a day, but this added up to 15 and a quarter hours over 366 days, and was the result of endless trawls through archive footage, old photographs and newspapers. And RTÉ does have some valuable archive material.

100 Years, narrated by Brian Farrell, proved very popular and drew a large audience. One viewer told of his local pub falling silent for the duration, the conversation resuming again afterwards. Many other viewers wrote about items which interested them personally or offered further information. A few were unhappy about the exclusion of certain events, but ultimately a choice had to be made and lots of good stories had to be left out. There were phone calls from distraught viewers who forgot to set their videos and missed a day!

For those and others, RTÉ repeated the series on a weekly basis in 2001.

– Nuala Ní Dhomhnaill *Editor*

Above Brian Farrell, Narrator of *100 Years*.

Opposite Page Scenes from *100 Years* – **Main Photograph** The Papal visit to Ireland 1979. **1** Douglas Hyde, First President of Ireland. **2** Count John McCormack (front left) at UCD, 1929. **3** President de Valera and Liam Cosgrave. **4** President John F. Kennedy in Wexford, 1963. **5** Erskine Childers and Jack Lynch at the funeral of Seán Lemass, 1971. **6** Cork v Kilkenny in the 1969 All-Ireland Hurling Final.

(All photographs courtesy of the RTÉ Archive-Stills Collection)

The Scattering

> *The Scattering* book project was born out of a longing to acknowledge and reflect the emigrant experience of the people of Co. Clare.

Millennium Committee Award €40,631 (IR£32,000)

Down through the years, thousands of people from Co. Clare have left to live and work in other lands. Today this Clare scattering can be found in every corner of the globe: The young girl who left Clare in the 1920s still dreams of the county in an old folks home in the Bronx; the geologist on the Amazon; the nun in Nairobi; the Killimer girl who left to become a sewing maid; the Ennis lad who brought his passion for hurling to Paris and the dry stone wall builder in America.

For some Clare people the experience is a happy and fulfilling one, for others it has meant loneliness and heartbreak, cut off from family and friends. An open invitation to the people of Clare to nominate friends and or relations around the world for inclusion in the book garnered an amazing response. Names and addresses in 33 countries were selected and for a 12 month period, six of Ireland's leading photographers, all living in the Mid-West, crisscrossed the world. There were many hurdles. Time zones and borders, currencies and languages, tropical diseases and war zones all presented their own challenge. Between them they visited 68 Clare people at work and in their homes. Twenty thousand images and a huge variety of stories were brought home.

Some of those included found fame. Writer Edna O'Brien features, as does singer Maura O'Connell and musician Martin Hayes. Other emigrants tell stories of success, achievement and often of generous and significant contributions to their new countries. But the book also records that many who left Clare to seek their fortune never realised their dream. *The Scattering* is for and about all Clare emigrants, those who made it and those who didn't. It is an attempt in this new Millennium to welcome them all back home.

Above Michael Power grew up in Barr-na-Gaoithe, Darragh. In 1987, after emigrating to the USA, he joined the NYPD and is now a Sergeant stationed in Manhattan.

Left Rachel "Blue" McDonnell, a native of Ennis, emigrated to the USA in 1994. After driving trucks for a year she took a course in theatre drama and is now pursuing a career in acting in Los Angeles.

Right John Glynn, a native of Kilkee, emigrated to Australia in the 1960s where he worked as a teacher. In 1981 he was ordained a priest in Papua New Guinea where he served until 1997. He now lives in retirement on the island of New Ireland.

Gardens

> Gardens, great and small, are enduring symbols of beauty, growth and regeneration. Many garden projects were developed for the Millennium, including the rescuing and refurbishing of the great and historic gardens at Woodstock, Co. Kilkenny, and Birr Castle, Co. Offaly.

Woodstock Garden Restoration

In the second half of the 19th century, Woodstock in Co. Kilkenny was regarded as one of the great gardens of Ireland, with its design and concept belonging mainly to the early and mid-Victorian period from 1840 to 1870. Sadly in recent decades, years of neglect, indifference and vandalism have left Woodstock a shadow of its once great profile. The ambitious restoration programme at Woodstock by Kilkenny County Council and other agencies is undoing many of the errors of the recent past and creating a heritage garden of beauty and tranquillity for public enjoyment.

Funding from the National Millennium Committee has helped to restore a number of historic features that were central to the original status of the gardens. The Grotto, built in the early Victorian era, has been rescued from a tangle of weeds and briars and lovingly restored. Historic paths in The Rose Garden and Yew Walk have been reconstructed and, to lend authenticity to the transformation back to former beauty, old Victorian varieties of roses have been purchased for planting.

Birr Castle Millennium Gardens

The recently restored Formal Gardens at Birr Castle, Co. Offaly, were opened in July 2000 and renamed "The Millennium Gardens" following a two-year-long restoration project carried out under the direction of the Earl and Countess of Rosse.

The project was carried out under The Great Gardens of Ireland Restoration Programme with patronage from Gallaher (Dublin) Limited and the endorsement of the National Millennium Committee.

The Earl and Countess of Rosse chose the new name, The Millennium Gardens, as "an appropriate means of marking Ireland's passage into the new Millennium". Lord Rosse said, it is hoped that "future generations will be reminded of the dedication, care and craftsmanship which this generation was prepared to invest in the preservation of this unique amenity, at a time when Ireland is entering an era in which the environmental value of such works may become even more important".

Above Woodstock Gardens.
Right Birr Castle Millennium Gardens.

Genetic History of Ireland

> Irish Origins is an all-Ireland investigation of the origins and genetic relationships of the prehistoric peoples of Ireland and their links with the ancient peoples of Europe, the Near East and North Africa. The latest genetic techniques are used in this fascinating quest to uncover clues about the histories of these peoples.

Millennium Committee Award €126,973 (IR£100,000)

Ireland was more or less covered by ice until about 13,000 years ago. The oldest archaeological human remains are about 9,000 years old though we do not know the extent of the contribution these early people made to the modern Irish population. The archaeological evidence shows that peoples in Ireland maintained strong and dynamic links with the populations of adjacent areas of Western Europe throughout the prehistoric and historic periods.

Geneticists, medical doctors, archaeologists, geographers and historians, North and South, are collaborating in using new molecular genetic techniques to carry out a geographical and historical survey of the genetic origins of the prehistoric peoples of Ireland. The main objective is to find genetic clues about the histories of the peoples who have inhabited Ireland during the 13,000 years since the end of the last Ice Age. This can be done in two ways. The first way is to compare the genetic material (DNA) of the modern Irish population and the neighbouring peoples. The second way is to examine the DNA in ancient bones.

It seems that genetic investigations of human origins are of wide general public interest. As Stephen Jay Gould of Harvard has said: "This research has great importance for the obvious and most joyously legitimate reason … our intense fascination with ourselves and details of our history." Many European and other world populations are being closely investigated using a variety of molecular genetic methodologies. This work often results in rich inference about ancestral relationships, population origins and the nature of human genetic diversity. For example we should be able:

(i) To discover the closeness of the genetic relationships between the modern Irish peoples and the peoples of chosen regions in Europe, the Near East and Africa. It will be especially interesting to look at the links with different parts of Scotland, England, Wales, Scandinavia, Iceland, France, Iberia − as well as Northwest Africa and the Near East. Mainly sampling of anonymous modern DNA, which contains the record of our ancient ancestors, can do this.

(ii) To discover whether the regional archaeological differences within our island might be explained by prehistoric arrivals of different peoples or by other processes of interactions between populations.

(iii) To discover whether there was a large incursion by Celtic people about 2,500 years ago. The question of a Celtic incursion is hotly debated and genetic research could make a valuable contribution to the issue.

(iv) To discover whether there is a genetic basis to the distribution of Irish surnames. The results may link the project with genealogy, and lead to methods of following modern Irish emigrations.

(v) To analyse selected genes that cause resistance or susceptibility to disease which may explain why some ancient peoples survived better under the very harsh conditions of Ice-Age Europe. These analyses may show patterns that reflect ancient migrations or other forms of population interaction in the past. As a side benefit, the results will be medically valuable.

(vi) To analyse DNA from ancient bones from Ireland and other places to test for their relationships. Human remains recovered from archaeological sites provide us with the most direct means of studying past populations of this island.

(vii) To compare the native breeds of domesticated plants and animals in Ireland with those in other regions of Europe, Africa and the Near East to find clues about where the ancient Irish owners may have come from or to identify the area with which they had contacts. The study could include cattle, horses, sheep, deer, oats, barley, wheat, apples, coarse fish and rabbits, all of which were brought to Ireland by human groups.

A research programme on this scale would be very ambitious, and would take many years. However, the National Millennium Committee decided that the general questions are so important that it would fund four pilot projects. The pilot research programme is being co-ordinated by the Royal Irish Academy and has been part funded by the Wellcome Trust. A competition was held and four research groups were chosen and funded to carry out the pilot studies. They are in Queen's University Belfast, Trinity College Dublin, the Royal College of Surgeons of Ireland and University College Cork.

The early results are exciting because they are indicating that the modern Irish population is sufficiently genetically distinct from the average European to indicate our closest relatives. We already had some indication of this from some early studies on the ABO blood groups by George Dawson and others (Figure 1). The frequencies of these groups change as you move across Europe from east to west and that is seen across Ireland too. For example, blood group O is more common in the West of Ireland than in the East. Consider hair colour and features of the skin. We are known for our red hair and our freckles and these too are more common in the West of Ireland than in the East (Figure 2). So these early genetic observations indicate that we are genetically slightly different from other Europeans and that the people in the West of Ireland may differ slightly from those from the East.

The question was, whether we could confirm and extend this data using the new techniques of DNA analysis. Dan Bradley and Emmy Hill at Trinity have shown we learn more using the DNA methods. They began by looking at the Y chromosomes of a few hundred Irish men. They discovered that Irish men tend to have Y chromosomes of a type called hg 1, especially if the men have Irish surnames and even more so if they come from Connaught or Munster. This type of Y chromosome is generally more common in Western Europe, it is very rare in the east of Europe and is hardly found at all in Turkey, for example. In Ireland it is not so common in men with English, Norman/Norse or Scottish surnames. Of course, men receive both their Y chromosome and their surname from their fathers, the surname in Ireland may be correlated with cultural origin and the Y chromosome with genetic origin. It appears that, in this case, the cultural origins can be traced by following the genetic origins. Once again the people of the West of Ireland differ from the people in the East. Maternally inherited mitochondrial DNA chromosomes also show an East-West diversity and together with the Y work, indicate similarity with the other populations commonly labelled Celtic and the Basques.

One feature of the genetic analysis is the way it can link with medical studies. David Croke, Philip Mayne and Charles O'Neill of the R.C.S.I. and the Temple Street Hospital, have been studying the incidence and cause of PKU (phenylketonuria), a rare genetic disorder, for which all children are tested. By studying the genetic basis of PKU in Ireland and neighbouring populations, they have demonstrated that the predominant defect causing PKU (known as R408W-1.8) also exhibits a gradient across Europe from east to west, reaching its highest frequency in Ireland (Figure 3).

These gradients of genetic variation crossing the European continent into Ireland must reflect the effects of human population movement and other forms of population interaction.

Derek Middleton and Alun Evans at Queen's University have been studying another set of genes called HLA. One of the most variable genetic systems, it is passed on from father and mother to both sons and daughters, and it is very important in determining whether donors and recipients are suited for organ transplantation. The Northern Ireland team has isolated DNA from 5,000 individuals from the Northern population. These have been typed for HLA genes, and 3,045 individuals have been typed by surname: 30% had an Irish surname, 14% an English surname, 14% a Scottish surname and 3% a Norman surname. To date, positive associations of HLA gene with origin of surname have been found as follows. HLA-A*01 with Irish, A*24, B*58 with English, A*02, A*03, A*24, B*49, DR9 with Scottish and B*51 with Normans. This data can be extended and related to peoples from other parts of Europe and will help to build up the evidence showing the different strands which contribute to the modern Irish population.

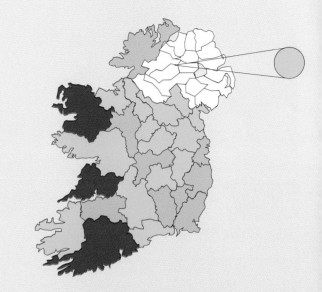

Fig.1 **B** Blood Group O

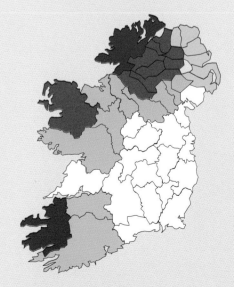

Fig.2 **A** Freckles

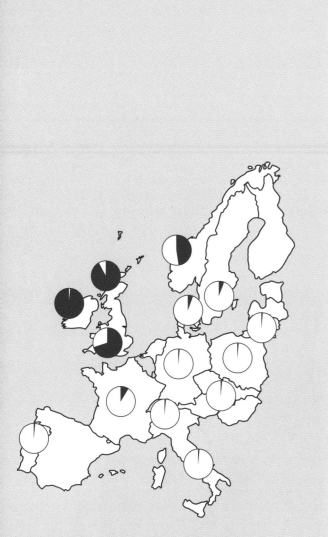

Fig.3 **R408W-1.8** Phenylketonuria Mutation

One of the most intriguing studies is being carried out by Barra Ó Donnabháin and colleagues at University College Cork on genetic material isolated from bones buried in cemeteries prior to and at the time of the Viking incursions.

The Vikings founded many settlements on the coast and gradually intermarried, converted to Christianity and merged culturally with the native Irish. The genes of the Vikings would have differed slightly from the pre-contact population and by looking at the genes from these ancient bones, it may be possible to advance our understanding of the nature of the interactions between both groups. While the immediate goal is to gain a fuller understanding of relations between Viking and local populations during the couple of centuries prior to 1000 A.D., characterising the population of this island at the time of the first Millennium will make a significant contribution to our understanding of the origins of the population of Ireland as we move into the third.

The *Irish Origins* project is just beginning, and it is very important that it be continued. The pilot studies have already shown that the tiny genetic differences between us can give us new insights into the ancestry of our peoples.

– David McConnell
Chairman, Advisory Committee on Genetic Anthropology, Royal Irish Academy

– Dan Bradley and Emmy Hill
Department of Genetics, Trinity College Dublin

– David Croke, Philip Mayne and Charles O'Neill
Department of Biochemistry, Royal College of Surgeons of Ireland and Department of Pathology, Temple Street Hospital

– Derek Middleton and Alun Evans, Northern Ireland
Regional Histocompatibility and Immunogenetics Laboratory and Department of Epidemiology and Public Health, Queen's University Belfast

– Barra Ó Donnabháin
Department of Archaeology, University College Cork

Battle of Aughrim

> The Battle of Aughrim in 1691 was the last big battle fought in Ireland. It was also the bloodiest battle on Irish soil and for this reason is sometimes referred to as "Ireland's Gettysburg". The battle determined much of the military, social and ecclesiastical future of Ireland for centuries. Today the battle site is a focus for peace and reconciliation.

The vast majority of those who use the Aughrim bypass on the main Ballinasloe to Galway road are unlikely to be aware that they are driving through one of the most historic places in Ireland which has significance, not only in Ireland, but also in several European countries.

On Sunday 12 July, 1691, a 20,000 strong Jacobite army drawn from many parts of Ireland with a number of French officers – the best known of whom, Lieut.-General the Marquis de St. Ruth, was in command – occupied a defensive position stretching over 1.5 miles along the ridge from Aughrim village to Urraghry.

On the opposite side of the impassible marsh bog which separated them, was a similar sized, but better equipped army which was commanded for King William by the Dutch General Godard van Reede Baron de Ginkel. His army was drawn from several European nations, 12 or 13 battalions of English, three Ulster battalions and Danish, Dutch and French Huguenot soldiers.

After five hours of fighting, some of Ginkel's officers were considering withdrawal but just then a section of his army succeeded in getting a cavalry force across a narrow causeway near Aughrim village. This bridgehead was quickly augmented and from then onwards everything went wrong for the Irish side. Just as the horse soldiers got across, St. Ruth was killed by a chance cannon shot. What had at one stage been near success now turned to rout and by nightfall the Irish army was destroyed, its dead numbering about 7,000. Some 2,000 of Ginkel's men were killed, bringing the total dead at Aughrim to approximately 9,000.

Aughrim heralded the end of the War of the Two Kings in Ireland and set the scene for all the unfortunate history that ensued.

Today, many point to the important potential of Aughrim as a focus for reconciliation on the whole of this island. The Aughrim-based Christian Training Institute of Ireland was founded in 1999 by Trevor Sullivan and Russ Parker as a resource for individuals and groups to further the healing of individuals, communities and institutions. One of its initiatives, which is being supported by the National Millennium Committee and the National Tree Council, is the *Aughrim Peace Wood*. This includes a tree-planting programme at focal points and regimental sites of the 1691 Battle. The tree planting is also to commemorate all those wounded by our history. The institute also facilitates inter-group and inter-institutional relations programmes on a North-South and Anglo-Irish basis.

Above "Crossing the Causeway".

Opposite Page "The First Assault" as the Williamites attack.

Both paintings reproduced with the kind permission of the artist, Ben Maile.

Francis Ledwidge Cottage

> On a sunny day in August 2001 hundreds of people gathered in Slane, Co. Meath, for the unveiling of a special memorial to the poet Francis Ledwidge and the opening of the extended museum in the house in which he was born.

Millennium Committee Award €12,697 (IR£10,000)

John Bruton

> A Personal Note

The funding of the Ledwidge Cottage project by the Millennium Committee is a very worthwhile initiative.

Francis Ledwidge, a world-renowned poet from Slane, who died in World War I, represented a generation of Irish people, 49,000 of whom lost their lives on Flanders. The Ledwidge Cottage will be a lifelong memorial to the promotion of peace and reconciliation, and to the life and poetry of Francis Ledwidge. A replica of the monument which the people of Ypres erected at the exact place where Francis died in World War I, now takes pride of place in the cottage garden – the stone for which has come from Belgium.

Visitors from all over the world will be able to learn of the life and poetry of Francis Ledwidge from the glass display panels inside the cottage depicting his works. The Ledwidge Cottage Museum will now become a focus for peace and reconciliation throughout the world – an excellent way to step forward into the new Millennium.

– John Bruton T.D. *Dáil Éireann*

Top A working party moving towards the Battle of Pilchem Ridge on 31 July, 1917. It was on this day that Ledwidge was killed while serving with another working party.

Above The River Boyne.

Right An exhibition panel from the Ledwidge Cottage Museum.

JOURNEY'S END

THE NEXT DAY, HE WAS OCCUPIED ON road making duty, on ground captured from the Germans early that same morning, in the area of Rose crossroads and the old railway line. In the afternoon, while on tea break, a shell exploded beside him and he was killed instantly. Francis Ledwidge lies buried in Artillery Wood Cemetery, Plot 2, Row B, Grave 5. It is almost a mile east of the village of Boesinghe (Boezinge) near Ypres (Ieper) and far from his home in Slane and the Boyne Valley he loved so well. In July 1998 a memorial to the poet, designed and commissioned by 'The In Flanders Fields Museum', was erected by the people of West Flanders on the exact spot where the poet was killed on 31st July, 1917.

Home

A burst of sudden wings at dawn,
Faint voices in a dreamy noon,
Evenings of mist and murmurings,
And nights with rainbows of the moon.

And through these things a wood-way dim,
And waters dim, and slow sheep seen
On uphill paths that wind away
Through summer sounds and harvest green.

This is a song a robin sang
This morning on a broken tree,
It was about the little fields
That call across the world to me.

1998

Athshloinniú - Reclaim Your Name!

> Most Irish people over the last few centuries have been saddled with anglicised versions of their original family and clan names. However, there is no law to say you have to keep using that version if you don't want to.

Tomás Mac Ruairí

The dawn of this new Millennium spawned many interesting projects and many people of all ages adopted the "*Athshloinniú* – reclaim your name" idea which Conradh na Gaeilge suggested as "*togra pearsanta mílaoise duitse*" or your own personal Millennium project. Simplicity itself – reverting to the original Irish-language version of your surname as your own personal, practical and positive way of celebrating the new Millennium – *agus ní gá duit a bheith lán-líofa sa teanga ag an am seo le tabhairt faoi "athshloinniú"*.

You don't even have to be fluent in Irish to "reclaim your name" and can make your personal Millennium statement through one or other of two equally legal ways.

You can simply start using the original Irish form of your surname from this moment forward, without any ceremony, or you can change it formally by making a simple declaration through a commissioner for oaths so that the Irish version is henceforth your official name.

Either way it's totally legal (unless, of course, you change your name for a deliberate unlawful purpose – *ach sin scéal eile ar fad*).

Agus ardóidh sé do mheanman – it will raise your spirits because it is your personal way of saying "I'm Irish and proud of it." *Beidh bróid mór ort as é sin a dhéanamh.*

Irish has been spoken on this island for possibly four Millennia. What else has lived so long here? The founding of Conradh na Gaeilge in 1893 not only helped to arrest a decline in use of the language but fuelled a great surge of cultural renewal and identity.

Census statistics over recent decades have shown increasing numbers of people claiming an ability to speak Irish – it's around the 1.4 million figure now, or some 30% of the state's population, and growing. Surveys indicate that about 40% of that number use at least a little Irish daily.

Conradh na Gaeilge is there to help you if you need a copy of the simple form required to change your surname formally to the Irish version.

Just call or write to:

Conradh na Gaeilge
6 Sráid Fhearchair
Baile Átha Cliath 2

or contact us by e-mail at eolas@cnag.ie,

or by sending a fax message to +353 (0)1 475 7844.

Tá go leor daoine ann a bhfuil Gaeilge líofa acu agus cé go n-úsáideann cuid mhaith acu an Ghaeilge go rialta – fiú go dtógann siad clann le Gaeilge – is é an sloinne Béarla amháin a úsáideann siad i ngach gné dá saol.

Tá sé le hargóint go gcuirfeadh sé go mór lena meanma phearsanta an leagan Gaeilge a úsáid feasta. Chuirfeadh sé freisin go mór le seasamh na Gaeilge sa tsocaí go mbeadh níos mó den phobal ag úsáíd an leagan Gaeilge dá sloinnte.

– Tomás Mac Ruairí *Uachtarán Chonradh na Gaeilge*

Mizen Head Visitor Centre

> The new Mizen Head Visitor Centre in West Cork is perched on the edge of rock in one of the most dramatic locations in Ireland. It introduces the visitors to the spellbinding attractions that follow, the historic Head Signal Station, the famous Suspension Bridge, the 99 steps down to the station and to that great spine of ancient rock, the peninsula's final push into the wild Atlantic.

Millennium Committee Award €88,881 (IR£70,000)

> A Personal Note

We were sure that Mizen Head, the most south-westerly point of Ireland, would have the last light of the Millennium, but we were pipped at the post by two minutes by Dursey Head. Not daunted we planned our own Last Light Ceremony. The day broke with mist and drizzle. But Mizen Head is charismatic in any weather. It is such a magical ancient place; there is a feeling of timelessness and peace there, contradictory for a rocky headland surrounded by the restless sea. The Irish Lights Fog Signal Station, protecting seafarers, stands sentinel on the cliffs. The mist swirled around giving a mystic feeling to the day.

Inside the shell of our visitor centre – no doors or windows, just a roof and walls to protect us from the rain. Derry and Justin fixed up a sound system for some music. Ed and Mary Jo ran down their list of readers, singers, poets. A sheet of paper was found for a Visitors' Book, placed on some concrete blocks and a small queue formed. We had advised everyone to bring a candle in a jam jar.

Suddenly there was a murmuring from outside, a growing, disbelieving excitement – the clouds and mist were clearing. Looking up the car park there was a stream of people making for the path to the station. Out west the sky cleared to a brilliant blue and the sun came out, a huge red ball, sinking slowly into the ocean. Ten minutes later it was over, candles lighting, rockets bursting in the sky, such community and well-being; then the prayers and recitations. A party night to celebrate that moment in a thousand years.

It was so good that it is now a tradition for every New Year's Eve – but this year we were inside our wonderful new Mizen Head Visitor Centre – thanks to the wonderful support of the National Millennium Committee.

The centre is the culmination of over ten year's work. It is testimony to persistence, never taking "no" for an answer, vision and imagination.

– Sue Hill *Project Manager, Mizen Head Visitor Centre 2001*

Top A scaled model of the Fastnet Rock Lighthouse in the Mizen Head Visitor Centre.

Above Mizen Head showing the Fog Signal Station and Suspension Bridge.

Seismograph House

> The restoration of the Seismograph House in Rathfarnham Castle and its opening as an exhibition centre will bring alive again a period of remarkable and innovative developments there in the detection and measuring of earthquake tremors from the early part of the last century.

Millennium Committee Award €38,092 (IR£30,000)

A unique element of the research was the pioneering work of Jesuit priest Rev. W.J. O'Leary S.J. who is reputed to have designed and built his own seismograph, a delicate instrument used by scientists to identify and record very small ground movements, and installed it in the house.

According to the Jesuit Yearbook of 1958 the first seismograph was installed at Rathfarnham in 1915 by Fr. O'Leary. This instrument remained in use for decades and was regarded as a highly original and accurate gauge of earthquake tremors. It remained in use until 1962 and was finally dismantled in 1979 to preserve what had been left of it after it was vandalised. In 1932 a new instrument with greater accuracy of recordings, the Milne-Shaw Seismograph, was installed in the house. The restoration of the Seismograph House by South Dublin County Council was carried out with the support of funding from the National Millennium Committee.

1 The Seismograph House in disrepair.
2 The restored building.
3 The original Seismograph (Photograph – Fr. Browne Collection).

Millennium Snapshots

> Ireland's rich heritage was central to many initiatives that emerged at community and local authority level for the Millennium and received support from the National Millennium Committee. This is a selection:

1 > Elphin Windmill

The 18th century Elphin Windmill in Co. Roscommon is the oldest of its kind in the country and is now fully restored. The windmill was perfectly located to harness the winds sweeping over the plains of Elphin. Unusual features include its thatched revolving roof and four sails that are turned into the wind by using a tailpole attached to a cartwheel on a circular track.

2 > Countess Markievich

One of the outstanding social and historical Irish figures will be celebrated with the erection of a striking sculpture in her home town of Sligo. Countess Constance Markievich was born into a privileged and wealthy lifestyle, but she gave it all up to help the disadvantaged and downtrodden. She played a critical role in the establishment of this state and was the first woman elected to a British Parliament. Appointed to the Ministry of Labour in the first Dáil, she was then the first woman Cabinet Minister in the world.

She died in 1927 in a public ward amongst Dublin's poor, where she had abandoned status for her beliefs and ideals in the service of the poor and disadvantaged. She is recognised today as a symbol of unity and tolerance that transcends party allegiances.

The work by Dublin sculptor, John Coll, combines the various elements of the Countess's life, from patriotism to her work with prisoners and the destitute. The bronze figure on a stone plinth with stainless steel gates is 20 ft high, 15 ft deep and 7 ft wide.

3 > Waterford Area Museum Society

Second year architectural students from the Waterford Institute of Technology undertook, at the request of the Waterford Area Museum Society, the task of researching and building a scaled model of the Co. Waterford coastline. The model will be particularly beneficial to those studying the geology, wildlife and botany of the Tramore area.

4 > Portumna Castle Crafts

The traditional skill of weaving continues with the expansion of the "Craft Workshop Project" at Portumna Castle Crafts, Co. Galway.

5 > Allihies Mining Museum

The parish of Allihies on the Beara Peninsula in West Cork was, in the last century, the setting for the largest copper mining enterprise ever undertaken in Ireland. The mines opened in 1812 and worked continuously until 1884. At their peak the mines employed up to 1,200 people. The extraordinary story will now be told in an exciting way in the Allihies Mine Museum using high quality graphics, photographs, illustrations and models. It is the captivating story of a part of the Industrial Revolution, transported to one of Ireland's most remote regions. It is also a tale of great human hardship with poverty, death and famine commonplace. The Museum is housed in the old Protestant church, built in 1845 to serve the Cornish miners, which has been re-roofed, refurbished and decorated with funding from the National Millennium Committee. Near the museum and standing over Allihies like watching sentinels, are the ruined towers and chimneys of the copper mines.

6 > Atlas of Historic Towns

The historic town of Kilkenny was the Royal Irish Academy's Millennium project for its Irish Historic Towns Atlas series. These historical atlases have been produced for the past 18 years, with nine towns already in print. Kilkenny is the largest to date and the atlas includes large maps to accommodate its size and rich topographical records and "the Marble City's" abundant historical sources.

7 > Inishowen Maritime Museum

Inishowen Maritime Museum is located in the old Coastguard Station in Greencastle, overlooking one of the busiest fishing fleets in Ireland. The museum has a large collection of marine artefacts, memorabilia and boats, including a fully rigged Drontheim (or Greencastle yawl). A Millennium Award assisted the establishment of a state-of-the-art Planetarium which has provided entertainment and education for many school groups and the general public.

8 > Offaly Historical & Archaelogical Exhibition

The Offaly Historical and Archaeological Society Millennium Exhibition ran for most of the year 2000.

Amongst the hundreds of photographs exhibited was this one from the Fetherson-Haugh Collection which shows the daughters of William Whelan, a solicitor in Tullamore. Matilda Emily Constance was born in 1883 and died in 1966 in Stoke, New Zealand, and Letitia Violet was born in 1885 and died in 1969 in Richmond, Nelson, New Zealand.

9 > Bere Island Project

The Bere Island Project involves the restoration of the Martello Tower and its conversion into a heritage centre specialising in exhibits on local military history.

10 > St. Mullins Monastic Ruins

The provision of floodlighting at the historic monastic ruins at St. Mullins, Co. Carlow, allows for longer viewing hours by the community and visitors.

11 > Stranorlar Millennium Town Clock

New Year's Day, 1960, marked the end of the Donegal railway system and with it the end of Stranorlar's railway history, which dates back to 1840. When the clock from the old railway station was uncovered, a local action group resolved to mark the passing of the Millennium with a new structure to carry the clock and the station bell.

We conceived of this simple structure as a tower and a

11

12

13

14

beacon, a reference to the past as well as a sign of optimism for the future. Situated across from St. Mary's Church and facing the bridge linking Stranorlar to Ballybofey, it creates a new entrance to the bus station that stands on the location of the former train station. The lower section of the tower is clad in limestone while the upper section has a skin of woven stainless steel mesh. Depending on the light, the upper section alternates between an impression of solidity (an extension of the stone base) and a diffuse volume. At night the searchlight within the structure further decomposes its presence. A slit in the side allows views of the clock mechanism and bell,

whilst the bus-yard entrance is balanced by an "oversized" bench on the other side of the tower. The lights were turned on at midnight on New Year's Eve, 2000.

– Martin Henchion *Architect*

12 > Cavan & Leitrim Railway

The restoration of a section of the Cavan & Leitrim railway line is a project steeped in history and nostalgia.

13 > St. Declan's

St Declan's Millennium Committee, Ardmore, Co. Waterford erected a sculpture as a tribute to St. Declan, patron saint of their diocese.

14 > Clonmel 350

Battles cries rang out, Oliver Cromwell's army advanced menacingly on the town and above it all a parachute squad floated down from the sky, bearing the Tipperary flag. The Bees Knees Summerfest, organised by Clonmel 350, mixed military spectacles, old and new, for a day of colour, pageant and excitement that was a highlight of the Millennium year. The event was held to mark the 350th anniversary of the Siege of Clonmel in 1650 in which Cromwell suffered his only defeat on Irish soil.

09 Social

Social

> For some countries the Millennium was pure celebration. In Ireland, celebration was a significant part of the marking of the Millennium but this was balanced with a genuine desire to use the historic event to make a more enduring impact. Support for those less well off or in need of a boost, at home and abroad, was the main priority.

One of the earliest themes adopted by the National Millennium Committee was the need to recognise the contribution of those whose energy and sacrifice helped shape and build modern Ireland. In particular, there was a debt of gratitude to our elderly citizens who lived through the social, economic and political turmoil and who experienced the heartbreak of forced emigration.

Their contribution was acknowledged in a number of ways. Centenarians received special awards from the Millennium Committee and communities in every corner of Ireland organised events to pay tribute at local level.

Some of our elderly are sadly most vulnerable as they now enter their sunset years. The Millennium Committee was able to play a role in addressing this issue by selecting particular projects for support.

The **S.H.A.R.E.** charity for the vulnerable elderly of Cork city should be an inspiration to all. The driving force behind it for the past 30 years has been the students of secondary schools in the city who visit and care for the elderly. An award of €952,303 (IR£750,000) from the Millennium fund is helping to build a new day-care centre at Sheare's Street. This will provide a full range of services for the elderly

while still allowing them the independence of living at home. Another project, **Gascoigne House** in Rathmines, Dublin, is now open as a residential home for the elderly with 44 beds, day care facilities, respite care and a specialised dementia unit.

In addition to projects for the elderly, hundreds of proposals to help others in a vulnerable state, or those with specialised needs, were received. The Millennium Committee selected many for support, from high profile national initiatives for the homeless and marginalised to the supply of vehicles to local care organisations.

An award of €1,269,738 (IR£1 million) to the **National Rehabilitation Hospital** in Dun Laoghaire is helping to build an accommodation facility for the families of patients who are victims of traumatic brain injury, stroke or spinal cord injury so that they can be close to their loved ones and offer valuable support on the road to recovery.

The provision of hospice accommodation where people will find comfort and friendly care in the twilight of their days is of the utmost importance. The National Millennium Committee donated €126,973 (IR£100,000) towards **The Whoseday Book**, a unique journal for the year 2000,

which was published in aid of the Irish Hospice Foundation. Separately, an award of €126,973 (IR£100,000) was made towards the building of the **Hospice in Co. Donegal.**

The St. Vincent De Paul Society and the **Simon Community** requested that the Millennium be marked for them with support for urgent projects. An award of €317,434 (IR£250,000) has helped the society develop a site at Mountjoy Square into a community resource centre and sport facility, while **Simon** is using its allocation of €266,644 (IR£210,000) to refurbish its four centres.

The Irish Wheelchair Association had its invaluable contribution rewarded with an award of €431,710 (IR£340,000) towards a national mobility centre at Clane, Co Kildare. In addition the association was assisted in a Millennium Awards initiative in every county to celebrate its 40th anniversary.

The greatest gift **Barretstown Gang Camp** in Co. Kildare can give is in helping children who have known the trauma of illness to rediscover what it means to be a normal child again. The Millennium Committee award for the construction of an additional cottage is in recognition of the contribution Barretstown makes towards helping seriously ill children rediscover their own inner strength, confidence and self esteem.

There were many other projects worthy of support; the **Bone Marrow for Leukaemia Trust** was helped purchase new high-tech medical equipment; **Bray Cancer Support** published a detailed guide to breast cancer; relief agencies **GOAL** and **Concern** were helped with specific projects and an award to **Bóthar** helped in the transporting of 100 goats to needy families in Tanzania. Amid all the hype and frenzy over celebrating the Millennium there emerged a

clear need to help those who may find it all emotionally overwhelming. An award of €76,184 (IR£60,000) to **The Samaritans** allowed them to launch an extensive public awareness campaign.

Chuir an Mhílaois, i ngeall ar a tábhacht mar ócáid stairiúil, iachall ar dhaoine ar fud na cruinne athbhreithniú a dhéanamh ar a saoil féin agus ar an sochaí inar mhair siad. In Éirinn, ba thréimhse é le machnamh a dhéanamh ar an méid dul chun cinn a bhi déanta againn mar náisiún neamhspleách, réasúnta óg. Sonraíodh ár bhforás aibíochta mar náisiún i mórán slite, trí na mílte achainíocha agus iarratais a fuair Coiste na Mílaoise agus trí theachtaireacht a soiléiriu go cruinn, da réir. Dob é sin, ag smaoineamh siar gan amhras ar an chaoi ar bhraith an tír seo in amanna thart ar thacaíocht o dhreamanna eile, gur theastaigh ó fhormhór de mhuintir na hÉireann, an Mhílaois a cheiliúradh go spleodrach ach go mbeadh fhios acu roimhré, go mbeadh an chuid ba mhó den maoiniú oifigiúil á thabhairt chun cuidiú le tionscnaimh fiúntacha agus le cúiseanna soisíalta, ach go háirithe.

Right Residents of Gascoigne House, relaxing in the new facility.

S.H.A.R.E. Day Care Centre

> S.H.A.R.E (Students Harness Aid for the Relief of the Elderly) is a unique organisation dedicated to caring for the elderly of Cork City and suburbs. Its most ambitious project to date is a new Day Care Centre on Sheare's Street, which is supported by the National Millennium Committee. The Centre will have 14 residential places and provide a full range of non-residential services to the elderly, such as physiotherapy and chiropody. It will cater for up to 100 people and will provide a daily hot meal service, TV room, refreshments, laundry and hairdressing facilities. The emphasis throughout is on reinforcing for the elderly their dignity and independence in pleasant, comfortable surroundings.

Millennium Committee Award €952,303 (IR£750,000)

> A Personal Note

Living in Cork in the 70s, the S.H.A.R.E Crib was part and parcel of Christmas, with the local teenagers fasting and collecting in Patrick Street. Who would have thought then

Micheál Martin T.D.

that a group of schoolboys (at that stage it was only boys) could have touched and changed the lives of so many of Cork's older citizens in such a remarkable way. Their efforts brought not only housing and accommodation, but comfort, support, cheer and friendship to the vulnerable in our society, offering them the prospect of secure and independent living for the remainder of their lives.

The example set by these school-children brought out a real sense of pride in the people of Cork. The enthusiasm of this small group of far-seeing and socially aware collectors was matched by the generosity of the people of Cork, who never failed to support the Christmas fast. Of course, it is inspiring to see the changes that S.H.A.R.E has made not only to the lives of the elderly, but also to the lives of those who work in the organisation itself.

The youth bring their enthusiasm and vibrancy while at the same time learning from the life experience and wisdom of the older people they meet. It has been my pleasure, both in a personal and professional capacity, to be associated with S.H.A.R.E. A project that began with a group of volunteers has grown to merit the admiration of all. The policy of the Department of Health and Children is to maintain older people in dignity and independence at home, in accordance with their own wishes, and eventually to restore to independent living in their own homes, those who become ill or dependant.

A very commendable S.H.A.R.E initiative is the development of the Day Resource Complex in Sheare's Street. This centre will provide a full range of services to support independent living at home. It will also promote community contact and social stimulation among older people, as well as providing carers with a well-earned break period.

May I convey my congratulations to S.H.A.R.E for its great work for the people of Cork and the example it sets. My wish is that you will continue this unique organisation from which we all gain so much.

– Micheál Martin T.D. *Minister for Health and Children*

Brother Jerome Kelly

The centre has been dedicated to the memory of Brother Jerome Kelly (1926-1999), who founded the S.H.A.R.E. Movement in 1970. The ethos of the movement is the encouragement of interaction between the elderly and Cork's youth. The boys and girls who participate in an annual Christmas fast to raise funds for S.H.A.R.E. are drawn from Transition Year students of the 24 secondary schools in Cork.

Clockwise from Top Left An artist's impression of the new Day Care Centre.
Young and old sharing together.

Donegal Hospice

> The Donegal Hospice is the result of unstinting efforts on the part of a core group of people who were determined to provide this caring service for the people in their own county. The new hospice in Letterkenny will have six en-suite apartments, day room, rest rooms, chapel, facilities for nursing and medical staff, ancillary accommodation and access to hairdressing and aroma therapy facilities.

Millennium Committee Award €126,972 (IR£100,000)

> A Personal Note

Ireland's Millennium celebrations were marked by many colourful and exciting events throughout the country. We saw imaginative pageantry, street theatre, notable musical events and what was perhaps the most spectacular fireworks display on the Liffey which illuminated the skies over Dublin, in a way we had never experienced before. It could be said that as a people we welcomed the new century in a style which reflected our warm neighbourly welcome for visitors, our traditional good humour and our undoubted flair for fun and enjoyment.

For me, however, the most memorable development in all our celebrations centred on the story of a little boy who sadly never saw the 21st century, but whose youthful courage in the face of relentless suffering inspired a movement which will serve people, and ease pain in my own county of Donegal in this new century and perhaps for many centuries ahead.

I refer to little Adrian Mitchell whose fortitude in his battle against fatal illness became a catalyst for the development of the hospice movement in Donegal. The need for a hospice was, of course, long evident but it could be said that the effort to alleviate Adrian's suffering galvanised us in our renewed and now, thankfully, successful efforts to ensure that we would have in Donegal a haven where people will find comfort and friendly care in the twilight of their days.

When, as a minister in the government and as one of the founders of the Donegal Hospice Movement I was privileged to turn the first sod for the Hospice in October 2000, little Adrian Mitchell's story was in my thoughts and I felt that the realisation of our hospice dream may have been a source of some solace and consolation to his parents in their grief.

The North Western Health Board has generously supported the hospice project to the tune of over €1,269,738 (IR£1 million). This was supplemented by truly marvellous fundraising activities which bought in €1,015,790 (IR£800,000). The dedication of our fundraisers and the generosity of the public is in itself a Millennium memory to cherish. In recognition of that superb fundraising effort, the government's Millennium fund allocated €126,974 (IR£100,000) for the project. That was a sizeable contribution to a very worthy cause.

The progress we have made in Donegal reflects a growing awareness nationwide of the invaluable work in medical and in human terms of the hospice movement. The unique initiative of the movement in preparing, organising and publishing *The Whoseday Book* celebrated the new century in a highly original way which reflected the genius of many gifted Irish men and women and above all the sense of compassion which will, I hope, always remain characteristic of our people.

– Dr. James McDaid T.D. *Minister for Tourism, Sport and Recreation*

Above and **Right** Two views of the new Donegal Hospice in Letterkenny. Photography – Clive Wasson.

The Whoseday Book

> *The Whoseday Book* was a unique diary for the year 2000, featuring contributions from 366 artists, writers and personalities. The book, which was supported by AIB, the National Millennium Committee and general donations, sold 40,000 copies in Ireland and raised more than €2,158,555 (IR£1.7 million) for the Irish Hospice Foundation. It was the most successful fundraising idea in the history of the foundation.

Millennium Committee Award €126,974 (IR£100,000)

Marian Finucane

> A Personal Note

The Millennium celebration provided ample opportunities for enthusiasm, for cynicism, for coming together and for splits. It was, in other words a splendid opportunity for all that we are.

In symbolism, my outstanding good memories are of the passing of a lit candle from Nelson Mandela to the younger generation in South Africa and our own Last Light ceremony – involving families and communities all over Ireland. The symbolism of candles is ancient. The moments of symbolism pass and one hopes the idea or ideal remains. Other Millennium projects were more tangible.

Among those, for me, the Irish Hospice Foundation's *Whoseday Book* is outstanding. A book lasts. *The Whoseday Book* may well last a very long time indeed. For many

reasons – 366 plus. Seamus Heaney was an enthusiastic and respected patron.

Three hundred and sixty five other writers and artists contributed words and images for each day of this significant calendar year. Each day of the year therefore has represented for it thoughts of significance from these diverse and remarkable people.

A snapshot of Irish ideas and images at the end of the 20th century. Perhaps more importantly, it focussed them and consequently hundreds of thousands of others, on the work of the hospice movement. A movement that treats the person rather than the disease, that believes in the quality of life rather then length in hours and minutes and facilitates all, including families, to benefit from life right to the end.

This beautiful, thoughtful and thought-provoking book succeeded beyond wildest imagination in spreading the hospice message and in raising €2,158,555 (IR£1.7 million)

for the Irish Hospice Foundation to help extend hospice care for adults, children and their families in Ireland.

The original idea came from John Waters and was adopted immediately by Marie Donnelly and worked on exhaustively by many others, most notably Eileen Pearson.

There was sponsorship and support from a variety of sources including the National Millennium Committee and AIB. If you haven't got a book of your own, the originals are now in the National Library – thanks to the partnership with AIB.

– Marian Finucane *Broadcaster*

Above John Rocha at the launch of *The Whoseday Book*.
Right *The Whoseday Book* – a source of inspiration for all ages.

Clockwise from Top Left Marie Donnelly with Paul McGuinness at the public signing by contributors to *The Whoseday Book* in the RDS, Dublin. Writer, Deirdre Purcell. Writer, Anthony Cronin. Singer, Gavin Friday.

The National Mobility Centre

> Irish people with disabilities who need their mobility levels assessed no longer have to face the inconvenience of travelling to Britain. The new National Mobility Centre in Clane, Co. Kildare, now provides an expert, high-tech assessment service as well as advice on all aspects of motoring for persons with physical disability.

Millennium Committee Award €317,434 (IR£250,000)

> A Personal Note

The Irish Wheelchair Association upgraded its National Driver Training and Assessment Service in 2001 with the addition of a National Mobility Assessment Centre at Clane.

This innovation was funded with a National Millennium Committee Award. The idea behind this centre is to ensure that persons with physical disability can have access to the most up-to-date mobility aids and motoring devices available. Heretofore, many people had to travel to Britain for high-tech assessment if their needs were out of the ordinary. Now, with further assistance from the motor trade, a real start has been made to providing this service within the island of Ireland.

As well as equipment, the centre provides advice on all aspects of motoring, driver training, safety and, of course, the issue of European parking badges. The service also provides a Centre of Excellence for 16 outreach assessment

and tuition units based across the country, and the centre features the most up-to-date internationally recognised vehicles and equipment. It is hoped that eventually these outreach units will extend to one per county in the Republic.

The benefits to persons with disability who avail of this service are enormous. Driving, or being driven, in a suitably adapted vehicle can change the lives of people previously marginalised. Our disabled driver/passenger scheme, which facilitates the purchase of a vehicle without having to pay VAT or VRT, is recognised as the best in the world.

Inclusion and independence has improved considerably through this novel Millennium funding programme.

– Séamus Thompson *Chief Executive,*
Irish Wheelchair Association

Above Motoring made easier for persons with physical disability.

Barretstown Gang Camp

> The Barretstown Gang Camp on a 500 acre estate at Ballymore Eustace, Co. Kildare, is the brainchild of actor Paul Newman. Each year this camp provides a stimulating range of therapeutic recreational programmes for more than 1,000 seriously ill children. The Millennium Cottage, funded by the National Millennium Committee, will increase capacity by over 10% which means an additional 120 children and family members can, each year, enjoy the Barretstown experience. On the recommendation of the National Millennium Committee an award of €1.27 million (£1 million) was made to the Barretstown Gang Camp by the Minister for Finance, Mr. Charlie McCreevy, in his Budget of December 2001.

Millennium Committee Award €190,460 (IR£150,000)

"When I first saw Barretstown Castle I knew this is where I wanted the first European camp to be.
I imagined a kind of medieval bazaar where sick kids from different countries could raise a little hell together. It's not just that the children say 'Thank you for a wonderful time …' It's that they say, 'Thank you for changing my life'. The beneficiaries of Barretstown appear to be everybody who gets connected with it. The caras [supervisors] and staff get as much from the kids as they give. It's an extraordinary circular experience."

– Paul Newman *Founder*

"You could offer me weeks in a tropical country and I'd prefer to come to Barretstown for a couple of days. Because no matter where you go in the world, you cannot guarantee the warmth, welcome and understanding that lies behind these magical gates. The wonderful feeling of happiness and of being wanted radiates around this exceptional magical fantastic place."

– Camper *aged 14*

"I have seen with my own eyes, repeatedly, that ten days at Barretstown helps return the person who was there prior to this disruption in their life. Before they leave, I see a sparkle in their eyes or a radiance in their voice that was barely present on day one. They can do this because of the community that is Barretstown."

– Paul M Zeltzer MD *Neuro-oncologist, USA*

Above Paul Newman at Barretstown Castle.
Right Barretstown Castle, home to the Gang Camp.

> A Personal Note

If there's one aspect of my career as a singer and entertainer that gives substance to what I do, it's to be able to bring some joy into the lives of people who are coping with all kinds of struggles.

There's never a day goes by that I'm not reminded of how I have been dealt a charmed life. I have been blessed with success in my career; I have been lucky to find a wonderful partner in Yvonne and we have two healthy young children.

But through the letters I receive on a daily basis, I am constantly made aware that so many people, both young and old, have terrible burdens and physical suffering to cope with in their lives.

In my nine years as a performer, I have been given many chances to make a difference to someone's life just by simply meeting that person before a show. I am always honoured and humbled to be able to do that.

But my greatest opportunity to do something really positive came when I was asked to become a member of the Millennium Committee. My personal aim, as a member, was that we would spend money on things that would enrich the lives of people and give them something they wouldn't forget.

One of the projects selected for funding was the Barretstown Gang Camp where seriously ill children are encouraged to do things they never thought possible. Through taking part in activities like horse riding and canoeing, they discover

that they are braver, stronger, more confident and independent than they ever thought they could be. It's a tonic no medicine can match.

Every year a thousand children from all over Europe, Ireland and the UK visit Barretstown. They are primarily cancer patients, although some have the HIV virus and others AIDS.

The wonderful centre, with its castle, lake, secret garden and theatre gives them a holiday full of fun and laughter.

Although it tears me apart to see children who are seriously ill, I love going down there and putting a smile on their faces. It's such a beautiful and emotional place. The children seem to forget all their troubles while they are there because they're having such a great time with the staff and other kids.

It gives me great satisfaction to know that the Millennium Committee has made a difference down there, and I hope that Barretstown is a facility that will last for a long, long time.

– Ronan Keating *Singer/Entertainer*
Member of the National Millenium Committee

Top Children enjoying an outdoor adventure.

Below A cara (supervisor) and a member of the Barretstown Gang Camp exploring.

Right Ronan Keating and eight-year-old Mark O'Neill feeding the swans beside the lake in Barretstown. Photograph – Maxwells.

Gascoigne House

> Gascoigne House in Dublin is a new residential home for the elderly with 44 beds, day care facilities, respite care and a specialised dementia unit. It is a Millennium flagship project of the Church of Ireland.

Millennium Committee Award €507,895 (IR£400,000)

The specialised care centre at Cowper Road, Rathmines, replaced a one-hundred-year-old facility. The new Gascoigne House will form part of a network of sheltered housing and nursing home developments throughout Dublin, which have traditionally been associated with the Church of Ireland. There are currently 17 such establishments, strategically located around the city, but the demand for places constantly outstrips supply. The ethos of the new home is to provide the highest quality of care while preserving the dignity and enhancing the quality of life of residents and their carers.

Gascoigne House will operate on a multi-denominational basis serving the entire community. Admissions will be on a "priority needs" basis established through a medical, nursing and social assessment. It will provide residential nursing care for 44 residents with a day care facility also available. The service provided will encompass respite and convalescent care, extended care for dependent older people and terminal care. Twelve places will be provided for dementia sufferers in a purpose-built unit which forms an integral part of the development. The National Millennium Committee donated

€507,895 (IR£400,000) to the inter-denominational project and the remainder of the overall cost is being met through public appeals and donations from private and business donors, parishes and other trusts.

This Page Gascoigne House residents and staff.
Opposite Page Time for a relaxing afternoon cuppa.
Photography – Maxwells.

"I believe that one of the most important elements in social justice is the care of the elderly. Because of the great strides made by medical science, life expectancy continues to increase, which, of course, is something about which we should rejoice. However, the elderly continue to be vulnerable and it is the duty of all the citizens of this state to ensure that the greatest care is taken of them."

– Walton N. F. Empey
Church of Ireland Archbishop of Dublin

St. Vincent De Paul Ozanam House Project

> The St. Vincent de Paul Millennium project was the major renovation and refurbishment of its property, Ozanam House at Mountjoy Square, Dublin, transforming it into a community resource centre and indoor sports facility.

Millennium Committee Award €317,434 (IR£250,000)

> A Personal Note

Ozanam House at Mountjoy Square in Dublin's inner city has been at the heart of the Society of St. Vincent de Paul's activities in the district for over 80 years. It is situated in an area with many needs and few community resources.

For years, society members visiting families have been frustrated by their inability to "go the extra mile" for the people they were visiting, as there was no central location to bring them together and provide necessary services.

Over the years we identified many activities to benefit the community – Personal Development/Home Management Courses, Homework Clubs, clubs for the elderly, and while we were able to meet some of these needs by renting premises, the lack of a permanent base made it difficult to sustain these facilities.

In the midst of this time of change, the society is seeking to improve its services by working with individuals, families and communities, to promote self-sufficiency and greater social justice for all. The development of Ozanam House as

a permanent resource for the local community is an investment in the future of the community.

Our vision for Ozanam House is a place for all – from our youngest to our most senior citizens. The crèche facilities will provide much needed childcare to allow young mothers to access education and other programmes which include: literacy, computer skills, personal development, arts and music and a sports centre (to include indoor sports hall and small gym).

We hope that the regeneration of the house in this Millennium Project will form part of the regeneration of a community fighting to make a better life, particularly for its younger members. The Society of St. Vincent de Paul is privileged to be part of the realisation of a dream for people who have been forgotten for generations.

– Rose McGowan *Chairperson, Ozanam House*
(Ozanam House was officially opened by the Taoiseach, Mr. Bertie Ahern T.D. in January, 2002.)

Above Inside Ozanam House **1** Meeting area .
2 Outdoor play area. **3** Gymnasium and sports area.

Millennium Goats

> Struggling families in third world countries have received "living gifts" of dairy goats as part of a National Millennium Committee sponsored initiative.

> ## A Personal Note

Picture the scene. An African mother surrounded by her children, all with hands outstretched to greet a visitor from a distant land who has arrived with a very special living gift that will provide the first opportunity of a nutritious diet for the whole family.

That gift is a dairy goat from Ireland. Fr. Derek Leonard from the Raheen/Mungret/Crecora Parish in Limerick was the visitor who, although filled with emotion, exuded composure, friendship and love.

Fr. Leonard visited 49 other families and made similar presentations. Shortly afterwards, the National Millennium Committee awarded Fr. Leonard's parish the sum of €15,872 (IR£12,500) towards the cost of sending a further 100 goats to individual families. One dairy goat yields an average of four litres of milk per day which is sufficient to support a full family. Any additional milk can be sold to raise funds to send children to school.

These animals enabled the families to welcome the new Millennium with a hope they never experienced before. Bóthar, now ten years old, has to date sent 1,020 heifers, 2,900 goats, 1,000 chicks, 40 pigs and 150,000 A.I. straws to destitute families worldwide.

This truly is a Millennium success story made possible by the generosity, energy and foresight of Irish people.

– John T. Garrett *Bóthar Limerick*

Above The inhabitants of a North Tanzanian village welcome the arrival of the goats.

Right Fr. Derek Leonard presenting one of the 100 Millennium goats to members of the Nushimbi family in North Tanzania.

National Rehabilitation Hospital

> The Millennium Hostel at the National Rehabilitation Hospital in Dun Laoghaire will offer accommodation to the families of recovering patients so that they can be close at hand to offer valuable support. A large number of patients who are victims of traumatic brain injury, stroke or spinal cord injury live outside Dublin, with the result that their families experience considerable difficulties supporting them through the post trauma crisis. At any one time in the hospital there are patients from all 26 counties being treated.

Millennium Committee Award €1.269 million (IR£1 million)

> A Personal Note

The National Rehabilitation Hospital (N.R.H.) is eagerly awaiting completion of our eight-bed hostel funded by the National Millennium Committee. As a national service, N.R.H. offers rehabilitation programmes to people who have sustained major disabilities. The process of achieving maximum recovery after a brain injury or spinal injury typically involves prolonged hospitalisation. Return home, when appropriate, is greatly facilitated by giving family members and carers the opportunity to learn at first hand the techniques and skills needed to support the person on their return home. The hostel will enable the family members and carers to stay within the hospital grounds while they acquire the essential caring techniques, by working with members of the hospital multidisciplinary rehabilitation team.

For some people with major disability the rehabilitation process needs to be broken up into phases spread over several years. For those people who return from their home for a further phase of rehabilitation, the opportunity to live in a hostel, rather than require admission to a hospital bed, enables the person to retain independence, while accessing further rehabilitation. For young children who sustain a major traumatic brain injury and require admission to the National Rehabilitation Hospital, the new hostel will enable the parents to stay with their children while they receive essential rehabilitation. As the design team finishes its brief, the N.R.H. looks forward to the increased flexibility and responsiveness it can offer in its rehabilitation programme as the new hostel comes on stream in mid-2002.

– Dr. Mark Delargy *Consultant in Rehabilitation Medicine, National Rehabilitation Hospital*

Above Dr. Mark Delargy.
Right The National Rehabilitation Hospital, Dun Laoghaire.

Simon Community

> The Simon Community of Ireland used the award from the Millennium Committee to refurbish its centres for the homeless in Dublin, Cork, Dundalk and Galway and to increase access and mobility for residents of the centres.

Millennium Committee Award €266,645 (IR£210,000)

>A Personal Note

The Simon Community of Ireland is delighted to report that the money received from the National Millennium Committee has greatly improved the facilities available to homeless people in our four communities.

Cork Simon used its money to provide better facilities in its emergency shelter and two residential houses. For instance, the installation of an extra shower unit and the upgrading of the laundry has benefited residents and up to around 70 people sleeping out, who come to the Simon day facility each day to wash, get clean clothes and have a hot meal.

Dublin Simon ear-marked its money for the refurbishment and relocation of its Settlement and Training Project. The money will provide for furnishing and decoration and the purchase of new equipment, including lockers, for a purpose-built kitchen.

Among the projects on which *Dundalk Simon* spent its money was the installation of a lift. This will provide residents who, for reasons of mobility or ill health, had

been confined to the ground floor without access to the upper floor. It also means that people with such problems do not have to be refused admission when the ground floor is fully occupied.

Galway Simon spent its money on a van to provide residents with greater mobility.

– Marnie Hay, *Communications Co-ordinator, Simon Community*

Above Relaxing in a Simon residential home.
Right Millhouse, a residential home of the Cork Simon Community.
Photography courtesy of The Simon Community.

Out On the Road

> Many caring groups and voluntary organisations regarded the Millennium as an opportune time to expand services and support for the less advantaged and vulnerable. Some viewed the provision of modern, independent transport facilities as the key to opening new horizons for the less mobile, isolated and disabled. For others, ownership of a new vehicle was the gateway to an improved and speedy response to emergency situations. The National Millennium Committee responded to many of these requests – here we feature some examples of the beneficiaries.

> A Personal Note

Coming from a rural background we were aware for some time of the problems that our members and potential members were faced with every day. Inadequate public transport, and the lack of adequate modes of transport for those suffering from disabilities, coupled with living a distance from facilities and services, can cause great difficulties and disenchantment. It can also lead to a feeling of isolation and social exclusion and a lack of enthusiasm for life in general.

For some time we in the Summerhill Active Retirement Group in Co. Meath knew of older people around the area who, because of lack of transport, were unable to attend our centre. This prompted a fundraising drive to purchase a 16 seater mini-bus with wheelchair facilities and easy access for people with a wide range of disabilities. The group's efforts received a major boost from a €21,586 (IR£17,000) Millennium Recognition Award.

The bus took its maiden voyage in July 2000 and since then it has brought the group on a variety of regular outings such as picnics, barbecues, shopping trips and social events. Our "Millennium Bus" has made a huge difference to the lives of our members, especially those disabled, giving them not only a means of transport but a fresh lease of life. In addition, these people now have access to the services our centre offers: from chiropody, library, Internet access, computer classes and drama to inter-generational projects and volunteering opportunities. Our Third Age Centre is also within close proximity to the doctor's surgery, the pharmacy and local shops. The availability of the "Millennium Bus" to the older members of the community now gives them a reason to get out of the house, meet new people, form new relationships, gain new skills and information and join in new activities.

– Mary Nally *Summerhill Active Retirement Group, Co. Meath*

1 > John Paul Centre, Galway

An award of €23,935 (IR£18,850) under the Millennium Recognition Awards allowed the John Paul Centre, Ballybane, Galway, to purchase a seven seater Mitsubishi Space Wagon for use by St. Clare's Training Unit which cares for young adults with severe learning disabilities. Activities at the unit include basic workskills, swimming, cookery, computer work, drama, arts and crafts and social training.

2 > Tullow Day Care Centre

The Tullow Day Care Centre, Co. Carlow, brings isolated elderly people daily to meet with other citizens and share the comfort of the facility. The purchase of a second vehicle to support their programme was an ambition achieved with the help of a Millennium Recognition Award of €35,553 (IR£28,000).

3 > Galway Mountain Rescue Team

The Galway Mountain Rescue Team used their award of €35,553 (IR£28,000) to purchase and fully equip a vehicle for use in emergency call-out rescues. The vehicle carries radio equipment, a mobile base station as well as a comprehensive range of rescue equipment.

4 > Order of Malta

Sgt. Ted Fearon of the Dundrum, Co. Dublin, Order of Malta, with a new ambulance purchased with support from the National Millennium Committee.

Right Summerhill Active Retirement Group on a day's outing.

Millennium Snapshots

The Millennium was seen by a large number of communities, voluntary organisations, caring groups, schools and individuals as an opportunity to develop beneficial social projects with support from the National Millennium Committee. Here we feature a selection:

1 > Mercy Family Centre

The Mercy Family Centre, South Brown Street, Dublin, developed a community garden as part of its family support initiative, and a club house for inner city children, with the assistance of €25,395 (IR£20,000) from the Millennium Recognition Awards.

2 > Clare Haven

A Millennium Recognition Award of €95,230 (IR£75,000) has facilitated the total upgrading of the accommodation at the Clare Haven Refuge in Ennis, Co. Clare. The newly built, six family unit is the culmination of a project which started in 1993. It provides safety, security, dignity and comfort along with the practical services of information and support for women and children who are victims of domestic violence.

3 > Ballyphehane/Togher Community Development Project

A Millennium award of €4,571 (IR£3,600) to Ballyphehane/ Togher Community Development Project in Co. Cork went to promote access to information technology within the local community.

4 > Bray Cancer Support

With the support of a €19,046 (IR£15,000) Millennium Recognition Award the Bray Cancer Support and Information Centre now provides a comprehensive outreach service through pamphlets and a series of public meetings, with special emphasis on health awareness related to cancer. The Centre also published *A Guide to Breast Cancer* prepared by *Friends Up Front*, a support group for women with breast cancer.

5 > Windgap Millennium Hall

The Windgap I.C.A. Women's group, Co. Kilkenny, renovated a house, which has social and cultural links going back to the 1940s, for use as a meeting place and community centre. The project received support of €27,934 (IR£22,000) under the Millennium Recognition Awards.

6 > Bone Marrow for Leukaemia Trust

The Bone Marrow for Leukaemia Trust enthusiastically believes the Real Time PCR Machine, a new piece of high-tech medical equipment, will revolutionise gene testing in leukaemia in Ireland and speed up diagnosis and treatment of the disease. The machine, purchased at a cost of €152,369 (IR£120,000), has been installed in the National Bone Marrow Transplant Unit at St. James's Hospital, Dublin. It was bought with support from the National Millennium Committee, fundraising groups associated with the trust and personal donations. The DNA gene testing procedure will initially be used in the treatment of childhood leukaemia and cancer. In making the diagnosis of leukaemia more precise it is hoped that better and earlier methods of treatment will be available to increase the cure percentage of patients. Pictured is Susan Campbell who was one of the first people in Ireland to receive a bone marrow transplant.

7 > Farney Workhouse Project

The €634,869 (IR£500,000) project entails the restoration and redevelopment of the Farney Workhouse into a One-Stop-Shop that will incorporate all community development initiatives, including a Resource and Information Centre, into a powerhouse of social, community and economic development for South Monaghan and its environs. Built in 1841 to house the most disadvantaged in society, the Workhouse will, when developed, once again serve the community by offering workspace, office and training facilities to those addressing local needs.

8 > Cura Kerry

Cura Kerry, based in Tralee, were awarded €73,645 (IR£58,000) to make the long-awaited move to a more accessible location with up-to-date facilities to cater for the growing demand for their services. This has allowed for additional services geared towards dealing with teenage pregnancies, counselling and aftercare.

9 > Samaritans

The hype and anticipation that surrounded the ushering in of the new Millennium raised genuine fears that the event might prove overpowering and traumatic for many people. The National Millennium Committee responded by awarding The Samaritans €76,184 (IR£60,000) to allow the support organisation launch its largest ever awareness campaign in Ireland.

The Samaritans were able to more than double their awareness strategy across Ireland, to include television advertising. It used the award-winning cartoon theme, designed as part of *The Samaritans Youth Matters* promotional drive, to encourage younger people to make contact when they were experiencing an emotional crisis.

The Samaritans had predicted that 10% more people than usual would make contact over the Millennium holiday period of 1999/2000. In the event, branches received 15-20% more calls, and one got 22% more. Paul O'Hare, Public Relations Manager, The Samaritans, said: "People expect to have a great time at Christmas and the New Year, but frequently this is not the case. The Samaritans know that Christmas stresses bring increased calls and the Millennium hype added to the pressure. We also felt many would experience a comedown after the holiday and statistics show that January is a month when, sadly, there are many suicides. The Millennium Committee enabled us to let people know we were there for them."

10 In Recognition

Casting a Wide Net

> Amongst the most important of the contributions that the National Millennium Committee has made to Irish life is that future generations of Irish people will always be aware that, as a country, Ireland did a lot more than just pay lip service to the memory of many people, institutions and organisations whose histories might have otherwise gone unrecognised, unreported and unmarked.

The Committee felt it important that such a significant date should not just celebrate joyous, happy events, but should also mark in a significant manner the fact that many people in society are less fortunate than most of us or, for example, have been the victims of institutional abuse and marginalisation. The special **Groves for Victims of Abuse** that have been created in a number of The People's Millennium Forests are intended to both record an injustice done and to offer a haven of peace and solace.

Many Irish mariners have been lost at sea off our coasts. Courageous lifeboat men, too, have selflessly and, without thought for their own safety, given their lives in attempting rescue. Both the **Dunmore East**, Co. Waterford, and **Rosguil**, Co. Donegal, **Maritime Memorials** were erected to record such tragedy and courage. Others have died in the pursuit of truth and justice, which the **Veronica Guerin Memorial** in the Dubhlinn Garden at Dublin Castle will witness in perpetuity. Over the years, too, many Irish men, women and children have inexplicably gone missing, to the confusion and heartbreak of family and friends, and a special **Sculpture**

to the Missing, a powerful and evocative work by artist Ann Mulrooney has been erected at Kilkenny Castle.

The tragedy of forced economic emigration is still a raw wound for many Irish families rent asunder by it, and the ambitious multi-million pound **Irish World Heritage Centre in Manchester** will become the definite resource centre documenting the life and times of those who had to leave Ireland to make a living for their families, celebrating the immense contribution they made to society and at the same time affirming the confidence and vision of the new Ireland.

Mar a thaispeánfaidh lárionad Manchester is beag clann in Éirinn nár chuir eisimirceacht isteach ortha. Síos trí na mbliain, nuair a bhi Éire mar náisiun óg ag streacháil, dob é an t-ordú poist ag teacht ó ghaolta i Sasana, Albain, san Bhreatain Bheag agus níos faide i gcéin, a sholáthraigh go minic, an t-airgead le baile agus dóchas a choinneáil beo. Ní gá do dhuine ach féachaint ar na figiúirí do sheoltáin poist ó dheoraithe le tuiscint ceart a bheith aige ar an ról lárnach a d'imir na heisimircigh i gcúnamh a thabhairt d'Éirinn in amannaí an ghannchuid.

And then there are those who are ill or suffering, whose lives will be made less painful and meaningful by a number of projects the Committee has supported – **Dun Laoghaire's Rehabilitation Hospital**, the **Barretstown Gang Camp**, the **Leukaemia Trust, Bray Cancer Support** and the **Samaritans** among them. For those who have handicaps or less mobility, funding was provided to groups such as the **Irish Wheelchair Associations** for its National Mobility Centre as well as for county-by-county recognition awards.

The uniqueness of the birth date of babies born on the 1/1/2000 was acknowledged in the presentation of a hand-crafted silver coaster and a commemorative edition of the £1 Millennium coin. Citizens who celebrated their 100th birthday in 2000 were also specially honoured.

And, finally, a number of organisations that have undertaken to help those who are experiencing marginalisation in our modern society were also backed by the National Millennium Committee, including **Westgate Sheltered Housing** in Cork, **Tralee's Cura Centre**, the **Simon Community** and **S.H.A.R.E** in Cork. The Committee was also pleased to endorse the **Bank of Ireland's Millennium Scholars Trust**, which offers the opportunity of third level education to those who could not otherwise afford it.

Right John Coll beside his bust of Veronica Guerin in the Dubhlinn Garden, Dublin Castle. Photograph – Maxwells.

Millennium Coin

> Coins as currency have been part of barter, trading and commerce for Millennia. The Millennium offered the opportunity for a final and distinctive Irish coin, before the arrival of the Euro. On the recommendation of the National Millennium Committee, the Central Bank of Ireland designed and minted five million special £1 Millennium coins.

The Millennium year coincided with a unique time in the history of Irish currency. Following a suggestion from the National Millennium Committee, the Central Bank struck the very last of the distinctive Irish coins that first went into circulation more than 70 years previously. Appropriately, that coin was a special one-off design of a £1 coin to mark the Millennium year. As the production of Irish coins ended, we had already begun a new era in Irish currency, with the production of a first run of almost one billion Euro coins.

Again and again, over the years, I have been struck by the comments made about Irish coins by overseas visitors. Our coinage has been recognised the world over for its distinctive design. While over the centuries men and women of importance have always understood the value of imprinting their heads and their achievements on the coinage, I believe that it is to our credit in Ireland that we went down a different road. In 1926, a committee chaired by William Butler Yeats met to choose a design for Irish coins. Their choice was inspired. Those original Percy Metcalfe designs, based on Irish animals and birds, have stood us in good stead. There have been some additions since – the designs of Gabriel

Hayes on the halfpenny, penny and two pence at the introduction of decimalisation; and the Red Deer design of the £1 coin by Thomas Ryan.

The design of the Millennium coin, by Alan Ardiff and Garret Stokes, follows admirably in this tradition. Based on the Broighter Boat, which is on display at the National Museum, the coin represents the past as much as it does the future. In addition to a commemorative edition, the Central Bank also produced five million Millennium £1 coins for general circulation. Everybody should have come across this special coin in the course of their normal daily business at some point during 2000 and 2001 and many of the public, I am sure, will have held onto one of these coins as a memento of the Millennium.

– Maurice O'Connell *Governor, Central Bank of Ireland 1994-2002*

Right The Millennium £1 Coin. The primary image is based on the Broighter Boat, a minature in gold which was found as part of the Broighter hoard in Co. Derry in 1896. It dates from 10 B.C.

Distinctive Coins Through the Years

Pre-Decimalisation Coinage

Decimal Coinage

United Nations Commemorative Coin, Dublin 1000 Years Commemorative Coin and the 50 Ecu coin.

Babies

> Babies born on the first day of the new Millennium and the 21st century will always be that little bit special. The uniqueness of the birth date of these babies was acknowledged in the presentation by the Millennium Committee of a hand-crafted silver coaster and a commemorative edition of the £1 Millennium coin.

Millennium babies receiving their Millennium gifts. **1** Councillor Pearse O'Hanrahan, Chairman, Dundalk UDC, making the presentation to baby Mílaoise Murphy and family. **2** The Cathaoirleach of Clare County Council, Mr. Séan Hillery, having a chuckle with baby Michael Kenny. **3** Carlow County Council Chairman Walter Lacey making the presentation to Cody Michael Murphy, Graiguecullen and mum Dawn. **4** Kerry Millennium babies with their parents.

5 Millennium twins Cathal and Lorcan Kissane, Dundrum, Dublin (at 13 months) with parents Antoinette and Brian. **6** Dublin babies receiving presentations from Minister Séamus Brennan at Government Buildings. **7** The Mayor of Waterford, Alderman Davy Daniels, making presentations to Waterford babies.

Centenarians

> Recognising those whose energies and sacrifices helped shape modern Ireland was to the forefront of Millennium commemorations. Centenarians throughout the country were honoured and received special silver mementos of the occasion.

Honouring the centenarians. **1** Kate Callan is presented with her awards by Councillor Nicky McCabe, Chairman, Louth County Council, and Brian Harten, Louth Millennium Officer. **2** Ellen (Cis) Ryan and the Cathaoirleach, Councillor Tom Wood, at the ceremony in St. Patrick's Hospital, Cashel. **3** Kate O'Sullivan, aged 104, Beaufort, Co. Kerry, with members of her family. **4** Patrick Kinsella receives his honours from Councillor Mary Elliott, Cathaoirleach, Dun Laoghaire-Rathdown County Council.

5 Margaret Kearney, Inagh, Co. Clare celebrates with Máirín Hill, Clare Millennium Officer. **6** Ellen McGuigan, assisted by Nurse Margaret Culbert, receives her presentation from Councillor Pearse O'Hanrahan, Chairman, Dundalk UDC. **7** Brigid Guinan, surrounded by her family, at the presentation by Ann Coughlan, Offaly Millennium Officer (left).

Maritime Memorials

> The populations of many coastal communities in Ireland are dependent on the sea for a livelihood. For fishermen, it is a living that involves danger and risk. The fishing communities of Dunmore East, Co. Waterford, and Rosguill, Co. Donegal, saw the Millennium as an appropriate time to recognise the bravery and sacrifice of those who lost their lives farming the restless sea or who were drowned in other accidents at sea. With support from the National Millennium Committee, sensitive and lasting memorials to those who lost their lives now stand proudly on the quays in Dunmore East and Rosguill.

> ## Rosguill Memorial ... A Personal Note

On Monday 3 January, 2000, over 500 people gathered at the spot overlooking Downings Pier to celebrate the unveiling of a Millennium Celtic Cross. The cross commemorates the lives of those who died tragically in the waters off the Rosguill Peninsula and those from the parish who were drowned elsewhere.

The cross, standing seven and a half feet high, is crafted in granite, adorned by an anchor and is surrounded by five megalithic standing stones, each connected by a chain. A memorial stone also crafted in black granite, bears the names of some 27 people, all of whom died at sea. The cross and memorial stand on elevated ground above Downings Pier, at Árd Na nEangach. It is lit by fibre optic beams at dark, and can be seen both on entering the village and on coming in from sea. The surrounding area has been landscaped and there is wheelchair access.

The idea for the Millennium Cross and Memorial came from a local Development Committee in Autumn 1999. Funding from the local community and substantial funding from the National Millennium Committee helped see the project through to completion. Local people helped in so many ways. Indeed, the cross and memorial are a tribute to local effort.

The Downings Millennium Memorial Cross is not only a reminder of the new Millennium, but it is an everlasting prayer, crafted in stone, for those loved ones lost at sea.

– Mary McGettigan *Secretary*
The Memorial Committee Rosguill Development Association

From Left to Right Sea Memorials, Rosguill, Co. Donegal, and Dunmore East, Co. Waterford.

> ## Dunmore East

The provision of a worthy memorial at Dunmore East to the 128 persons recorded as having lost their lives along the Waterford seaboard over the last century or so, was the culmination of the work and dreams of the local community and, particularly, the committee which brought the project to fruition. President Mary McAleese unveiled the bronze and marble sculpture on 6 March, 2000. She said that the memorial would provide "a focus for the collective grief of the community". The project was originally conceived following the sinking of the *Jenalisa*, with the loss of two crewmen, in 1996.

The cost was met mainly through voluntary work, local fundraising and assistance from the National Millennium Committee.

Since the unveiling, many bereaved relatives from along the Waterford coastline, as well as other parts of the country and beyond, have come to pay tribute to their own loved ones and to all those lost at sea. Sadly the list of names on the memorial is growing, with the addition of those who have lost their lives tragically since.

The local community echo the words of the President and "pray that all who have suffered will find some strength and peace here".

Victims of Abuse Groves

> The final decades of the 20th century and the second Millennium witnessed the disclosure of many failures of society in the treatment of children, particularly those in the care of state institutions. It has been, and still is, a painful and traumatic experience for those abused and mistreated.

On 11 May, 1999, the Taoiseach, Mr. Bertie Ahern said: "A light has been shone into the dark corners of both our past and present, and these victims have performed an immense service in challenging our collective complacency. They have shown us that we cannot put the past behind us by ignoring it. We must confront it and learn its lessons. This is the least we can do to address the injustices of the past and the dangers of the present."

As a further gesture of support and reconciliation, the National Millennium Committee has, in response to a request from the Association for the Healing of Institutional Abuse, Aislinn Centre, dedicated groves in forests, one in each of the four provinces, as areas of contemplation and reflection. A bench of native wood in each grove bears the inscription: "*This grove is dedicated to all those who, as victims of institutional abuse, suffered incalculably. Let us all pledge ourselves to ensuring that those most vulnerable never again suffer such pain and deprivation.*"

The groves are located in The People's Millennium Forests in Ballygannon, Co. Wicklow, Tourmakeady Wood, Tourmakeady, Co. Mayo, Derrygorry, Co. Monaghan, and Glengarra, Cahir, Co. Tipperary.

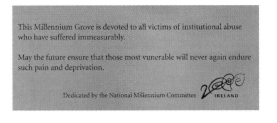

This Millennium Grove is devoted to all victims of institutional abuse who have suffered immeasurably.

May the future ensure that those most vunerable will never again endure such pain and deprivation.

Dedicated by the National Millennium Committee

Above The inscription on benches in each of the Groves of Reflection.

Right Christine Buckley of the Association for the Healing of Institutional Abuse, Aislinn Centre, at the Grove of Reflection dedicated to victims of abuse in Ballygannon Wood, Rathdum, Co. Wicklow.

Bank of Ireland Millennium Scholars Trust

> The Bank of Ireland Millennium Scholars Trust of €12,697,381 (IR£10 million) will provide financial backing for talented individuals wishing to participate in further education, but who, for economic or social reasons or because of physical disabilities, are prevented from fulfilling their ambition. The Trust is Bank of Ireland's main Millennium initiative and the largest single such Millennium endeavour from either state or private sources.

The scheme is attracting applications from all walks of life. Recipients of scholarships include single parents, community activists, students with disabilities, those currently in college and mature students entering third level education for the first time. Successful Leaving Certificate students and students with exceptional talents in the creative/performing arts area have also benefited from the Trust. The National College of Ireland administers the Trust on behalf of the Trustees and Bank of Ireland.

Since its inception almost 2,000 applications have been received and €2.6 million (IR£2.05 million) has been awarded to 133 students throughout Ireland. It is clear from the applications that they all share a burning ambition to realise their full potential, and, in many cases, have overcome major obstacles before embarking on their journey to third level education. Scholarships provide funding from €3,800 (IR£3,000) with an upper limit of €38,000 (IR£30,000) for the duration of the coarse as determined by the Board of Trustees. Scholarships range from one year up to five years and the Trust is committed to awarding 60 scholarships a year for a further eight years.

But the Trust goes beyond financial support with a Mentoring Programme provided by bank staff who help the scholars recognise and develop their own skills.

The Trust is about nurturing and harvesting the talents of the scholars for their individual benefit and for the good of society.

Above Two of the 2001 recipients. Declan Kinsella from Tallaght who is studying for a four year history degree and Jimmy Griffin from Walkinstown who commenced a four year theology and biblical studies degree. Both are attending Trinity College, Dublin.

Right Isabelle O'Connell was awarded a scholarship in 2000 to study for a Masters in Performance in the Manhattan School of Music, New York.

The Irish World Heritage Centre

> The Irish World Heritage Centre in Manchester was the chosen Millennium project to recognise the worldwide contribution of the Irish diaspora. The centre has been designed to reflect two Millennia of Ireland's past and to acknowledge the immense contribution of Irish emigrants, as well as celebrating the confidence and vision of the new Ireland.

Millennium Committee Award €2,539,476 (IR£2 million)

The new centre will be an exciting venue, reflecting contemporary Ireland and offering multipurpose facilities to a wide range of customer groups. The facilities will include a museum, tracing through a large collection of artefacts and historical documents the story of Irish emigration: a social venue for the local expatriate community, visitors from Ireland and international Irish communities; an Arts Centre for designers, artists and performers; a Business Centre attractive to the business community; hotel, shops, restaurants and a health club, and sports pitches for the promotion of Gaelic games.

Minister Séamus Brennan, speaking in Manchester in September 1999 at the announcement of Millennium funding for the project, said: "There are few families in Ireland that have not been affected in some way by emigration. Through the decades when Ireland as a young nation was struggling, it was the postal order or money order arriving in the post from family members in England, Scotland, Wales and further afield, that often provided the finance to keep homes and hopes alive."

Above Denis Irwin. Photograph — David Maher, Sportsfile.
Right Computer-generated impression of the Irish World Heritage Centre.

I am proud to support a project like this which has great vision and merit. It will cherish Ireland's rich heritage while at the same time evolving to meet the needs of a more diverse, confident and outgoing Irish community.

It will provide an outlet for young people of all generations and in particular second-generation Irish children to express their cultural heritage and identity and I have no doubt it will play a key role in promoting and sustaining both.

– Denis Irwin *Soccer star, Manchester United F.C. and Republic of Ireland*

Irish people have helped shape the destiny of many nations and this centre will celebrate the immense legacy of their success and that of their descendants.

Today, throughout the world, their monuments endure but the men and women are largely forgotten. This centre will ensure that their contribution will be remembered forever. If *we* do not keep their names alive, who will?

– Michael Forde *Chairman, Irish World Heritage Centre*

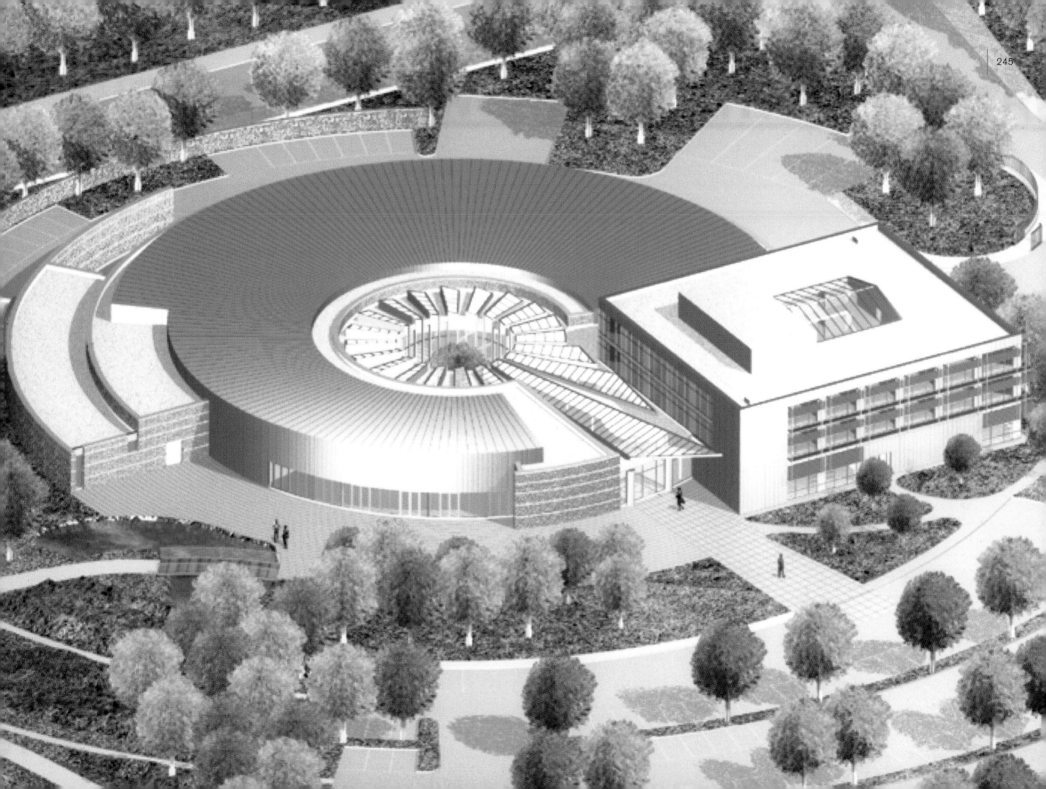

The Irish in Britain – The Middle Nation

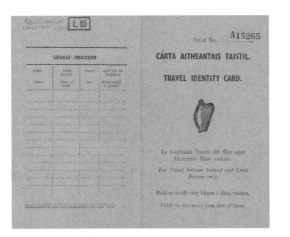

We in Ireland are justly proud of the considerable influence and achievements of the Irish in North America. In recent times Ireland, both North and South, has benefited enormously from their attachment to this country and its political destiny. The pride which Irish-Americans have always taken in their heritage is reflected, not only in a concern for Ireland, but in the untiring efforts of Irish-descent American academics to analyse and document that heritage. As a consequence this element of the diaspora dominates the popular history of the Irish abroad.

The Irish-British, by contrast, are sadly neglected in the annals of the Irish diaspora. Ironically it was a Canadian historian of Irish descent, Professor Donald Harman Akenson, who wrote that the Irish in Britain, although they are the second most important Irish emigrant community abroad, are the least analysed and the least understood. I would go further and say they are also the least appreciated.

They followed in the footsteps of the Spailpíns and Tattie Hokers, the maids and servants, and became nurses and navvies in order to pay their way and maintain countless others left at home. Between 1951 and 1961 alone over half a million, in almost equal gender proportions, went to Britain. While responding to Britain's pressing need for labour they carried with them not only the burden of familial obligation but also the handicap of history; as one female emigrant put it, after a lifetime spent in Britain, "They taught us to hate England – and then they sent us over here!"

Today, they are the largest emigrant ethnic minority in Europe. Many of them hold key positions in the upper echelons of British political and economic life. The groundworks aspects of the British construction industry, historically the largest single employer of Irish male emigrants, is dominated by Irish-owned companies. Second generation Irish graduates have developed a thriving Irish studies community which is not only analysing the experience of the Irish in Britain, but also focusing official attention on the plight of the less fortunate in that community, particularly amongst the elderly.

It is therefore to the eternal credit of the present government in Ireland that the sacrifices, achievements, and standing of the Irish in Britain have been recognised in the granting of the largest National Millennium Committee award for a project outside Ireland, €2,539,476 (IR£2 million), towards the building of the new Irish World Heritage Centre in Manchester. It represents some acknowledgement of the great debt owed by the new Ireland to the Irish in Britain – The Middle Nation.

– Ultan Cowley *Author of The Men Who Built Britain*

Top Left Travel Identity Card from the 1940s, used courtesy of Ultan Cowley.

Left Irish workers "pulling cable" on a construction site in 1952. Photograph – Courtesy McNicholas Construction.

Right Tunnel Tigers: Irish and Polish Tunnellers break through Lough Sloy, Scotland, 1949. Photograph – National Museums of Scotland.

Missing Persons' Sculpture

> Every year in Ireland up to 2,000 people are reported to the Gardaí as officially missing. Many of these people return home voluntarily or are located safe. However, a few do disappear without trace.

Millennium Committee Award €31,743 (IR£25,000)

So begins the long and agonising wait for their families and loved ones; a vigil that will end, they know not when.

The Jo Jo Dullard Memorial Trust – named after the young woman who disappeared on the night of 9 November, 1995 – through the National Millennium Committee sought recognition for all missing persons. The Committee responded with funding for a sculpture which is located in the ancient, sweeping grounds of Kilkenny Castle.

The sculpture, an 8ft high structure, consists of handprints of family members of missing people. It is cast in bronze and shaped in a lattice-like open column. Relatives and friends of missing persons visiting this area of reflection will be invited to plant perennial bulbs – everlasting symbols of renewed hope.

> A Personal Note

From the beginning, I realised that this was a very sensitive project. I knew that if this sculpture was to have any real significance, it had to be more than a dead lump of metal. The families had to be involved, had to feel a sense of ownership of the piece. It needed to become a real part of their lives. Any other approach seemed arrogant, presumptuous. It had already occurred to me that the best way in which to involve people in a public sculpture was for them to "give a hand" in the making. And that is literally what has happened. For months, I travelled the country casting handprints from family members of missing people. These have been built into a lattice-like open column, and cast in bronze. The bronze will outlast all of us.

Whilst I knew in an abstract sense that the families would be involved, I hadn't foreseen the depth or intensity of my own involvement. I have been invited into people's homes and lives. I've seen their photos, heard fragments of their stories – if they felt like telling them. For some it's a relief to talk, for others it's visibly too painful. At times I have been like Parzifal, wondering whether to ask, "brother, what ails thee"?

A missing person is not the same as a death; they cannot be grieved over and dealt with in the same way. Instead it becomes something lived with, day-by-day. I feel fortunate to have met these people, who openly live their pain.

I hope that some sense of this humanity expresses itself in the finished piece. And I hope that all their stories find endings.

– Ann Mulrooney *Sculptor*

Above Sculptor Ann Mulrooney.

Right The Sculpture to Missing Persons in the grounds of Kilkenny Castle. Photograph – Tom Brett.

Veronica Guerin Memorial

> On 26 June, 1996, *Sunday Independent* investigative journalist Veronica Guerin was murdered by Dublin criminals. The National Millennium Committee and Independent News and Media (Ireland) jointly honoured her courage and sacrifice by commissioning a sculpture from John Coll. The bust of Veronica was unveiled by the Taoiseach, Mr. Bertie Ahern T.D. on 22 June, 2001, and is now a permanent feature of the Dubhlinn Garden in the grounds of Dublin Castle.

The monument bears the inscriptions *Be Not Afraid* and *Greater justice was her ideal and it was her ultimate achievement. Her courage and sacrifice saved many from the scourge of drugs and other crimes. Her death has not been in vain.*

It has been five years since my mother passed away, but in that short space of time, so much work has been done in relation to the crime and drug trafficking in Ireland. I'm glad and proud to say that this could not have been achieved without the work of my mum … and now the people of Ireland can come to Dublin Castle and see this beautiful bust of a brilliant woman who gave us all so much. I love you mum.

– Cathal Turley (aged 11) *Son of Veronica Guerin speaking at the unveiling ceremony.*

The name Veronica means 'image of truth'. Veronica wrote the truth about those criminals who eventually had her assassinated.

School trips regularly visit Dublin Castle. A visit to Veronica's garden might be included in the future. Here, they [schoolchildren] should have no problem relating to Veronica and her work. In fact it may be more effective than lectures in a classroom.

– Mrs. Bernie Guerin *Mother of Veronica Guerin.*

Right The late Veronica Guerin. Photograph courtesy of *The Sunday Independent.*

Opposite Page The Taoiseach Bertie Ahern T.D. with Veronica Guerin's son, Cathal, husband, Graham Turley, and mother, Mrs Bernie Guerin, after the unveiling of the bust..

Veronica Guerin
1959-1996

Be Not Afraid

Millennium Events Awards

> The Millennium Events Awards were designed to allow people throughout the country become involved in the excitement generated by the Millennium, presenting them with a means to express their desire to mark the momentous occasion in their own neighbourhood, in their own individual manner.

Millennium Committee Award €3,809, 214 (£3 million)

The first meetings of the National Millennium Committee were crucial in shaping the direction of Ireland's celebration of this once-in-a-lifetime occasion. The meetings had to tackle a potentially divisive question – how the €41,901,357 (IR£33 million) voted by the government to mark this remarkable milestone would be spent. In the view of the Chairman of the Committee, Séamus Brennan T.D., the Government Chief Whip and Minister of State at the Department of An Taoiseach, the Committee arrived at the right answer, rejecting, after considerable debate, the idea of a single celebratory party like that in Sydney, or a multi-million pound monument like the Millennium Dome or London Eye. The Committee's feeling was that public money must involve the people, so some ten per cent of the Millennium Fund was set aside for a scheme to allow communities all around the country to decide what they wanted to do to mark the transition. The scheme was called the **Millennium Events Awards**, and it eventually supported a total of 1,959 events. In support of this major undertaking, the 34 city and county local authorities appointed a special Millennium Officer who worked enthusiastically

and tirelessly with the national Millennium Office on behalf of their local communities.

The only criteria were that the events should be lasting, rewarding and, above all, celebratory. Each region was awarded an overall budget of €88,882 (IR£70,000), each event was subject to a maximum subvention of €5,079 (IR£4,000) and required the local community to raise a matching sum. The response was overwhelming! Throughout the country, myriad committees were formed and, in an outpouring of community creativity, thousands of schemes were developed. They ranged from town and village festivals, theatrical productions, youth events, recognition receptions for senior citizens, musical celebrations, dance shows, exhibitions of all kinds, historical parades and pageants, local environmental improvements and the publication of books of local history.

The majority of the projects funded sought to make the community a better place for those who live in it. In Carlow town, for instance, the Friends of the Elderly were awarded €2,539 (IR£2,000) to help create a Millennium Garden of

Peace, Hope and Tranquillity in the grounds of the District Hospital overlooked by the hospice rooms. In Co. Louth the Rathnescar Wildfowl and Habitat Management Project received €4,393 (IR£3,460) to create public access to the beautiful Rathnescar Lake and Wood, a move which will have a high amenity value for the local community, as will the restoration of a 16th century bridge at Durrow, Co. Laois, a project that involved the use of old traditional manual skills in danger of dying out.

Some of the entertainment projects were spectacular. Cork city's Corca Dorca Theatre Company received €4,825 (IR£3,800) for a huge outdoor theatrical event, a Passion Play called *The Trial of Jesus* written by Conal Creedon, and Co. Donegal's An Grianán Theatre got €5,079 (IR£4,000) for *Trasnú*, a large scale celebration in Letterkenny featuring the best of the country's artists including Altan, Cathal Ó Searcaigh, Mairéad and Tríona Ní Dhomhnaill and Brendan Gallwey.

Bhí na deontais de €635 (IR£500) díreach chomh tábhachtach céanna do chaitheamh aimsire agus fleánna sráide a chuidigh le mion-phobail a theacht le chéile agus an Mhilaois a cheiliúradh in a mbealach féin. Tá creidiúint ag dul don Choiste de bharr go raibh slí ann ins na Duaiseanna do Imeachtaí le haghaidh roinnt grinn agus amadaíochta, ar nós "Bliain na Báistigh" le Seán Taylor. D'iompaigh an cumadóir, sonraí báisteach bliana, go dtí nodaireacht ceoil agus b'éigean don Ceolfhoireann Aragail an toradh a sheinnt. Bravo!

Joe Barry

> Millennium Committee Favourites

It was a wonderful experience to work on the National Millennium Committee. It had an excellent Chairman in Séamus Brennan T.D. and an excellent cross-section of people dedicated to coming up with good results. What I found particularly exciting were the many and diverse presentations from hopeful award recipients. It didn't matter whether they were for very major projects or for smaller community-based ideas; there was equal passion and commitment from their proposers.

I was particularly pleased about the inclusiveness of the Committee's awards. The monies allocated spread throughout the community. I wouldn't like to pick any one particular Millennium event above any other. They were, each and every one of them, equally important in the eyes of those people who devised them, worked hard to make them happen and to the communities in which they took place.

– Joe Barry *Former RTÉ Director-General and Member of the National Millennium Committee*

Right Local history enthusiasts marching through a field of corn dressed as Knights Templar at the launch of Loughshinny Historical Millennium Walk, Skerries, Co. Dublin. The Templars are closely associated with the nearby Baldungan Castle. Photograph – Maxwells.

Millennium Snapshots – Events Awards

1 > Loughshinny Historical Millennium Walk

The Loughshinny Historical Millennium Walk is intended to capture the rich history and tradition of the North County Dublin seaside village. The walk includes the ruins of Baldungan Castle, which date back to the Knights Templar, the Copper Mines, Flag Quarry, Smugglers Cave and Martello Tower.

2 > Castlemahon History Group

The Castlemahon History Group, Co. Limerick, published a special Millennium Edition of the Castlemahon-Feohanagh Parish Annual. The painting on the cover by Gerard

O'Connor is based on an original photograph of the village taken around 1937 by Billy Sexton. It shows the River Deel and Bridge in Castlemahon with the old St. Nicholas Church and Liston's Corner House pub in the background.

3 > Ahiohill Millennium Park

The Ahiohill Millennium Garden and Park, devised and developed by the staff and pupils of Scoil Náisiúnta Achaidh Eóchoill, Co. Cork, draws its inspiration from the heritage and environment of the area. The originals of all the monuments recreated in scaled models can be found locally. Local schoolchildren staged an historical pageant for the official opening.

4 > Kilmessan Dunsany Book

The parish of Kilmessan and Dunsany in Co. Meath produced a book to mark the Millennium. The 300-plus page publication contains over 400 photographs contributed by local people as a record of life in the area over many decades. The book also features pictures from the long-running TV series The Riordans (above), history of the area and profiles some well known local people, including Sir Horace Plunkett, founder of the Co-operative Movement and Ireland's first Agriculture minister, and Cheltenham Gold Cup winning jockey, Adrian Maguire. Titled On the Banks of the Skane, it was launched at Bellinter House, former home of Lord Tara.

5 > Riverstown Enterprise Development

Riverstown Enterprise Development, Co. Sligo, organised Millennium celebrations in the village.

6 > Connacht Veteran Motor Club

Style and nostalgia were the order of the day when the Connacht Veteran Motor Club celebrated the history of motors of all sizes and shapes.

7 > Rockwood Rowing Club

The Rockwood Rowing Club took to the water in celebration of the Millennium with a regatta on Lough Gill, Co. Sligo.

8 > Carlow Youth Artists Choir

Carlow Young Artists Choir brought astonishing rhythm and harmony to their music-making in a special Millennium concert in the Cathedral of the Assumption. The Choir received a Millennium Events Award, which enabled them to perform "Millennium Melodies" with professional musicians under director, Mary Amend.

9 > Ballymote Community Enterprise Ltd.

Presentations to Millennium babies included Siorse O'Dowd who is pictured above with her parents and Mr. John Perry T.D.

10 > Will on the Hill

Scenes from plays by William Shakespeare were performed by the Rush Dramatic Society in an open-air presentation on the town's historic Millbank site in North Co. Dublin. A bustling medieval bazaar, complete with stocks, jugglers and archery competitions, set the mood. It had started out formally titled "Shakespeare on the Millbank" but by the end of a day of boisterous fun and entertainment, it was dubbed "Will on the Hill". The photograph above shows Andy Monks as King Lear and Marcia Weldon as Regan, Lear's daughter. Photograph – Kieran Corrigan.

11 > Phoenix Players
The Phoenix Players, Tubbercurry, Co. Sligo, invested their Millennium Award in a Millennium pageant.

12 > Cork Tea Dances
Millennium Events involved city and rural communities all over the country. In Cork, they joined together for a series of Tea Dances for the Young at Heart *"Next Dance Please"* was the call sent out from the combined Cork City and County Councils' Millennium Committees. Six Tea Dances were held around the county. Almost 2,500 senior citizens enjoyed dancing to the nostalgic music of their youth with the Cork Pops Orchestra conducted by Lyric FM's Evelyn Grant.

13 > Bímís Dílis
A CD entitled *Bímís Dílis: the Spirit of Offaly, in Music, Words and Song* was produced. It includes three original works, specially commissioned by Offaly County Council to celebrate the Millennium, a *Fanfare for Chamber Orchestra*, by Adele O'Dwyer; the poem *Esto Fidelis* for voice and cello and *Bímís Dílis* by Ann Egan and Adele O'Dwyer. It was first performed by the Offaly Youth Choir with Tommy Keene on pipes, and vocals by Finola Ó Siochrú on 31 December, 2000, in conjunction with a performance of Handel's *Messiah*. The poem, which is dedicated to Anne Coughlan, Offaly's Millennium Officer, encapsulates the essence of the spirit of Offaly which will be a lasting memorial to Offaly's Millennium Year.

14 > Irish Guide Dogs For the Blind
The Irish Guide Dogs for the Blind in Co. Sligo used their Millennium Award to create a new website.

15 > Dualla Millennium Project
Dualla Parish Millennium Pageant, Cashel Co. Tipperary. Photograph is of the recreation of an ancient baptismal scene.

Right Celebrating under cover.

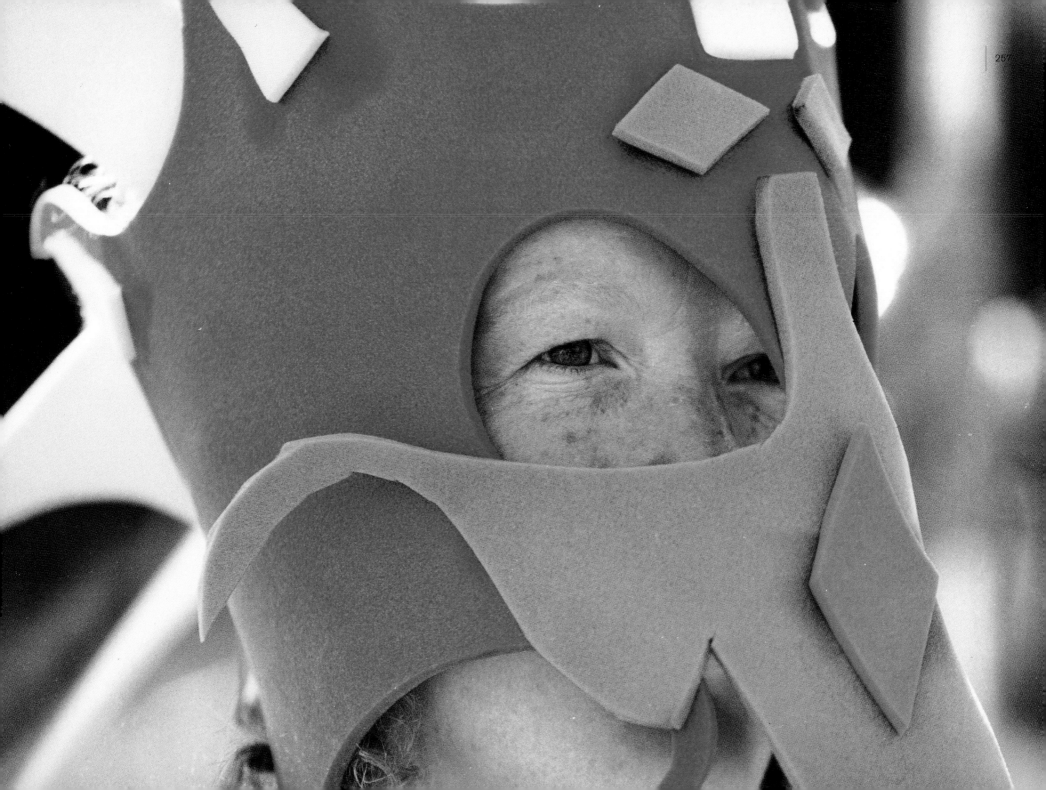

Millennium Recognition Awards

> The Millennium Recognition Awards were designed to recognise, build on or add value to existing community projects or enable new projects to be developed. No Award exceeded €95,230 (£75,000) and there was no lower limit.

Millennium Committee Award €3,809, 214 (£3 million)

The Millennium was a remarkable benchmark everywhere, and here in Ireland a decision was made to attempt to involve as many people as possible in marking this truly unique moment in history. One of the important Millennium endeavours was to try to create a vehicle to acknowledge the huge value to the fabric of Irish society of community enterprise and spirit.

Thus, in an effort to appreciate in a tangible fashion the energy, commitment and resourcefulness of the thousands of local community and voluntary groups who do so much for the economic, social and cultural development of their area, the **Millennium Recognition Awards** were born. The Awards were designed to recognise, build on or add value to existing community projects or enable new projects to be developed. In all, more than 1,400 applications were received. After a lengthy appraisal period, 193 ventures got the go-ahead and Area Development Management Ltd. (A.D.M.), an independent government-EU agency, was assigned responsibility for the design, implementation and monitoring of the scheme. Many of the bigger undertakings funded by the Millennium Recognition Awards were of a

bricks and mortar nature, designed to be of benefit to their communities for many years into the future. **Cura Kerry**, for instance, received €73,644 (£58,000) to move from an inadequate location in Tralee to a more accessible premises in the town, with up-to-date facilities to cater for the growing demand for their services in the community, tackling the problem of teenage pregnancies, and providing expert counselling and aftercare. **The Mountmellick Development Association** in Co. Laois was granted €50,789 (£40,000) to transform and renovate an old building into a craft and heritage centre to display Mountmellick embroidery. The display area will promote and reiterate the importance of this specialised craft as part of Ireland's Quaker history and heritage. **The Bere Island Heritage Centre** in Co. Cork is an example of one of a number of relatively isolated communities that received grants for heritage centres. In Bere Island's case the new space will provide a home for the wealth of literature and artefacts that exist about the island.

Among the directly targeted projects were those that met the needs of specific groups with special needs within the

community, particularly those for people with disabilities, youth at risk and women's groups. **The Kerry County Network** of People with Disabilities, for instance, was granted €27,934 (£22,000) to purchase two mini-buses and special equipment for "Transport-Us" Kerry's first community-based transport service. Among the bigger of the projects was the €95,230 (£75,000) funding for the **Clare Haven** House Project in Ennis, Co. Clare, to furnish and equip a new refuge for victims of domestic violence. On a less ambitious scale, the **Rathangan Parish Council** in Co. Kildare was given €7,618 (£6,000) to develop a community-run laundry service to meet the needs of the infirm, confined and less able among the elderly of the area.

Amongst the more visually arresting of all the projects was the one mooted by the **Shoot The Scattering Trust** based in Ennis, Co Clare. The Trust received €40,631 (€32,000) to capture images of Clare people around the world and to publish the results in a handsome book of text and photographs.

Anuas trí na blianta d'fhág na milte daoine Co. an Chláir le maireachtáil agus le saothrú i dtiortha eile. Inniu is féidir teacht ar an scaipeadh Cláirineach seo ins gach cearn den domhan. Is eachtra sonasach sásúil é do roinnt de mhuintir an Chláir, do roinnt eile ba uaigneas agus briseadh croí é gearrtha amach ón a ngaolta agus ón a gcairde. Tá An Scaipeadh ar son agus faoi eisimircigh an Chláir; iadsan gur éirigh leo agus iadsan nár éirigh leo. Is iarracht é sa Mhílaois nua seo fáilte a chur rompu abhaile.

> Millennium Committee Favourites

Howard Kilroy

I suppose that, in a way, I am a little disappointed that we didn't decide, as a Committee, to go for a big signature-type project to mark the Millennium. But, having said that, I think there were some wonderful things done that, most importantly, brought joy and pleasure to the people at large on what was a major milestone in the history of our planet. It was great to see people out on the streets enjoying themselves or at events, meaningful to them in terms of their memories of what it was about. I think that was done well at national level (with a couple of exceptions, that rightly got slated) and reached right down into the community at large, small town and village level.

I was impressed by the impact of the **Millennium Recognition Awards** and Millennium Events Awards, which matched pound for pound local community fundraising for special Millennium projects throughout the country. Between these two €7,618,428 (IR£6 million) was distributed. I think it's wonderful when government can speak to ordinary people in this way and make something special happen in their lives.

– Howard Kilroy *Former Governor of Bank of Ireland and Member of the National Millennium Committee*

THE NATIONAL MILLENNIUM COMMITTEE
MILLENNIUM RECOGNITION AWARDS

THIS AWARD RECOGNISES THE UNIQUE CONTRIBUTION MADE BY

TO IRELAND'S ECONOMIC, SOCIAL AND CULTURAL DEVELOPMENT

IRELAND

Tugann an gradam seo, atá á bhronnadh ag an gCoiste Náisiúnta na Mílaoise, aitheantas d'fhis agus d'inspioráid an tionscnaimh, agus do leas an tionscnaimh don phobal in an Mhíleaoise nua

This Award, presented by the National Millennium Committee, acknowledges the vision and inspiration of the project and its contribution to the community in the new Millennium

Séamus Brennan T.D.
Chairman, National Millennium Committee

Millennium Snapshots – Recognition Awards

1 > Irish Wheelchair Association

The year 2000 coincided with the 40th anniversary of the founding of the Irish Wheelchair Association. This was a significant landmark for this countrywide association which was acknowledged by the National Millennium Committee. In every county, recognition was given to the many people whose commitment and dedication has helped develop the Association as caring and effective campaigners for those with physical disability. At the anniversary celebration in the Croke Park Hospitality Complex, 188 people from all over the country were each presented with a statuette of Cuchulain, symbolising strength and courage, by the Taoiseach, Mr. Bertie Ahern T.D.

2&3 > Drogheda Community Forum

Drogheda Community Forum invited the locals to nominate their own "Local Hero" for an award in recognition of their contribution to the community.

Among the Millennium Heroes were: Susan Maguire of the Drogheda Travellers Initiative (No.2), who has "pushed through the glass ceiling expectations of her from society and from her own community". Susan holds a Diploma in Childcare and works with both the settled and travelling community as manager of an after-school project. She has lobbied for the interest of her own people, in particular the children. Kitty Byrne (No.3) runs a regular Montessori Play School, that accepts children with learning difficulties. Parents are

welcomed with the children and given a sense of hope in a time of despair. Kitty sets an individual regime for each child preparing for school and helps others do simple tasks for themselves. Her "Hero" nomination says "Kitty has given hope to our community, especially the young and vulnerable who cannot speak for themselves".

4 > Ballymahon Vocational School Millennium Garden

"Our Geography teacher, Mrs. Marian Barrins, instigated our project. Our aim was to clear a derelict site that was strewn with rubble from the building of our new Gym several years previously. It was a lovely sunny site but at the time a real eyesore. The 4th Year students tackled this and cleaned up the area, painted the posts, cleared away

bushes and planted some trees. The 2nd Years' aim was to create a natural haven for birds and insects. We took this to heart and studied various gardening books on creating a habitat which would attract animals, birds and insects and, of course, "stressed-out students" who could unwind in a haven of tranquillity. So far, we have done major cleaning on site, planted trees, lawns and many special shrubs to attract butterflies. We have also planted an orchard with apple, pear and plum trees.

We were greatly supported by the 4th Years who did most of the major construction work. We also built an archway into the garden and planted lots of climbers such as clematis, honeysuckle and roses to attract the bees. One more special thing we want to do is to plant a rose garden in memory of one of our 4th/5th year students, Barry Anderson, who died tragically."

– Joseph Croughan, Edwin Cummins, John Mulvanney, Lorraine Lenehan and Patrick Clarke, *Vocational School, Ballymahon, Co. Longford*

5 > Loughboy Area Resource Centre

The Loughboy Area Resource Centre, Kilkenny, works extensively with women and it used an award of €12,697 (IR£10,000) under the Millennium Recognition Awards to support a community response programme, including the Women and Well Being Group, the "Hands On" community arts initiative and the *Women's Writers Group*.

6 > Maam Children's Playscheme

Children from Maam, Co. Galway, assisted by others from surrounding towns and villages in Galway and Mayo, worked during their summer holidays on scripting, directing, producing and filming two movies, *Is My Teacher An Alien?* and *Maam TV*. They were helped by The Nerve Centre from Derry, an Oscar-nominated multimedia arts centre. The project received €25,395 (IR£20,000) in Millennium funding.

7

8

9

10

7 > Bornacoola Community Development Association
The Bornacoola Community Development Association, Co.
Leitrim, which was awarded €16,507 (IR£13,000), developed
a Millennium Garden and Sculpture. The sculpture, "Returning"
by Éamon O'Doherty, is of four wild geese in bronze on a
granite plinth, set in a garden of flowers and shrubs.

8 > Castletara Community Development Association
The Castletara Community Development Association, with
support from the National Millennium Committee, has
developed a Millennium heritage path to the famous Finger
Stones on Shantemon Mountain in Cavan. The five standing
stones are reputed, in Gaelic Mythology, to be the fingers
of legendary warrior Finn MacCumhail.

9 > Bailieborough Development Association
An allocation of €38,092 (IR£30,000) from the Millennium
Recognition Awards allowed Bailieborough Development
Association, Co. Cavan, to develop the ICT Centre offering
a range of computer training facilities. The high take-up of
courses by trainees, both young and old, means more people
are now better prepared to embrace the information age.

10 > Newcastle West & Area Arts Committee
The Newcastle West & Area Arts Committee involved a
range of community groups in their Street Theatre Company,
making it a truly inclusive project: The Desmond Women's
Group for disadvantaged and marginalised women, the
Arts 2000 Percussion Group and the Brothers of Charity

group of mentally and physically challenged, were all
thrilled with their participation. Our photograph is of Tutor
Trish Corbett working with trainees of the Brothers of Charity.

11 > Newport Millennium Photographic Competition
The Newport Millennium Photographic Exhibition in the Co.
Tipperary town was on the theme of "People, Places, Activities",
and included a section for old historic photographs.

12 > Sports Against Racism in Ireland
In September 2000 aided by a Millennium Recognition
Award, Sports Against Racism in Ireland (S.A.R.I.) staged
their annual sports event in Dublin's North Inner City.
The football competition, with teams from Travellers to

Transylvanians, was won by the Thin Blue Line team from the Gárda Síochana.

Smithfield Square was the venue for the wonderfully colourful Community Mardi Gras which attracted over one thousand participants. The entire event was shot on video and will be used as a centrepiece in the forthcoming education video pack which will be distributed to schools throughout the country. Support from state and private sector sponsorship is vital to voluntary bodies such as S.A.R.I. in order to action projects that tackle racism and promote multicultural integration within communities. The work of S.A.R.I. is highly regarded and their methods have been adopted by other European-based organisations.

Our patrons include Paul McGrath, Pelé, Roger Milla, Curtis Fleming, Benjamin Zephaniah, Ossie Ardiles, Eric Cantona, Chris Houghton and George Best.

– Frank Buckley *Sports Against Racism in Ireland*

13 > St. Michael's Family Life Centre

The St. Michael's Family Life Centre, Sligo, put a Millennium Award of €15,015 (IR£11,825) to good use, renovating and upgrading the centre which provides essential support for families. The work included changing to a warm inviting glow the building's previous drab grey image.

14 > St. Johnston Lecture Hall

The renovation by the St. Johnston Lecture Hall Management Committee to the Community Hall, St. Johnston, Co. Donegal, was assisted with an award of €10,158 (IR£8,000) under the Millennium Recognition Awards and included the installation of a stair lift, disabled toilets and ramps.

15 > Keadue Development Association

The beauty of the village of Keadue, Co. Roscommon, was enhanced when the Keadue Development Association used a Millennium Recognition Award of €63,487 (IR£50,000) to upgrade an historic well which dates back to the 1850s, and to renovate and extend the local Community Hall.

16 > Kilcummin Recreation Hall

The renovation and upgrading of Kilcummin Recreation Hall, Co. Kerry, involved the re-roofing of the building, exterior improvements and the laying inside of a new timber floor.

17 > Jubilee Bells, Cork

Hand bell ringing is considered unique to Cork and an allocation of €4,444 (IR£3,500) under the Millennium Recognition Awards allowed the Jubilee Bells Committee in the parish of Dennehy's Cross to form a new adult group of eight ringers as well as extending the scope of the existing performers.

18 > Mullinavat Women Shared Threads

The Mullinavat Women Shared Threads Group produced a patch-work quilt from scenes of the local area.

19 > Monasterevan Millennium Committee

The Monasterevan Millennium Committee undertook the repair and restoration of the gates at the entrance to Moore Abbey in the Co. Kildare town. Moore Abbey was the family home of John Count McCormack from 1927-1939.

20 > Tallanstown Youth Group

The Tallanstown Youth Group undertook to record everyday life over the past one hundred years in their village in Co. Louth. This picture from the early 1930s has a large number of boys missing from the group because many did not attend school when potatoes were being gathered or turnips thinned.

Many of the children in the main photograph are now senior citizens and a good number of them still live in the

19

Tallanstown area. They have stories and past traditions to share with everyone and their memories of school days are of particular interest to young people. They recall that the absence of a boy from the school could result in the parents receiving a summons or a fine of one shilling.

The school is still used by the community for events, meetings and training, and it is well landscaped in keeping with the rest of the village, which maintains a very high standing in the National Tidy Towns Awards.

21 > Tullamore Travellers Movement

Tullamore Travellers Movement is a partnership of Traveller and settled people committed to Travellers' right to self-determination and equality within Irish society. The project seeks to promote the recognition of Travellers as a nomadic ethnic group within Irish society, having its own distinctive culture and lifestyle.

The Millennium Award provided the opportunity to record this message by showing the lives of Travellers in Tullamore in the first year of the new Millennium. The video portrays the living conditions, culture, economics and family structures in a manner that is open, frank and understandable. It is hoped to use the video in schools, communities, state agencies, local authorities and the media to promote Travellers' rights and their way of life. The project has been developed by members of the Culture Working Group and is being used as a vehicle for Travellers to train in video production.

22 > Cloughleigh Development Group

A Millennium award to Cloughleigh Development Group, Ennis, Co. Clare, went towards an extension to the Community Centre. The extension includes two meeting rooms, a games room for young people and upgraded playschool facilities. One of the meeting rooms is devoted to technology classes using computers donated by Eircom.

11 Appendices

A Word of Thanks …

When the chairman of the NMC suggested the appointment of dedicated Local Authority Millennium Officers, it won enthusiastic and heartfelt approval from City and County Managers around the country.

The appointment of the Millennium Officers followed a meeting between Minister Séamus Brennan, City and County Managers and senior local authority personnel.

Thirty four officials took on the responsibility in addition to an already full agenda. They went on to play a pivital role in co-ordinating Ireland's special community-based marking of the Millennium. The thrill for many of the officers was that they could ask communities how they wanted to mark the Millennium in their own neighbourhood without outside interference or influence. Communities the length and breadth of the country were greatly spurred on by their own resident administrators who came right out into their midsts and helped make their local celebration relevant and memorable.

The Millennium Officers and the local authorities in each city and county were central to the success of the Millennium. They were the people in touch with what was happening in their area, the contact point for those who wanted in a variety of ways to make their own contribution to the marking of the Millennium, and the valuable link between organisations and events countrywide and the National Millennium Committee. We owe all these people a debt of gratitude for helping us to achieve in Ireland our ambition of turning this historic event into a memorable 'People's Millennium'.

– The Taoiseach, Bertie Ahern T.D.

City and County Managers and Senior Local Authority Officials

Munster Millennium Officers

Leinster Millennium Officers

Connacht & Ulster Millennium Officers

National Projects List

> The following list details those projects that received funding from the National Millennium Committee's National Projects Allocation. In a small number of instances either the award in its entirety was not availed of or to date some projects have not been completed due to unanticipated planning and technical delays. Where savings were identified, funds were reallocated to Church Floodlighting Projects.

PROJECT	€
MILLENNIUM EVENTS AWARDS	3,809,214
MILLENNIUM RECOGNITION AWARDS	3,809,214
CHILDREN'S HOUR FUND	2,539,476
LIFFEY BOARDWALK / LIFFEY OF LIGHTS	2,539,476
IRISH WORLD HERITAGE CENTRE, MANCHESTER	2,539,476
MILLENNIUM CANDLE	2,407,958
THE PEOPLE'S MILLENNIUM FORESTS	2,031,581
NATIONAL REHABILITATION HOSPITAL HOSTEL FOR FAMILIES, DUN LAOGHAIRE, DUBLIN	1,269,738
MILLENNIUM BRIDGE / CHILDREN'S PARK, GALWAY	1,269,738
MILLENNIUM FESTIVALS	1,269,738
NEW YEAR'S EVE / LAST LIGHTS CEREMONY	1,171,797
WATERFORD CITY MILLENNIUM PLAZA	1,079,277
S.H.A.R.E. HOUSING FOR THE ELDERLY, CORK	952,304
MESSIAH XXI FOR THE NEW MILLENNIUM	888,817
LIMERICK CITY MILLENNIUM PROJECTS	761,843
CINEMOBILE TRAVELLING CINEMA	674,231
LIGHTHOUSEKEEPERS' COTTAGES (IRISH LANDMARK TRUST)	634,869
CORK CITY MILLENNIUM BRIDGE	634,869
GAIETY THEATRE RESTORATION, DUBLIN	634,869
CORK OPERA HOUSE DEVELOPMENT	571,382

GASGOIGNE HOUSE, DUBLIN	507,895
CORK CITY BRIDGES, MILLENNIUM ILLUMINATION	380,921
FRANCIS BACON STUDIO (HUGH LANE MUNICIPAL GALLERY)	380,921
SAINT VINCENT DE PAUL OZANAM HOUSE RESTORATION, DUBLIN	317,435
IRISH WHEELCHAIR ASSOCIATION NATIONAL MOBILITY CENTRE, KILDARE	317,435
BATTLE OF THE BOYNE SITE	317,435
MILLENNIUM PEACE PARK, MURRISK, MAYO	317,435
GLENDALOUGH MILLENNIUM HERMITAGES, WICKLOW	317,435
LARCON CENTRE, LIBERTY HALL, DUBLIN	317,435
SIMON COMMUNITY OF IRELAND – CORK, DUBLIN, DUNDALK, LIMERICK	266,645
MÍLEAOISE NA GAELTACHTA 2000, GAILLIMHE	253,948
LARTIGUE MONORAIL RESTORATION, KERRY	222,204
BARRETSTOWN GANG CAMP MILLENNIUM COTTAGE, KILDARE	190,461
GREENTOWN 2000 ENVIRONMENT AWARDS	190,461
IRELAND'S MILLENNIA CD-ROM FOR SCHOOLS (RTÉ)	190,461
SKYFEST 2000 – SAINT PATRICK'S FESTIVAL	165,066
MILLENNIUM FIREWORKS NEW YEAR'S EVE 1999, DUBLIN	154,106
DONEGAL HOSPICE	126,974
IRISH HOSPICE FOUNDATION WHOSEDAY BOOK	126,974
MILLENNIUM YOUTH CENTRE, KILLARNEY	126,974

ATHLONE TOWN PARK, WESTMEATH	126,974
CARLOW MILLENNIUM BRIDGE	126,974
MAYO MILLENNIUM SPIRE, BALLYHAUNIS	126,974
SAINT FIN BARRE'S CATHEDRAL BEYOND 2000, CORK	126,974
NATIONAL FIELD STUDY CENTRE, SLIGO	126,974
GENETIC HISTORY & GEOGRAPHY OF IRELAND (ROYAL IRISH ACADEMY)	126,974
TALLAGHT PLAZA SCULPTURE, DUBLIN	101,579
"WRITE HERE WRITE NOW" MILLENNIUM BOOK	101,579
CHRISTIAN ARCHITECTURE EXHIBITION (ROYAL INSTITUTE OF ARCHITECTS IN IRELAND)	92,691
MIZEN HEAD INTERPRETIVE CENTRE, KERRY	88,882
ALLIHIES MINING MUSEUM, KERRY	88,882
CITIES' MILLENNIUM EVENTS – WATERFORD/ CORK/LIMERICK/GALWAY	86,342
THE SAMARITANS MILLENNIUM AWARENESS CAMPAIGN	76,184
GOAL MILLENNIUM CAMPAIGN	63,487
CONCERN MILLENNIUM CAMPAIGN	63,487
ROSCOMMON TOWN PARK	63,487
WOODSTOCK GARDENS RESTORATION, KILKENNY	63,487
GOLDEN EAGLES REINTRODUCTION, DONEGAL	63,487
THE HERITAGE COUNCIL PILGRIM PATHS	63,487
SAINT GEORGE'S BELLS RELOCATION, DUBLIN	63,487
THE ARK CULTURAL CENTRE FOR CHILDREN, DUBLIN	63,487
PLANETARIUM, INISHOWEN, DONEGAL	63,487
CO-OPERATION IRELAND ISLAND JOURNEY CONCERTS	54,599
SAINT PETER'S BELFRY RESTORATION, DROGHEDA	50,790
MILLENNIUM FARM HERITAGE PROJECT (IRISH FARMERS' ASSOCIATION)	50,000
20TH CENTURY ART EXHIBITION	46,980
NATIONAL SAFETY COUNCIL AWARENESS CAMPAIGN	44,441
COOLEY BRIDGE OF PEACE, CARLINGFORD LOUGH, LOUTH	38,092
RESTORATION OF SEISMOGRAPH HOUSE, RATHFARNHAM CASTLE, DUBLIN	38,092

LOUGH DERG SAINT PATRICK'S STATUE, DONEGAL	38,092
GAISCE MILLENNIUM GOLD ENCOUNTER	38,092
SCOUTING IRELAND ADVENTURE FACILITIES	38,092
SLIGO MILLENNIUM COUNTESS MARKIEVICZ SCULPTURE	38,092
WICKLOW FILM TRAIL, WICKLOW	31,743
MISSING PERSONS SCULPTURE, KILKENNY CASTLE	31,743
VERONICA GUERIN MEMORIAL SCULPTURE, DUBLIN CASTLE	31,743
MILLENNIUM ECUMENICAL SERVICE, DUBLIN	30,657
MULTI PURPOSE RESOURCE COMPLEX, NEWCASTLEWEST, LIMERICK	25,395
THURLES MILLENNIUM PROJECT, TIPPERARY	25,395
SPIRITUALITY CENTRE, DONAGH PARISH, MONAGHAN	25,395
CHRIST CHURCH MILLENNIUM BELLS, DUBLIN	25,395
MILLBANK THEATRE EXTENSION, RUSH, DUBLIN	25,395
COORACLARE MILLENNIUM RESTORATION PROJECT, CLARE	24,125
BALLINTUBBER ABBEY CELTIC FURROW, MAYO	24,125
LUMEN CHRISTI CHORAL SYMPHONY PREMIER PERFORMANCE	23,490
DUBLIN CHAMBER OF COMMERCE DUBLIN A CELEBRATION PIANO COMPOSITION	19,046
SLIGO BAY LIFEBOAT STATION	17,776
TURLOUGH ROUND TOWER AND CHURCH OF IRELAND ILLUMINATION, MAYO	17,776
CORCA DORCA THEATRE COMPANY MILLENNIUM PASSION PLAY, CORK	15,872
ALL IRELAND AMATEUR DRAMA FESTIVAL	12,697
O'CONNELL MEMORIAL PIPE ORGAN RESTORATION, CAHERCIVEEN, KERRY	12,697
LEDWIDGE COTTAGE MUSEUM EXPANSION, MEATH	12,697
CAVAN / LEITRIM RAILWAY RESTORATION	12,697
FERMOY MILLENNIUM BANDSTAND	12,697
KILLESHANDRA CHURCH ILLUMINATION, CAVAN	12,697
SAINT COLUMBA'S CHURCH BELL TOWER, BURTONPORT, DONEGAL	12,697
STRANORLAR & MEENGLASS CHURCH OF IRELAND BELL TOWER & BELLS	12,697
CATHOLIC YOUTH COUNCIL WORLD YOUTH DAY TRIP TO ROME	12,697

SAINT JOSEPH'S CHURCH RESTORATION OF CHIMES, CARRICKMACROSS, MONAGHAN	12,697
ROYAL IRISH ACADEMY OF MUSIC MILLENNIUM CONCERT SERIES, NATIONAL GALLERY, DUBLIN	12,697
DUBLIN INTERNATIONAL PIANO COMPETITION IRISH QUALIFYING ROUND, DUBLIN	12,697
NATIONAL YOUTH ORCHESTRA OF IRELAND	12,697
CLARE SCOUT COMMITTEE REGIONAL CAMP-SITE	12,697
ORDER OF MALTA AMBULANCE, DUBLIN	12,063
COMMUNITY RADIO MILLENNIUM PROGRAMMES, DUBLIN	11,664
RHODE PARISH COMMUNITY CENTRE, OFFALY	11,428
BATTLE OF AUGHRIM RECONCILIATION PROJECT, GALWAY	11,428
STRANORLAR MILLENNIUM CLOCK TOWER, DONEGAL	11,428
BALLYMACWARD CHURCH SPIRE, BALLINASLOE, GALWAY	11,428
BLACKPOOL COMMUNITY MILLENNIUM HALL, CORK	10,158
PILLARS OF LIGHT GARDEN, COOLMINE COMMUNITY SCHOOL, DUBLIN	10,158
LOST AT SEA MEMORIAL, ROSGUILL, DONEGAL	9,523
KNOCKLYON ECUMENICAL PASTORAL CENTRE, DUBLIN	9,523
IRISH MISSIONARY UNION FILM ARCHIVES	8,888
HOLMPATRICK SELECT VESTRY BELFRY PROJECT, DUBLIN	8,888
PLACE OF PILGRIMAGE RESTORATION, OUR LADY'S WELL, CLARE	8,888
FAMINE CHURCH RESTORATION, MAYO ABBEY	8,888
KILDALLON CHURCH BELLS RESTORATION, CAVAN	8,431
MILLENNIUM SCULPTURE & GARDEN, DUNDRUM	8,253
SAINT VINCENT DE PAUL MILLENNIUM YOUTH DAY	6,349
CATHOLIC HOUSING AID REFURBISHMENT OF APARTMENTS FOR THE ELDERLY, DUBLIN	6,349
IRISH HISTORIC TOWNS ATLAS, KILKENNY (ROYAL IRISH ACADEMY)	6,349
MEANUS CHURCH ILLUMINATION, LIMERICK	6,349
SAINT MARY'S CHURCH ILLUMINATION, CARRICK-ON-SHANNON, LEITRIM	6,349
FENAGH ABBEY & CHURCH OF IRELAND ILLUMINATION, LEITRIM	6,349
BROOMFIELD CHURCH ILLUMINATION, MONAGHAN	6,349
STAR OF THE SEA CHURCH ILLUMINATION, SANDYMOUNT, DUBLIN	6,349

SACRED HEART CHURCH ILLUMINATION, MONKSTOWN, CORK	6,349
CHURCH OF THE ASSUMPTION ILLUMINATION, DALKEY, DUBLIN	6,349
GURTEEN CHURCH OF IRELAND ILLUMINATION, SLIGO	6,349
COURTNACUDDY CHURCH ILLUMINATION, WEXFORD	6,349
HOLY YEAR CROSS ILLUMINATION, COMERAGH MOUNTAINS, TIPPERARY	6,349
SAINT PATRICK'S CHURCH ILLUMINATION, RINGSEND, DUBLIN	6,349
SAINT COLMAN'S CHURCH ILLUMINATION, CLAREMORRIS	6,349
MILLENNIUM RESTORATION OF ORIGINAL BELL, GLENTIES	6,349
CHURCH OF SAINT NICHOLAS OF MYRA ILLUMINATION, KINSEALY, DUBLIN	6,349
CORPUS CHRISTI CHURCH ILLUMINATION, DRUMCONDRA, DUBLIN	6,349
SAINT ANDREW'S CHURCH ILLUMINATION, WESTLAND ROW, DUBLIN	6,349
SAINT PATRICK'S CHURCH ILLUMINATION, MONKSTOWN, DUBLIN	6,349
SAINT PATRICK'S CHURCH ILLUMINATION, BANDON, CORK	6,349
SAINT PETER'S CHURCH OF IRELAND ILLUMINATION, BANDON, CORK	6,349
DUBLIN A CELEBRATION – FROM THE 1ST TO THE 21ST CENTURY (PAT LIDDY)	6,349
CHURCH OF THE HOLY CHILD ILLUMINATION, LARKHILL / WHITEHALL, DUBLIN	5,960
CHURCH OF SAINT THERESE GARDEN & ILLUMINATION, MOUNT MERRION, DUBLIN	5,748
SAINT ANNE'S CHURCH ILLUMINATION, BOHERNABREENA, DUBLIN	5,714
MILLENNIUM GARDEN, MAYNOOTH BOYS' NATIONAL SCHOOL, KILDARE	5,079
MILLENNIUM FIRST CHRISTMAS STORY, HAROLD'S CROSS, DUBLIN	4,444
SAINT KEVIN'S CHURCH ILLUMINATION, HARRINGTON STREET, DUBLIN	4,003
CHURCH OF THE NATIVITY OF THE BLESSED VIRGIN MARY, CHAPELIZOD, DUBLIN	3,914
IRISH SEAL SANCTUARY SEAL RELEASE	3,809
SAINT COLMCILLE'S CHURCH BELL, AUGHNACLIFFE, LONGFORD	3,809
SAINT JOSEPH'S CHURCH ILLUMINATION, GLASTHULE, DUBLIN	3,756
CHURCH OF THE ASSUMPTION ILLUMINATION, NAVAN, MEATH	3,605

SAINT PATRICK'S CHURCH ILLUMINATION, STRANDHILL, SLIGO	3,400
SAINT THOMAS' CHURCH ILLUMINATION, DUBLIN	3,301
SAINT ANNE'S HERITAGE CENTRE, MALLOW, CORK	3,174
SAINT CIARAN'S NATIONAL SCHOOL MILLENNIUM PLAZA, DUBLIN	3,174
CARNA PARISH CHURCH ILLUMINATION, GALWAY	3,174
GOOD SHEPHERD CHURCH ILLUMINATION, CHURCHTOWN, DUBLIN	3,174
MILLENNIUM SCULPTURE, MOUNTMELLICK, LAOIS	3,174
MILLENNIUM SUNDIAL, BALTIMORE, CORK	3,174
SÉIPÉAL UINSEANN NAOFA, BAILE AN FHEIRTEARAIGH & SÉIPÉAL NA CARRAIGA, CILL CHUILE, BAILE NA NGALL, CIARRAÍ	2,633
GOOD COUNSEL GAA CLUB DEVELOPMENT, DUBLIN	2,539
WOODLAND PARK PROJECT, BALLYROAN NATIONAL SCHOOL, DUBLIN	2,539
SAINT JOSEPH'S CHURCH ILLUMINATION, TERENURE, DUBLIN	2,539
CHURCH OF THE ASSUMPTION ILLUMINATION, MILLTOWN, DUBLIN	2,539
SAINT MATTHEW'S CHURCH BELL, MAGHERA, CAVAN	2,539
MILLENNIUM MONUMENT, DROMINA, CORK	2,539
MILLENNIUM THEMED GARDEN, AHIOHILL NATIONAL SCHOOL, CORK	2,539
METHODIST CHURCH ILLUMINATION, BANDON, CORK	2,428
TALLOW CHURCH ILLUMINATION, WATERFORD	2,349
BALLYBUNION CHURCH, KERRY	2,228
CELTIC SYMBOLS MONUMENT, BALLYFIN, LAOIS	2,222
GALWAY COUNTY SHOW MILLENNIUM ROSETTES	2,208
CHURCH OF THE ANNUNCIATION ILLUMINATION, FINGLAS WEST, DUBLIN	2,133
AGHABOE ABBEY ILLUMINATION, LAOIS	1,981
KILTERNAN CHURCH OF IRELAND ILLUMINATION, DUBLIN	1,905
THINK THURLES TIDY INITIATIVE, TIPPERARY	1,651
HOLY CROSS MILLENNIUM GARDEN, DUBLIN	1,587
CASTLEMAHON HISTORY GROUP MILLENNIUM ANNUAL, LIMERICK	1,587
CHURCH OF SAINT MARY & SAINT MICHAEL ILLUMINATION, RATHDRUM, WICKLOW	1,549
SAINT JOHN'S CHURCH ILLUMINATION, DUNFANAGHY, DONEGAL	1,422

MOY CHURCH ILLUMINATION, MILTOWN MALBAY, CLARE	1,301
LIMERICK ARCHIVAL RECORD 1800 – 1900, LIMERICK	1,270
MILLENNIUM SUN DIAL, DERRINACHARA NATIONAL SCHOOL, CORK	1,270
SCULPTURE & MURAL, BALLYNARRY NATIONAL SCHOOL, CAVAN	1,270
HISTORY OF HOWTH / MALAHIDE PRESBYTERIAN CHURCH, DUBLIN	1,270
MILLENNIUM PAGEANT, GLENCULLEN , DUBLIN	1,207
SAINT PATRICK'S CHURCH ILLUMINATION, ROSSLARE HARBOUR, WEXFORD	1,136
MILLENNIUM CELEBRATION FOR SENIOR CITIZENS, TUBBERCURRY, SLIGO	952
CALASANTIUS COLLEGE TAPESTRY, GALWAY	952
KILRUSH COMMUNITY SCHOOL MILLENNIUM BOOK, CLARE	889
CHURCH OF THE IMMACULATE CONCEPTION ILLUMINATION, BALLYMORE EUSTACE, KILDARE	786
ANNAGRY'S CHURCH ILLUMINATION, DONEGAL	776
HOLY CROSS CHURCH ILLUMINATION, DUNFANAGHY, DONEGAL	584
SAINT MACHONOG'S CHURCH TOWER ILLUMINATION, KILMACANOGUE, WICKLOW	567

Millennium Recognition Awards

> The following is the list of 193 projects selected for funding under the Millennium Recognition Awards. The Awards were designed to recognise, build on or add value to existing community projects and to enable new projects to be developed. The Awards scheme was administered by Area Development Management Limited (ADM).

Millennium Committee Award €3,809, 214 (£3 million)

SMART (ST. MULLIN'S AMENITY & RECRET. TOURISM LTD). CARLOW. CULTURAL.
€12,071.16

TULLOW DAY CARE CENTRE (FOR THE ELDERLY) CARLOW. COMMUNITY.
€35,578.14

CROSSERLOUGH OLD SCHOOL REPAIR PROJECT COMMITTEE. CAVAN. COMMUNITY.
€20,965.69

BAILIEBORO DEVELOPMENT ASSOCIATION LTD CAVAN. COMMUNITY DEVELOPMENT.
€38,119.44

CASTLETARA COMMUNITY DEVELOPMENT CAVAN. CULTURAL.
€6,226.18

DOONBEG COMMUNITY DEVELOPMENT LTD CLARE. COMMUNITY RESOURCE.
€10,165.18

SHOOT THE SCATTERING TRUST (MCMAHON GROUP) CLARE. CULTURAL.
€40,660.74

CLARE HAVEN HOUSE PROJECT CLARE FAMILY SUPPORT.
€95,298.60

COMMUNITY ARTS & SPORTS EDUCATION (CASE) CLARE. COMMUNITY DEVELOPMENT.
€2,541.30

CLOUGHLEIGH DEVELOPMENT GROUP CLARE. COMMUNITY RESOURCE.
€23,506.99

CLARE MUSIC MAKERS PARENTS ASSOCIATION CLARE. CULTURAL.
€12,706.48

SCOIL SAMHRAIDH WILLIE CLANCY TEORANTA. CLARE. CULTURAL.
€8,894.54

TOGHER INTEGRATED DEVELOPMENT PROJECT. CORK. COMMUNITY RESOURCE.
€38,119.44

MAHON YOUTH DEVELOPMENT PROJECT CORK. COMMUNITY RESOURCE.
€33,036.85

BALLYPHEHAN/TOGHER COMMUNITY DEVELOPMENT PROJECT. CORK COMMUNITY DEVELOPMENT.
€4,447.27

BISHOPSTOWN COMMUNITY ASSOCIATION LIMITED. CORK. COMMUNITY RESOURCE.
€20,838.63

FERMOY CHORAL SOCIETY. CORK. CULTURAL.
€6,353.24

KNOCKRAHA AREA COMMUNITY ASSOCIATION CORK. COMMUNITY RESOURCE.
€7,623.89

BALLINCOLLIG SENIOR CITIZENS CLUB LTD. CORK. COMMUNITY RESOURCE.
€38,119.44

GLEN & DISTRICT NEIGHBOURHOOD YOUTH PROJECT. CORK. YOUTH.
€6,353.24

TULLYLEASE COMMUNITY COUNCIL. CORK. CULTURAL.
€3,811.94

CAIRDE CORCAÍ. CORK. SPECIAL INTEREST.
€12,706.48

BERE ISLAND PROJECTS GROUP. CORK. CULTURAL.
€76,238.88

BOHERBUE PARENT, BABY & TODDLER GROUP. CORK. FAMILY SUPPORT.
€25,412.96

KNOCKNAGREE MILLENNIUM COMMITTEE CORK. COMMUNITY RESOURCE.
€15,247.78

KANTURK & DISTRICT COMMUNITY COUNCIL LTD. CORK. COMMUNITY RESOURCE.
€9,529.86

JUBILEE BELLS. CORK. CULTURAL.
€4,447.27

SHANDON/NORTH CATHEDRAL COMMUNITY ASS. LTD. CORK. COMMUNITY DEVELOPMENT.
€9,529.86

STOP DRUGS NOW. CORK. ECONOMIC.
€10,165.18

SELECT VESTRY, ROSSNOWLAGH PARISH CHURCH. DONEGAL. COMMUNITY RESOURCE.
€21,601.02

ST. JOHNSTON LECTURE HALL MANAGEMENT COMMITTEE. DONEGAL. SPECIAL INTEREST.
€10,165.18

SWILLY MULROY COMMUNITY DEVELOPMENT PROJECT. DONEGAL. COMMUNITY DEVELOPMENT
€31,766.20

COUNTY DONEGAL CHORAL PROJECT. DONEGAL, CULTURAL.
€3,176.62

LEGHOWNEY COMMUNITY GROUP. DONEGAL. CULTURAL.
€2,318.93

COMHARCHUMANN FORBARTHA ARAINN MHOR. DONEGAL. CULTURAL.
€12,134.69

SOUTHSIDE WOMAN'S ACTION NETWORK. DUBLIN. COMMUNITY RESOURCE.
€12,706.48

MOUNT MERRION PARISH COMMUNITY CENTRE. DUBLIN. COMMUNITY DEVELOPMENT.
€25,412.96

LUCAN COMMUNITY COUNCIL. DUBLIN. ENVIRONMENT.
€3,811.94

DUBLIN CITYWIDE DRUGS CRISIS CAMPAIGN.DUBLIN 1. SPECIAL INTEREST.
€18,526.05

DUBLIN SIMON COMMUNITY. DUBLIN 1. SPECIAL INTEREST.
€29,224.90

SUNFLOWER RECYCLING (CITYLIFE). DUBLIN 1. ECONOMIC
€25,921.22

SPORTS AGAINST RACISM IN IRELAND LTD (S.A.R.I.). DUBLIN 1. URBAN. CULTURAL
€37,484.12

I.S.P. PLAY FACILITIES DEVELOPMENT GROUP. DUBLIN 1. FAMILY SUPPORT.
€18,424.40

ORCHARD COMMUNITY CENTRE. DUBLIN 10. COMMUNITY DEVELOPMENT.
€5,082.59

THE MILLENNIUM PROJECT GROUP. DUBLIN 10. ENVIRONMENT.
€6,900.89

SENIOR CITIZENS PARLIAMENT FINGLAS DIVISION. DUBLIN 11. COMMUNITY RESOURCE.
€3,811.94

FORUM FOR ARTS IN BALLYMUN. DUBLIN 11. YOUTH.
€48,919.95

ST. HELENA'S WOMEN'S AWARENESS GROUP. DUBLIN 11. FAMILY SUPPORT.
€39,358.32

FINGLAS SPORTS DEVELOPMENT GROUP. DUBLIN 11. COMMUNITY RESOURCE.
€3,811.94

CRUMLIN COMMUNITY YOUTH BAND. DUBLIN 12. YOUTH.
€5,082.59

TARGET. DUBLIN 13. COMMUNITY RESOURCE.
€6,353.24

CITY OF DUBLIN DIVISION, ST. JOHN AMBULANCE BRIGADE. DUBLIN 15. COMMUNITY RESOURCE.
€58,449.81

THE BLANCHARDSTOWN CENTRE FOR THE UNEMPLOYED. DUBLIN 15. COMMUNITY RESOURCE.
€25,412.96

BLANCHARDSTOWN YOUTH SERVICE. DUBLIN 15. YOUTH.
€29,828.46

NETWORKING DUBLIN 15. DUBLIN 15. COMMUNITY RESOURCE.
€10,165.18

LEICESTER CELTIC. DUBLIN 16. COMMUNITY RESOURCE.
€25,412.96

OUR LADYS SCHOOLS LOTTO COMMITTEE. DUBLIN 16. COMMUNITY RESOURCE.
€9,529.86

COMHARCHUMANN CUMARSÁIDE. DUBLIN 17. CULTURAL.
€1,270.65

PARENTS ALONE COMING TOGETHER (PACT). DUBLIN 17. FAMILY SUPPORT.
€2,541.30

ACTIVE AGE GROUP DARNDALE. DUBLIN 17. CULTURAL.
€6,353.24

STANHOPE GREEN SANCTUARY GARDEN PROJECT. DUBLIN 2. ENVIRONMENT.
€46,031.77

TEENAGE CARE DEVELOPMENT TRUST. DUBLIN 2. YOUTH.
€30,495.55

WALKINSTOWN ASSOCIATION FOR THE HANDICAPPED PEOPLE. DUBLIN 22. SPECIAL INTEREST.
€4,447.27

THE IRISH TRADITIONAL YOUTH BAND. DUBLIN 24. CULTURAL.
€3,176.62

TALLAGHT COMMUNITY ARTS CENTRE. DUBLIN 24. YOUTH.
€22,871.66

BEG BARROW AND STEAL THEATRE CO. DUBLIN 3. CULTURAL.
€17,789.07

COUNCIL FOR CO-ORDINATION OF SOCIAL SERVICES. DUBLIN 5. COMMUNITY DEVELOPMENT.
€56,670.90

SMASHING TIMES THEATRE COMPANY LTD. DUBLIN 7. CULTURAL.
€11,435.83

BALLYMUN ECHO. DUBLIN 7. CULTURAL.
€2,160.10

MERCY FAMILY CENTRE. DUBLIN 8. FAMILY SUPPORT.
€25,412.96

SWICN YOUTH SERVICES. DUBLIN 8. CULTURAL.
€6,353.24

BONE MARROW FOR LEUKAEMIA TRUST. DUBLIN 8. ALTERNATIVE INTEREST.
€38,119.44

ST JOHN OF GOD MENNI SERVICES. DUBLIN 8. SPECIAL INTEREST.
€25,412.96

THE FRANCISCAN SOCIAL JUSTICE INITIATIVES. DUBLIN 8. SPECIAL INTEREST.
€38,119.44

GLASNEVIN CORE GROUP. DUBLIN 9. CULTURAL.
€3,811.94

BALLINAKILL ACTIVE AGE CLUB. GALWAY. COMMUNITY RESOURCE.
€1,461.25

MAAM VALLEY CRAFT GROUP. GALWAY. CULTURAL.
€762.39

MONIVEA PARK RESIDENTS ASSOCIATION. GALWAY. COMMUNITY DEVELOPMENT.
€35,069.89

PARENTS AND FRIENDS ASSOCIATION. GALWAY. COMMUNITY RESOURCE.
€23,951.72

MAAM CHILDREN'S PLAYSCHEME. GALWAY. CULTURAL.
€25,412.96

WESTSIDE COMMUNITY RESOURCE & DEVELOPMENT CENTRE. GALWAY. YOUTH.
€5,082.59

LOUGHREA ATHLETIC CLUB. GALWAY. YOUTH.
€2,541.30

ORANMORE COMMUNITY DEVELOPMENT ASSOCIATION LTD. GALWAY. COMMUNITY DEVELOPMENT.
€3,811.94

GALWAY MOUNTAIN RESCUE TEAM. GALWAY. ALTERNATIVE INTEREST.
€35,578.14

GALWAY ADULT LITERACY GROUP LTD. GALWAY. COMMUNITY DEVELOPMENT.
€17,789.07

PORTUMNA CASTLE CRAFTS. GALWAY. CULTURAL.
€6,353.24

MOUNTBELLEW DISTRICT DEVELOPMENT ASSOCIATION. GALWAY. ENVIRONMENT.
€6,353.24

BEAGH RURAL DEVELOPMENT LTD. GALWAY. ENVIRONMENT.
€1,905.97

WOMEN OF NORTH EAST GALWAY. GALWAY. COMMUNITY RESOURCE.
€7,623.89

C.Y.M.S. COMMITTEE. KERRY. COMMUNITY RESOURCE.
€5,082.59

KERRY COUNTY NETWORK OF PEOPLE WITH DISABILITIES. KERRY. SPECIAL INTEREST.
€27,954.26

SNEEM DEVELOPMENT CO-OPERATIVE SOCIETY. KERRY. RURAL. COMMUNITY DEVELOPMENT.
€12,706.48

CAHERCIVEEN CELTIC MUSIC COMMITTEE. KERRY. CULTURAL.
€36,848.79

KILCUMMIN RECREATION HALL COMMITTEE. KERRY. COMMUNITY RESOURCE.
€3,811.94

CURA KERRY. KERRY. RURAL. FAMILY SUPPORT.
€73,697.59

TRALEE COMMUNITY DEVELOPMENT PROJECT. KERRY. COMMUNITY DEVELOPMENT.
€95,298.60

KILCUMMIN RURAL DEVELOPMENT LTD. KERRY. CULTURAL.
€4,447.27

TEMPLENOE COMMUNITY COUNCIL. KERRY. CULTURAL.
€2,541.30

THE RATHANGAN PARISH WELFARE ASSOCIATION. KILDARE. COMMUNITY RESOURCE.
€7,623.89

FAMILY ORIENTED COMMUNITY ACTIVE SCHEME (F.O.C.A.S). KILDARE. YOUTH.
€5,082.59

MONASTEREVAN MILLENNIUM COMMITTEE. KILDARE. CULTURAL.
€21,601.02

THE HUMPTY DUMPTY CLUB (PARENT & CHILD SUPPORT GROUP). KILDARE. FAMILY SUPPORT.
€986.02

CASTLEDERMOT COMMUNITY GAMES. KILDARE. YOUTH.
€3,176.62

KILKENNY TRAVELLERS WOMEN GROUP. KILKENNY. SPECIAL INTEREST.
€2,541.30

RIVER THROUGH TIME. KILKENNY. CULTURAL.
€34,307.50

MULLINAVAT WOMEN SHARED THREADS GROUP. KILKENNY. CULTURAL.
€635.32

GOWRAN DEVELOPMENT ASSOCIATION. KILKENNY. ENVIRONMENT.
€6,353.24

WINDGAP I.C.A. WOMEN'S GROUP. KILKENNY. FAMILY SUPPORT.
€27,954.26

NEWMARKET TIDY TOWNS AND COMMUNITY ARTS GROUP. KILKENNY. CULTURAL.
€32,401.52

LOUGHBOY AREA RESOURCE CENTRE. KILKENNY. COMMUNITY DEVELOPMENT.
€12,706.48

CULLOHILL MILLENNIUM COMMITTEE. LAOIS. ENVIRONMENT.
€3,811.94

MOUNTMELLICK DEVELOPMENT ASSOCIATION. LAOIS. CULTURAL.
€50,825.92

LAOIS YOUTH ARTS/LAOIS LEADER. LAOIS. YOUTH.
€69,885.64

ROSSINVER COMMUNITY DEVELOPMENT COMPANY LTD. LEITRIM. COMMUNITY DEVELOPMENT.
€12,706.48

BORNACOOLA COMMUNITY DEVELOPMENT. LEITRIM. CULTURAL.
€16,518.42

MOHILL TRAVELLERS DEVELOPMENT GROUP. LEITRIM. SPECIAL INTEREST.
€2,642.95

DRUMSHAMBO MILLENNIUM GROUP. LEITRIM. CULTURAL.
€6353.24

BEE PARK RESOURCE CENTRE. LEITRIM. YOUTH.
€12,706.48

ST MARY'S ARTS GROUP. LIMERICK. CULTURAL.
€13,977.13

OUR LADY'S OF LOURDES COMMUNITY SERVICES GROUP. LIMERICK. URBAN. COMMUNITY RESOURCE.
€15,247.78

RAHEEN MUNGRET CRECORA BOTHAR SUPPORT GROUP. LIMERICK. ALTERNATIVE INTEREST.
€15,883.10

SOUTHILL INTEGRATED DEVELOPMENT PROGRAMME (S.I.D.P.). LIMERICK. URBAN. COMMUNITY RESOURCE.
€33,799.24

NORTH CORK/SOUTH LIMERICK SPECIAL OLYMPICS. LIMERICK. SPECIAL INTEREST.
€2,541.30

NEWCASTLE WEST & AREA ARTS COMMITTEE. LIMERICK. CULTURAL.
€7,115.63

IRISH GIRL GUIDES. LIMERICK. URBAN. YOUTH.
€25,412.96

ST MUNCHIN'S SOCIAL EDUCATION YOUTH INITIATIVE. LIMERICK. YOUTH.
€1,270.65

CAHERCONLISH – CAHERLINE COMMUNITY COUNCIL LTD. LIMERICK. COMMUNITY RESOURCE.
€12,706.48

4TH YEAR CLASS VOCATIONAL SCHOOL. LONGFORD. ENVIRONMENT.
€2,541.30

COUNTY MARKETS HANDCRAFT ADVISORY COMMITTEE. LONGFORD. CULTURAL.
€5,082.59

KILLOE DEVELOPMENT GROUP. LONGFORD. CULTURAL.
€17,026.68

KENAGH COMMUNITY CO.-OPERATIVE SOCIETY LTD. LONGFORD. ECONOMIC.
€25,412.96

TALLANSTOWN YOUTH GROUP. LOUTH. CULTURAL.
€15,476.49

DROGHEDA COMMUNITY FORUM. LOUTH. CULTURAL.
€21,601.02

ANIMAL RESCUE CENTRE. LOUTH. ALTERNATIVE INTEREST.
€15,247.78

BLACKROCK MILLENNIUM PROJECT COMMITTEE. LOUTH. CULTURAL.
€41,931.39

MUIRHEVNAMORE COMMUNITY YOUTH PROJECT. LOUTH. YOUTH.
€3,073.70

BALLA TOWN PARK LTD. MAYO. ENVIRONMENT.
€75,857.69

LINENHALL ARTS CENTRE. MAYO. CULTURAL.
£44,472.68

KILMOVEE/URLAUR COMMUNITY COUNCIL. MAYO. CULTURAL.
€31,766.20

KNOCK AREA DEVELOPMENT ASSOCIATION. MAYO. COMMUNITY RESOURCE.
€25,412.96

CONG COMMUNITY DEVELOPMENT ASSOCIATION. MAYO. COMMUNITY RESOURCE.
€6,353.24

KILLALA CHRISTMAS LIGHTS COMMITTEE. MAYO. CULTURAL.
€6,353.24

SUMMERHILL ACTIVE RETIREMENT GROUP. MEATH. COMMUNITY RESOURCE.
€21,601.02

AMEN – NAVAN BRANCH. MEATH. ALTERNATIVE INTEREST.
€25,412.96

BATTERSTOWN VILLAGE ENHANCEMENT ASSOCIATION. MEATH. ENVIRONMENT.
€2,541.30

NORTH MEATH COMMUNITIES DEVELOPMENT ASSOCIATION. MEATH. SPECIAL INTEREST.
€6,353.24

ST. OLIVER PLUNKETT COMMUNITY CENTRE. MEATH. COMMUNITY DEVELOPMENT.
€57,179.16

MONAGHAN DRAMATIC SOCIETY. MONAGHAN. CULTURAL.
€5,082.59

DONAGHMOYNE COMMUNITY DEVELOPMENT CO. LTD. MONAGHAN. COMMUNITY RESOURCE.
€25,412.96

LEITRIM COMMUNITY DEVELOPMENT ASSOCIATION. MONAGHAN. COMMUNITY DEVELOPMENT.
€6,099.11

FARNEY COMMUNITY RESOURCE AND INFORMATION CENTRE. MONAGHAN. COMMUNITY RESOURCE.
€12,706.48

ST. MARY'S YOUTH CENTRE. OFFALY. YOUTH.
€19,059.72

OFFALY MENTALLY HANDICAPPED ASSOCIATION. OFFALY. SPECIAL INTEREST.
€7,623.89

OFFALY HISTORICAL AND ARCHAEOLOGICAL SOCIETY. OFFALY. CULTURAL.
€7,623.89

TULLAMORE TRAVELLERS MOVEMENT. OFFALY. SPECIAL INTEREST.
€4,858.96

TULSK ACTION GROUP LTD. ROSCOMMON. CULTURAL.
€25,412.96

ELPHIN AREA COMMUNITY ENTERPRISE LTD. ROSCOMMON. CULTURAL.
€54,637.87

KILBRIDE COMMUNITY CENTRE COMPANY LTD. ROSCOMMON. COMMUNITY RESOURCE.
€25,412.96

KEADUE DEVELOPMENT ASSOCIATION. ROSCOMMON. COMMUNITY DEVELOPMENT.
€63,532.24

O'CAROLAN INTERNATIONAL HARP FESTIVAL COMMITTEE. ROSCOMMON. CULTURAL.
€16,518.42

ST. MICHAEL'S FAMILY LIFE CENTRE. SLIGO. COMMUNITY DEVELOPMENT.
€15,025.41

WOMEN AWAKE GROUP. SLIGO. COMMUNITY RESOURCE.
€2,265.57

KEASH COMMUNITY DEVELOPMENT GROUP. SLIGO. CULTURAL.
€5,082.59

MOYTURA 2000 STEERING GROUP. SLIGO. CULTURAL.
€12,706.48

MCR COMMUNITY CENTRE COMMITTEE. SLIGO. COMMUNITY DEVELOPMENT.
€12,706.48

COOLANEY COMMUNITY COUNCIL. SLIGO. COMMUNITY RESOURCE.
€2,541.30

C.J. KICKHAM BRASS AND REED BAND. TIPPERARY. CULTURAL.
€10,800.51

CAPPAGHWHITE COMMUNITY COUNCIL. TIPPERARY. RURAL. COMMUNITY RESOURCE.
€19,059.72

THE BRIDEWELL CENTRE. TIPPERARY. CULTURAL.
€3,811.94

CULLEN DEVELOPMENT ASSOCIATION MILLENNIUM PROJECT. TIPPERARY. SPECIAL INTEREST.
€5,082.59

GLENGOOLE COMMUNITY DEVELOPMENT GROUP. TIPPERARY. ENVIRONMENT.
€2,541.30

CLONMEL TASK FORCE. TIPPERARY. CULTURAL.
€7,623.89

ST. DECLAN'S MILLENNIUM COMMITTEE, ARDMORE. WATERFORD. CULTURAL.
€5,082.59

WATERFORD FOROIGE. WATERFORD. YOUTH.
€5,717.92

WATERFORD AREA MUSEUM SOCIETY. WATERFORD. CULTURAL.
€3,811.94

WATERFORD ACCESS SUPPORT PROGRAMME (W.A.S.P.). WATERFORD. URBAN. YOUTH.
€26,302.41

DUNMORE EAST MEMORIAL COMMITTEE. WATERFORD. RURAL. CULTURAL.
€6,353.24

CITY OF WATERFORD BRASS. WATERFORD. CULTURAL.
€19,059.72

ATHLONE YOUTH COMMUNITY PROJECT. WESTMEATH. CULTURAL.
€7,623.89

MOYVORE MUINTIR COUNCIL. WESTMEATH. COMMUNITY RESOURCE.
€12,706.48

CASTLEPOLLARD YOUTH CLUB. WESTMEATH. YOUTH.
€1,270.65

IRISH WHEELCHAIR ASSOCIATION. WESTMEATH. SPECIAL INTEREST.
€25,412.96

MULLINGAR TRAINING DEVELOPMENT AGENCY. WESTMEATH. RURAL. COMMUNITY RESOURCE.
€52,096.57

BUNCLODY SWIMMING POOL COMMITTEE. WEXFORD. RURAL. COMMUNITY RESOURCE.
€29,224.90

WEXFORD ARTS CENTRE. WEXFORD. CULTURAL.
€16,518.42

KILMORE QUAY COMMUNITY DEVELOPMENT ASSOCIATION. WEXFORD. COMMUNITY DEVELOPMENT.
€25,412.96

ENNISCORTHY FILM PROJECT. WEXFORD. RURAL. CULTURAL. £14,000

BRAY CANCER SUPPORT & INFORMATION CENTRE. WICKLOW. SPECIAL INTEREST.
€19,059.72

WICKLOW WORKING TOGETHER LTD. WICKLOW. YOUTH.
€32,719.19

CARNEW COMMUNITY CARE. WICKLOW. COMMUNITY RESOURCE.
€36,213.47

BRAY MILLENNIUM JAZZ FESTIVAL 2000. WICKLOW. CULTURAL.
€31,766.20

BRAY SCHOOL PROJECT ASSOCIATION. WICKLOW. CULTURAL.
€25,412.96

TINAHELY COURTHOUSE LTD. WICKLOW. CULTURAL.
€7,369.76

Millennium Events Awards

> The following is the full list of the original 1,959 Millennium Events Awards approved by the National Millennium Committee. The Awards were funded by the Millennium Committee on the basis of matching funding. The Awards were administered by the relevant Local Authority through the appointed Millennium Officers. The following list is of the recipients and of the events involved. Support from the Millennium Committee for the events varied from €253 (£200) to €5,078 (£4,000). The events took place in 1999, 2000 and 2001.

Please Note This is the list of Awards made in 1999. Subsequently, slight variations may have occurred and some projects may have been withdrawn and others added.

CO. CARLOW
MILLENNIUM OFFICER: BERNIE O'BRIEN

ARDATTIN TIDY VILLAGE: ERECTION OF GRANITE MILLENNIUM CANDLE IN CHURCH GROUNDS.

BALLON RATHOE DEVELOPMENT ASSOCIATION: "MILLENNIUM CLOCK" – VILLAGE CENTRE.

BORRIS BELFRY RESTORATION MILLENNIUM PROJECT: "MILLENNIUM BELFRY" – BELL RESTORATION.

BORRIS DEVELOPMENT COMMITTEE: FLOODLIGHTING OF BORRIS VIADUCT.

FEILE AND FHOMHAIR: "FEILE 2000" – AUTUMN FESTIVAL PROMOTING THE IRISH LANGUAGE.

FRIENDS OF THE ELDERLY DISTRICT HOSPITAL: "MILLENNIUM GARDEN OVERLOOKING HOSPICE ROOMS.

CO. CARLOW WHEELCHAIR ASSOCIATION: MILLENNIUM RECOGNITION AWARDS.

EIGSE CARLOW ARTS: ARTS FESTIVAL TO CELEBRATE THE NEW MILLENNIUM.

YOUNG ARTISTS CHOIR: "MILLENNIUM MELODIES" – 100 VOICES FROM JUNIOR, SENIOR AND CHAMBER ENSEMBLE- IN CARLOW CATHEDRAL.

CARLOW CHORAL SOCIETY: "ELIJAH 2000 – MENDELSSOHN FOR THE MILLENNIUM".

CARLOW STAGE SCHOOL: "MILLENNIUM VARIETY" FEATURING 340 CHILDREN.

WRITER'S GROUP C/O SEAMUS O'ROURKE: "STORIES OF THE MILLENNIUM".

CARLOW MILLENNIUM COMMITTEE: "MILLENNIUM CAPSULE" – COMMUNITY PROJECT IN CONJUNCTION WITH SCHOOLCHILDREN.

METHODIST COMMUNITY: FLOODLIGHTING OF CARLOW METHODIST CHURCH.

PRESENTATION STUDENTS: EVENT TO PROMOTE PEACE & UNDERSTANDING.

CARRIGDUFF DEVELOPMENT: "MILLENNIUM GREEN" – AMENITY PROJECT.

KEEP CLONEGAL TIDY COMMITTEE: CONVERSATION OF DERELICT VILLAGE PIG HOUSE TO CHILDREN'S PLAY AREA.

HACKETSTOWN COMM. DEV.: "MILLENNIUM WALK" – AMENITY PROJECT.

LEIGHLINBRIDGE IMPROVEMENT GROUP: "MILLENNIUM GARDEN" – AMENITY PROJECT.

LEIGHLIN PARISH PASTORAL COUNCIL: RECOGNITION TO MERCY ORDER IN LEIGHLIN.

DUNLECKNEY GROUP OF PARISHES: FLOODLIGHTING OF ST. MARY'S CHURCH.

MILLENNIUM COMMITTEE: "MILLENNIUM ECUMENICAL SERVICE".

MILLENNIUM COMMITTEE: "MILLENNIUM RIVER / MUSIC FESTIVAL".

MILLENNIUM COMMITTEE: "MILLENNIUM STREET PUPPET THEATRE".

MILLENNIUM COMMITTEE: "MILLENNIUM CRAFTS" EXHIBITION.

MILLENNIUM COMMITTEE: "MILLENNIUM PARK" – AMENITY PROJECT.

MYSHALL NATIONAL SCHOOL PARENT TEACHER ASSOC: SCHOOL MURAL INVOLVING 101 CHILDREN.

FOROIGE CLUB: "MILLENNIUM TIME CAPSULE".

MYSHALL I.C.A.: "MILLENNIUM RURAL SHOW".

SENIOR CITIZEN'S COMMITTEE: "SENIOR CITIZENS MILLENNIUM MEMORIES" – RECEPTION.

RATHVILLY COMMUNITY COUNCIL: "MILLENNIUM WALK" – AMENITY PROJECT.

ROYAL OAK DEVELOPMENT: "MILLENNIUM OAKS" – AMENITY PROJECT.

TULLOW DAY CARE CENTRE: RECEPTION TO RECOGNISE SENIOR CITIZENS.

TULLOW VARIETY GROUP: CONCERT TO CELEBRATE MILLENNIUM.

TOPS OF THE TOWN: "CARLOW MILLENNIUM TOPS" – MUSIC/DRAMA EVENT.

TULLOW COMMUNITY DEVELOPMENT INITIATIVE: "MILLENNIUM WALK" – COMMUNITY PROJECT.

CO. CAVAN
MILLENNIUM OFFICER: SEAMUS NEELY

CORNAFEAN G.F.C, BRUS, ARVA: FUNCTION TO COMMEMORATE JOHN JOE O'REILLY.

LAVEY COMMUNITY GROUP, LEITER, POLES: EVENT AND SHOW FEATURING ALL AGES FROM AREA.

MILLTOWN NATIONAL SCHOOL, BELTURBET: COMPILE BOOK BASED ON FOUR LOCAL SCHOOLS.

CAVAN MILLENNIUM CELEBRATIONS COMMITTEE: TO STAGE CELTIC MILLENNIUM EXPERIENCE.

CAVAN MUSICAL SOCIETY, KILGARRY, CAVAN: LOCAL CAST AND STUDENTS IN MUSICAL SHOW.

P.J. DUNNE, DRUMELIS, CAVAN: BOOK ON CO. CAVAN FEATURING OLD POSTCARDS.

GREAGHRAHAN NATIONAL SCHOOL, STAGHALL, BELTURBET: PROJECT ENTITLED OUR HERITAGE.

CAVAN AMATEUR BOXING CLUB: HOSTING OF SPECIAL BOXING TOURNAMENT.

CORNAFEAN VINTAGE PLOUGHING ASSOCIATION: EVENT 'CAPTURING THE PAST TO BUILD A NEW FUTURE.'

ST. CLARE'S COLLEGE, BALLYJAMESDUFF: PERFORMANCE BY STUDENTS.

CAVAN G.A.A. SUPPORTERS CLUB: LOCALS SELECT TEAM OF THE MILLENNIUM.

BALLYHUGH ART AND CULTURAL CENTRE, BALLYHUGH, BALLYCONNELL: RE-ENACTMENT OF LIFESTYLES AT TURN OF CENTURY.

BALLYJAMES DUFF CULTURAL CLUB: HISTORICAL PAGENT DEPICTING HISTORY OF CAVAN.

BALLYCONNELL COMMUNITY THEATRE: MODERN INTERPRETATION OF THE PUBLIC LIFE OF CHRIST.

CAVAN PARISH MILLENNIUM COMMITTEE: DISPLAY OF MILLENNIUM ARTWORK.

KNOCKBRIDE VINTAGE AND HERITAGE COMMITTEE: A MILLENNIUM OF WHEEL TRANSPORT IN IRELAND.

MILLENNIUM COMMITTEE, ROSEHILL, MULLAGH: EXHIBITION OF VIDEO, FILM, PHOTOGRAPHS.

MAUDABAWN COMMUNITY ALERT, DOOHALLET, SHERCOCK: COMMUNITY EVENT FEATURING MUSIC AND STORY-TELLING.

MOYNEHALL SET DANCERS: LAST CÉILÍ OF THE MILLENNIUM.

MASIE SMITH, STRADONE: MILLENNIUM BASH FOR THE GOLDEN OLDIES.

LARAGH AREA DEVELOPMENT GROUP: PHOTOGRAPHING ALL THE PEOPLE IN THE PARISH.

KILLESHANDRA COMMUNITY COUNCIL: EVENT CELEBRATING LOCAL HISTORY.

CAVAN FAMILY RESOURCE GROUP: THE FAMILY-THE NEW MILLENNIUM.

MARTIN DONOHOE, SWELLAN UPPER, CAVAN: "MUSIC IN DRUMLINS" PROJECT.

FR. LIAM KELLY, CASTLETARA, BALLYHAISE: "RESTORING JUSTICE-LIVING THE JUBILEE".

CUILCHA WALKER, MONAGHCASHEL, BLACKLION: CUILCHA WALKERS MILLENNIUM CELEBRATION.

CAVAN PARISH MILLENNIUM COMMITTEE: DISPLAY IN CATHEDRAL OF OBJECTS OF HISTORICAL INTEREST.

DRUMGOON COMMUNITY CENTRE, COOTEHILL: DOCUMENTING A RURAL ENVIRONMENT.

CAVAN FOROIGE DISTRICT COUNCIL: WORKSHOPS ON CHALLENGES OF NEW MILLENNIUM.

MARGARET MATTHEWS, DUNANCORY, VIRGINIA: WINDOW DISPLAYS AND MERIT AWARDS FOR ELDERLY.

CAVAN FEDERATION OF THE ICA: CELEBRATION 'A STEP INTO THE NEW MILLENNIUM'.

COMHALTAS CEOLTÓIRÍ ÉIREANN, COOTEHILL BRANCH: A CELEBRATION OF THE MILLENNIUM FEATURING TRADITIONAL MUSIC AND SONG.

SILLAN COMMUNITY PLAYERS, GLASLECK, SHERCOCK: PRODUCTION OF "SON OF MAN" BY DENIS POTTER.

VIRGINIA HERITAGE GROUP: PRODUCTION OF MILLENNIUM CALANDER.

SELECT VESTRY, KILMORE CATHEDRAL: FLOWER FESTIVAL AND EXHIBITION.

PHILIP CLARKE, CAVAN TRADITIONAL MILLENNIUM COMMITTEE: PRESERVING

UNPUBLISHED MATERIAL ABOUT TRADITIONAL MUSIC .

KILLYGARRY MILLENNIUM COMMITTEE, EDENTICLARE: SENIOR CITIZEN PARTY.

BUTLERSBRIDGE MILLENNIUM COMMITTEE: RE-UNION FOR ALL ASSOCIATED WITH THE AREA.

MAUDABAWN MILLENNIUM EVENT: SCHOOLCHILDREN RECORD PRESENT-DAY SOCIETY THROUGH VIDEO AND PRINT.

CAVAN MILLENNIUM FESTIVAL: CHORAL CONCERT IN CAVAN CATHEDRAL.

COOTEHILL TIDY TOWNS: EVENT TO RECOGNISE CONTRIBUTION OF SENIOR CITIZENS.

PERCY FRENCH FESTIVAL: ART EXHIBITION CELEBRATING FAMOUS CAVAN EMIGRANTS.

CASTLETARA CHURCH AND SCHOOL COMMITTEE: FUNCTION TO MARK RE-DEDICATION OF ST. PATRICK'S CHURCH.

BALLINAGH CHRISTMAS LIGHTS COMMITTEE: EVENT ASSOCIATED WITH SWITCHING ON OF FESTIVE LIGHTS.

MARGARET KELLY, HIGHFIELD ROAD, CAVAN: MILLENNIUM EVENTS LINKED TO ST. PATRICK'S DAY PARADE.

KINGSCOURT COMMUNITY DEV. COUNCIL: EVENT CENTRED ON A MUSIC AND RECREATIONAL THEME.

ERNE RALLY COMMITTEE, BELTURBET: BOAT RALLY AND AERIAL DISPLAY.

DRUMLANE G.F.C., KILCONNY, BELTURBET: SERIES OF NIGHT'S OUT FOR SENIOR CITIZENS.

BELTURBET INLAND WATERWAY ASSOCIATION: BOAT TRIPS TO LOUGH OUGHTER CASTLE AND HISTORIC RE-ENACTMENTS.

REDHILLS DEVELOPMENT ASSOCIATION: HISTORY OF KILLOUGHTER PARISH.

WESLIAN METHODISTCHAPEL, BALLIEBOROUGH: HISTORY OF METHODIST RELIGION IN CAVAN.

BALLYHAISE G.F.C.: PRESENTATION TO FOOTBALLERS OF THE DECADES.

LACKEN G.F.C.: HONOURING PLAYERS OF THE PAST.

BELTURBET TRADER'S ASSOCIATION: ENHANCING AMBIENCE OF THE TOWN.

BELTURBET FESTIVAL COMMITTEE: SPECIAL MILLENNIUM INPUT FOR FESTIVAL.

COOTEHILL TRADER'S ASSOCIATION: PROVISON OF YEAR 2000 LIGHTING.

COOTEHILL CHAMBER OF COMMERCE: GALA MILLENNIUM BALL.

IRISH WHEELCHAIR ASSOCIATION: HONOURING PEOPLE INVOLVED IN DISABILITY.

VOCATIONAL SCHOOL, VIRGINIA: MILLENNIUM BOOK.

KILLYCONNAN NATIONAL SCHOOL: PICTURES FOR THE MILLENNIUM BY PUPILS.

COOTEHILL ARTS FESTIVAL: MILLENNIUM ARTS FESTIVAL.

PATRICK J. CORRIGAN P.P., BELTURBET: PARISH RE-UNION EVENT.

ST. PATRICK'S COLLEGE, CAVAN: CHORAL ORCHESTRAL CONCERT.

SHERCOCK TOWN DEVELOPMENT: GALA EVENT FOR YOUNG PEOPLE.

BALLYHAISE CAMOGIE CLUB: RE-UNION OF 1968 COUNTY FINAL TEAMS.

CO. CLARE
MILLENNIUM OFFICER: MAÍRÍN HILL

MRS ANNETTE CLEARY KILMIHIL: PUBLIC NOVENA FOLLOWING THE RESTORATION OF ST. MICHAEL'S SHRINE.

TULLA MILLENNIUM COMMITTEE: COMPETITION FOR THE DESIGN OF A TULLA "CREST".

TOM GLYNN, ENNIS, PAT MURPHY, SIXMILEBRIDGE: QUADRANGULAR / TRIANGULAR CLARE MILLENNIUM CUP.

LISDOONVARNA COMMUNITY COUNCIL LTD: MILLENNIUM TIME CAPSULE COMPETITION.

CLLR. PAUL EDSON, KILRUSH: KILRUSH MILLENNIUM FESTIVAL.

FLOATING THEATRE COMPANY: "THE MILLENNIUM VOYAGE" IN MOUNTSHANNON AND CHILDREN'S PAGEANT.

EAST CLARE DEVELOPMENT ASSOCIATION, FEAKLE: EXHIBITION COVERING THE LAST 150 YEARS.

R.N.L.I. LIFEBOATS "LOCAL BRANCHES": CLARE'S TRADITIONAL MILLENNIUM TRIBUTE TO THE LIFEBOATS.

MILLENNIUM COMMITTEE SHANNON: MILLENNIUM CELEBRATIONS PARADE.

ANNAGH N.S.: VIDEO AND BOOK TO CELEBRATE SCHOOLS 100 YEARS.

ENNIS ARTS INITIATIVE: DIGITAL VIDEO PROJECTION.

MULLAGH BRIDGE CLUB: SENIOR CITIZENS PARTY.

CLARE AUDIO AND SOUND PROJECT: EVENTS, INCLUDING FOOTBALL AND CYCLING, AT SPANISH POINT.

EAST CLARE HERITAGE CO.: "O'GRADY" CLANRALLY.

BRIDGETOWN TIDY TOWNS ASSOC.: PLANTING SHRUBS AND FLOWERS.

WILLIE MCGRATH, KILKEE: WEST CLARE CANCER SUPPORT GROUP MINI MARATHON.

FR. PASCAL HANRAHAN, KILRUSH: FESTIVAL OF SACRED MUSIC.

CLONFERT TO MOUNT BRANDON 2000 MILLENNIUM PILGRIMAGE: WALK FROM CLONFERT TO BRANDON THROUGH PARTS OF CO. CLARE.

PETER KEANE, ENNIS: "THE GATHERING" – 21ST CENTURY CLARE – MILLENNIUM VIDEO.

TRADITIONAL FESTIVAL, ENNIS: ENNIS TRADITIONAL FESTIVAL.

CARRIGAHOLT PARISH MILLENNIUM COMMITTEE: MILLENNIUM ALBUM, OUTDOOR CRIB AND CHIME BELLS.

MILLENNIUM COMMITTEE, MULLAGH: MASS FOR DECEASED MEMBERS OF MULLAGH & QUILTY SETS.

QUILTY ACTION GROUP: OFFICIAL OPENING OF RECREATION AREA.

CREE DEVELOPMENT ASSOCIATION: SENIOR CITIZENS PARTY MASS & SOCIAL EVENING.

CLARECASTLE DAY CARE CENTRE: SENIOR CITIZENS PERFORMING IN A MILLENNIUM CONCERT.

KILLALOE DIOCESAN MILLENNIUM COMMITTEE: NUMBER OF EVENTS INCLUDING WATER & LIGHT CEREMONY AND YOUTH ROCK MASS.

KILRUSH CHAMBER OF COMMERCE: EVENT TO CELEBRATE THE MARITIME & MARKET HERITAGE OF KILRUSH.

COIS NA HABHNA TRAD: MUSIC ARCHIVE, ENNIS. CONCERT.

DENIS LIDDY, ENNIS: CD – BAREFIELD N.S., CONCERT

BILLY LOUGHNAN, CAHER: THEATRICAL PROD-UCTION HONOURING POET BRIAN MERRIMAN.

ENNISTYMON & DISTRICT BRANCH CCE: "MILLENNIUM FEILE" TRAD. NIGHT

AN FHEILE, SCOIL DRAMAIOCHTA DON MHILAOIS, RAE NA GEISEACH, CILLMHAILE, INIS: FESTIVAL OF SCHOOLS DRAMA IN IRISH.

KNOCK COMMUNITY GROUP: OFFICIAL OPENING OF NEW PIER IN VILLAGE.

BALLYEA PARISH COUNCIL: MUSICAL EVENING.

MARY HOGAN, KILCRONA, KILKEE: RESEARCH LOCAL HISTORY.

FR. PATRICK CARMODY P.P., COORACLARE: RESTORATION OF OUR LADY'S WELL.

CAROLINE RYAN, QUIN: ERECTION OF CELTIC CROSS.

IRISH WHEELCHAIR ASSOCIATION: SPECIAL RECOGNITION AWARDS.

JOHN DEELY, KILRUSH: OPENING OF BLESSED WELL IN TULLYCRINE.

EAST CLARE ACCESSIBLE TRANSPORT: COMMUNITY TRANSPORT CONFERENCE AND WORKSHOPS.

TUBBER GAA & COMMUNITY DEV. COMMITTEE, TUBBER: OFFICIAL OPENING OF GROUNDS AND NEW INDOOR SPORTS FACILITIES.

COOLEEN BRIDGE SCHOOL, TUAMGRANE: BRINGING CHILDREN AND THE ELDERLY TOGETHER.

KILMIHIL COMMUNITY DEV. LTD.: MILLENNIUM WEBSITE, DESIGN AND ESTABLISH.

DOMHNALL O'LOINSIGH, INIS: "FEILE NA H-INSE 2000".

DOONBEG DRAMA FESTIVAL, DOONBEG: DRAMA FESTIVAL, ART & PHOTOGRAPHIC EXHIBITION.

BIRDWATCH IRELAND: ALL IRELAND CONFERENCE ON BIRDS .

BROADFORD DEVELOPMENT ASSOC.: RELIGIOUS & ECUMENICAL THEME.

COROFIN DRAMATIC SOCIETY: COLOURFUL STREET PAGEANT.

COORACLARE NATIONAL SCHOOL: SPECIAL EDITION OF PARISH MAGAZINE.

IRISH CHAMBER ORCHESTRA, UNIVERSITY OF LIMERICK: CLASSICAL MUSIC FESTIVAL .

ST. FLANNAN'S COLLEGE, ENNIS: IMPROVEMENT WORKS TO GROUNDS AND WALKS.

LISSYCASEY DEVELOPMENT ASSOCIATION: SENIOR CITIZENS PARTY, MASS AND SOCIAL EVENING.

CLARE COUNTY COUNCIL: OFFICIAL OPENING OF COUNTRY MUSEUM.

CLARE COUNTY COUNCIL: OFFICIAL OPENING OF ENNIS SWIMMING POOL.

CLARE COUNTY COUNCIL: "HISTORY OF LOCAL GOVERNMENT IN CO. CLARE 1899-1999".

CLARE COUNTY COUNCIL: OFFICIAL OPENING OF SIXMILEBRIDGE CONSERVATION PROJECT.

CLARE COUNTY COUNCIL: PROJECT COMMEM-ORATING ANNIVERSARY OF THE BIRTH OF CHRIST.

CO. CORK
MILLENNIUM OFFICER: IAN MCDONAGH

PARISH OF ALLIHIES BEARA: ECUMENICAL SERVICE AND ERECTION OF A CROSS.

ALLIHIES COMMUNITY CARE: MASS FOLLOWED BY A MEAL AND SOCIAL EVENING FOR SENIOR CITIZENS.

COMHARCUMANN CHLEIRE TEO: CLEAN UP AND FLOWER PLANTING OF THE NORTH HARBOUR.

CAPE CLEAR ISLAND MUSEUM: EXHIBITION DEPICTING THE EARLY CHRISTIANISING ACTIVITY OF ST. CIARAN.

CUMAN NA CROISE DEIRGE: SÍLE UÍ CEADAGÁIN – OILEÁN CHLEIRE. OUTING FOR ELDERLY ON THE ISLAND.

DAY CARE CENTRE – ST. JOSEPH'S HOSPITAL SKIBBEREEN: PUBLICATION OF "THINGS I HAVE SEEN…." A COMPILATION OF STORIES.

SKIBBEREEN BUSINESS PROMOTIONS: POPULATION JOIN HANDS FORMING A CIRCLE OF PEOPLE A MILE LONG.

WEST CORK ARTS CENTRE: MILLENNIUM ARTS WEEK, TRADITIONAL KNOW-HOW PROJECT: RECONSTRUCTING THE ENVIRONMENT, FLORA, FAUNA, AGRICULTURE, CRAFTS, COOKING TRADITIONS AND LOCAL HISTORY.

WEST CORK ARTS CENTRE: CHRISTIAN MILLENNIUM EXHIBITION.

FRIENDS OF SKIBBEREEN DAY-CARE CENTRE: WRITING A BOOK INCORPORATING THE LIFETIMES OF THOSE WHO ATTEND THE CENTRE.

MILLENNIUM GOLDEN YEARS ART FESTIVAL: ARTS FESTIVAL FOCUSING ON THE WORK OF RETIRED PEOPLE.

SCHULL SPRING MEITHEAL: ARTS FESTIVAL, INCLUDING WORKSHOPS, LECTURES AND PERFORMANCES.

SULT SCOIL MHUIRE – SCHULL: STREET THEATRE PROJECT.

DRIMOLEAGUE COMMUNITY DEV. ASSOCIATION: MILLENNIUM RECEPTION FOR SENIOR CITIZENS.

FRIENDS OF ST. JOSEPH'S HOSPITAL: MASS AND DAY OF MUSIC, DANCE AND STORY TELLING FOR RESIDENTS.

AIDEEN MCCARTHY – THE WARNER CENTRE: THE "PATRICK'S MILLENNIUM PARADE BANTRY"

KILCROHANE DEVELOPMENT ASSOC.: MILLENNIUM REGISTER CATALOGUING THE DEMOGRAPHICS OF THE TOWN.

CAPTAIN FRANCIS O'NEILL MEMORIAL COMPANY: TO ERECT MONUMENT COMMEMORATING CAPT FRANCIS O'NEILL.

WEST CORK MUSIC LTD: THREE CONCERTS IN COMMEMORATION OF JOHANN SEBASTIAN BACH.

BALTIMORE, RATH, SHERKIN & CLEIRE COMMUNITY COUNCIL: MILLENNIUM PAGEANT AND CHILDREN'S DRAMA.

RATHBARRY TIDY TOWNS: CELEBRATION TO LAUNCH THE NEWLY RESTORED "SPRIGGING SCHOOL".

ARDFIELD OLD GRAVE YARD MILLENNIUM RESTOR-ATION PROJECT: CREATE A SMALL SCALE PLAN OF THE GRAVEYARD AND PLACE A SMALL WOODEN CROSS ON EACH OF THE UNMARKED GRAVES.

CLONAKILTY MILLENNIUM COMMITTEE: MILLENNIUM AWARDS FOR INDIVIDUALS WHO HAVE CONTRIBUTED TO THE TOWN.

MIDLETON TIDY TOWNS: FLORAL DISPLAYS TO MARK THE MILLENNIUM.

BRINGING THE BIBLE TO LIFE CHRISTINE HILLIARD – MIDLETON: LARGE DISPLAY UNITS FILLED WITH AUTHENTIC ARTEFACTS DEPICTING LIFE IN BIBLICAL TIMES.

TRACTON COMMUNITY ASSOCIATION: RIVER WALK AND MILLENNIUM FESTIVAL SET IN A VILLAGE THEME.

MILLENNIUM CROSS – MINANE BRIDGE: ERECT MILLENNIUM CROSS IN CEMETERY.

MACROOM MILLENNIUM COMMITTEE: MILLENNIUM ST. PATRICK'S WEEKEND FESTIVAL.

CANOVEE PANTOMIME GROUP: SINGING IN THE NEW YEAR.

KILBRITTAIN TIDY TOWNS ASSOC.: ERECTION OF SUNDIAL AT THE END OF VILLAGE.

LISLEVANE COMMUNITY ASSOC.: ERECTION OF MILLENNIUM STONE AT CENTRE OF VILLAGE.

TOP OF THE HILL RESIDENTS ASSOC. COBH: STREET CARNIVAL ON NEW YEAR'S EVE .

TOWER COMMUNITY DEVELOPMENT ASSOC: A REPLICA STONE TOWER AT THE ENTRANCE TO THE VILLAGE.

CHERNOBYL CHILDREN'S PROJECT: MILLENNIUM CONVOY TO BELARUS.

NORA BRETT, LADYSBRIDGE: A MILLENNIUM CHRISTMAS PARTY FOR CHILDREN.

KINSALE U.D.C.: ERECT SCULPTURE BASED ON THEME OF BIRDS.

RATHPEACON COMMUNITY ASSOC.: DEVELOPMENT OF OPEN AIR FACILITY.

BALLINCOLLIG HURLING & FOOTBALL CLUB: PLANTING OF MILLENNIUM TREES.

CORRIN CROSS MILLENNIUM PROJECT: HIGHLIGHT CORRIN CROSS AS A COMMUNITY FACILITY.

BALLYHOOLY TIDY TOWNS: AN CLADH DUBH LOCAL AMENITY WALK.

BANTEER COMMUNITY SPORTSFIELD LTD.: WELCOME HOME WEEKEND AND THE OPENING OF BANTEER MILLENNIUM PARK.

GLEN THEATRE: ARTS AND DRAMA FESTIVAL TO PROMOTE DRAMA FOR CHILDREN.

CASTLELYONS COMMUNITY COUNCIL: MILLENNIUM PAGEANT OF TIME PAST.

CASTLELYONS COMMUNITY COUNCIL: VISITING OLDER PEOPLE AND ORGANISING SOCIAL EVENINGS.

BALLYHEA MILLENNIUM COMMITTEE: SCULPTURE IN CHURCH YARD AND SUPPORT PARISH IN AFRICA. PLANTING 1,000 TREES.

COLÁISTE AN CHRAOBHÍN / OPENMIND THEATRE: ANTHOLOGY OF PROSE AND POETRY PRESENTED BY STUDENTS AND TEACHERS.

I.C.A. GLANWORTH: BOOK CONTAINING HISTORY THOUGH THE MEMORIES OF SENIOR CITIZENS.

RAHAN HISTORICAL GROUP: COMPILING A BOOK ON THE LOCAL AREA.

KILDORRERY COMMUNITY DEVELOPMENT LTD: HONOUR PEOPLE IN THE PARISH.

BALLINDANGAN MILLENNIUM FLOWER FESTIVAL COMMITTEE: FESTIVAL WITH THEME OF CHRIST YESTERDAY, TODAY AND FOREVER.

MITCHELSTOWN PARISH MILLENNIUM COMMITTEE: PROCESSION TO THE ANCIENT ABBEY OF ST. FANAHAN AT BRIGOWN.

KILKORREY HISTORICAL SOCIETY: MEMORIAL TREES AND TIME CAPSULE ON THE ROADSIDE BETWEEN FARRAHY AND ROCKMILLS.

KNOCKNAGREE MILLENNIUM COMMITTEE: PROVIDE A VARIETY OF EVENTS FOR THE COMMUNITY.

CORK POPS ORCHESTRA: MILLENNIUM TEA DANCES FOR SENIOR CITIZENS IN YOUGHAL, BANTRY AND MALLOW.

IRISH WHEELCHAIR ASSOCIATION: SPECIAL RECOGNITION AWARDS.

CORK CITY
MILLENNIUM OFFICER:
PAT DUGGAN/NOÍRÍN MULCAHY

ST. FIN BARRE'S BEYONE 2000: SERVICE OF LIGHT CEREMONY WITH 1,000 CANDLES.

JUNIPER PRODUCTIONS: A FILM RETRACING THE PATH TAKEN BY ST. FIN BARRE FROM GOUGANE BARRA TO CORK CITY.

CORK MILLENNIUM FESTIVALS COMMITTEE: LAUNCH FOR THE MILLENNIUM EVENTS AWARDS.

CORK MILLENNIUM FESTIVALS COMMITTEE: CELEBRATION OF THE TRADITIONAL DAY OF COUNTRY SHOPPING IN TOWN.

TRISKEL ARTS CENTRE: CONCERTS, TALKS AND COLLABORATIONS ON INNOVATIONS IN CORK MUSIC.

CORK MILLENNIUM FESTIVAL COMMITTEE: A FREE OPEN AIR CONCERT FEATURING THE MUSIC OF THE '60'S.

CORK CITY LIBRARY: ACTIVITIES TO ACKNOWLEDGE THE IMPORTANCE OF THE ARTS IN THE DEVELOPMENT OF CORK.

THE IRISH GIRL GUIDES: HONOUR THE OLDER CITIZENS OF CORK.

ST. FINBARR'S HOSPITAL, CORK: PRESENTATION OF MILLENNIUM CLOCK.

CORK AIDS ALLIANCE: CANDLE LIT HUMAN CHAIN THROUGH THE CORK CITY CENTRE BRIDGES.

JUBILEE BELLS: LITURGICAL AND SOCIAL RECITALS FOR THE MILLENNIUM YEAR.

CORK MILLENNIUM FESTIVALS COMMITTEE: THE COUNTRY COMES TO TOWN (HARBOUR EVENT).

JAN DE MAN ENTERTAINMENTS: STREET CARNIVAL ENTERTAINMENT AND PAGEANT.

CORK MILLENNIUM FESTIVALS COMMITTEE: CONCERT TO WELCOME NEW MILLENNIUM.

CORK MILLENNIUM FESTIVALS COMMITTEE: LAST LIGHTS OF THE MILLENNIUM CEREMONY.

CORK MILLENNIUM FESTIVALS COMMITTEE: CHILDREN'S DISCO AND AFTERNOON EVENT TO CELEBRATE THE NEW MILLENNIUM.

ST. VINCENT'S SECONDARY SCHOOL: ERECTION OF MOSAIC PANEL USING LOCAL ART.

CORK MILLENNIUM FESTIVALS COMMITTEE: CHILDREN INVITED TO TRY DIFFERENT SPORTING EVENTS.

CORK MILLENNIUM FESTIVALS COMMITTEE: INAUGURATION OF A TIME CAPSULE PROJECT.

DENIS MCGARRY: SONG 2000 SPECIALLY COMPOSED FOR THE MILLENNIUM.

CORK MILLENNIUM FESTIVAL COMMITTEE: TEA DANCE FOR FOR SENIOR CITIZENS.

CANON HARTE DRAMA SCHOOL: MUSIC CONCERT.

COMHAR NA MUINTEOIRI GAEILGE: POETRY COMPETITION IN IRISH LANGUAGE IN HONOUR OF SEAN O'RIORDAN.

MAHON COMMUNITY ACTION PLAN: HISTORICAL FOLKLORE VIDEO.

CORK MILLENNIUM FESTIVAL COMMITTEE: TEA DANCE FOR SENIOR CITIZENS.

CORK INTERNATIONAL CHORAL FESTIVAL: ONE-OFF PERFORMANCE BY CHAMBER CHOIR – ANUNA.

CORCA'DORCA THEATRE COMPANY: "THE TRIAL OF JESUS" OUTDOOR THEATRE SPECTACULAR.

CORK WOMEN'S POETRY CIRCLE: PUBLICATION OF A BOOK OF POETRY FROM IRISH SCHOOL CHILDREN.

TOGHER FESTIVAL OF PHOTOGRAPHY: CELEBRATING THE 15TH YEAR OF THE FESTIVAL.

CORK MILLENNIUM FESTIVAL COMMITTEE: A TEA DANCE FOR CITIES SENIOR CITIZENS.

ASSOCIATION OF IRISH FLORAL ARTISTS: NATIONAL FLOWER FESTIVAL IN CORK CITY.

NATIONAL YOUTH FEDERATION CORK: AWARDS TO PARTICIPANTS IN "MY COMMUNITY IN THE MILLENNIUM" THEME.

POETRY CORK: A FILM – DAY IN THE LIFE OF POETIC CORK.

C.S.P.C.A.: DISPLAY OF BIRDS/FISH/TREES OF THE LOUGH AREA.

IRISH OFFICER – OIFIGEACH GAEILGE CORK CORPORATION: 2000 SET DANCERS PERFORM A CELEBRATION SET AT THE GRAND PARADE.

SENSE OF CORK – ARTS FESTIVAL: BONFIRE NIGHT CELEBRATION AT EMMET PLACE.

BEREAVED PARENTS SUPPORT GROUP: WATER FOUNTAIN MEMORIAL DEDICATED TO ALL DECEASED CHILDREN.

MIDDLE PARISH COMMUNITY CENTRE: STREET SHOW PORTRAYING CORK THROUGH THE YEARS.

MUNSTER LITERATURE CENTRE: STORIED CORK – CELEBRATING THE ART OF STORY TELLING.

LEEDS UTD. (CORK) SOCCER CLUB: INTERNATIONAL SOCCER TOURNAMENT CATERING FOR BOYS AND GIRLS AT SCHOOL LEVEL.

FIRKIN CRANE DEVELOPMENT AGENCY: TO DEVELOP AN EDUCATION PROCESS USING DOCUMENTARY DANCE FOOTAGE AND COMPUTER IMAGES.

CORK FOLK FESTIVAL: FOCUS ON PASSING ON THE MUSICAL STYLE WITHIN FAMILIES.

MUNSTER LITERATURE CENTRE: FRANK O'CONNOR LITERATURE FESTIVAL.

MUNSTER LITERATURE CENTRE: ASSEMBLING THE IMPORTANT LITERARY OUTPUT OF CORK.

SCOUTING IRELAND: ACTIVITY WEEKEND TO CELEBRATE 21ST ANNIVERSARY.

CORK MILLENNIUM FESTIVAL COMMITTEE: LINKING NORTH CATHEDRAL AND ST. FINBARRE'S CATHEDRAL IN CELEBRATION.

CORK MILLENNIUM FESTIVAL COMMITTEE: SEALING OF TIME CAPSULE IN CITY HALL GROUNDS.

CORK MILLENNIUM FESTIVAL COMMITTEE: CEREMONY TO HONOUR FAMOUS SONS AND DAUGHTERS OF CORK.

MILLENNIUM MUNSTER YOUTH DANCE: SPECIAL CHRISTMAS BALLET

CO. DONEGAL
MILLENNIUM OFFICER: LIAM Ó RONÁIN

AN TAISCE, DONEGAL NORTH WEST: MILLENNIUM LANDSCAPES – DONEGAL PHOTO 2000.

JOHN JUDE DEVENNEY: MILLENNIUM EVENT RECORDING THE HISTORY/CULTURE OF DONEGAL 1900-1999.

CÁIT NIC GIOLLA BHRÍDE: PREAMHACHA MILAOSIE (MILLENNIUM ROOTS) – RECORDING THE HISTORY/CULTURE OF GAOTH DOBHAIR.

ARTLINK, BUNCRANA: RECORDING THE HISTORY/CULTURE OF BUNCRANA AND ENVIRONS.

ROSSNOWLAGH ORANGE CULTURAL ASSOCIATION: VIDEO RECORDING THE HISTORY/CULTURE OF THE ORANGE ORDER OF SOUTH DONEGAL.

PEADAR MCDAID, TERMON : RECORDING THE HISTORY/CULTURE OF GARTAN IN A VIDEO.

CHARLIE O'DONNELL, ARDARA: RECORDING THE HISTORY/CULTURE OF THE LEAC CHONAILL AREA OF ARDARA.

CARRIGART DEVELOPMENT ASSOC.: RECORDING THE HISTORY/CULTURE OF CARRIGART AND MEVAGH.

CUMANN SEANCHAS CLOICH CHEANN FHAOLA: COMORADH AN MHÍLAOISE: CÉAD BLIAN Ó SHÍN. RECORDING THE HISTORY/CULTURE OF THIS GAELTACHT AREA.

JOHN BARRY O'DONNELL: RECORDING THE HISTORY/CULTURE OF THE ROSSES.

ANNE MCMENAMIN, LETTERKENNY HOSPITAL: RECORDING THE HISTORY/CULTURE OF PEOPLE DURING MILLENNIUM WEEKEND, INCLUDING PATIENTS AND STAFF IN HOSPITALS IN DONEGAL.

AN GRIANÁN THEATRE: LARGE-SCALE MUSIC/DRAMA EVENT WITH A MILLENNIUM FOCUS.

POBALSCHOIL CHARN DOMHNACH: 'OLIVER' – LARGE SCALE MUSIC/DRAMA EVENT WITH A MILLENNIUM FOCUS .

INISHOWEN TRADITIONAL SINGERS' CIRCLE: LARGE-SCALE MUSIC/DRAMA EVENT FEATURING IRISH, ENGLISH AND WELSH SINGERS.

LETTERKENNY MUSICAL SOCIETY: MILLENNIUM PRODUCTION OF 'JESUS CHRIST SUPERSTAR'.

SAOL BEO COMMUNITY PAGEANTRY: MILLENNIUM MARDI GRAS.

LEGHOWNEY COMMUNITY GROUP: SENIOR CITIZENS MILLENNIUM RECOGNITION.

SCOIL GHEIMHRIDH FRANKIE KENNEDY: SCOIL GHEIMHRIDH AN MHÍLAOISE – LARGE SCALE MUSIC/DRAMA EVENT.

EARAGAIL ARTS FESTIVAL: EARAGAIL ARTS MILLENNIUM FESTIVAL 2000 AND MILLENNIUM BALL.

GAA DONEGAL: CELEBRATION HONOURING THE 'GREAT SERVANTS OF THE GAA IN DONEGAL'.

LETTERKENNY UDC MILLENNIUM COMMITTEE: 'PEOPLE OF THE CENTURY' NIGHT.

BRIDIE CONEFRY, SILVER & GOLD CLUB, GLENTIES: 'GRANDPARENTS MILLENNIUM BALL' .

IRISH WHEELCHAIR ASSOCIATION, DONEGAL: SPECIAL RECOGNITION AWARDS .

CONWAL PARISH: RELIGIOUS/SPIRITUAL MILLENNIUM EVENT.

MOVILLE PRESBYTERIAN CHURCH: MILLENNIUM REFLECTION, A SPIRITUAL MILLENNIUM EVENT.

ST. JOHN'S CHURCH OF IRELAND, ROSSNOWLAGH: MILLENNIUM WILD FLOWER FESTIVAL.

CONWAL UNION, CHURCH OF IRELAND: RELIGIOUS/SPIRITUAL MILLENNIUM EVENT FOCUSING ON ST. COLUMBA.

CANON BRIAN SMEATON: 'THE CHRISTIAN MILLENNIUM' ART EXHIBITION AND CHURCH SERVICE.

GLENFIN AREA COUNCIL: 'MILLENNIUM ECUMENICAL SERVICE'.

CANON DAVID CROOKS. ST. BAITHIN 2000: RELIGIOUS/SPIRITUAL MILLENNIUM EVENT IN THE CARRIGANS.

FR. MACATEER, RATHMULLAN: RELIGIOUS/ SPIRITUAL EVENT TO HERALD THE MILLENNIUM.

DONEGAL TOWN PRESBYTERIAN CHURCH: MILLENNIUM ECUMENICAL SERVICE.

CLONMANY MILLENNIUM PROJECT: OPEN AIR CONCERTS TO WELCOME EMIGRANTS HOME.

DOHERTY CLAN REUNION: MILLENNIUM RALLY OF DONEGAL'S SECOND LARGEST CLAN.

INISHOWEN TOURISM COMMITTEE: MILLENNIUM SCALP CHALLENGE ON HILL ROAD AT SCALP.

BORDER REACH ARTS FESTIVAL, LIFFORD: PAGEANT OF DANCE, DRAMA, LATIN AND TRADITIONAL MUSIC.

LIFFORD-CLONLEIGH RESOURCE CENTRE: YOUTH PROJECT, INVOLVING CAROLS AND RECREATION OF HIRING FAIR.

COUNTY DONEGAL YOUTH ORCHESTRA: MILLENNIUM YOUTH CONCERT IN LETTERKENNY .

CASTLEFINN MILLENNIUM FESTIVAL COMMITTEE: FESTIVAL OF DANCE.

CRAIC (CULTURAL REVIVAL AMONGST INTEGRATED COMMUNITIES): MILLENNIUM JOHNNY CRAMPSIE – TRADITIONAL MUSIC WEEKEND.

SPECIAL NEEDS MILLENNIUM GROUP, BALLYSHANNON: SPECIAL NEEDS MILLENNIUM PROGRAMME.

TIONSCNAMH LUGH: SRAITH CEOLCHOIRMEACHA NA MÍLAOISE.

ABBEY VOCATIONAL SCHOOL, DONEGAL: ROTHA MÓR NA TSAOIL. SMALLER SCALE MUSIC/ CULTURAL EVENT .

FINN FARM HOSTEL COMMITTEE: JOHN 'SIMI' DOHERTY MILLENNIUM WEEKEND CELEBRATING LIFE AND MUSIC OF TRAVELLING FIDDLER.

SCEIM FORBAIRT POBAL CHROITHLÍ: MILLENNIUM FESTIVAL IN SMALL GAELTACHT COMMUNITY.

OLD LETTERKENNY RE-UNION: RE-UNION 2000 OF EMIGRANTS FROM TOWN.

CROSSROADS/KILLYGORDON ENTERPRISE: MILLENNIUM DREAM- LOCAL COMMUNITY MILLENNIUM CELEBRATION.

COUNTY DONEGAL GRAND LODGE: CELEBRATING 205 YEARS OF ORANGE CULTURE IN SOUTH DONEGAL.

TAUGHBOYNE DEV ASSOC.: MILLENNIUM CARNIVAL.

CLONMANY YOUTH CENTRE: MILLENNIUM CELEBRATION FOCUSING ON YOUTH GROUPS FROM NORTH INISHOWEN AND CARRICKFERGUS, CO. ANTRIM,

CONVOY COMMUNITY ASSOCIATION: MILLENNIUM CELEBRATION BRINGING EMIGRANTS BACK TO CONVOY.

RATHMULLAN COMMUNITY CENTRE: A JOURNEY WELL TRAVELLED- LOCAL COMMUNITY CELEBRATION.

BRIDIE LYNCH FUND, ST.JOHNSTON/LIFFORD: CELEBRATION OF BRIDIE LYNCH, GOLD WINNER AT LAST SPECIAL OLYMPIC GAMES.

MOVILLE CULTURAL PROMOTION: COMMUNITY CELEBRATION BEGINNING ON ST. PATRICK'S DAY.

ROYAL & PRIOR SCHOOL, RAPHOE: MILLENNIUM CELEBRATION BASED IN SECOND LEVEL SCHOOL.

INISH FREE MILLENNIUM COMMITTEE: COMMUNITY MILLENNIUM CELEBRATION BRINGING EMIGRANTS FROM INISH FREE ISLAND AND THEIR CHILDREN BACK TO ISLAND.

MILFORD WOMEN'S GROUP: MILLENNIUM CELEBRATION WITH A SPECIAL FOCUS ON OLDER WOMEN.

SIMPLY MUSIC: ENCOURAGING CHILDREN TO COMPOSE AND PERFORM MUSIC.

DUBLIN CITY.
MILLENNIUM OFFICER: GERARD EGAN

BALLYGALL YOUTH PROJECT: WEEKEND TRIPS TO COUNTRY FOR DEPRIVED CHILDREN.

LOWER CRUMLIN COMMITTEE: FAMILY NIGHT IN LOCAL SCHOOL.

CHERNOBYL CHILDRENS PROJECT: (FINGLAS OUTREACH GROUP). GIVING 20 CHILDREN FROM CHERNOBYL FOUR WEEKS IN IRELAND.

RINGSEND DISTRICT RESPONSE TO DRUGS: LOCAL GROUP/RECOVERING ADDICTS TO PERFORM PLAY.

BLUEBELL OLD FOLKS ASSOCIATION: MUSICAL EVENT TO CELEBRATE THE THEATRE ROYAL/THE QUEENS.

IRISH NATIONAL YOUTH BALLET CO.: EVENING OF DANCE AND MUSIC OF IRELAND.

JUBILEE 2000 COMMITTEE – O.L.V. PARISH: LITURGICAL PROGRAMME; TIME CAPSULE; HISTORICAL WALK; MILLENNIUM BOOK.

CEOL PROJECT: CONCERT BY SCHOOL CHILDREN AND YOUTH CLUBS IN BALLYFERMOT AREA.

MR. JAMES MORRIN: ERECTION OF GRANITE MEMORIAL BOULDER AT HAMPSTEAD COURT SENIOR CITIZENS' COMPLEX.

MCCANN MCGUIRK PRESENTATIONS: THE MILLENNIUM STORY OF THE FIRST CHRISTMAS.

SAOR – OLLSCOIL NA HÉIREANN: VISIONS OF PEACE CONFERENCE.

IRISH TAEKWONDO ACADEMY : EXHIBITION OF TAEKWONDO FOR FAMILY AND FRIENDS OF STUDENTS.

MARIGOLD CRESCENT 2000: VARIETY OF ENVIRONMENTAL IMPROVEMENT PROJECTS.

CEANNT FORT RESIDENTS' ASSOC.: AWARDS FOR SPECIAL PEOPLE IN AREA, GARDENING COMPETITION, PLAYGROUND/SMALL PARK.

ROYAL HORTICULTURAL SOCIETY OF IRELAND: MILLENNIUM ROSE FESTIVAL 2000, ST. ANNE'S PARK, CLONTARF.

BRABAZON STREET RESIDENTS ASSOC.: COMPLETE RENOVATION OF OLD GROTTO TO OUR LADY.

CABRA MOUNTAINEERING GROUP AND O.B.A.C.: CABRA YOUTH MILLENNIUM EXPEDITION, NEPAL 2000.

IRISH SQUASH / FITZWILLIAM LTC: MILLENNIUM IRISH SQUASH OPEN.

ST. PETER'S SENIOR COLLEGE: JOINT CURRICULUM PROJECT WITH MAYHULL HIGH SCHOOL, LIVERPOOL.

IRISH COUNTRYWOMEN'S ASSOC. (DUBLIN FED): ARTS AND CRAFTS EXHIBITION AND 5-WEEK SPONSORED WALK.

ST. PAUL'S SENIOR CITIZENS' CLUB: ECUMENICAL SERVICE AND EXHIBITIONS OF ARTS AND CRAFTS.

CHARLEMONT RESIDENTS' ASSOC.: ILLUMINATION OF THE ENTRANCES TO CHARLEMONT ESTATE.

SYLVAN YOUTH BALLET: THE MILLENNIUM FESTIVAL OF DANCE.

BALLYFERMOT DRAMA COMMITTEE: TRIPS TO THE THEATRE FOR 18 GROUPS OF CHILDREN AND PARENTS.

ST. PAUL'S PARISH, AYRFIELD: UNVEILING OF MILLENNIUM WINDOW.

FAIRVIEW PRODUCTIONS LIMITED: PLAN AND PRODUCE SHORT FILM WITH YOUNG PEOPLE IN BALLYMUN.

DUBLIN CORPORATION, COMMUNITY DEVELOPMENT SECTION: PROMOTION OF MILLENNIUM AWARDS.

WOMEN'S AID: THE MILLENNIUM AND BEYOND EVENT.

GIRLS' FRIENDLY SOCIETY IN IRELAND: CELEBRATION SERVICE IN ST. PATRICK'S CATHEDRAL FOR 2,000 MEMBER AND FRIENDS FROM 32 COUNTIES.

CITY QUAY YOUTH SAMBA PROJECT: SPECIAL PROJECT FOR THE SOUTH DOCKS FESTIVAL PARADE.

ST. LAURENCE O'TOOLE'S JUNIOR BOY'S SCHOOL: CONCERT INVOLVING ALL AGE GROUPS OF THE COMMUNITY.

FINGLAS WEST YOUTH CLUB: MILLENNIUM DISCO AND SANTA FOR 250 FINGLAS WEST CHILDREN.

CITY QUAY PRIMARY SCHOOL: DEVELOPMENT OF PART OF SCHOOL YARD AS GARDEN WITH SEATING.

NORTHSIDE ARTS AND CULTURAL CENTRE LTD: DRAMA, DANCE AND ART WORKSHOPS FOR CHILDREN OF COOLOCK.

NORTH COUNTY DUBLIN CRAFT WORKERS ASSOCIATION: TO DISPLAY MEMBERS' CRAFTS IN MILLENNIUM ROSE FESTIVAL.

ST. AGNES PRIMARY SCHOOL: MILLENNIUM GARDEN. TREE PLANTING AND FLOWER BASKETS.

MR WILLIAM BYRNE: A WEEK OF ACTIVITIES FOR THE ELDERLY IN UPPER BALLYFERMOT.

DUBLIN YOUTH THEATRE: DUBLIN YOUTH THEATRE ONE ACT FESTIVAL.

FEDERATION OF RAHENY RESIDENTS: LIST OF ACTIVITIES THROUGHOUT YEAR 2000.

8TH DUBLIN MILLENNIUM LESBIAN & GAY FILM FESTIVAL: DEVELOP IRISH INTERNATIONAL 'FUTURES' THEME FOR FILM FESTIVAL.

DOROTHY HAYDEN: TO PROVIDE SEASONAL DISPLAYS IN ST. ANNE'S PARK.

WOMEN'S EDUCATION RESEARCH AND RESOURCE CENTRE: HOST A MAJOR CONFERENCE ON THE THEME 'INSPIRING WOMEN'.

MS DOROTHY HAYDEN: ENTERTAINMENT FOR THOSE ATTENDING ROSE FESTIVAL.

MS DOROTHY HAYDEN: PROVIDE A SERIES OF LECTURES ON THE MILLENNIUM ROSE FESTIVAL.

MS DOROTHY HAYDEN: ST. ANNE'S PARK – TO PROVIDE ACTIVITIES / WORKSHOPS TO INCREASE AWARENESS OF NATURE, PLANT CULTIVATION.

MS DOROTHY HAYDEN: TO SELECT BEST ROSES, BASED ON GARDEN MERIT.

ACTIV 8 MILLENNIUM FESTIVAL: 3 DAY FESTIVAL IN CHARLEMONT STREET.

NAVAN ROAD COMMUNITY COUNCIL: HISTORY OF THE AREA FOR CULTURAL & HISTORICAL WEEK.

MILLENNIUM LIFFEY SWIM: SPONSORSHIP FOR MILLENNIUM SWIM.

SALVATION ARMY: CONCERT TO RAISE AWARENESS OF HOMELESS PEOPLE IN DUBLIN.

FR. DAVID HALPIN: FUND RAISING DRIVE TO SUPPORT HEALTH CENTRE IN VILLAGE OF AROR IN KENYA.

MR. JEREMIAH SULLIVAN: MILLENNIUM CONCERT IN CHURCH AND SUPPER DANCE.

PARISH TEAM: PUBLIC READING OF BOOKS OF THE NEW TESTAMENT, BALLYMUN .

DOLLYMOUNT AVENUE MILLENNIUM STREET PARTY: STREET PARTY TO BURY TIME CAPSULE.

DUBLIN 5 HORTICULTURAL SOCIETY: FLOWER SHOW TITLED 'DUBLIN 5 MILLENNIUM VISTA'.

SR. NUALA DOLAN: HONOUR OLDER PERSONS IN DARNDALE/BELCAMP COMMUNITY.

MID BLACKHORSE AVENUE RESIDENTS ASSOCIATION: LANDSCAPING AND PLANTING TREES AND FLOWER BEDS.

BALLYMUN LADIES CLUB: ART EXHIBITION AND MUSIC FESTIVAL.

DRAMA LEAGUE OF IRELAND: 'A NEWLY COMMISSIONED PLAY DEVISED WITH AMATEUR DRAMA GROUPS IN DUBLIN CITY.

DRAMA LEAGUE OF IRELAND (D.I.T.): 'A CELEBRATION OF DUBLIN WIT'.

NATIONAL BOTANIC GARDENS: EXHIBIT AT THE MILLENNIUM ROSE FESTIVAL.

ROYAL IRISH ACADEMY OF MUSIC: RIAI INTERMEDIATE ORCHESTRA PARTICIPATES IN EUROPEAN YOUTH MUSIC FESTIVAL.

DUBLIN BRANCH INLAND WATERWAYS OF IRELAND: 'THE TWO CANAL MILLENNIUM RALLY'.

CARMICHAEL CENTRE FOR VOLUNTARY GROUPS: A MILLENNIUM GOOD FRIDAY CONCERT IN ST. PATRICK'S CATHEDRAL.

IRISH VARIETY CONCERT BAND : 10 CONCERTS FOR SENIOR CITIZENS.

LORCAN & DISTRICT ACTIVE RETIREMENT: ART AND CRAFT EXHIBITION AND ST. PATRICK'S DAY CONCERT BY LOCAL CEOLTUS CEILTEORÍ ÉIREANN.

BALLYMUN MILLENNIUM AWARDS: PRESENTATION OF AWARDS TO GROUPS AND INDIVIDUALS IN THE COMMUNITY.

TEAM EDUCATIONAL THEATRE CO: SERIES OF PUBLIC PERFORMANCES LOOKING AT YOUNG PEOPLE'S PERCEPTION AT TIME OF MILLENNIUM.

E.C.O. COMMUNITY TREE NURSERY: FUN DAY FOR ALL COMMUNITY TO CELEBRATE THE MILLENNIUM.

SUGRADH CHILDCARE CENTRE: TO CREATE A MILLENNIUM GARDEN.

IRISH WHEELCHAIR ASSOCIATION: SPECIAL RECOGNITION AWARDS.

EDMUND RICE OFFICE: THE NAGLE-RICE FAMILY WALK 2000.

COBBLESTONE MANAGEMENT LTD.: ERECTION OF STATUE, SUNDIAL AND ARCH IN MILLENNIUM PLATEAU.

BALLYFERMOT APPLE ORCHARD MILLENNIUM PROJECT: PLANT AN APPLE TREE IN THE GARDENS OF EACH HOUSEHOLD.

DUBLIN YOUTH THEATRE: ONE ACT FESTIVAL PRODUCED BY DYT MEMBERS.

DUBLIN DEAF ASSOCIATION: EXHIBITION ON THE HISTORY OF IRISH DEAF PEOPLE.

MS MAIREAD STERIO: STREET PARTY AND MUSIC EVENTS TO CELEBRATE THE MILLENNIUM.

CLONLIFFE NEIGHBOURHOOD WATCH: FITTED LOCKS AND OUTDOOR LIGHTS FOR PEOPLE LIVING ALONE.

DUBLIN ADULT LEARNING CENTRE: (D.A.L.C.): A 'WRITING DAY' TO HELP LEARNERS.

ASHINGTON RESIDENTS ASSOC.: PARADE FEATURING COSTUMES OF THE PAST CENTURY.

INCHICORE VILLAGE INITIATIVE SERVICES: A VILLAGE CELEBRATION TO EMBRACE THE WHOLE COMMUNITY.

DUBLIN NORTH REGION BRIDGE FESTIVAL 2000: A FESTIVAL OF BRIDGE DESIGNED TO SUIT ALL STANDARDS.

RIVERMOUNT F.C.: TOURNAMENT COMPRISING OF LEAGUE OF IRELAND TEAMS AND LOCAL TEAMS.

UNITED ARTS CLUB: EXHIBITION O PAINTINGS AND SCULPTURE BY DECEASED MEMBERS .

DUBLIN HEALTHY CITIES: CELEBRATE THE MILLENNIUM WITH A DAY OF DANCE.

DARK HORSE VENTURE: AWARD SCHEME FOR OLDER PEOPLE.

DUBLIN STEEL ORCHESTRA: CELEBRATORY MUSIC IN DUBLIN AS PART OF LATIN AMERICA WEEKS.

CHAPELIZOD OLD VILLAGE ASSOC.: SET UP A LOCAL CULTURE MAGAZINE ON THE WORLD WIDE WEB.

CHAPELIZOD COMMUNITY FESTIVAL: WEEK LONG COMMUNITY FESTIVAL.

PORT OF DUBLIN SEA SCOUTS, PARENTS ASSOC-IATION: ROWING INTO THE MILLENNIUM EVENT.

TERENURE 2000: FOUR-DAY COMMUNITY FESTIVAL 25-28 MAY 2000.

ARTANE BEAUMONT BASKETBALL CLUB: UNDERAGE BASKETBALL TOURNAMENT.

ARTANE / BEAUMONT RECREATION CENTRE: DESIGN A MILLENNIUM GARDEN IN THE GROUNDS.

ROSARY COLLEGE: DEVELOP A LARGE COURTYARD INTO A MILLENNIUM GARDEN.

ST. DAVID'S BOYS NATIONAL SCHOOL: UNVEILING OF MILLENNIUM STONE IN GROUNDS OF SCHOOL.

COUNCIL FOR CO-ORDINATION OF SOCIAL SERVICES: AWARDS CEREMONY FOR MEALS ON WHEELS DRIVERS.

MEN'S MULTI-MEDIA PHOTO GROUP: THREE PHOTOGRAPHIC EXHIBITIONS.

NORTH STRAND RESIDENTS ASSOC.: PRODUCTION OF A SPECIAL MILLENNIUM CALENDAR.

RIALTO ENVIRONMENT GROUP: RIALTO ART ON THE ROUNDABOUT PROJECT.

FINGLAS CELEBRATION 2000: FINGLAS CREATIVE MINDS 2000 (ARTS WEEK).

DONORE DRAMA GROUP: ASSISTANCE TOWARDS COST OF PRODUCING A PLAY IN LOCAL COMMUNITY.

CATHOLIC GUIDES OF IRELAND (DUBLIN DIOCESES): 'THINKING DAY IN THE NEW MILLENNIUM' EVENT.

FIONA LOUISE KING: YOUTH MILLENNIUM ART EXHIBITION.

MINISTRIES DEVELOPMENT GROUP: JUBILEE BOOK – EACH STUDENT CONTRIBUTES A REFLECTIVE PIECE.

NEAR FM NORTH EAST ACCESS RADIO: DUBLIN SCHOOLS MILLENNIUM ENVIRONMENTAL PROJECT.

SAMHAIN 1999: DUBLIN'S HALLOWEEN PARADE.

BUNGALOW FAMILY RESOURCE CENTRE: 10TH ANNIVERSARY OF THE BUNGALOW RESOURCE CENTRE.

RAHENY HERITAGE SOCIETY: LOCAL HISTORY EXHIBITION.

SOUTH DOCK'S FESTIVAL: 'SOUTH DOCKS MILLENNIUM FESTIVAL'.

ST. ANDREW'S RESOURCE CENTRE: LIGHT FAÇADE OF ST. ANDREW'S RESOURCE CENTRE.

COMMUNITY ALLIANCE OF LOWER CRUMLIN: FESTIVAL TO CELEBRATE ASSOCIATION'S 25TH ANNIVERSARY.

CATHOLIC YOUTH COUNCIL: SUMMER PROJECTS.

CATHOLIC YOUTH COUNCIL: A MULTIMEDIA PROJECT TO CAPTURE A MOMENT IN TIME.

BALLYFERMOT GRAND CANAL FESTIVAL: ORGANISING AND RUNNING OF A CANAL BASED FESTIVAL.

GURTEEN YOUTH CENTRE: ORGANISING A COMMUNITY WIDE YOUTH FESTIVAL.

ARDLEA UNITED FOOTBALL CLUB: 'MILLENNIUM FESTIVAL OF FOOTBALL'.

GRANGE WOODBINE CLUB: DINNER AND ENTERTAINMENT FOR ACTIVE RETIREMENT AND SENIOR CITIZENS.

OLDE DUBLIN SOCIETY: FILM ARCHIVE OF DUBLIN IN 1999.

MUSCULAR DYSTROPHY IRELAND: A MILLENNIUM SUMMER CAMP FOR YOUNG PEOPLE WITH MUSCULAR DYSTROPHY.

NORTH WEST INNER CITY YOUTH INTEREST GROUP: COMMUNITY FESTIVAL CELEBRATING YOUNG PEOPLE.

IRISH MODERN DANCE THEATRE: LARGE SCALE OUTDOOR DANCE/THEATRE EVENT.

CANZONA CHAMBER CHOIR: MILLENNIUM BACH FESTIVAL.

DUBLIN COMMUNITY GAMES: MILLENNIUM BOOK.

ACCESS IRELAND REFUGEE SOCIAL INTEGRATION PROJECT: LECTURES ON 'CELEBRATING CULTURAL DIVERSITY IN THE NEW MILLENNIUM'.

CITYWIDE FACILITY SUPPORT NETWORK: A YEAR OF ACTIVITIES AROUND THE ISSUE OF FAMILY SUPPORT .

UPR BLACKHORSE LANE & DARLING ESTATE MILLENNIUM GROUP: SEVEN DAY LIVE EXHIB-ITION OF LIFE AS IT WAS ON BLACKHORSE LANE.

VESUVIUS THEATRE COMPANY: THEATRE PRODUCTION OF 'MOTHER COURAGE AND HER CHILDREN'.

ALCHEMY ART: MILLENNIUM PORTFOLIO DESIGN COMMUNITY WORKSHOPS.

MR NOLLAIG HANNAWAY: CHILDREN OF RATHMINES DESIGN AND PLANT A MILLENNIUM GARDEN.

RATHMINES TERENURE INTEGRATED DEVELOPMENT PLAN: MURAL ON THE WALL OF THE REAR OF RATHMINES SWIMMING POOL.

SMITHFIELD HERITAGE AND ARTS REGENERATION PROJECT: EVENT TO CELEBRATE RE-OPENING OF SMITHFIELD CIVIL SPACE.

EAST WALL VIKING LONGSHIP: TO INVITE PEOPLE ON A VISIT TO THE VIKING LONGSHIP.

NATIONAL ASSOCIATION FOR YOUTH DRAMA: 'GHOSTS OF THE MILLENNIUM'.

IRELAND'S VOICES FOR PEACE: CONCERT BRINGING TOGETHER CHOIRS AND SOLOISTS FROM NORTH AND SOUTH.

ST. RAPHAEL'S N.S.: PUBLISH A POETRY BOOK ENTITLED 'A DREAM FOR THE MILLENNIUM'.

VIRGIN MARY SCHOOLS: PROJECTS INVOLVING PARENTS AND PUPILS.

GLÓR NA NGAEL: LEISURE GARDEN FOR SENIOR CITIZENS, COULTRY AREA.

DUBLIN DIOCESAN CHILDREN'S PILGRIMAGE: PILGRIMAGE, VIDEO, COLOURED NEWSLETTER, SWEATSHIRTS.

ST. MONICA'S COMMUNITY COUNCIL: SERIES OF CULTURAL EVENTS.

GLASNEVIN DOWNS RESIDENT ASSOC.: TIME CAPSULE TO BE BURIED IN GREEN.

ST. PATRICK'S CATHEDRAL DUBLIN: SERIES OF MONTHLY TALKS.

ST. FINAN'S YOUTH GROUP: ACTIVITIES FOR LOCAL CHILDREN.

NORTHSIDE TRAVELLER SUPPORT GROUP: RESEARCHING TRAVELLER HISTORY IN COOLOCK AREA.

KILMORE WEST EDUCATION & DEVELOPMENT GROUP: CHILDREN'S ART, POETRY AND WRITINGS DEPICTING CHANGING LIFE OF AREA.

THE LIBERTIES SENIOR CITIZEN GROUP: MILLENNIUM CHRISTMAS DINNER DANCE IN MANSION HOUSE FOR SENIOR CITIZENS.

DUBLIN–FINGAL
MILLENNIUM OFFICER: SHAY BARKER

HOWTH / SUTTON LIONS CLUB: EXHIBITION OF HISTORY OF HOWTH IN MARTELLO TOWER.

PORTMARNOCK PARISH: PERFORMANCE OF HANDEL'S MESSIAH.

MILLENNIUM EXPRESSION 'YOUNG PEOPLE REPRESENTING OURSELVES' (FINGAL): EXHIBITION, BOOK, MILLENNIUM WALL.

RING COMMONS SPORTS CENTRE: MILLENNIUM RECREATIONAL AND TENNIS COURT ARENA.

YOUTHOPIA THEATRE CO. LTD: NEW MILLENNIUM PLAY – 28 YOUNG PEOPLE DEVISING A NEW PLAY.

LUSK TIDY TOWNS: JOSE BRIDGE: CLEAN UP OF AN OLD STONE WALL AND STREAM.

LUSK TIDY TOWNS: MILLENNIUM EASTER CARD.

LUSK TIDY TOWNS: LAUNCH OF BOOKLET.

LUSK TIDY TOWNS: PORTFOLIO OF PHOTOS.

LUSK HERITAGE GROUP: WALL HANGING.

D 15 COMMUNITY ARTS FESTIVAL: CARNIVAL DAY, COMPETITIONS, CEILIS, ETC.

HOWTH / SUTTON HORTICULTURAL SOCIETY: LAUNCH OF MAGAZINE.

RUSH DRAMATIC SOCIETY: SHAKESPEARE ON THE MILLBANK-"WILL ON THE HILL".

ICA: ARTS, CRAFTS & PHOTO EXHIBITION

ST MARNOCK'S PARENTS ASSOC: TREE / SHRUB PLANTING.

GARRISTOWN COMM COUNCIL: PROVISION OF MILLENNIUM STONE.

GARRISTOWN HISTORICAL SOCIETY: PUBLICATION OF MILLENNIUM BOOK.

DRAIOCHT: STREET CARNIVAL AND EXHIBITION.

MALAHIDE CAMERA CLUB: PRODUCTION OF A BOOK.

BLANCHARDSTOWN YOUTH FORUM: CULTURAL VISIT FOR 12 YOUNG PEOPLE – WILL PROMOTE POSITIVE ASPECT OF IRISH YOUTH CULTURE.

CAIRDE LE CHEILE: NORTHERN IRELAND EXCHANGE.

MOYNE PARK TRAVELLERS COMMUNITY GROUP: BOOKLET AND VIDEO TELLING THE STORY OF LIFE IN MOYNE PARK HALTING SITE.

DRAMA FEVER: FESTIVAL FOR YOUNG PEOPLE.

THE BYT GROUP (AFTER SCHOOLS PROJECT OF ST. CRONANS SENIOR NATIONAL SCHOOL: MILLENNIUM DRAMA FESTIVAL.

BALDOYLE FORUM LIMITED: NEW YEARS EVE CONCERT.

ST. FINAN'S COMMUNITY COLLEGE: ARTS FESTIVAL AND LANDSCAPING OF MILLENNIUM GARDEN.

PADDY A. BOYLE: PUBLICATION OF BOOK ON THE HISTORY OF THE PROMONTORY FORT OF DRUMANAGH, LOUGHSHINNY.

LOUGHSHINNY & DISTRICT DEVELOPMENT ASSOCIATION: DEVELOPMENT OF A WALKING TRAIL ALONG HISTORICAL ROUTE.

MALAHIDE & DISTRICT PIPE BAND: MALAHIDE MILLENNIUM FESTIVAL OF PIPING AND DRUMMING.

IRISH WHEELCHAIR ASSOCIATION: SPECIAL RECOGNITION AWARDS.

WEB PROJECT: SIX MONTH PROGRAMME TARGETING TEN, 13-16 YR OLDS WHO ARE IN TROUBLE WITH LAW AND AT RISK.

YOUTH WORKING GROUP (BAP): COMPILATION OF A MILLENNIUM COOKBOOK BY YOUNG PEOPLE.

MALAHIDE CHESS CLUB: WEEKEND CHESS TOURNAMENT.

BALDOYLE FAMILY RESOURCE SERVICES LTD: MAY MILLENNIUM FESTIVAL.

SWORDS PRIDE OF PLACE COMMITTEE: AN EXTENSION OF THE ANNUAL SWORDS HERITAGE FESTIVAL.

ANNE EGAN: ECUMENICAL SERVICE ON NEW YEAR'S EVE.

DUBLIN HEALTHY CITIES: DAY OF DANCE.

DARK HOUSE VENTURE. SCHEME FOR OLDER PEOPLE.

MARY KELLY ROGERS: A WEEKEND OF BRIDGE PLAYING.

MARY KIERNAN, SWORDS, CHURCH COMMITTEE MEMBER: PRODUCTION OF A BOOK – EACH FAMILY HAVE HALF A PAGE TO WRITE ABOUT THEIR FAMILY AND EVENTS.

THE SHEAMUS ENNIS CENTRE, NAUL : CENTRE FOCUSING ON TRADITIONAL MUSIC AND CULTURE.

PORTMARNOCK COMMUNITY SCHOOL / TANGIBLE TECHNOLOGY: SIGNIFICANCE OF PORTMARNOCK IN THE HISTORY OF AVIATION.

DUBLIN-SOUTH
MILLENNIUM OFFICER: MICHAEL COLEMAN

ST JOSEPH'S BOYS SCHOOL, CLONDALKIN VILLAGE: OPENING A MILLENNIUM GARDEN .

TALLAGHT TRAVELLERS YOUTH SERVICE: 5-DAY MILLENNIUM FESTIVAL. MARDI GRAS TYPE OF EVENT.

CATHOLIC YOUTH COUNCIL: TRAVELLERS JUBILEE PILGRIMAGE TO GLENDALOUGH.

SOCIETY OF ST. VINCENT DE PAUL TALLAGHT REFUGEE FUND: 2 DAY ART EXHIBITION AND WORKSHOPS TO PROMOTE INTEGRATION THROUGH MUTUAL UNDERSTANDING.

IRISH VETERAN AND VINTAGE MOTOR CYCLE CLUB: MILLENNIUM MOTOR CYCLE SHOW.

TALLAGHT COMMUNITY ARTS CENTRE: OUTDOOR THEATRE AT THE ART TOWER TO CELEBRATE THE DAWNING OF THE NEW MILLENNIUM.

DUBLIN YOUTH ORCHESTRAS: MILLENNIUM CELEBRATION CONCERTS INVOLVING FOUR ORCHESTRAS, A TOTAL OF OVER 300 MUSICIANS RANGING IN AGE FROM 10 TO 21 YEARS.

ST. PAUL'S SECONDARY SCHOOL, GREENHILLS: POETRY, SPIRITUAL, LITURGICAL READINGS AND DANCE TO CELEBRATE THE MILLENNIUM.

PARISH OF DIVINE MERCY, BALGADDY, LUCAN: POTTERY AND PLAQUES TO BE PAINTED AND INSERTED IN CHURCH WALL.

TALLAGHT COMMUNITY COUNCIL: MILLENNIUM PERSON OF THE YEAR AWARD LOOKING BACK ON 16 YEARS .

KILLAKEE RESIDENTS ASSOCIATION: SPECIAL PLANTING OF NATIVE BROADLEAF TREES.

CLONDALKIN HERITAGE TRUST: PUBLISHING A BOOK ENTITLED CLONDALKIN THROUGH THE MILLENNIUM.

CLONDALKIN HISTORY SOCIETY: PUBLICATION OF SPECIAL MILLENNIUM LEAFLET 'A WALK THROUGH THE PAST'.

KNOCKLYON HISTORY SOCIETY: PUBLICATION IN BOUND FORM OF TALKS, LECTURES.

KINGSWOOD HEIGHTS RESIDENTS ASSOCIATION: CREATION OF WORK OF ART BY THE YOUTH OF THE AREA.

TALLAGHT COMMUNITY RADIO: AN HOUR LONG RADIO PROGRAMME FOCUSING ON THE PEOPLE OF TALLAGHT.

SCOIL MHUIRE, BALLYBODEN: DEVELOPMENT OF ECO-FRIENDLY PRIMARY SCHOOL INCORPORATING MILLENNIUM COMMUNITY LIBRARY, GARDEN AND COMMUNITY WEB-SITE.

WANDERERS G.A.A. CLUB, ROCKBROOK, RATHFARNHAM: FREE MILLENNIUM CONCERT / CULTURAL EXTRAVAGANZA IN FOOTBALL PARK.

RATHFARNHAM CONCERT BAND SOCIETY: 'PROM' TYPE CONCERT USING 3 BANDS FROM THE SOCIETY INVOLVING LOCAL CHOIRS AND DANCE GROUPS.

WOODVILLE DISTRICT RESIDENTS ASSOCIATION: MILLENNIUM CHILDREN'S PAGEANT.

DODDER VALLEY RESIDENTS: CREATION OF MILLENNIUM PEACE FLOWER AND SHRUB BEDS.

TALLAGHT MILLENNIUM YOUTH TATTOO: YOUTH TATTOO BASED ON EXPERIENCE OF PERFORMING IN THE EDINBURGH MILITARY TATTOO IN 1998.

DODDER VALLEY PARK RESIDENTS ASSOCIATION: RIVER DANCE 2000 PERFORMED BY IRISH DANCERS RESIDENT IN THE ESTATE.

BRITTAS & DISTRICT COMMUNITY ASSOCIATION: CREATION OF MILLENNIUM GARDENS.

TALLAGHT ARTS SQUAD: MILLENNIUM MOSAIC QUAKE 2000. LAUNCH OF MOSAIC QUAKE TO BE DEVELOPED WITH A MILLENNIUM CELEBRATION THEME THROUGH A SERIES OF WORKSHOPS INVOLVING CHILDREN 8-12 YEARS OLD.

CLONDALKIN ARTSQUAD: PRODUCTION OF C.D. TO CELEBRATE THE MILLENNIUM USING LOCAL MUSICIANS.

CHERRYFIELD RESIDENTS ASSOC, WALKINSTOWN: MILLENNIUM SUMMER EXTRAVAGANZA FUN DAY WITH BANDS.

TALLAGHT YOUTH SERVICE: COMING TOGETHER OF YOUTH GROUPS IN THE TALLAGHT AREA.

BALLYBODEN/WHITECHURCH RESIDENTS ASSOCIATION: A PLAY BY A LOCAL PLAYWRIGHT WHICH WILL BE A LAMPOON ON LIFE IN A COUNCIL HOUSING ESTATE AT THE TURN OF THE MILLENNIUM.

ST. MARY'S BOYS NATIONAL SCHOOL, GRANGE ROAD, RATHFARNHAM: THE SALMON OF KNOWLEDGE MILLENNIUM PROJECT. INCLUSION OF WATER ELEMENT AND PLANTED AREA .

ST. MARY'S PARISH, LUCAN: CREATION OF MILLENNIUM GARDEN AND HAND PRINTS ON THE GARDEN WALL .

CONSERVATION IRELAND VOLUNTEERS: COMMUNITY PARTICIPATION IN THE CELEBRATION OF THE MILLENNIUM BY PLANTING 5,000 NATIVE TREES IN ONE DAY.

EDMONDSTOWN NATIONAL SCHOOL, RATHFARNHAM: OPENING OF SPECIAL MILLENNIUM PARK.

BODEN PARK RESIDENTS ASSOC. RATHFARNHAM: MILLENNIUM GARDEN FEATURING TREES.

CLONDALKIN COMMUNITY COUNCIL, NEWLANDS RESIDENTS ASSOC.: LECTURES, TALKS AND WORKSHOPS TO CELEBRATE THE MILLENNIUM.

SAGGART AND RATHCOOLE, COMMUNITY COUNCIL: STREET FESTIVAL INVOLVING THE LOCAL COMMUNITY.

CLONDALKIN ARTSQUAD: STAGING OF A JOINT EXHIBITION BETWEEN CLONDALKIN ARTSQUAD AND COMMUNITY ARTS TALLAGHT.

TALLAGHT FOROIGE DISTRICT COUNCIL: UNIQUE MILLENNIUM FUND DAY.

DUBLIN HEALTHY CITIES PROJECT: DARK HORSE VENTURE FOR OLDER PEOPLE.

DUBLIN HEALTHY CITIES PROJECT: MILLENNIUM DAY OF DANCE.

ST. KEVIN'S GOLDEN AGE CLUB, KILNAMANAGH: MILLENNIUM CELEBRATION IN RECOGNITION OF CONTRIBUTION TO THE CLUB.

INSTITUTE FOR FEMINISM AND RELIGION: CELEBRATION OF THE CRONES; THE WISE WOMEN OF IRELAND.

CHURCH OF IRELAND PARISH, LUCAN: CONCERT AND PANTOMIME TO CELEBRATE THE MILLENNIUM.

SOUTH DUBLIN MILLENNIUM COMMITTEE: CELEBRATION OF COMMUNITY DEVELOPMENT VOLUNTEERS IN THE COUNTY.

IRISH WHEELCHAIR ASSOCIATION: SPECIAL RECOGNITION AWARDS.

DUN LAOGHAIRE-RATHDOWN
MILLENNIUM OFFICER: PETER CORCORAN

HARRY V. WOODS, HARWOOD MARKETING, EDMONSTOWN ROAD: COMPILING BOOK "MARKETING AT THE MILLENNIUM".

DUBLIN HEALTHY CITIES: DAY OF DANCE IN DUBLIN.

BALLYOGAN DRIVE/PARK RESIDENTS ASSOCIATION: STREET PARTY AND ACTIVITIES FOR CHILDREN AND ADULTS.

EATON SQUARE RESIDENTS ASSOCIATION: CENTENARY CELEBRATION OF EATON SQUARE.

JOHN RUDDOCK, ULVERTON ROAD, DALKEY: CHAMBER MUSIC WEEKEND FESTIVAL.

MARIE O'REILLY, BLACKGLEN ROAD, SANDYFORD: PROJECT TO HONOUR COUNTESS CONSTANCE GORE-BOOTH.

SWIM IRELAND: DUN LAOGHAIRE HARBOUR RACE.

GLASTHULE RESIDENTS ASSOCIATION: FLORAL DISPLAYS.

IRISH WHEELCHAIR ASSOCIATION: SPECIAL AWARDS.

THE GRAINSTORE YOUTH ARTS CENTRE: ART BASED PROJECTS.

DEPARTMENT OF ARCHITECTURE AND TOWN PLANNING, DUBLIN INSTITUTE OF TECHNOLOGY: INTERNATIONAL MILLENNIUM CONFERENCE.

CILL INION CHURCHYARD GROUP: BROCHURE ON HISTORY OF 6TH CENTURY GRAVEYARD.

BALLINACLEA HEIGHTS RESIDENTS ASSOCIATION: PLANTING OF LARGE SCALE FLOWER BED IN SHAPE OF MILLENNIUM LOGO.

SHANKILL BOWLING CLUB: OPENING OF ALL-WEATHER BOWLING GREEN.

SCULPTURE IN CONTEXT: EVENT GIVING ARTISTS SPACE TO EXHIBIT.

ST. CATHERINE'S RESIDENTS ASSOCIATION,GLENAGEARY: BURYING OF A TIME CAPSULE.

DARK HORSE VENTURE: AWARDS SCHEME FOR OLDER PEOPLE.

BALALLY PARISH MILLENNIUM COMMITTEE: ECUMENICAL/LITURGICAL CELEBRATION.

GOOD SHEPARD PRIMARY SCHOOL, CHURCHTOWN: MILLENNIUM GARDEN POND PROJECT.

NUTGROVE AND LORETO RESIDENTS ASSOCIATION: CHILDREN'S PARTY AND FIREWORKS.

QUEEN OF ANGELS NATIONAL SCHOOL, WEDGEWOOD: TALKS FOR PARENTS IN DISADVANTAGED AREA.

QUEEN OF ANGLES NATIONAL SCHOOL, WEDGEWOOD: GARDENING PROJECT.

PINE VALLEY RESIDENTS ASSOCIATION, RATHFARNHAM: CELTIC BOX HEDGE IN LOCAL PARK.

THE MOTHERS' UNION-IRELAND: MILLENNIUM JOURNEY TO CELEBRATE 2000 YEARS OF CHRISTIANITY.

SANDYFORD VILLAGE FESTIVAL COMMITTEE: VILLAGE FESTIVAL.

KILCROSS RESIDENT'S ASSOCIATION, SANDYFORD: VIDEO AND FILM MAKING FOR YOUNG PEOPLE.

BALLINTEER FAMILY HISTORY: BOOK ON THE "BIG HOUSES" IN THE AREA.

BEECH GROVE RESIDENTS ASSOCIATION, BOOTERSTOWN: RESTORATION OF PEDESTRIAN WALKWAY.

JOHNSTOWN/KILLINEY ACTIVE RETIREMENT ASSOCIATION: PHOTOGRAPHIC ALBUMS OF PLACES OF HISTORICAL INTEREST.

DALKEY CASTLE AND HERITAGE CENTRE: CONTEMPORARY GLASS EXHIBITION.

CO. GALWAY
MILLENNIUM OFFICER: TONY MURPHY

ATHENRY FESTIVAL: MAJOR CELEBRATION OF 1000 YEARS OF ATHENRY'S HISTORY.

CONNEMARA LIVE ARTS: A SERIES OF EVENTS AROUND NORTH WEST CONNEMARA CELEBRATING ITS HISTORY, CULTURE AND HERITAGE. .

WOMEN CREATING SPACE: A MIXED MEDIA AND MULTIMEDIA CELEBRATION OF WOMEN'S WORK AND LIVES.

COMHAIRLE MUINTIRAN CHAISEAL TEO: CAISEAL 2000 COMHAIRLE MUINTIR AN CHAISEAL TEO, CAISEAL. PRODUCTION OF MILLENNIUM CALENDAR.

ELLIS TATE CENTRE FOR THE ARTS: MAJOR VISUAL ARTS EXHIBITION FEATURING AWARD WINNING GALWAY BASED ARTISTS.

LADY GREGORY AUTUMN GATHERING: LAUNCH OF MILLENNIUM VOLUME ON THE HISTORY AND LITERATURE OF LADY GREGORY'S GALWAY.

ATHENRY MILLENNIUM MUSIC: ORIGINAL MUSIC COMPOSITION PERFORMED BY 100 GALWAY SCHOOL CHILDREN.

MONIVEA MILLENNIUM COMMITTEE: A CELEBRATION MASS IN MONIVEA MAUSOLEUM FOLLOWED BY COMMUNITY MILLENNIUM CELEBRATION.

BALLINDEREEN COMMUNITY COUNCIL: LAUNCH OF 'AN DOIRIN' – A MILLENNIUM HISTORY OF BALLNDEREEN.

ATHENRY TIDY TOWNS COMMITTEE: MILLENNIUM TREE PLANTING CEREMONY.

TUAM TRAVELLERS EDUCATION & DEVELOPMENT ASSOCIATION: TRAVELLER FOLKLORE, STORIES AND SONGS – LAUNCH OF A MILLENNIUM VOLUME.

COMMUNITY DEVELOPMENT GROUP: LAUNCH OF A HISTORY OF KILKERRIN 500 AD – 2000 AD.

AN COISDE GAELACH, MILLTOWN: ORGANISING, PUBLISHING AND LAUNCHING A LIST OF PLACE NAMES IN BILINGUAL FORM.

CLAREGALWAY YOUTH MUSIC: THE GALWAY YOUTH ORCHESTRA PERFORM A MILLENNIUM SHOWCASE CELEBRATION .

ST. CUANA'S NATIONAL SCHOOL: A MILLENNIUM CELEBRATION OF THE LIFE OF ST. CUANA, PATRON SAINT OF THE AREA .

MOYLOUGH TIDY TOWN: OPENING OF THE MILLENNIUM GARDEN.

ANNAGHDOWNS PARENTS ASSOC.: A MOSAIC OF CERAMIC TILES CONSTRUCTED FOR THE MILLENNIUM BY THE CHILDREN OF THE AREA.

COISTE POBAL AR AIRE, AN CHEATHRU RUA: MILLENNIUM GALA EVENING FOR THE ELDERLY WITH ARTS, MUSIC AND STORYTELLING.

SCOIL BAILE NUA, MOYCULLEN: BOOK LAUNCH, MILLENNIUM EXHIBITION AND CELEBRATION EVENT.

ROUNDSTONE OPEN ARTS WEEK: CELEBRATION OF THE ARTS, CULTURE & HERITAGE OF WEST CONNEMARA.

BALLYMOE MILLENNIUM COMMITTEE: NOSTALGIC NIGHT AND SENIOR CITIZENS EVENTS.

MOYLOUGH SOCIAL SERVICE: MILLENNIUM EVENTS FOR SENIOR CITIZENS.

WOODFORD MUMMERS FEILE: MILLENNIUM TRADITIONAL MUSIC & MUMMARY FESTIVAL.

PLEARACA TEO: MORSHIUIL MHORDAIN / CARACTAIR CONNEMARA / CEOLCHOIRM DAMHSA NA MILAOISE. COMMUNITY SPECTACLE & MILLENNIUM CELEBRATIONS.

CLONBERN HERITAGE: LAUNCH OF PUBLICATIONS ON HISTORY OF CLONBERN.

CLOONCUREEN MENLOUGH, COMMUNITY CENTRE: LAUNCH OF MILLENNIUM BOOK AND MILLENNIUM CELEBRATION.

ST. RAPHAEL'S COLLEGE, LOUGHREA: MILLENNIUM GARDEN, MURAL, CAROL SERVICE FOR THE ELDERLY.

BALLYCONNEELY NATIONAL SCHOOL: NIGHT OF MILLENNIUM CELEBRATION WITH THE COMMUNITIES OF WEST AND NORTH WEST CONNEMARA.

BALLYCONNEELY 2000, FAIRWAYS: BALLYCONNEELY 2000 – TREE PLANTING, TIME CAPSULE, OLD FOLK AND COMMUNITY MILLENNIUM EVENTS.

LETTERFRACK WRITERS GROUP: CONNEMARA / DERRY MILLENNIUM LITERATURE AND MUSIC FESTIVAL.

TYNAGH & DISTRICT DEV. CO.: LAUNCH OF MILLENNIUM PUBLICATION.

LISHEENKYLE NATIONAL SCOIL, ORANMORE: MILLENNIUM PAGEANT OF CHILDREN'S LITERATURE.

FLOATING THEATRE COMPANY: MILLENNIUM VOYAGE TO BALLINASLOE AND ONE WEEK OF

WORKSHOPS FOLLOWED BY A PAGEANT ABOARD THE FLOATING THEATRE.

ATHENRY HERITAGE & TOURISM CO.: MILLENNIUM EXHIBITION OF MEDIEVAL TAPESTRIES, COSTUMES AND CRAFT FAIR.

FOLDING LANDSCAPES: LAUNCH OF MILLENNIUM PRIME NUMBER CELEBRATION BOOKLET.

ST. CAILLIN'S DAY COMMITTEE, BALLYCONNEELY: A SPECIAL NIGHT OF MUSIC AND DANCE FOR THE SENIOR CITIZENS ON THE NIGHT OF THEIR PATRON SAINT.

OUGHTERARD G.A.A. CLUB: EVENT TO ACKNOWLEDGE THE CONTRIBUTION OF OLDER CLUB MEMBERS.

OUGHTERARD MILLENNIUM MUSIC: A COMING TOGETHER OF 1000 YEARS OF INDIAN & IRISH MUSIC.

ATHENRY AGRICULTURAL SHOW: SPECIAL MILLENNIUM EVENTS AT AGRICULTURAL SHOW.

KILBEGNET / BALLINAKILL HISTORICAL SOCIETY: MILLENNIUM PUBLICATION & BURIAL OF TIME CAPSULE .

CONRADH NA GAEILGE: MILLENNIUM SEACHTAIN NA GAEILGE. CELEBRATING A 1,000 YEARS OF IRISH CULTURE.

'TRUELIGHT' COMMITTEE, CLIFDEN: MILLENNIUM CELEBRATIONS CONNECTED TO THE HISTORICAL RE-LAUNCH OF THE LAST CLADDAGH HOOKER.

COMHARCHUMANN INIS MEAIN, ARAN ISLANDS: SEACHTAIN SYNGE, 2000, INIS MEAIN / SPECIAL MILLENNIUM PRODUCTION OF SYNGE'S PLAYS.

CREGGS RURAL DEVELOPMENT: SPECIAL MILLENNIUM EVENTS IN HONOUR OF CHARLES STEWART PARNELL'S VISIT TO CREGGS.

KILTEVNA FESTIVAL COMMITTEE: LAUNCH OF A MILLENNIUM HISTORY OF 17 DUNMORE VILLAGES.

KINVARA MILLENNIUM COMMITTEE: MULTI-CULTURAL MILLENNIUM SPECTACLE AND FESTIVAL.

SOUTH EAST GALWAY TOURISM: COMMUNITY MILLENNIUM FESTIVAL IN PORTUMNA, ON LOUGH DERG.

CALASANCTIUS COLLEGE, ORANMORE: LAUNCH OF SCHOOL / COMMUNITY TAPESTRY.

CONNAUGHT ANGLING COUNCIL: EVENTS TO LAUNCH THE NAMING OF THE ISLANDS IN LOUGH CORRIB FOR THE MILLENNIUM.

KILLIMOR BRANCH OF THE GALWAY MENTALLY HANDICAPPED: A NIGHT OF ENTERTAINMENT.

LOUGHREA ENVIRONMENTAL GROUP: MILLENNIUM WALK WAY AND ARCHAEOLOGY DOCUMENTATION PROJECT.

DONNAGHPATRICK COMMUNITY COUNCIL: FAILTE ARAIS WEEK FOR EMIGRANTS.

MUINTEARAS: MILLENNIUM SAILING AND EDUCATIONAL PROJECT INVOLVING THE SCHOOL CHILDREN OF THE REGION.

IRISH GIRLGUIDES / WEST AND CENTRAL MIDLANDS REGION: SPECIAL MILLENNIUM ACTIVITY CAMP.

ORANMORE COMMUNITY DEVELOPMENT ASSOCIATION: ORANMORE MILLENNIUM TWO-DAY WALKING FESTIVAL.

AUGHRIM FESTIVAL COMMITTEE: MILLENNIUM HOME COMING FESTIVAL .

KILCOONA PARISH: FESTIVAL CELEBRATING THE CULTURE, CHRISTIANITY AND HERITAGE OF HEADFORD.

MAAM WOMEN'S GROUP: EXHIBITION CELEBRATING THE WOMEN OF THE MAAM VALLEY.

CUMANN STAIRE MHAIGH CUILINN: CEREMONY OF CONSECRATION FOR THE CHILDREN'S BURIAL GROUNDS OR LISINS IN THE MOYCULLEN AREA.

WOODFORD DEVELOPMENT COMMITTEE: RE-PLANTING AND ENHANCEMENT OF ST. JOHN'S GRAVEYARD, WOODFORD.

COLDWOOD COMMITTEE, ATHENRY: MILLENNIUM CELEBRATION AND PLANTING COLDWOOD MASS ROCK.

BALLINAKILL DEVELOPMENT ASSOC. LOUGHREA: COMMUNITY LAUNCH AND PLANTING FOR MILLENNIUM MONUMENT.

KILLIMOR PASTORAL COUNCIL: LAUNCH OF MEMORIAL GARDEN FOR THE MILLENNIUM .

MILLTOWN COMMUNITY CARE ASSOC.: SPECIAL MILLENNIUM AWARDS TO RECOGNISE THE EFFORTS OF COMMUNITY CARERS FOR ELDERLY CITIZENS.

OILITHREACHT NA GAELTACHTA, 2000, CARRAROE: ALL IRISH SPEAKING MILLENNIUM AWARDS TO RECOGNISE THE EFFORTS OF COMMUNITY CARERS FOR ELDERLY CITIZENS.

THE MULTIPLE SCLEROSIS SOCIETY: A CELEBRATION OF YOUTH AND LIFE FOR MS FAMILY CARERS THROUGH EXCHANGE PROGRAMME BETWEEN NORTHERN IRELAND AND GALWAY.

ATHENRY FRIENDS OF PEOPLE SPECIAL NEEDS: HOLIDAYS FOR 11 PEOPLE WITH SPECIAL NEEDS.

GALWAY CITY
MILLENNIUM OFFICER: MARTINA MOLONEY

KNOCKNACARRA AMATEUR THEATRE SOCIETY: PASSION PLAY.

RINCE LE CHÉILE THEATRE COMPANY: COMMUNITY WORKSHOPS AND SHOW.

PEARSE AVENUE, MERVUE RESIDENTS: ENVIRONMENTAL ENHANCEMENTS.

BALLYBANE YOUTH DEVELOPMENT PROJECT: COMMUNITY VARIETY SHOW.

GALWAY YOUTH THEATRE: MILLENNIUM YOUTH DRAMA FESTIVAL.

FÉILE 2000: IRISH LANGUAGE ARTS FESTIVAL.

RENMORE RESIDENTS ASSOCIATION: BOOK ON HISTORY OF RENMORE .

COMMUNITY MUSIC CREW: COMMUNITY MUSIC SHOWCASE .

COMMUNITY MUSIC CREW: POSTER CELEBRATING GALWAY'S MUSICIANS.

MERVUE SENIOR CITIZENS COMMITTEE: HONORARY PIN FOR PRESENTATION TO SENIOR CITIZENS.

MOBILE MUSIC COMPANY: MILLENNIUM MUSIC MOVIE.

CASTLEGAR COMMUNITY ALERT: MILLENNIUM OUTING FOR SENIOR CITIZENS .

GALWAY BOYS SINGERS: MILLENNIUM CONCERT IN GALWAY CATHEDRAL.

OAKLANDS RESIDENTS ASSOCIATION: PLANTING OF MATURE TREES.

RENMORE PANTOMIME SOCIETY: CINDERELLA MILLENNIUM PANTOMIME.

ICON 2000: EXHIBITION OF ICONS IN GALWAY CATHEDRAL.

ST. BRIGID'S WOMEN'S GROUP: EXHIBITION ON HISTORY OF THE GROUP.

BROTHER'S OF CHARITY: BLUE TEAPOT THEATRE COMPANY-MILLENNIUM FABLE .

COLÁISTE EINDE PARENTS COUNCIL: MILLENNIUM ART AND CRAFT EXHIBITION .

CRESTWOOD RESIDENTS ASSOCIATION: PLANTING OF LARGE MATURE TREE

MERVUE LADIES CLUB . MILLENNIUM CONCERT.

GALWAY WOMEN'S NETWORK: MILLENNIUM EXHIBITION.

SCOIL NICHOLÁIS NAOFA, CLADDAGH: CHILDREN AND COMMUNITY ART AND CRAFT FAIR.

MOININ NA GCISEACH COMMUNITY COLLEGE: MILLENNIUM ART'S WEEK.

BEACH COURT RESIDENTS ASSOCIATION: ENVIRONMENTAL WORKS AND TIME CAPSULE.

RENMORE MILLENNIUM COMMITTEE: WEEKEND COMMUNITY FESTIVAL.

CONRADH NA GAEILGE: SEACHTAIN NA GAEILGE.

GALWAY TRAVELLERS SUPPORT GROUP: CELEBRATION OF TRAVELLERS CULTURE.

IRISH WHEELCHAIR ASSOCIATION: SPECIAL RECOGNITION AWARDS.

MACNAS: PARADE OF LIGHT INVOLVING LOCAL CHILDREN.

DYKE ROAD ARTISTS: WATER TOWERS MILLENNIUM PROJECT.

IRELAND/INDIA MUSIC2000: COMING TOGETHER MUSIC EVENT.

FIDELMA HEALY-EAMES: PUBLICATION-"WRITE A POEM FOR THE MILLENNIUM".

SIGHLE MEEHAN: MILLENNIUM FESTIVAL OF MEDIEVAL PLAYS.

GALWAY EARLY MUSIC: INTERNATIONAL CHORAL EXCHANGE.

LADY GREGORY COMMEMORATION COMMITTEE: MILLENNIUM FESTIVAL OF PLAYS.

GALWAY MILLENNIUM ARTISTS: CELEBRATION SYMBOLISING THE DAWN OF A NEW AGE .

CO. KERRY
MILLENNIUM OFFICER: MARIE NÍ CHEALLAIGH

KILCUMMIN COMMUNITY CARE: MILLENNIUM PARTY FOR THE DAY CARE CENTRE OF THE ELDERLY.

KILGARVAN COMMUNITY CARE: MUSIC EVENT TO CELEBRATE THE MILLENNIUM.

KILFLYN VINTAGE RALLY: THE KILFLYNN MILLENNIUM VINTAGE RALLY .

KENMARE CHURCH OF IRELAND CHORAL GROUP: ECUMENICAL GATHERING OF THE COMMUNITY IN A CHORAL STREET CONCERT.

KILLARNEY SENIOR CITIZEN DAY CARE: MILLENNIUM MASS IN DAY CARE CENTRE, EXCHANGE VISIT WITH RATHMORE SENIOR CITIZENS FOLLOWED BY IRISH TRADITIONAL MUSIC.

THE MILLENNIUM GROUP, KNOCKANURE: TRANSFORMING OLD CHURCH BELL FROM MANUAL TO ELECTRIC.

JOAN COLLINS: SIGNPOST AND OPEN THE OLD ROAD TO AGHADOE GRAVEYARD.

CASTLECOVE COMMUNITY GROUP: ANNUAL OPEN-AIR MASS 'MILLENNIUM' AND NEW TANNOY PUBLIC ADDRESS SYSTEM.

WATERVILLE TIDY TOWNS COMMITTEE: ILLUMINATING LOCAL CHURCH OF IRELAND BUILDING AND THE GROTTO IN THE VILLAGE.

INCH COMMUNITY COUNCIL: HISTORY OF LIVES IN INCH SINCE THE 13TH CENTURY.

CROMANE COMMUNITY COUNCIL: TRADITIONAL CONCERT FOR THE ENTIRE COMMUNITY AND MASS.

BALLYDONOGHUE PARISH COMMITTEE: UPGRADING AND ENHANCEMENT OF ST. BATH'S

WELL AND RESTORATION OF FAMINE BURIAL GROUND .

KEEL CEMETERY RESTORATION GROUP: CLEAN UP AND PRESERVE CEMETERY AND WALLS OF AN ANCIENT MONASTERY DATING FROM THE 6/7TH CENTURY .

MILLENNIUM HARVEST: POSITIONING AND UNVEILING OF A HOLY YEAR CROSS AND PILGRIM PATHS THROUGH THE PARISH TO BE OPENED.

COISTE FORBARTHA BAILE AN SCEILG: CONSTRUCT A GROTTO DEDICATED TO OUR LADY IN THE VILLAGE OF DUNGEGAN, INCORPORATING A VARIETY OF THEMES RELATING TO THE LOCAL AREA AND DATING BACK TO THE 6TH CENTURY.

KILFEIGHNEY BURIAL GROUND COMMITTEE: CONSTRUCT A GROTTO AS PART OF THE MILLENNIUM PROJECT FOR LIXNAW PARISH.

JOHN MANGAN , KILCUMMIN OLD GRAVEYARD AND MEDIEVAL CHURCH: OPEN DAY FOR VISITORS TO NEWLY RENOVATED SITE AND OFFICIAL UNVEILING OF PLAQUE.

LISTOWEL BUSINESS AND RETAIL ASSOCIATION LTD: ERECTING FESTOON LIGHTING AND FEATURES AT LOCATIONS IN LISTOWEL.

ASDEE COMMUNITY DEVELOPMENT ASSOCIATION: PLANT NATURE TREES AND PLANT SHRUBS FOR THE MILLENNIUM.

JOE WALSH: OFFICIAL OPENING OF THE ALL-WEATHER SYNTHETIC ATHLETICS TRACK IN CASTLEISLAND.

COISTE FORBARTHA AN GLEANNA: OPENING AND CELEBRATION OF THE FIRST PHASE OF THE MILLENNIUM COMMUNITY HOUSING SCHEME.

FORBAIRT NA DROMODA TEORANTA: MILLENNIUM EXHIBITION – TO CELEBRATE THE OFFICIAL OPENING OF COMMUNITY PROJECT AT CILLIAN LIATH.

CAHERCIVEEN LIBRARY MILLENNIUM COMMITTEE: EXHIBIT OF ASPECTS OF LOCAL HERITAGE AND ONE DAY SEMINAR.

KERRY TRAVELLERS DEVELOPMENT PROJECT, TRALEE: A CELEBRATION OF TRAVELLER CULTURE. LOOKING AT MUSIC AND CRAFTS IN THE PAST AND FORWARD TO EXPLORE THE ROLE OF TRAVELLERS.

KERRY COUNSELLING CENTRE: WORKSHOPS REFLECTING ON IMAGES OF GOD FOR THE NEXT MILLENNIUM.

CPI ADULT RESOURCE CENTRE, TRALEE: HIGHLIGHTING THE NEED FOR SUPPORTED EMPLOYMENT FOR ADULTS WITH SIGNIFICANT PHYSICAL DISABILITIES.

BERNADETTE CUNNINGHAM, KERRY SCHOOL OF ART, KILLARNEY: MILLENNIUM EXHIBITION OF ART WORKS CREATED BY ADULTS AND CHILDREN .

MOYVANE DEVELOPMENT ASSOC: WORKSHOPS ON THE ORIGINS OF MAKING BODHRANS AND THE ART OF PLAYING .

DUAGH RESOURCE AND CULTURAL CENTRE: TO FURNISH AND FIT OUT AN AUDIO VISUAL ROOM CELEBRATING THE LIFE AND WORKS OF THE LATE PLAYWRIGHT GEORGE FITZMAURICE.

DUAGH HISTORICAL AND HERITAGE SOCIETY LTD: RESEARCH, CO-ORDINATE AND PUBLISH HISTORY OF DUAGH.

TRALEE WOMEN'S FORUM AND RESOURCE CENTRE: INTERNATIONAL WOMEN'S CONFERENCE WITH SPEAKERS FROM IRELAND, EUROPE AND THE US.

KERRY ACTION FOR DEVELOPMENT EDUCATION: A MULTICULTURAL, MULTIFAITH SEMINAR – MILLENNIUM YEAR 2,000 CULTURAL DIVERSITY.

FR. PAT O'DONNELL: DOCUMENTARY PHOTOGRAPH WORKSHOP AFTER WHICH PARTICIPANTS WILL PHOTOGRAPH LIFE IN KILFLYNN AND ABBEYDORNEY DURING THE YEAR 2000.

CHRAOBH BAILE AN MHUILINN / LIOS A TRÍ: THE COMMISSION OF A COMMEMORATIVE SCULPTURE OF MICHAEL HANNIFIN - RENOWNED FIDDLE PLAYER FROM CALLINAFERCY, MILTOWN

ST. MICHAEL'S COLLEGE,KILLARNEY: MILLENNIUM BALL, FLORAL DISPLAY AND RESTORATION OF A PIECE OF BOG OAK.

KILGARVAN COMMUNITY COUNCIL: 'SCULPTED IN THE FIRST MILLENNIUM, FORGOTTEN IN THE SECOND AND REVEALED BY KERRY COUNCIL IN HE THIRD MILLENNIUM'.

MNÁ CUAN AN CAISLEÁN: ERECTING HAND CARVED STONE BEARING THE NAMES OF THE 17 TOWNLANDS ON THE COMMUNITY AS GAEILGE AND IN ENGLISH .

FINUGE GAA CLUB: MILLENNIUM WALL TO INCLUDE THE HISTORY OF FINUGE GAA SINCE THE FOUNDATION OF THE GAA.

KENMARE MOTHER AND TODDLER GROUP: IMPRINT OF CHILDREN'S HANDS, NAME AND DATE OF BIRTH AND MILLENNIUM LOGO ON CERAMIC PLAQUES AND CONCRETE PAVING.

BALLYMACELLIGOTT MILLENNIUM GROUP: TO ERECT A MASS ROCK IN CLOGHER CEMETERY WITH A ST. BRENDAN THEME.

DAN V. O'CONNOR: UNVEILING OF A PLAQUE ON THE WALL OF SHRONE NATIONAL SCHOOL COMMEMORATING THE TEACHERS.

CAUSEWAY SOCIAL, SPORTS, CULTURAL AND ECONOMIC COMMITTEE: ERECTION OF MARBLE STATUE OF CHRIST THE KING ON CHURCH GROUND.

DINGLE CHAMBER OF COMMERCE: MILLENNIUM EVENTS PROGRAMME INCLUDING ERECTING BRONZE SCULPTURE OF FUNGI THE DINGLE DOLPHIN.

COISTE CHLÓR NA NGAEL: A MILLENNIUM CALENDAR.

CASTLEMAINE COMMUNITY COUNCIL, AUDIO VISUAL FACILITIES: BUILDING ON EXISTING RESEARCH, COMPILING AND PUBLISHING FACTS AND FOLKLORE, PRINTING BOOKLET.

KNOCKNAGOSHEL HERITAGE AND HISTORICAL SOCIETY: PUBLISH A KNOCKNAGOSHEL MILLENNIUM BOOK ON ITS HISTORY AND HERITAGE.

KERRY DIOCESAN JUSTICE MILLENNIUM COMMITTEE: PRODUCTION OF A JUSTICE DIARY BY THE COMMITTEE FOR THE YEAR 2000.

BIRD WATCH IRELAND: A UNIQUE SEA BIRDS POSTER WILL CONCENTRATE ON ILLUSTRATING THE WEALTH OF SEA BIRDS AND RICH NATURAL HERITAGE.

COMHCHOISTE GHAELTACHTAI CHIARRAI THEAS: TO COMPILE A CD OF THE TRADITIONAL SONGS AND MUSIC OF THE SOUTH KERRY GAELTACHT.

KERRY CHORAL UNION: CONCERT FEATURING WORKS BY COMPOSERS FROM THE LAST 1,000 YEARS.

SOCIETY OF ST. VINCENT DE PAUL: SPECIAL MILLENNIUM PARTY / BINGO TO CATER FOR APPROX. 600 PATRONS.

KERRY SKELLIG REGION: WALKING FESTIVAL, EVENING ENTERTAINMENT AND GOURMET FESTIVAL.

COISTE EIGSE: TO ORGANISE 'EIGSE NA MILAOISE' IN HONOUR OF DR SEÁN Ó SUILLEABHAIN 1903 – 1996. FOLKLORIST AND HISTORIAN .

TRALEE MILLENNIUM COMMITTEE: ERECTION OF A PIECE OF PUBLIC ART TO COMMEMORATE THE MILLENNIUM.

WATERVILLE FESTIVAL COMMITTEE: A FAMILY ORIENTED FESTIVAL. MUSIC, SPORT AND CULTURAL EVENTS.

KILLARNEY MILLENNIUM COMMITTEE: RESTORING TOWN CENTRE CLOCK, FLOODLIGHTING THE OLD MONASTIC 7TH CENTURY SETTLEMENT ON INNISFALLEN ISLAND ON KILLARNEY'S LOWER LAKE AND FLOODLIGHTING ROSS CASTLE.

TARBERT MILLENNIUM COMMITTEE: STREET PARADE ENHANCED WITH A PAGEANT AND STREET ENTERTAINMENT.

ABBEYDORNEY PLOUGHING SOCIETY: TO HOLD ANNUAL PLOUGHING MATCH AND DANCE.

PORTMAGEE DEVELOPMENT GROUP: MILLENNIUM CELEBRATIONS.

PUCK FAIR: CORONATION DETHRONEMENT PARADE FEATURING AN HISTORIAL LOOK AT PUCK FAIR THROUGH THE CENTURIES.

IRD FOIL MORE-KELLS CO. LTD.: 'DAWN TIL DARK' FESTIVAL.

KILLORGLIN CREDIT UNION CYCLING CLUB: THREE PART EVENT ON THE ROADS OF CO. KERRY.

KILLARNEY ROARING 1920'S FESTIVAL: MILLENNIUM CHILDREN'S FUN DAY.

KERRY DIOCESAN YOUTH SERVICE: 2000 YOUNG PEOPLE WILL PARTICIPATE IN OVER 30 EVENTS.

BALLYHEIGUE RACE COMMITTEE: TWO DAY RACE MEETING ON BALLYHEIGUE BEACH.

ST. JOHN'S THEATRE AND ARTS CENTRE, LISTOWEL: 'SAN KOFA' – AFRICAN DANCE PERFORMANCE, CLASSICAL RECITAL AND EXHIBITION.

BROSNA HERITAGE: MILLENNIUM HOME COMING FESTIVAL.

SLIABH LUACHRA WOMEN'S RESOURCE: SERIES OF MILLENNIUM EVENTS ON THEME 'PAST, PRESENT AND FUTURE.

CAHERCIVEEN SEA AND SHORT ANGLING CLUB: DEEP SEA ANGLING FESTIVE.

LISTOWEL FOOD FAIR: FOODS FROM THE FARM TO THE TABLE INCLUDING TRADITIONAL RECIPES.

ABBEYDORNEY COMMUNITY MILLENNIUM PROJECTS COMMITTEE: MILLENNIUM LIGHTING AND OUTDOOR SILHOUETTES /SIGNING OF MILLENNIUM SCROLL / BURYING OF TIME CAPSULE IN ST. BERNARD'S CHURCH.

DAN PADDY ANDY COMMITTEE, LISTOWEL: A FESTIVAL TO PROMOTE AND ENCOURAGE MORE VISITORS TO THE DECLINING RURAL AREA.

SEAN MCCARTHY MEMORIAL WEEKEND, LISTOWEL: INTERNATIONAL BALLAD FESTIVAL.

FEILE CHULTUR CHIARRAI,KILLARNEY: CELEBRATE AND PROMOTE AN AWARENESS OF FOLKLIFE, HERITAGE AND CULTURE OF CO. KERRY.

MILTOWN TWINNING COMMITTEE: MILLENNIUM VISIT TO BRETON TWINNED TOWN.

REV. DONAL O'NEILL: SCHOOL BASED COMPETITION TO FOCUS YOUNG PEOPLES ENERGIES AND CREATIVITY.

FR TOMÁS Ó CAOIMH : WALK FROM CLONFERT TO MOUNT BRANDON TO CELEBRATE NEW MILLENNIUM.

TÍIR NA NÓG, AN NEIDÍN: GIVING LOCAL PLAYGROUND A CELTIC THEME.

CAHERCIVEEN PARISH COUNCIL: MILLENNIUM GARDEN IN GROUNDS OF O'CONNELL MEMORIAL CHURCH.

FINUGE TIDY TOWNS COMMITTEE: CREATE A MILLENNIUM GARDEN ON SITE OF DERELICT HOUSE.

IRD WATERVILLE: DEVELOP A MILLENNIUM CHILDREN'S PLAYGROUND.

BALLYBUNION SEA AND CLIFF RESCUE SERVICE: LAUNCH OF RESCUE SERVICE. INTRODUCTION OF 2ND LIFEBOAT.

KERRY CABLE STATIONS COMMITTEE: ERECTION OF BRONZE PLAQUE AT EACH OF THE CABLE STATIONS IN VALENTIA, BALLINSKELLIGS AND WATERVILLE .

KERINS O'RAHILLYS GAA CLUB, TRALEE: RECOGNITION OF COMMUNITY SPIRIT AND COMMITMENT BY GROUPS IN THE STRAND ROAD.

PEIGÍ MHIC GHEARAILT: MILLENNIUM COMP-ETITIONS FOR MEMBERS OF THE ICA IN KERRY.

KENMARE DISTRICT SCHOOL OF MUSIC: COMPOSITION PROJECT USING ORIGINAL SCORE, BASED ON THE LEGEND OF INBHEAR SCEINE.

IRISH WHEELCHAIR ASSOC., TRALEE: SPECIAL RECOGNITION AWARDS .

AITAINMNEACHA CHIARRAI, RATHMORE: SURVEY BY SCHOOLS TO RECORD MINOR PLACENAMES OF KERRY.

KENMARE COMMUNITY CARE: CELEBRATION TO RECOGNISE THE CONTRIBUTION MADE BY THE ELDERLY .

CHRISTY BROWN CENTRE, TRALEE: MILLENNIUM MOBILITY PROJECT TO GIVE CHILDREN WITH SEVERE PHYSICAL DISABILITY THE EXPERIENCE OF MOVING INDEPENDENTLY.

KERRY COUNTY COUNCIL MILLENNIUM COMMITTEE: VARIOUS PROJECTS TO CELEBRATE AND MARK THE MILLENNIUM.

FÉILE NA BEALTAINE, DINGLE : LARGEST INTERNATIONAL CELTIC CELEBRATION.

CO. KILDARE
MILLENNIUM OFFICER: CHARLIE TALBOT

IRISH WHEELCHAIR ASSOCIATION: SPECIAL RECOGNITION AWARDS.

HANG OUT CLUB, CLANE: THREE OUTINGS FOR PHYSICALLY AND/OR MENTALLY DISABLED CHILDREN.

CURRAGH LOCAL HISTORY GROUP: PUBLISH VIDEO AND BOOK OF PHOTOGRAPHS TO PORTRAY LIFE IN THE AREA IN FIRST YEAR OF MILLENNIUM.

DARK HORSE VENTURE, KILCOCK: AWARDS PRESENTATION FOR PARTICIPATION IN ACTIVITIES WITH MILLENNIUM THEME.

KILDARE YOUTH SERVICES: ARTS EVENT CULMINATING IN KILDARE YOUTH ARTS FESTIVAL 2000.

KILDARE FEDERATION I.C.A.: DINNER AND SOCIAL TO HONOUR FOUNDER MEMBERS.

DERRINTURN GUILD I.C.A.: WOMEN FROM OMAGH INVITED TO DERRINTURN IN INTERESTS OF PEACE AND RECONCILIATION.

FRIENDS OF THE ELDERLY, MONASTEREVIN: COMMUNITY SERVICE AWARDS FOR ELDERLY WHO HAVE MADE OUTSTANDING CONTRIBUTIONS.

CARBURY PLAYERS, DERRINTURN: PRIMARY SCHOOLS TALENT SHOW WITH MILLENNIAL THEME.

SCOIL MHUIRE SOIRSEARACH BALLYMANY, NEWBRIDGE: PROMOTE VISUAL MUSICAL AND DRAMATIC ARTS IN SCHOOL.

SALLINS FAMILY SUPPORT GROUP: PROVIDE FAMILY SUPPORT AND CARING FOR THE ELDERLY.

CLANE YOUTH CLUB: COMPILATION OF RECORD OF ACTIVITIES & ORGANISATIONS CATERING FOR YOUNG PEOPLE.

KILCULLEN COMMUNITY DEVELOPMENT: STREET ENTERTAINMENT AND THEATRE WITH PERIOD COSTUMES AND RE-ENACTMENT OF HISTORIC EVENTS.

LEIXLIP FESTIVAL: RE-ENACTMENT OF VIKING INVASION.

VISITOR CENTRE, ST. PATRICK'S COLLEGE, MAYNOOTH: VIDEO, RELIEF MAP AND MODEL OF CO. KILDARE.

BEALTAINE MILLENNIUM FESTIVAL, NEWBRIDGE: STREET PARTY AND THEATRE, INCLUDING CEREMONIAL LIGHTING OF BEALTAINE FIRE.

GUTH ÓN PHORTACH, THE CURRAGH: WORKSHOPS AND COMMUNITY ART EXHIBITION ON MILLENNIUM THEMES.

TÍR NA MÓNA, NAAS: ECUMENICAL PAGEANT WITH SPIRITUAL THEME AND CHORAL EVENT.

FLOATING THEATRE CO., PROSPEROUS: PERFORMANCE AREA ON CONVERTED BARGE. AND MILLENNIUM VOYAGE INVOLVING CHILDREN.

CÁIRDE BRIDE: A SCULPTURE OF ST. BRIGID AT KILDARE.

IRISH SOCIETY FOR AUTISM, ENFIELD: EXHIBITION OF RESIDENT'S ART WORK.

NETWORK KILDARE, COMMUNITY EDUCATION: WOMEN OF KILDARE JOIN WITH FRIENDS FROM NORTHERN IRELAND TO EXPLORE ROLE OF WOMEN IN IRISH CULTURE.

MNÁ NA COILLE, DONORE NAAS: EXPLORATION OF BIRTH OF CHRIST THROUGH FLOWERS, FOLIAGE AND DECORATIONS.

KARE, NEWBRIDGE: MILLENNIUM BALL TO CELEBRATE CONTRIBUTION OF VOLUNTARY WORKERS.

CO. KILDARE ARCHAEOLOGICAL SOCIETY, MAYNOOTH : SEMINAR ON EARLY CHRISTIANITY IN COUNTY KILDARE.

LEIXLIP TOWN COMMISSIONERS: ERECTION OF PLAQUE TO DEAD OF BOTH WORLD WARS WITH NAMES OF LOCAL PEOPLE.

LEIXLIP TOWN COMMISSIONERS: PUBLISH SOCIAL HISTORY OF LEIXLIP WITH OLD PHOTOGRAPHS .

LEIXLIP TOWN COMMISSIONERS: PUBLICATION OF A SOUVENIR BROCHURE WITH NEW YEAR'S EVE AND NEW YEAR'S DAY EVENTS .

LEIXLIP TOWN COMMISSIONERS: SEMINARS ON HISTORY, ENVIRONMENT, TRANSPORT AND INFRASTRUCTURE OF LEIXLIP.

CO. KILKENNY
MILLENNIUM OFFICER: JOHN MCCORMACK

ABBEY HALL COMMITTEE: MILLENNIUM CONCERT OF ALL LOCAL TRADITIONAL BANDS AND LOCAL TALENT.

BALLYRAGGET COMMUNITY: PROPOSED JONATHON SWIFT MEMORIAL SCULPTURE AT SWIFTS HEATH AND SWIFT LITERARY FESTIVAL.

BALLYRAGGET COMMUNITY HALL: PROPOSED CLEAN-UP AND RE-PAINT OF COMMUNITY HALL INSIDE AND OUTSIDE.

BALLYRAGGET SCOUT GROUP: BURY A TIME CAPSULE CONTAINING ITEMS OF LOCAL SOCIAL AND HISTORICAL INTEREST, IN THE GROUNDS OF LOCAL CATHOLIC CHURCH.

BARNSTORM-KILKENNY THEATRE ARTS: A TOURING THEATRE SPECTACULAR FOR SUMMER 2000. A CROSS-COMMUNITY THEATRE PROJECT USING A CARNIVAL STYLE PRESENTATION AND TOURING FORM VILLAGE TO VILLAGE.

BISHOP BIRCH PLACE ACTION LTD.: YEAR 2000 CALENDAR DEPICTING, THROUGH PHOTOS AND ARTICLES, EVENTS, ACHIEVEMENTS AND SUCCESSES OF THE COMMUNITY OVER THE PAST 10 YEARS.

BLACK & WHITES GAA CLUB: MILLENNIUM FESTIVAL OF HURLING.

BRENNAN CLAN: REUNION OF THE CLAN IN CASTLECOMER. LECTURES, GENEALOGICAL SEMINARS, BUS TOURS, ECUMENICAL SERVICES ETC.

BROOKFIELD RESIDENT'S ASSOCIATION, BALLY-RAGGET: DECORATIVE SEAT IN THE GREEN AREA TO BE SURROUNDED ON ALL SIDES BY STONE TILES.

BUTLER GALLERY: MILLENNIUM EXHIBITION SHOWCASING NEW WORK OF YOUNG ARTIST EAMON O'KANE.

CASTLECOMER COMMUNITY SCHOOL: EDUCATIONAL PROGRAMME TO RETAIN ALL

FIRST YEAR STUDENTS IN SCHOOL AS FAR AS JUNIOR CERT.

CASTLECOMER DEMESNE COMPANY LTD: ESTABLISHING A BLUE BELL GARDEN FOR FUTURE GENERATIONS TO ENJOY.

CASTLECOMER LIBRARY: PAGEANT DEPICTING THE LAST 2000 YEARS OF CIVILISATION IN COSTUME, LITERATURE, PRINTING AND ART.

CASTLECOMER MILLENNIUM CELEBRATION STEERING COMMITTEE: SERIES OF EVENTS, SPORTING, CULTURAL, EDUCATIONAL AND ENTERTAINING OVER THE BANK HOLIDAY WEEKEND.

CASTLECOMER WELLINGTON RACE COMMITTEE: WELLINGTON RACE, FLOAT PARADE AND MARCHING BANDS.

CEOLTÓIRÍ KILKENNY: SUMMER ENTERTAINMENT, INCLUDING INVITING SWEDISH GROUP OF IRISH DANCERS AND MUSICIANS TO KILKENNY AND THE STAGING OF A SERIES OF IRISH ENTERTAINMENT SHOWS.

CLOGH PARISH FAITH TEAM: ECUMENICAL AND LITURGICAL CELEBRATION OF THE LIFE OF THE 'MILLENNIUM CHILD'.

CLONTUBRID MILLENNIUM GROUP: TO CONVERT WASTE GROUND INTO A GARDEN AND PROVIDING INDIGENOUS TREES, BUSHES, WILD FLOWERS AND FOOTPATHS.

COLÁISTE POBAIL OSRAÍ: MILLENNIUM COMPUTER PROJECT: PURCHASE AND INSTALL COMPUTER FACILITIES.

COMERAGH VIEW RESIDENTS ASSOCIATION: DEVELOP LARGE GREEN AREA, PLANT NATIVE TREES AND INSTALL FOUNTAIN.

COMHALTAS CEOLTÓIRÍ ÉIREANN – MARBLE CITY BR: PRESENTATION OF AN IRISH MUSIC PAGEANT, CONCERT AND VIDEO, THE PUBLICATION OF A BOOK AND THE MOUNTING OF A VISUAL DISPLAY.

CONAHY LADIES CLUB: ALL SENIOR CITIZENS IN PARISH PRESENTED WITH A SPECIALLY DESIGNED PIECE.

COOLAGH PATTERN COMMITTEE: ERECT WATER FEATURE/FOUNTAIN ADJACENT TO COOLAGH CHURCH.

COON AREA DEVELOPMENT ASSOCIATION: FLOODLIGHTING OF CHURCH IN COON.

CROSSPATRICK COMMUNITY DEVELOPMENT GROUP: MULTIMEDIA CULTURAL EXHIBITION AND CELEBRATION OF THE COMMUNITIES HERITAGE AND CULTURE.

DANESFORT GAA CLUB AND FORT RANGERS AFC: HOSTING OF ALL IRELAND AND FIVE NATIONS SHEEP SHEARING CHAMPIONSHIPS.

DIOCESE OF OSSORY MILLENNIUM COMMITTEE: JUBILEE PILGRIMAGE THROUGH THE DIOCESE TO TAKE PLACE OVER 8 WEEKENDS IN 2000.

DUISKE CONCERTS LTD. MILLENNIUM COMMITTEE: MILLENNIUM CONCERT TO BE GIVEN IN DUISKE ABBEY, GRAIGUENAMANAGH FEATURE THE VIENNA BOYS CHOIR.

FIDDOWN DEVELOPMENT ASSOCIATION: RESTORING THE OLD CHURCH IN FIDDOWN, PROVIDING FLOODLIGHTING AND REPLACING THE OLD BELL.

FIRODA NATIONAL SCHOOL: MILLENNIUM STONE AND ROCKERY AT FRONT OF SCHOOL.

FRESHFORD HERITAGE & DEVELOPMENT GROUP: MILLENNIUM PARK INCORPORATING WILD LIFE MEADOW, LAY PATHWAYS, SEATING, PICNIC AREAS, AND TREES.

GLENMORE MILLENNIUM COMMITTEE: PUBLICATION OF MILLENNIUM MAGAZINE, PARISH EXHIBITION AND MILLENNIUM NEW YEAR'S GATHERING.

GOWRAN DEVELOPMENT ASSOCIATION: "NOIMÉAD AM" (MOMENT IN TIME)-TO CREATE A GARDEN TO REFLECT THE PASSING OF TIME AND TO EMPHASISE THE NEED TO TAKE TIME TO LINGER.

GOWRAN PARISH DEVELOPMENT: "TEACH MHUIRE" COMMUNITY CRAFT SHOP.

GRANNAGH ICA: CRAFT DISPLAY AND DEMON-STRATION OF 12 TRADITIONAL IRISH CRAFTS.

INISTIOGE RIVERSIDE COMMITTEE: DEVELOP A RIVERSIDE WALK FROM CENTRE OF INISTIOGE VILLAGE ALONG RIVER NORE THROUGH THE FORESTS.

IRISH WHEELCHAIR ASSOCIATION: SPECIAL RECOGNITION AWARDS.

JAMES STEPHEN'S PIPE BAND: HOLD A 3-DAY FESTIVAL OF PIPING AND DRUMMING, PRODUCE A DOUBLE CD RECORDING THE EVENTS AND PRODUCE A TELEVISION PROGRAMME.

JOHNSWELL LITURGY GROUP: SOWING OF BEECH/LIME TREES AROUND JOHNSWELL GRAVEYARD.

KEEP KILKENNY BEAUTIFUL: PROPOSED CLEAN-UP OF NEWPARK FEN AND REINSTATE WALKWAYS, PLANT SHRUBS AND TREES AND CREATE AMENITY AREA.

KILKENNY ACTIVE RETIREMENT ASSOCIATION : A SPIRITUAL RETREAT FOR 70 MEMBERS WITH A THEME FOR THE MILLENNIUM OF "AGAINST THE ODDS".

KILKENNY ARTS FESTIVAL: "TANGO" AT BALLYKEEFFE QUARRY-AN OUTDOOR MUSICAL EVENT AS AN OPENING TO KILKENNY ARTS WEEK 2000.

KILKENNY COMMUNITY ACTION NETWORK: LAUNCH A TIME CAPSULE CONTAINING THE HIDDEN HISTORY OF COMMUNITY MEMBERS IN KILKENNY .

KILKENNY COUNTY COUNCIL: MILLENNIUM FOUNTAIN IN THE GROUNDS OF COUNTY HALL.

KILKENNY MILLENNIUM CONCERT: MILLENNIUM CONCERT IN KILKENNY CASTLE, A SHOWCASE FOR LOCAL KILKENNY TALENT.

KILKENNY MUSIC CLUB: ORGANISE A SERIES OF CONCERTS USING THE NEWLY FORMED CAMERATA (SIX INTERNATIONAL MUSICIANS LIVING IN KILKENNY).

KILKENNY MUSIC FESTIVAL: PIANO AND CHORAL COMPETITIONS.

KILKENNY WATER SAFETY ASSOCIATION: HISTORY OF KILKENNY WATER SAFETY ORGANISATION.

KILMACOW MILLENNIUM COMMITTEE: CELEBRATION OF LOCAL TALENTS, LANDSCAPING OF AREA AND COMMEMORATIVE STONE AND CREST.

KILMANAGH BALLYCALLAN/KILALOE COMMUNITY ENTERPRISE: DEVELOPMENT OF QUARRY, WHICH IS A NATURAL AMPHITHEATRE, AS AN AREA CAPABLE OF HOLDING OUTDOOR EVENTS.

LISDOWNEY DEVELOPMENT ASSOCIATION: PLANING PROGRAMME FOR THE VILLAGE OF LISDOWNEY.

LORETO SECONDARY SCHOOL: STAGING OF PIANO MILLENNIUM CONCERT IN THE WATERGATE THEATRE TO RAISE FUND TO PURCHASE MILLENNIUM PIANO FOR THE SCHOOL.

LOUGHBOY WOMEN'S WRITERS GROUP: A BOOK OF WOMEN'S SHORT STORIES AND POEMS.

MONEENROE COMMUNITY COUNCIL: CREATE VIEWING AREA WITH STONE WALL BOUNDARY.

MONEENROE COMMUNITY COUNCIL: 'MILLENNIUM MINGLE' FOR MEMBERS OF SENIOR COMMUNITY.

MULLINAVAT COMHALTAS CEOLTÓIRÍ ÉIREANN: ERECTION OF MILLENNIUM PLACE NAME STONES AT THE BOUNDARY OF EACH TOWNSLAND.

OFFICIAL LAST LIGHT CEREMONIES: IN KILKENNY CITY AND AT VENUES IN THE COUNTY.

OSSOY YOUTH: VOLUNTEER ACHIEVEMENT AWARDS TO RECOGNISE INPUT OF VOLUNTEER YOUTH LEADERS IN THE COMMUNITY.

OUTRATH RESIDENTS: RESTORATION OF GRAVE-YARD UNDER SUPERVISION OF ARCHAEOLOGIST.

OWNING I.C.A.: ERECTION OF STONE PILLAR AND HOLDING OF MILLENNIUM SENIOR CITIZENS RECEPTION.

PAULSTOWN FARÓIGE CLUB: FLOWER BEDS CONSTRUCTED, LANDSCAPED AND PLANTED BY LOCAL TEENAGERS AND ADULT LEADERS AT THE ENTRANCE TO PAULSTOWN CEMETERY.

PILTOWN MILLENNIUM CELEBRATIONS: FIREWORKS, PUBLIC ADDRESS SYSTEM, AMPLIFICATION, STAGE, LIGHTING AND SECURITY.

RADIO KILKENNY: SERIES OF 20 PROGRAMMES REFLECTING KILKENNY OVER THE LAST MILLENNIUM.

SLATE QUARRIES FESTIVAL OF ART AND CULTURE. ECHOES IN THE WIND-DRAMA, CHOIR PERFORMANCE, OPEN AIR MASS AT MASS ROCK, INTERNATIONAL POETRY COMPETITION, AND MILLENNIUM SCULPTURE.

SOUTH EAST NETWORK OF YOUTH THEATRES: LARGE SCALE FESTIVAL WHERE EIGHT MEMBERS FROM EACH COUNTY IN THE SOUTH EAST WILL ATTEND AND PARTICIPATE IN A WEEK LONG EVENT.

ST. BRIGID'S NATIONAL SCHOOL ,COON: PROPOSED CLEAN-UP OF THE SALMON POOL AREA IN USKERTY BY CHILDREN, PARENTS AND TEACHERS.

ST. CANICE'S INSTRUMENTAL MUSIC PROGRAMME: 450 CHILDREN WILL PARTICIPATE IN CONCERT IN WATERGATE THEATRE FOLLOWING A TWO-DAY WORKSHOP.

ST. FIACRE'S PATTERN COMMITTEE: MASS AT GROTTO IN KILFERA AND REPAIR AND UPDATING OF CROSS.

ST. JOHN'S LITURGY GROUP: MILLENNIUM MASS, CHILDREN'S COMPETITIONS, LITURGICAL CELEBRATIONS AND MILLENNIUM PILGRIMAGE TO FERRYHOUSE.

ST. JOHN'S SIDE BY SIDE CLUB: ERECTION OF MEMORIAL STONE IN GARDEN OUTSIDE DAY CENTRE OF ST. JOHN'S SENIOR CITIZENS.

ST. JOSEPH'S PASTORAL COMMITTEE: DISPLAYS OF LOCAL HERITAGE, TOWNLANDS, CLANS AND FAMILIES.

ST. KIERAN'S COLLEGE MILLENNIUM COMMITTEE: CONSTRUCTION OF A MILLENNIUM GARDEN.

ST. PATRICK'S NATIONAL SCHOOL, CLOGH: LAUNCH AND READING OF POETRY FROM CHILDREN OF ST. PATRICK'S NATIONAL SCHOOL AND CLOGH WRITERS ADULT WRITING GROUP.

ST. PATRICK'S PARISH MILLENNIUM CELEBRATION: STAINED GLASS WINDOW FOR ST. PATRICK'S CHURCH, DISTRIBUTION OF CANDLE WITH MILLENNIUM LOGO AND FAMILY PRAYER TO EACH HOUSEHOLD IN THE PARISH.

THE O'NEILL CENTRE: THE ORIGINAL BAND, TWEED, WILL COME TOGETHER FOR A ONCE OFF NIGHT OF NOSTALGIA WITH A SOUVENIR BOOKLET.

THOMAS MOORE SOCIETY: SOLO SINGING COMPETITION FOR PUPILS OF PRIMARY AND SECONDARY SCHOOLS.

TULLAHOUGHT LADIES GUILD: EXHIBITION OF PHOTOS OF LOCAL INTEREST OVER LAST 100 YEARS.

TULLAHOUGHT TIDY TOWNS: CREATE TWO MILLENNIUM GARDENS, ONE AT EACH END OF VILLAGE.

TULLAROAN NATIONAL SCHOOL: TAKING SCHOOL CHOIR TO PERFORM IN SCOTLAND, PLAYING SHINTY MATCHES AND VISITING PLACES OF INTEREST.

TULLAROAN MILLENNIUM CHURCH FLOWER FESTIVAL: FLORAL FESTIVAL FOR TULLAROAN CHURCH.

TULLAROAN MILLENNIUM COMMITTEE: MILLENNIUM BOOK DETAILING THE HISTORY OF TULLAROAN PARISH OVER THE PAST CENTURY.

UNITY SINGERS: CONCERT IN ST. MARY'S CATHEDRAL FEATURING IRISH SOPRANO, CARA O'SULLIVAN.

URLINGFORD MILLENNIUM ACTION GROUP: ERECTION OF MILLENNIUM MONUMENT WHICH WILL CONTAIN TIME CAPSULE WITH A CENSUS OF PERSONS RESIDING IN THE PARISH OF URLINGFORD AND GRAINE IN THE MONTH OF DECEMBER 1999.

CO. LAOIS
MILLENNIUM OFFICER: DOLORES MURPHY

FR. THOMAS O'SHEA, ATHY: FLOODLIGHTING TO ARLES CHURCH IN CONJUNCTION WITH "LAST LIGHT MILLENNIUM" CEREMONY.

HAWTHORN COMMUNITY COMMITTEE, BALLACOLLA: EXHIBITIONS OF PHOTOGRAPHS AND ITEMS OF LOCAL HISTORICAL SIGNIFICANCE FROM THE PARISH OF AGHABOE.

ERKINA DEV. ASSOC.: MILLENNIUM PAGEANTS – 10 LOCAL PAGEANTS REPRESENTING CENTURIES IN THE MILLENNIUM.

ERKINA DEV. ASSOC.: SERIES OF TABLEAUX INTERPRETING KEY EVENTS IN THE 20TH CENTURY.

PORTARLINGTON XMAS LIGHTS: ERECTION OF ILLUMINATED DISPLAY "2000-PEACE 2000" ON CHRISTMAS TREE.

PORTARLINGTON COM. DEV. ASSOCIATION: RIVER BARROW AMENITY WALK LAUNCH.

IRISH WHEELCHAIR ASSOCIATION: SPECIAL RECOGNITION AWARDS .

ST. BRIGID'S PL. FIELD COMMITTEE: OFFICIAL OPENING OF MILLENNIUM FIELD PROJECT.

LIGGACURREN MILLENNIUM PROJECT: PLANTING OF 10 TREES TO COMMEMORATE TEN EVENTS THAT HAPPENED IN LUGGACURREN IN THE LAST 100 YEARS.

SHAKE THE SPEAR- YOUTH THEATRE: NEWLY COMMISSIONED PLAY BY NATIONAL & INTERNA-TIONALLY RECOGNISED WRITER MICHAEL HARDING.

DURROW MILLENNIUM COMMITTEE: RESTORATION OF 16TH CENTURY BRIDGE IN DURROW, REVIVING OLD SKILLS AND USING LOCAL EMPLOYMENT TO ENHANCE THE BRIDGE AREA.

MILLENNIUM PASSION PLAY, BALLYLINAN: PASSION PLAY – 3-HOUR PRODUCTION IN ST. ANN'S HALL.

TIMAHOE MILLENNIUM COMMITTEE: MILLENNIUM DAY – MASS SERVICE AND FAMILY DAY PAGEANT PERFORMED BY YOUTH CLUB.

STRADBALLY PARISH: UNVEILING OF STRADBALLY MURAL DEPICTING THE SIGNIFICANT FOOTSTEPS OF THE COMMUNITY THROUGH HISTORY.

VICARSTOWN MILLENNIUM COMMITTEE: CEREMONY IN THE CHURCH, WHICH WILL INCLUDE SYMBOLIC ACTS TO MARK THE END OF ONE MILLENNIUM AND TO WELCOME THE NEW.

VICARSTOWN MILLENNIUM COMMITTEE: "VICARSTOWN MILLENNIUM DAY" – SPECIAL DAY FOR REFLECTION ON THE LAST MILLENNIUM.

KILLABBAN DRAMA GROUP: GRANGE. NIGHTS OF MUSIC AND DRAMA.

KILLEEN BADMINTON CLUB: ALL DAY DEMONSTRATION OF SPORTS, BOARD GAMES ETC. TO ENCOURAGE PEOPLE TO TAKE UP A NEW ACTIVITY.

KILLEEN HALL COMMITTEE: OLD FOLKS PARTY AND OFFICIAL OPENING OF NEW COMMUNITY CENTRE.

KILLABBAN ICA ARTS & CRAFTS: ART & CRAFT DISPLAY AND SALE.

TIMAHOE COMMUNITY DEV & I.W.A. TIMAHOE: MILLENNIUM PARK PROJECT – ESTABLISHING PARK AND FISHING AREA, INCLUDING RAISED FLOWER BEDS AND PATHS FOR WHEELCHAIR ACCESS ALONG THE BANKS OF THE RIVER.

MOUNTMELLICK MACRA NA FEIRME: "SLEEPING BEAUTY WAKES IN 2000" - PANTOMIME.

PHYL O'BRIEN, KILCAVAN: LABYRINTH – A SYMBOLIC PATH WHICH LEADS FROM EARTH TO GOD – TO BE CONSTRUCTED IN GROUNDS OF CLONAGHADOO CHURCH USING PAVING STONES AND BOX HEDGES.

CAMROSS COMMUNITY DEV. 60'S CLUB: BOOK ON THE SOCIAL HISTORY OF THE AREA.

CULLOHILL MILLENNIUM COMMITTEE: MILLENNIUM AUGUST WEEKEND FIESTA AND OFFICIAL OPENING OF MILLENNIUM MEMORIAL GARDEN.

MOUNTMELLICK MILLENNIUM COMMITTEE: RANGE OF EVENTS INCLUDING FESTIVAL OF

LIGHTS, MILLENNIUM BALL, MILLENNIUM DRUM CELEBRATIONS AND HALL OF MEMORIES EXHIBITION.

MOUNTMELLICK WOMENS GROUP: NEW OPPORTUNITIES FOR WOMEN'S NETWORKING IN CO. LAOIS 2000.

CASTLETOWN FOREOIGE CLUB: MILLENNIUM DAY – BURYING OF TIME CAPSULE AND UNVEILING OF MONUMENT.

NATIONAL PLOUGHING ASSOC OF IRELAND: UNVEILING OF MILLENNIUM PLAQUE, ECUMENICAL SERVICE, AND FUNCTION TO RECOGNISE ACHIEVEMENTS OF PLOUGHING CHAMPIONS DOWN THROUGH THE YEARS.

MOUNTMELLICK WORK EMBROIDERY GROUP: DISPLAY OF MOUNTMELLICK WORK-ORIGINAL EMBROIDERY DURING 2000 IN VARIOUS PLACES THROUGHOUT THE COUNTY.

STRADBALLY COMMUNITY GAMES: PUBLICATION AND LAUNCH OF COMMEMORATIVE BOOKLET CELEBRATING 25 SEASONS OF TRIBALLY COMMUNITY GAMES.

ARLES COMMUNITY DEVELOPMENT ASSOC.: ST. ABBAN'S WELL MILLENNIUM WALK – RESTORATION OF 7TH CENTURY WELL.

THE FITZPATRICK CLAN: BOOK WITH MILLENNIUM THEME ON THE FITZPATRICKS MCGIOLLA PHADRAIGS IN UPPER OSSORY – LAUNCHED AT CLAN GATHERING IN DURROW.

BORRIS-IN-OSSORY DEV. ASSOC: CONSTRUCTION OF A "GARDEN OF REFLECTION" IN A TRIANGULAR GRASSED AREA AT THE JUNCTION OF THE N7 AND THE ROCK ROAD.

JOHN KEEGAN SCHOOL, ABBEYLEIX: WEEKEND OF CELEBRATORY EVENTS TO MARK THE SIGNIFICANT CONTRIBUTION OF SAINTS AND RELIGIOUS ORDERS TO THE CULTURE AND HISTORY OF CO. LAOIS.

UN-LAOIS-ING MILLENNIUM SOUNDS: REMEMBERING THE GENESIS OF THE MILLENNIUM TAKING ITS CONCEPTION FORM THE CHRISTIAN STORY – A SERIES OF EVENTS, LECTURES, CONCERTS FOR THE MANY SACRED PLACES THROUGHOUT THE COUNTY.

LAOIS YOUTH MILLENNIUM ORCHESTRA, PORTLAOISE: LAUNCH OF LAOIS YOUTH MILLENNIUM ORCHESTRA.

MILLENNIUM BELL PROJECT: WORK ON AN INNOVATIVE COLLABORATION: DESIGNING, MODELLING, MAKING, TUNING, DOCUMENTING, EDUCATING AND FINALLY PERFORMING THE ACTUAL PLAYING OF 20 BELLS TO RING IN THE MILLENNIUM.

LAOIS YOUTH THEATRE MILLENNIUM SPECTACULAR: COMMISSIONING OF A PIECE OF

THEATRE INVOLVING ALL 2ND LEVEL SCHOOLS IN THE COUNTY.

LAOIS RECREATION, LEISURE & SPORTS FORUM, PORTLAOISE: TRAINING AND EDUCATION PROJECT – SERIES OF TRAINING COURSES MEETING THE NEED FOR TRAINING IN SPORT AND RECREATION.

LAOIS RECREATION, LEISURE & SPORTS FORUM, PORTLAOISE: CO. LAOIS MILLENNIUM GAMES – INTER SCHOOLS GAMES FOR ALL PRIMARY AND SECONDARY I SCHOOLS.

BALLYFIN PARISH COUNCIL MILLENNIUM COMMITTEE: ERECTION OF MONUMENT TO MARK THE YEAR 2000 IN THE CHRISTIAN TRADITION.

ABBEYLEIX JUBILEE 2000 PARISH COMMITTEE: ECUMENICAL OPEN AIR PAGEANT BASED ON MAJOR HISTORIC EVENTS PERTAINING TO 2000 YEARS OF LOCAL HISTORY FROM CELTIC TIMES TO THE COMING OF IRISH MONKS TO FRANAMANAGH (LAND OF THE MONKS) IN 7TH AND 8TH CENTURIES.

CO. LEITRIM
MILLENNIUM OFFICER: MICHAEL MCAULEY

DROMOD DEVELOPMENT ASSOCIATION: A CULTURAL COMMEMORATION OF THE MILLENNIUM

VISUAL LEITRIM: MILLENNIUM ELECTRONIC ART-NETWORKING PROJECT.

BALLINAMORE WOMEN'S GROUP: CULTURAL ACTIVITIES INCLUDING CREATIVE DANCING AND WRITING.

AN NAOINRA COMMUNITY PLAYGROUP: WEEK OF ART WORKSHIPS USING RECYCLED MATERIALS

BALLINAGLERA I.C.A.: MUSIC EVENTS AND EXHIBITION TO CELEBRATE MILLENNIUM.

GLENVIEW RESIDENTS ASSOCIATION: ENTERTAINMENT FOR RESIDENTS AND SURROUNDING AREAS.

NORTH LEITRIM GLENS DEVELOPMENT GROUP: SPECIAL SAMHAIN FESTIVAL AND HALLOWEEN SPECTACULAR.

JOE MOONEY SUMMER SCHOOL: CLASSES IN TRADITIONAL MUSIC AND SONG.

KESHCARRIGAN DEVELOPMENT ASSOCIATION: MILLENNIUM STREET PAGEANT AND GARDEN PROJECT.

BALLINAMORE CULTURAL COMMITTEE: ART AND SCULPTURE EXHIBITION.

AUGHNASHEELIN PARISH COUNCIL: COMMEMORATIVE GARDEN AND GROTTO, ST. MARY'S CHURCH.

MOHILL MILLENNIUM COMMITTEE: HISTORICAL EXHIBITION WITH FOCUS ON TOWN.

KINLOUGH COMMUNITY COUNCIL: OPENING OF WALK TO THE SHORE OF LOUGH MELVIN.

DROMAHAIRE DEVELOPMENT ASSOCIATION: OPEN AIR ECUMENICAL SERVICE AND TRADITIONAL MUSIC.

BREFFINI PLAYERS: MILLENNIUM PRODUCTION OF "FIDDLER ON THE ROOF"

DRUMKEERIN COMMUNITY COUNCIL: CELTIC FIRE FESTIVAL AND CONCERT.

CLOONE PARISH COUNCIL: BOOKLET ON MILESTONES IN PARISH DURING 20TH CENTURY.

DRUMSHAMBO MILLENNIUM COMMITTEE: FOUR EVENTS INCLUDING PAGEANT AND SCULPTURE.

AUGHAVAS I.C.A.: REVIVAL OF OLD CRAFTS AND CULTURAL DAY.

DRUMSHAMBO C.C.E.: CO. LEITRIM FLEADH CHEOIL.

LEITRIM PARTNERSHIP BOARD: "SCEITHIMINI LIATROMA" -CELEBRATING THE ART LIFE OF THE COUNTY.

LEITRIM ASSOC. OF PEOPLE WITH DISABILITIES: MILLENNIUM CONFERENCE.

BORNACOOLA DEVELOPMENT ASSOCIATION: MILLENNIUM RE-UNION AND FAILTE FESTIVAL

ST. CLARE'S N.S., MANORHAMILTON: MILLENNIUM BOOK OF CONTRIBUTIONS FROM ALL STUDENTS.

LEITRIM COUNTY COUNCIL: BOOKLET FOR WOMEN CURATORS.

LEITRIM COUNTY COUNCIL: PUBLICATION OF PHOTOGRAPHS "LEITRIM AT THE MILLENNIUM".

LEITRIM COUNTY COUNCIL: COMPOSITION OF PIECE FOR STRING QUARTET.

SLIABH-AN-IARAINN ARTS GROUP: MILLENNIUM ART AND CRAFT FAIR.

BREFFINI SINGERS/DRUMSHAMBO CHOIR: "MILLENNIUM MIRTH" PERFORMED BY FOUR LEITRIM CHOIRS.

DRUMSNA BRANCH C.C.E.: CONCERT AND SCHOOL RE-UNION.

DRUMKEELANMORE N.S.: SCHOOL RE-UNION AND LAUNCH OF MAGAZINE.

LEITRIM G.A.A.: LEITRIM TEAM OF THE MILLENNIUM.

LEITRIM COUNTY COUNCIL: EXHIBITION ON "CARING FOR THE ENVIRONMENT IN NEW MILLENNIUM."

NORTH LEITRIM MEN'S GROUP: VIDEO DEALING WITH PROBLEMS FACING MEN IN RURAL REGION.

MOHILL MILLENNIUM STORYTELLING: STORYTELLING FESTIVAL.

LEITRIM VILLAGE DEVELOPMENT ASSOCIATION: LIGHT OF VILLAGE AND PARISH FAMILY PHOTO ALBUM.

DRUMSHAMBO MUSIC SCHOOL: "THE MILLENNIUM TOUR" SERIES OF CONCERTS.

MOSSI WHELAN, AUGHAVAS PARISH: MILLENNIUM MASS AND ECUMENICAL EVENING.

LOUGH ERRILL DEVELOPMENT GROUP: ERECTION OF BOG OAK REFLECTION POINT BESIDE LAKE.

ROSSINVER COMMUNITY DEVELOPMENT GROUP: EXHIBITION OF SNAPSHOTS AND BURING OF TIME CAPSULE.

ESLIN DEVELOPMENT GROUP: ILLUMINATION OF MILLENNIUM GROTTO AND RECORD BOOK OF AREA.

SHANNON ERNE GUILD OF FOLK ARTISTS: FOLK ART SHOW AND EDUCATION PROGRAMME.

BALLINAMORE MILLENNIUM COMMITTEE: MILLENNIUM FLEADH COMPETITION AND SENIOR CITIZENS APPRECIATION PARTY.

LURGANBOY CRAFT GROUP: MILLENNIUM CRAFT EXHIBITION.

BORDER AREA CINEMA CO-OP: SHOWCASING "MOVIES OF THE MILLENNIUM".

IRISH WHEELCHAIR ASSOCIATION: SPECIAL RECOGNITION AWARDS.

NEWTOWNMANOR COMMUNITY COUNCIL: PLACE NAME STONE MONUMENTS AND WATER FEATURE.

DROMAHAIR ANGLERS ASSOCIATION: PIKE FISHING FESTIVAL ON CORRIGEENCOR LAKE.

CARRIGALLEN DEVELOPMENT COUNCIL PAINTING OF MURALS LINKED TO HISTORIC LOCAL EVENTS.

DRUMLEASE RESIDENTS ASSOCIATION: PLACENAME STONE, ROCKERY AND AERIAL PHOTOGRAPHY.

BEEZNEEZ THEATRE COMPANY: "LOVELY LEITRIM", ORIGINAL PLAY DEALING WITH IMMIGRATION.

EMERALD REVELLERS: SUPPORT FOR CROSS-BORDER GROUP OF SINGERS, DANCERS AND MUSICIANS.

O'NEILL SCHOOL OF IRISH DANCING: DEMONSTRATION AND PERFORMANCES.

MANORHAMILTON CARE OF THE AGED: EXHIBITION OF ARTS AND CRAFTS AND ARTEFACTS OF LOCAL INTEREST.

MELVIN GAELS G.A.A. CLUB: THE MILLENNIUM ROSE PAGEANT.

KILTOGHERT MILLENNIUM BOOK: HISTORY OF PROJECTS UNDERTAKEN BY ALL VOLUNTARY ORGANISATIONS.

KILTOGHERT ACTION COMMITTEE: "MILLENNIUM CHOIR" PERFORMING IN THREE CONCERTS.

MANORHAMILTON COMMUNITY COUNCIL:

UPGRADING CHRISTMAS LIGHTS AND WELCOME HOME FOR EMIGRANTS.

LEITRIM COUNTY LIBRARY: PUBLICATION OF LEITRIM MILLENNIUM BOOK.

LEITRIM TOURISM: AUDIO-VISUAL EXHIBITION OF PHOTOS OF COUNTY.

FARNAUGHT CEMETERY: GRAVEYARD IMPROVEMENTS.

MANORHAMILTON PARISH COUNCIL: ERECT MILLENNIUM CROSS AT CHURCH.

DRUMSHAMBO PASTORAL COUNCIL: ERECT STATUE OF ST. PATRICK IN CHURCH.

LIMERICK CITY
MILLENNIUM OFFICER: FERGUS QUINLIVAN

ST. MARY'S FIFE & DRUM BAND: MILLENNIUM EVE STREET PARADE & CONCERT.

UNIVERSITY CONCERT HALL: MILLENNIUM EVE GALA CONCERT.

TOM RYAN ARTIST: CROSSING PATHWAY / MILLENNIUM LIGHT PRESENTATION.

JANESBORO PARISH COUNCIL: INTER GENERATION CELEBRATION EXHIBITION OF ARTS, CRAFTS, PHOTOGRAPHY.

BELLTABLE ARTS CENTRE: INTERNATIONAL FESTIVAL OF FRINGE THEATRE.

ST. MARY'S LOCAL ARTS GROUP: MILLENNIUM HOPES FOR LOCAL CHILDREN.

LIMERICK YOUTH THEATRE: THEATRE OUTREACH PROJECT – DRAMA FOR THE DISADVANTAGED.

JOHN AND OWEN GILHOOLY: A TRIBUTE TO JOHN MCCORMACK – MILLENNIUM RECITAL.

GERRY O'BRIEN / DENIS CAREY: PREMIER OF THE MILLENNIUM SUITE IN A CELEBRATION OF LIMERICK MUSICAL HERITAGE.

LIMERICK CIVIC WEEK FESTIVAL: INTERNATIONAL MILLENNIUM CHORAL FESTIVAL.

UNIVERSITY CONCERT HALL: CATHERINE HAYES MILLENNIUM COMMEMORATIVE CONCERT.

ST. PATRICK'S WEEK FESTIVAL: CITY STREET PARADE / THEATRE.

ST MARY'S PARISH ADULT EDUCATION GROUP: A COMMUNITY TAPESTRY BASED ON PARISH HERITAGE.

LIMERICK SOUTH CITY INITIATIVE: RECOGNITION OF YOUTH ACHIEVEMENT & CONTRIBUTION OF SENIOR CITIZENS.

LIMERICK CHORAL UNION: SPECIAL RECITAL OF HAYDN CREATION.

MUNSTER SOC. OF MAGICIANS: MAGICAL MILLENNIUM – INTERNATIONAL CONVENTION.

LIMERICK YOUTH SERVICES: LIMERICK MILLENNIUM DANCE PROJECT.

DIOCESE OF LIMERICK, KILLALOE AND ARDFERT: MILLENNIUM ECUMENICAL PROJECT FOR THE DISADVANTAGED .

LIMERICK FOOD FESTIVAL: COMMUNITY COOKERY COMPETITION FOR THE MILLENNIUM.

SOUTHILL INTEGRATED DEVELOPMENT: CREATING THE TALENTS OF THE YOUTH IN THE COMMUNITY.

THE SUNFLOWER PROJECT, MOYROSS: COMMUNITY DEVELOPMENT THROUGH THE AGES.

UNIVERSITY CONCERT HALL: YOUTH MUSICAL THEATRE SUMMER SCHOOL.

KIERAN CAREY: OUT OF THE ASHES AT THE MILLENNIUM PUBLICATION.

THE UMBRELLA PROJECT: ACT YOUR AGE IN THE NEW MILLENNIUM.

LIMERICK YOUTH SERVICE: YOUTH AND COMMUNITY MILLENNIUM MUSIC PROJECT.

MAUREEN SPARLING: PUBLICATION OF SHORT STORIES.

ST. MARY'S CATHEDRAL: PROVISION OF LIGHTING FEATURE FOR THE NEW MILLENNIUM.

IRISH WHEELCHAIR ASSOCIATION: SOLDIERS OF CUCHULAINN – RECOGNITION AWARD.

LIMERICK SCHOOL PROJECT: ART DEVELOPMENT FROM AN EARLY AGE.

REAL ART PROJECT: MILLENNIUM IN FUSION.

LIMERICK SCHOOL OF ART: THE MILLENNIUM DESIGN SHOW.

IRISH CHAMBER ORCHESTRA: MILLENNIUM FAREWELL MESSIAH.

JOHN HUNT: THE STATE OF THE ARTS IN LIMERICK CITY/COUNTY PUBLICATION.

CO. LIMERICK
MILLENNIUM OFFICER: JOAN MACKERNANN

BEARNA RESIDENTS: BUILD A GROTTO TO OUR LADY.

MUNGRET / ST. PAUL'S MILLENNIUM FESTIVAL: ARTS AND SPORTS EVENTS FOR ALL AGES.

ASKEATON / BALLYSTEEN WOMEN'S GROUP: HISTORICAL PAGEANT ON NEW YEARS EVE. TOWN LIGHTING.

RATHKEALE COMMUNITY ARTS GROUP: MILLENNIUM SLANDERS FESTIVAL – STREET PARADE WITH MEDIEVAL AND MILLENNIUM BANNERS.

SEAN TAYLOR, BLIAN NA BAISTEACH: CONVERT RAINFALL DATA OVER ONE YEAR INTO MUSICAL NOTATION.

DAWN PUBLICATION BRUFF: MILLENNIUM MAGAZINE, 'THE DAWN' EDITION.

MAURA FITZGERALD, REGIONAL HOSPITAL: PLANTING A MILLENNIUM ROSE GARDEN AND A MAJOR ART EXHIBITION.

CONRADH NA GAEILGE : MILLENNIUM TELEPHONE DIRECTORY FOR THE IRISH SPEAKING POPULATION OF THE CITY AND COUNTY.

LIMERICK FEDERATION I.C.A.: MILLENNIUM 'KNEES UP' DAY OF CELEBRATION.

GLIN DEVELOPMENT ASSOC.: ERECT A SCULPTURE OF THE ONLY HARBOUR MISTRESS IN IRELAND.

PALLESCREEN G.A.A. AND COMMUNITY: ERECT A MONUMENT TO PADDY RYAN – WORLD AND OLYMPIC HAMMER CHAMPION.

FRIENDS OF ABINGTON CHURCH: CONSERVATION OF BELFRY OF ABINGTON CHURCH OF IRELAND.

MILTOWN MILLENNIUM COMMITTEE: SPECIAL FLORAL DISPLAY – EXHIBITION OF FARM MACHINERY.

TOURNAFULLA DEVELOPMT ASSOC.: COMPLETION OF 'TEACH SIAMSA' & GRAND OPENING ON MILLENNIUM EVE.

GLENBROHANE COMMUNITY ASSOC: MILLENNIUM PARISH SURVEY & RESTORATION OF CHURCH PROPERTY.

CLONFERT TO BRANDON MILLENNIUM WALK: TO VISIT ANCIENT CHRISTIAN SITES AND HOLY PLACES.

OOLA TIDY TOWNS: RESEARCH & PUBLISH HISTORY OF OOLA IN BOOK FORM .

LIMERICK YOUTH SERVICE: CELEBRATION OF TALENTS AND GIFTS OF YOUNG PEOPLE IN THE COUNTY.

LIMERICK PANTO SOCIETY: MILLENNIUM PANTOMIME IN UNIVERSITY CONCERT HALL.

BALLYHOURA BEARS WALKING CLUB: LIGHTING OF MILLENNIUM LIGHT ON TOP OF SLIABH REAGH.

CRECORA I.C.A.: ECUMENICAL SERVICE TO CELEBRATE THE MILLENNIUM AND DISPLAY OF ARTS AND CRAFTS.

CEREBRAL PALSY IRELAND: MILLENNIUM ART EXHIBITION – A PUBLIC CELEBRATION OF THE ACHIEVEMENTS OF PERSONS WITH PHYSICAL DISABILITIES.

BRUFF RUGBY FOOTBALL CLUB: MILLENNIUM UNDER 12 RUGBY FESTIVAL.

MARKET ARTISTS: VISUAL CELEBRATION OF THE ARTS AT THE TURN OF THE CENTURY.

CAISLÉAN NUA THIAR: MILLENNIUM PRODUCE AND CRAFT SHOW.

A-Z PHOTOGRAPHY EXHIBITION: 14 PHOTOGRAPHERS COMMISSIONED TO

PRESENT A COLLECTION OF 100 PHOTOGRAPHS DEPICTING THE ARTS IN LIMERICK CITY AND COUNTY.

ABBEYFEALE FOLK LTD: EVENTS TO PROMOTE FOLKLORE CULTURE AND HERITAGE IN RURAL LIMERICK.

ADARE BRANCH OF RED CROSS SOCIETY: MILLENNIUM CELEBRATION OF DIAMOND JUBILEE OF BRANCH .

ADARE MANOR GOLF CLUB: ERECTING BOG OAK SCULPTURE.

ADARE MILLENNIUM COMMITTEE: VIDEO OF ALL ASPECTS OF LIFE IN ADARE AT THE END OF MILLENNIUM.

REGIONAL HOSPITAL DOORADOYLE: ARK PROJECT DEPICTING THE STORY OF NOAH .

IRISH WHEELCHAIR ASSOC.: SPECIAL RECOGNITION AWARDS.

MANISTER MILLENNIUM COMMITTEE: NEW YEARS EVE MILLENNIUM CELEBRATION.

KILLEEDY MILLENNIUM COMMITTEE: COMMUNITY CELEBRATION OF THE NEW YEAR WITH THE ERECTION OF A MARBLE PLAQUE.

CAPPAMORE DEVELOPMENT ASSOC: STREET PARTY – SERIES OF EVENTS – BINGO, CARNIVAL, MILLENNIUM GET TOGETHER.

SAMHLÚ STREET THEATRE: EXTRAVAGANZA OF WORKSHOPS WITH DRUMS, DRAMA, MASK MAKING.

CAPPAMORE HISTORICAL SOCIETY: A SERIES OF EVENTS TO MARK THE MILLENNIUM.

RURAL OUTREACH PROJECT: MILLENNIUM DANCE AND MUSIC SHOW INVOLVING YOUTH CLUBS.

FRIARSGATE THEATRE AND ARTS: MILLENNIUM WEEKEND- LAUNCH OF MILLENNIUM BOOK, SENIOR CITIZENS CONCERT AND ECUMENICAL SERVICE.

LIMERICK MUSIC ASSOCIATION: CHAMBER MUSIC FESTIVAL .

DONOUGHMORE SCHOOL PARENT TEACHER ASSOC.: WEEKEND OF CELEBRATION WITH TREE PLANTING, TIME CAPSULE, AND EXHIBITION OF PAST AND PRESENT PHOTOGRAPHS.

ABBEYFEALE HERITAGE GROUP: LAUNCH OF LOCAL HISTORY MAGAZINE .

OOLA SENIOR CITIZENS COMMITTEE: WEEKEND IN WEXFORD FOR SENIOR CITIZENS TO MARK THEIR CONTRIBUTION .

KNOCKADERRY CLOUNCAGH COMMUNITY COUNCIL: NEW YEARS EVE CELEBRATION AND RECORDING OF THE HERITAGE OF THE PARISH AND COMMUNITY.

CO. LIMERICK YOUTH THEATRE: VIDEO OF YOUNG PEOPLE ON HOW THEY VIEW THEMSELVES.

IRISH CHAMBER ORCHESTRA: SERIES OF MILLENNIUM FAMILY CONCERTS.

LIMERICK COUNTY COUNCIL: RECONSTRUCTION OF PAGODA IN ADARE PUBLIC PARK.

CO. LONGFORD
MILLENNIUM OFFICER: MICHAEL CLANCY

CLONDRA VILLAGE MILLENNIUM COMMITTEE: TRADITIONAL IRISH SESSION AND CÉILÍ MÓR STAGED BY CHILDREN.

FINTAN FARRELLY: CHOIR OF 100 SINGERS, ACCOMPANIED BY AN ORCHESTRA , PERFORM IN ST. MEL'S CATHEDRAL .

LOUISE DONOHOE, SEC, GRANARD BRANCH COMHALTAS: SEAS NOS WORKSHOP CONDUCTED BY SÉAMUS MACMATHÚNA.

KILLOE DEVELOPMENT GROUP: TAR ABHAILE CHIUG 'KILLOE' MILLENNIUM CELEBRATION.

ENNYBEGS I.C.A. GUILD: I.C.A. MEMBERS AND FRIENDS – HERITAGE TOUR.

MOYDOW GUILD I.C.A.: RECEPTION TO HONOUR CONTRIBUTION OF PEOPLE TO LOCAL COMMUNITY .

ABBEYSHRULE & DISTRICT DEV. ASSOCIATION: SCULPTURE OF CANDLE IN LIMESTONE TO BE ERECTED IN THE VILLAGE.

NEWTOWNCASHEL MILLENNIUM PHOTO ALBUM COMMITTEE: COMPILE ALBUM OF ALL FAMILIES LIVING IN THE PARISH AT THE TURN OF THE CENTURY.

LOUGH REE DEVELOPMENT ASSOC.: LANESBORO'S ST. PATRICK'S DAY PARADE STAGED ON RIVER SHANNON.

IRISH WHEELCHAIR ASSOC.: SPECIAL RECOGNITION AWARDS.

MERCY SECONDARY SCHOOL, BALLYMAHON: PRODUCTION OF MILLENNIUM MAGAZINE.

MICHAEL GREALLY, ROYAL CANAL AMENITY GROUP: RESTORATION OF DERELICT BUILDING INTO TICKET OFFICE, FOR THOSE TRAVELLING ON THE CANAL BOAT SYSTEM.

BALLYMAHON TIDY TOWNS: RECEPTION TO HONOUR CONTRIBUTIONS BY INDIVIDUALS OR GROUPS .

CLUB 91, BALLYMAHON: RECEPTION TO RECOGNISE CONTRIBUTION OF SENIOR CITIZENS.

BALLYMAHON MUSIC FESTIVAL: STREET PAGEANT AND PARADE DEPICTING BALLYMAHON PAST AND PRESENT.

RATH MHUIRE RESOURCE CENTRE, GRANARD: A COMMUNITY EVENT, INCLUDEING POETRY READING AND ART EXHIBITION .

BALLYMAHON TOWN TWINNING COMMITTEE:

RECEPTION TO MARK THE TWINNING WITH HANDEVENT IN BRITTANY.

MULLINALAGHTA COMMUNITY DEVELOPMENT: CONCERT INVOLVING THE NEW ADULTS OF THE 21ST CENTURY.

MARIE MATTHEWS: COMPETITION FOR JUNIOR SCOR LOSERS .

DOLMEN FÁILTE CLUB & SERVICES: A CROSS BORDER EXCHANGE WITH SOCIAL / CULTURAL DIMENSION.

NORTH LONGFORD ANGLERS, LOUGH GOWNA: INTERNATIONAL BOAT FISHING COMPETITION £2000 PRIZE FUND .

EDGEWORTHSTOWN DISTRICT DEVELOPMENT ASSOCIATION: OFFICIAL OPENING OF COMMUNITY PARK.

CORBOY PRESBYTERIAN CHURCH: RELIGIOUS CONCERT TO CELEBRATE 2000 YEARS OF CHRISTIANITY.

ST. THERESE'S NATIONAL SCHOOL: MILLENNIUM CONCERT IN THE COMMUNITY INVOLVING SCHOOL CHILDREN.

HILLSIDE CLUB, BALLINALEE: OPENING OF CLUB FOR THE ELDERLY, HOUSE BOUND AND DISABLED IN THE AREA, AS A 'THANK YOU' FOR THEIR CONTRIBUTION.

SCOIL MHUIRE, NEWTOWNFORBES: ERECTION OF MILLENNIUM FOUNTAIN IN 'MILLENNIUM QUADRANGLE'.

CLONGUISH PASTORAL COUNCIL: CO-ORDINATE EFFORTS OF CLUBS AND GROUPS WITHIN THE CLONGUISH/NEWTOWNFORBES AREA IN ORGANISING EVENTS.

DROMARD G.F.C.: PLANTING OF 13000 IRISH OAK TREES IN A MILLENNIUM GARDEN.

DROMARD HISTORY GROUP: LAUNCH OF HISTORY BOOK OF DROMARD.

DROMARD RURAL DEVELOPMENT GROUP: VIDEO LINK UP WITH DROMARD EXILES IN LONDON, USA, ETC.

KENAGH COMMUNITY CO-OP SOC.: MUSIC EVENT TO CELEBRATE THE MILLENNIUM.

ST. DOMINIC'S N. S. KENAGH: CHILDREN OF 3RD – 6TH CLASSES TAKE PART IN 'THE HALLELUJAH MILLENNIUM CONCERT'.

KENAGH COMMUNITY CO-OP SOC: EXHIBITION OF ARTS, CRAFTS AND OLD PHOTOGRAPHS.

THE FARRELL CLAN: SIX DAY FARRELL CLAN RALLY – CELEBRATING 1000 YEARS IN COUNTY LONGFORD.

PARISH OF TEMPLEMICHAEL & BALLYMACROMACK: HISTORY OF PARISH WITH PARTICULAR REFERENCE TO PATRON SAINT.

LONGFORD SUMMER FESTIVAL: MONSTER FIREWORKS DISPLAY.

CLUB 89, ST. MEL'S ROAD, LONGFORD: SENIOR CITIZENS AND VOLUNTARY WORKERS VISIT BACKSTAGE THEATRE, LONGFORD.

FARNAGH YOUTH & COMMUNITY DEVELOPMENT ASSOCIATION: ERECTION OF A SCULPTURE AS TRIBUTE TO GENERAL SEÁN MACEOIN.

ST. MEL'S COLLEGE, LONGFORD: PUBLICATION AND LAUNCH OF MILLENNIUM MAGAZINE.

LONGFORD I.C.A. (NOW) LTD: OPENING OF NEW WOMEN'S CENTRE.

MELVIEW N.S. PARENTS COMMITTEE.: PLANTING OF TREE TO MARK THE MILLENNIUM AND ERECTION OF STONE PLAQUE.

MALL, LONGFORD: ERECTION OF MILLENNIUM STONE CIRCLE.

LONGFORD I.C.A, GRANARD: MILLENNIUM CELEBRATION OF WOMEN'S INTERNATIONAL DAY AND LAUNCH OF I.C.A. HISTORY BOOK.

BANTRACHT NA TUAITHE: OICHE GAILGE AGUS CEACHTEANNA GAEILGE.

CO. LONGFORD HISTORICAL SOC.: MILLENNIUM EXHIBITION OF PHOTOGRAPHS AND POSTCARDS.

CO. LONGFORD SOCIAL SERVICES: OLD FOLKS PARTY FOR RESIDENTS OF ST. JOSEPH'S HOSPITAL .

CUMANN LUTHCHLEAS GAEL COISTE CHONTAE LONGFOIRT: PAGEANT TO COINCIDE WITH OFFICIAL UNVEILING OF PAINTING OF MURALS ON WALLS.

ST. MEL'S CATHEDRAL MILLENNIUM CONCERT COMMITTEE: MILLENNIUM CONCERT

CHAMBER OF COMMERCE: RÁS TAILTEANN – STAGE END IN LONGFORD .

LONGFORD CHAMBER OF COMMERCE: AISLING CHILDREN'S ARTS FESTIVAL.

ANGLER'S DEVELOPMENT ASSOC.: ALL IRELAND MILLENNIUM PIKE PAIRS COMPETITION.

GRANARD AGRICULTURAL SHOW SOCIETY: 'TURN BACK THE CLOCK' CHILDREN'S HOSTORICAL PAGEANT AND DISPLAY OF VINTAGE FARM MACHINERY.

RATHARNEY MILLENNIUM COMMITTEE: ERECTION OF POST AND RAIL FENCING IN VILLAGE AND RESTORATION OF EXISTING ROAD SIGNS.

EDGEWORTHSTOWN TRADERS : ERECTION OF CHRISTMAS STREET LIGHTING.

ARDAGH/CLONMACNOISE DIOCESE: PAGEANT CELEBRATING THE MILLENNIUM – ST MEL'S CHURCH, ARDAGH.

CO. LOUTH
MILLENNIUM OFFICER: BRIAN HARTEN

ST. MARY'S PRESBYTERY, DROGHEDA: THEATRICAL PRESENTATION BY MORE THAN 100 YOUNG PEOPLE .

LOUTH YOUTH FEDERATION: PROJECT INVOLVING YOUNG PEOPLE FROM DUNDALK, NEWRY AND SURROUNDING AREAS.

ANNE-MARIE MORONY/ SUSAN CONNOLLY, TULLYALLEN: PUBLICATION AND LAUNCH OF BOOK ENTITLED 'OGHAM'-AN EXPLORATION IN ART AND POETRY OF EARLY IRISH SCRIPT.

FR. SEAN WALSH P.P. DUNDALK: ERECTION OF 6FT HIGH ILLUMINATED ST. BRIGID'S CROSS AT SHRINE.

BOYNE AUDIO VISUAL PRODUCTION: FRAMED PHOTOGRPAHIC EXHIBITION RECREATING DROGHEDA IN YEARS GONE BY.

IRISH RED CROSS SOCIETY: ASSISTANCE TOWARDS PURCHASE OF A 'MILLENNIUM BUS'.

DUNDALK TRAVELLERS COMMITTEE: A BOOK PROJECT FOR SETTLED AND TRAVELLER CHILDREN IN MID-LOUTH.

ST. MALACHY'S DOMINICAN FRIARY: SERIES OF CHORAL AND INSTRUMENTAL EVENTS CENTRE.

DUNDALK AGRICULTURAL SHOW: SPECIAL MILLENNIUM EXHIBITIONJ OF 'AGRICULTURE THROUGH THE AGES".

ST. MALACHY'S G.N.S. AND ST. NICHOLAS N.S.: PUBLICATION OF 'DUNDALK'S MILLENNIUM BOOK'.

DROGHEDA MILLENNIUM 2000: A 'JIM WILL FIX IT' IDEA OPEN TO CHILDREN AND SENIOR CITIZENS.

MELL RESIDENTS COMMITTEE, DROGHEDA: PHOTOGRAPHIC AND CHILDREN'S ART EXHIBITION CELEBRATING THE LIVES OF OUR SENIOR CITIZENS.

BLACKROCK MILLENNIUM PROJECT: ERECTION OF A STYLISED SUNDIAL, WITH CIRCULAR PAVED AREA.

CONRADH NA GAELIGE: PROGRAMME OF EVENTS – COMPETITIONS IN ART, POETRY, SPOKEN IRISH.

PATRICK WHYTE AND EOIN QUINN DUNDALK: THE PURCHASE AND INSTALLAITON OF NEW ANGELUS BELLS, WHICH WILL BE RUNG FOR THE FIRST TIME ON 12 MIDNIGHT DECEMBER 31ST.

SCOIL MHUIRE NA TROCAIRE: FULL PROGRAMME OF EVENTS BOTH WITHIN AND WITHOUT THE SCHOOL.

DARVER HISTORICAL RESEARCH GROUP: PROFESSIONAL VIDEO OF THE LOCAL AREA.

ORIEL DISTRICT SCOUTING IRELAND: A SPECIAL MILLENNIUM JAMBORETTE IN RAVENSDALE.

RATHNESCAR WILDFOWL & HABITAT MANAGEMENT PROJECT: TO CREATE PUBLIC ACCESS TO LAKE AND WOOD.

BAY ESTATE DEVELOPMENT GROUP, DUNDALK: FOUR SEATING AREAS AT THE RED BARNS ENTRANCE INTO THE ESTATE.

LOUTH VILLAGE MILLENNIUM: CONSTRUCTION OF A MEMORIAL MILLENNIUM GARDEN.

STEPHENSTOWN POND TRUST: TWO DAY EVENT WITH CHILDREN'S ADVENTURE WORKSHOPS.

COOLEY MOUNTAIN ASSOCIATION: A DISPLAY OF BEACONS ALONG CARLINGFORD LOUGH.

DUNDALK YOUTH THEATRE: COMMISSIONING OF A PLAY BY A PROFESSIONAL PLAYWRIGHT.

REV STANLEY MILLEN, DUNDALK: AN EVENT INCORPORATING THE LAUNCH OF A BOOKLET WITH A VISUAL AND MUSICAL PRESENTATION .

UNIVERSAL MARTIAL ARTS AND HEALTH CENTRE, ARDEE: A DRUG AND ALCOHOL AWARENESS PROJECT.

ARDEE UNION OF PARISHES: THE REPAIR OF THE BELFRY AND BATTLEMENTS OF ST. MARY'S CHURCH OF IRELAND .

DROGHEDA CHAMBER OF COMMERCE: THE PURCHASE OF MILLENNIUM CENTREPIECES FOR FESTIVE LIGHTING .

DROMISKIN GARDEN SOCIETY: PLANTING OF A MILLENNIUM BIBLICAL GARDEN IN THE GROUNDS OF A DEMOLISHED CHURCH.

BOYNE MILLENNIUM REGATTA C/O DROGHEDA LOCAL VOICES: ROWING CLUBS FROM NORTH AND SOUTH ROW ON THE BOYNE.

IRISH WHEELCHAIR ASSOC.: SPECIAL RECOGNITION AWARDS.

DUNDALK SPORTS CENTRE: COMMISSIONING OF MILLENNIUM PLAQUES AND TROPHIES FOR FINALISTS IN MILLENNIUM SCHOOLS COMPETITION.

ST PETER'S GUILD OF BELL RINGERS, DROGHEDA: PURCHASE OF NEW ROPES AND PROVISION OF TRAINING FOR BELL RINGERS.

COLLON CHURCH OF IRELAND: INSTALL AN ELECTRONIC UNIT TO THE EXISTING BELL IN CHURCH.

ST. VINCENT'S SECONDARY SCHOOL, DUNDALK: THE CREATION OF A MILLENNIUM SCULPTURE GARDEN IN THE SCHOOL GROUNDS.

TURAS LAR LÚ, DUNLEER: A PROGRAMME OF EVENTS FOR NEW YEAR'S EVE.

DROGHEDA PHOTOGRAPHIC CLUB: CREATION OF PHOTOGRAPHIC ARCHIVE OF THE TOWN AT THE TURN OF THE MILLENNIUM.

ST. MARY'S CHURCH OF IRELAND ARDEE: REPAIRS TO THE MAIN BELL AND THE INSTALL-ATION OF AN ELECTRONIC RINGING UNIT.

MICHAEL HOLOHAN, DROGHEDA: PERFORMANCE OF 'A SNAIL IN MY PRIME' .

VERONICA MCCARTHY, DUNDALK: THE PUBLICATION OF AN ILLUSTRATED BOOK CALLED 'MILLIE MILLENNIUM' A YOUNG CHILD'S WALK AROUND DUNDALK.

CO. MAYO
MILLENNIUM OFFICER: JOHN MAUGHAN

MAYO LEISURE CYCLING: THE PERPETUAL MILLENNIUM CYCLING TOURNAMENT AROUND CASTLEBAR

ARDAGH DEVELOPMENT GROUP: EXHIBITION AND LECTURES RELATING TO THE HERITAGE, HISTORY AND CULTURE OF THE LOCALITY.

KILLAWALLA MILLENNIUM MAGAZINE: COMPILATION OF A MAGAZINE SPANNING FROM 1800'S TO THE PRESENT DAY.

TONRAGEE N.S.: PRODUCTION OF A VIDEO ENTITLED "FROM ONE MILLENNIUM TO THE NEXT" – A CELEBRATION OF YOUTH – THE FUTURE.

NATIONAL COUNCIL FOR THE BLIND: SERIES OF WORKSHOPS-"MILLENNIUM DIMENSIONS IN ALTERNATIVE CREATIVITY FOR VISUALLY IMPAIRED PEOPLE."

CRANN MÓR RESOURCE CENTRE: MILLENNIUM ART EXHIBITION BY CRANN MÓR ARTS ABILITY GROUP TO PROMOTE THE GIFTS, TALENTS AND DREAMS OF THE SERVICE USERS.

MEELICK COMMUNITY COUNCIL: PERMANENT FLOODLIGHTING OF MEELICK ROUND TOWER.

GLOS RÉIM NA BPÁISTI: 800 CHILDREN WILL PARTICIPATE IN HISTORICAL PAGEANT IN BALLINA.

GLÓR MHAIGHEO: CULTURAL EVENTS INCLUDING IRISH TRADITIONAL CONCERTS.

BREAFFY N.S.: CREATION OF A GARDEN AND A WEBSITE TO RECORD PAST, PRESENT AND THE NEW MILLENNIUM.

BALLINA COMMUNITY CENTRE: A DAY TRIP TO CLONMACNOISE TO MARK THE CONTRIBUTION TO THE VOLUNTARY GROUPS IN BALLINA BY ITS SENIOR CITIZENS.

BELLACORICK WOMENS GROUP: SENIOR CITIZENS OF THE AREA ON A DAY TRIP TO KNOCK SHRINE AND MUSEUM.

MUINTIR MHAIGHEO GALWAY: MAYO ASSOCIATIONS WORLDWIDE MILLENNIUM CONVENTION 2000 – DELEGATES FROM IN EXCESS OF 20 ASSOCIATIONS WORLDWIDE.

CUSHLOUGH COMMUNITY COUNCIL LTD.: A NEW SET OF BELLS AT THE CHURCH OF THE SACRED HEART, CUSHLOUGH.

SHRULE MILLENNIUM COMMITTEE: THE CONSTRUCTION OF A STONE LABYRINTH TO MARK THE MILLENNIUM IN A PERMANENT WAY.

MUINTIR MAIGHEO DUBLIN: TO BRING 20 MAYO EMIGRANTS WHO HAVE FALLEN ON HARD TIMES HOME FOR A HOLIDAY.

MOYGOWMAGH COMMUNITY COUNCIL: "THE DIARY OF AN EXILE" – CELEBRATING THE PAST, PRESENT AND FUTURE THROUGH WEEKLONG EVENTS.

BELMULLET PLAYGROUND COMMITTEE: THE SETTING UP OF A CHILDREN'S PLAYGROUND FOR THE YOUTH OF THE AREA.

ST. JAMES N.S., SWINFORD: A SERIES OF CONCERTS – CHORAL AND INSTRUMENTAL MUSIC, IRISH SONGS.

PARKE MILLENNIUM CONCERT: STAGING OF A MILLENNIUM CONCERT TO INCLUDE LOCAL HISTORY, CULTURE, SET DANCING, AND IRISH MASS.

STRAIDE COMMUNITY COUNCIL: A DAY-LONG MUSICAL CELEBRATION ENTITLED "THE WIND QUINTET MILLENNIUM DAY ".

TURLOUGH COMMNUNITY DEVELOPMENT ASSOCIATION: ACKNOWLEDGING THE CONTRIBUTIONS OF SENIOR CITIZENS.

MAYO FOROIGE CLUBS: VISUAL MONTAGE OF ISSUES AND LIFE AS PERCEIVED BY YOUNG PEOPLE IN THE COUNTY.

CLAREMORRIS PASTORAL COUNCIL: NATIVITY PLAY TO CELEBRATE THE BIRTH OF CHRIST WITH INVOLVEMENT FROM YOUNG OF THE COMMUNITY.

IRISH WHEELCHAIR ASSOCIATION: SPECIAL RECOGNITION AWARDS .

SAULA SENIOR CITIZENS/ COMMUNITY ALERT/ GRÚPA MNÁ COIS NA LOCHA SAILE: VARIETY CONCERT IN ACHILL CONSISTING OF LOCAL TALENTS, IN IRISH AND ENGLISH, IN CONJUNCTION WITH SENIOR CITIZENS FUNCTION.

CLARE LAKEMCMAHON PARK PROJECT: THE SETTING OF STONE SUNDIAL CLOCK AT 12 NOON ON 21/06/00, AND THE SEEDS OF NATIVE TREES.

CEOL NA LOCHA: CONCERT OF TRADITIONAL IRISH MUSIC AND SONG TO PROMOTE THE IRISH LANGUAGE AND CULTURE).

MUSEUMS OF MAYO: INVITATION TO EVERY HOUSEHOLD IN MAYO FOR FREE ADMISSION TO ALL MEMBER CENTRES IN THE COUNTY.

FIS MILLENNIUM CONFERENCE: CONFERENCE, WITHIN THE COMMON GROUND OF CHRISTIANITY, TO EXAMINE AND REFLECT ON THE CULTURE OF WHICH WE ARE A PART.

WESTERN CARE ASSOCIATION: "MAYO MILLENNIUM MANUSCRIPT" IN WHICH PEOPLE OF ALL AGES ARE ASKED TO RECORD THEIR NAME, ADDRESS AND ANY MESSAGE/ COMMENT.

ST. JOSEPH'S N.S.: CONCERT COMPRISING OF A NATIVITY PLAY, A BELL CHOIR, CHORAL PRESENTATION AND TRADITIONAL MUSIC.

CÓR MHUIGHEO: CHORAL AND ORCHESTRAL PRESENTATION OF SCHUBERT'S MASS IN G.

OIDHREACHT CHOILLTE MACH: PRODUCTION OF A TAPESTRY OF THE PARISH OF KILTIMAGH IN ART FORM, AND IN IRISH, USING TWEED MATERIALS AND PAINTS.

LORCAN & UNA LEAVY: PUBLICATION OF A PHOTOGRAPHIC RECORD OF WILDFLOWERS RELATING TO THE FLORA OF THE AREA.

THREE SCHOOLS MILLENNIUM PROJECT: PRODUCTION OF A MILLENNIUM BOOK MADE FROM HANDMADE PAPER DOCUMENTING LOCAL HISTORY, PLACES OF INTEREST, STORIES.

CUMANN NA MBUNSCOL MHAIGHEO: "MILLENNIUM FUN DAY" FOR 194 PRIMARY SCHOOLS AT 20 VENUES ACROSS THE COUNTY.

BALLINROBE: A NATURE RESERVE TO BE USED EXCLUSIVELY FOR THE CHILDREN OF BALLINROBE NATIONAL SCHOOLS.

IRISHTOWN DRAMA AND HERITAGE GROUP: PAGEANT, LAUNCHING OF A BOOK ON LOCAL HISTORY AND CLEAN UP OF PATRICIAN SITE.

CLOONTIA DEVELOPMENT ASSOICATION: HONOUR THE SENIOR CITIZENS AND ENCOURAGE YOUTH OF THE AREAS WITH AN EVENT ENTITLED "PASSING ON THE TORCH".

LOUISBURGH MILLENNIUM FESTIVAL: "HERITAGE DAY" HIGHLIGHTING TRADITIONAL VALUES, I.E. BLACKSMITH, THATCHING AND TIN MAKING.

COISTE MHAOLAOISE DHU THUAMA: PRODUCING A CD-ROM TO RECORD THE SIGNIFICANT EVENS OF THE PAST 2000 YEARS IN THE AREA.

WESTPORT MILLENNIUM PROJECT: ECUMENICAL PRAYER SERVICE AT CROAGH PATRICK WITH MUSIC AND CHOIRS.

CHRIS DORAS: RECORD OF EVENTS AS A RESULT OF A JOURNEY TO BE UNDERTAKEN COVERING 2000 KMS.

WESTPORT/LIMAVADY LINKAGE COMMITTEE: "CROSS-BORDER CHOIRS MILLENNIUM CELEBRATION CONCERT".

SCOIL RAIFTEIRÍ: CREATION OF A NATURE RESERVE TO INCLUDE MIXED DECIDUOUS AND CONIFEROUS TREES, BUSHES, FLOWERBEDS.

MAYO ART SQUAD: TO OBTAIN VISUAL IMPRESSIONS FROM 1000 PEOPLE THROUGHOUT THE COUNTY.

FITE FUAITE COMMUNITY ARTS: 3 OLDER PERSONS AND 3 YOUNG PEOPLE IN EACH OF

THE 55 PARISHES IN MAYO TO DESIGN AND PRODUCE A PARISH MILLENNIUM FLAG.

CROSSMOLINA COMMUNITY COUNCIL: NATURE RESERVE ALONG THE BANKS OF THE RIVER DEEL.

SONAS: RESEARCH ON THE TRAVELLER CULTURE, LANGUAGE AND WAY OF LIFE AND PRESENT RESULTS IN LOCAL SCHOOLS.

CARNACON DEVELOPMENT ASSOCIAITON LTD.: UNVEILING OF A MILLENNIUM STONE ERECTED IN THE VILLAGE.

BALLINA MILLENNIUM COMMITTEE: CEREMONY AT CROSSROADS INVOLVING PARTICIPATION OF THE COMMUNITY AT DIFFERENT LEVELS.

BALLINTUBBER G.A.A.: MILLENNIUM HISTORY PROJECT. PRODUCTION OF MAGAZINE AND VIDEO "FROM 1885 TO THE MILLENNIUM".

FOROIGE: COMPILE AND PRINT A "MILLENNIUM BOOK" REPRESENTING HISTORY AND CULTURE OF AREA.

BELCARRA MILLENNIUM COMMITTEE: PLANTING OF THREE TREES TO SYMBOLISE THE LAST TWO, AND THE FUTURE, MILLENNIA.

BALLINTUBBER TOURIST CO-OP & BALLINTUBBER ABBEY TRUST: THE "STORY" OF BALLINTUBBER TO BE TOLD THROUGH DRAMA, SONG, MIME, STORY-TELLING AND DANCE.

KILLALA N.S.: THE COMPILATION OF A HISTORY LIFELINE OF MAJOR EVENTS IN IRELAND ESPECIALLY IN THE KILLALA REGION.

FÉILE IORRAS: FOUR EVENTS TO PROMOTE IRISH CULTURE – DRAMA, SONG, DANCE AND TALKS.

AGHAGOWER MILLENNIIUM PROJECT: ERECTION OF A STONE MONUMENT AND FLOODLIGHTING.

WOMEN ON TRACK: RECEPTION TO RECOGNISE AND REWARD THE CONTRIBUTION OF SENIOR CITIZENS.

CLOONLYON COMMUNITY ALERT: DAY TRIP TO KNOCK SHRINE FOR SENIOR CITIZENS.

PHILOMENA CRONIN: TO RECORD, AND PUBLISH A BOOK OF TRADITIONAL HOME CURES WHICH WERE WIDELY USED IN COUNTY MAYO.

GLENCORRIB MILL COMMUNITY PROJECT: ERECTION OF A SQUARE BASED PYRAMID, 20 FEET HIGH – ONE FOOT FOR EACH CENTURY OF THE PAST TWO MILLENNIA.

LAHARDANE FESTIVAL COMMITTEE: FESTIVAL TO REVIVE THE TRADITION, CULTURE AND WAY OF LIFE ASSOCIATED WITH THE DONKEY.

ACHILL YAWL: A PURPOSE BUILT ACHILL YAWL TO CELEBRATE THE NEW MILLENNIUM.

DEALBHOIREACHT 5000 TEO: MILLENNIUM SCULPTURE FOR THE MAYO 5000 SCULPTURE TRAIL.

CUMANN NA MBUN SCOIL: MILLENNIUM FUNDING FOR INDEPENDENT PROJECTS IN 185 SCHOOLS.

SECONDARY SCHOOLS ASSOCIATION: MILLENNIUM FUNDING FOR INDEPENDENT PROJECTS IN 29 SCHOOLS.

KILLAWALLA MILLENNIUM PROJECT COMMITTEE: REFLECTIVE AND SPIRITUAL MEMORIAL GARDEN.

INNISTURK COMMUNITY COUNCIL: ONE DAY MUSIC WORKSHOP FOR THE CHILDREN OF THE ISLAND.

BALLINA TRAINING CENTRE: CREATION OF A MILLENNIUM GARDEN FOR USE BY TRAINEES, PATIENTS AND ELDERLY OF THE LOCALITY.

HOPE HOUSE, FOXFORD: A MILLENNIUM CONCERT IN THE NEWLY RENOVATED CHAPEL OF HOPE HOUSE.

BRACKLOON & DRUMMIN COMMUNITY CO. LTD.: TREE PLANTING AT COMMUNITY HALL, FOLLOWED BY A RECEPTION AND CONCERT TO RECOGNISE THE CONTRIBUTIONS OF SENIOR CITIZENS AND DISABLED MEMBERS OF THE COMMUNITY.

ATTYMASS PARISH MILLENNIUM ASSOCIAITON LTD.: HONOUR THE ELDERLY AND RETIRED FOR THEIR CONTRIBUTION TO THE PARISH.

AGHAMORE VOLUNTARY HOUSING ASSOCIAITON LTD.: STONE SCULPTURE ERECTED AT THE FRONT OF A 10 HOUSE SCHEME FOR ELDERLY PERSONS.

ST. PATRICK'S CHURCH PARISH COMMITTEE: ERECT 12 FT "MILLENNIUM STAR" ON THE TOWER OF ST. PATRICK'S CHURCH, NEWPORT.

MAYO WATER SAFETY COMMITTEE: THE "MAYO MILLENNIUM LIFESAVING CHALLENGE" OPEN TO ALL SWIMMERS FROM MAYO.

CO. MEATH

MILLENNIUM OFFICER: GERARDETTE BAILEY

ROSEMARY WALLACE, RATOATH: A MILLENNIUM CONCERT INVOLVING 48 GUILDS OF ICA.

MICHAEL HOLOHAN, BRÚ NA BOINNE, DONORE: PERFORMANCE OF 'A SNAIL IN MY PRIME', COLLABORATION BETWEEN THE POET PAUL DURCAN AND COMPOSER MICHAEL HOLOHAN.

BARE BODKIN THEATRE COMPANY: 'MEATH'S MILLENNIUM MOBILE MEALTIME THEATRE'. TWELVE PERFORMANCES OF THE PLAY 'A GALWAY GIRL' AT CAFES/RESTAURANTS/HOTELS AROUND THE COUNTY.

KILMESSAN/DUNSANY MILLENNIUM COMMITTEE: PUBLISH AND LAUNCH OF 'KILMESSAN AND DUNSANY AT THE MILLENNIUM' A HISTORY OF THE PARISH AND PEOPLE.

SCOIL MHUIRE, TRIM: PURCHASE OF GENERATOR FOR THE KATILU BOYS SECONDARY SCHOOL IN THE REMOTE AREA OF TURKANA, KENYA.

SINÉAD UÍ GHIBNE, PASCALE MENARD, DONORE: 'MILLENNIUM SUMMER SOLSTICE FESTIVAL', AT DONORE, CO. MEATH.

NAVAN ROAD CLUB, SLANE: MILLENNIUM LEISURE CYCLING FESTIVAL FOR ALL AGES.

MOYNALTY MILLENNIUM BOOK COMMITTEE: BOOK TO CELEBRATE PARISH OF MOYNALTY, INCLUDING PHOTOS OF EVERY FAMILY IN THE PARISH.

MEATH TOURISM LTD.: PROJECT INVOLVING ALL. SCHOOLS IN THE COUNTY – PRIMARY AND SECONDARY IN A LIMERICK COMPETITION.

KENTSTOWN NATIONAL SCHOOL: ERECT GRANITE PLAQUE ON SCHOOL OUTSIDE WALL SHOWING THE NAMES OF ALL PUPILS AND TEACHERS AT THE SCHOOL 1999-2000.

KILCLOON JUBILEE COMMITTEE: COMPREHENSIVE PROGRAMME OF EVENTS AND PROJECTS INCLUDING PUBLICATION OF 'HISTORY OF KILCLOON PARISH'.

ASHBOURNE AND DISTRICT SENJIOR CITIZENS ASSOCIATIONS: SENIOR CITIZENS AND STUDENTS OF GAELSCOIL NA CILLE COLLABORATE ON A NUMBER OF MILLENNIUM PROJECTS IN MUSIC, ART AND LIVING HISTORY.

T.I.D.E. YOUTH DEVELOPMENT WORKER, TRIM: ART AND CRAFT CLASSES FOR DISADVANTAGED CHILDREN TAKING PART IN THE T.I.D.E. HOMEWORK CLUBS.

N.M.C.D.A., KELLS: ART AND CRAFT CLASSES FOR UNDERPRIVILEGED CHILDREN TAKING PART IN N.M.C.D.A. HOMEWORK CLUBS.

AITEANN BUÍ FOIROIGE CLUB, NAVAN: PUBLISH BOOK ON AITEANN BUÍ ON ITS TENTH ANNIVERSARY, TEENAGERS AGED BETWEEN TWELVE AND EIGHTEEN RESEARCH MATERIAL, TRACK FORMER MEMBERS AND COMPARE CLUB WHEN IT FIRST STARTED TO NOW.

MEATH COUNTY COUNCIL ARTS OFFICE, DUNSHAUGHLIN LIBRARY: CHILDREN'S MILLENNIUM ARTS FESTIVAL.

MARTIN TULLY, OLDCASTLE: PRODUCE A CD OF TRADITIONAL AND CONTEMPORARY MUSICIANS IN MEATH.

ASHBOURNE MILLENNIUM/JUBILEE COMMITTEE: TO HOST A FORUM 'OUR TOWN IN THE NEW MILLENNIUM' TO DISCUSS FUTURE OF THE VILLAGE.

ST. FINIANS DIOCESAN TRUST, MULLINGAR: DIOCESAN PILGRIMAGE TO THE HILL OF SLANE.

IRISH CULTURAL CENTRE, KELLS: A PROJECT INVOLVING SCHOOL CHILDREN IN THE AREA MEETING WITH, INTERVIEWING AND RECORDING MUSICIANS OF MEATH.

O'CAROLAN HARP, CULTURE AND HERITAGE FESTIVAL, CASTLETOWN, NAVAN: MILLENNIUM CHOIR AND HARP RECITAL.

MARIE MCCONNELL, NAVAN: TO RESTORE 'OUR LADY'S GROTTO' AND FLOODLIGHT DUNDERRY CHURCH.

IRISH GIRL GUIDES, ASHBOURNE DISTRICT: MILLENNIUM PROJECT TO PROVIDE TRAINING TO NINE LEADERS IN YOUTH AND DEVELOPMENT WORK.

ST. PATRICK'S PARK RESIDENTS ASSOCIATION, NAVAN: LIGHT UP TREE IN PARK IN MEMORY OF YOUTH NOW DECEASED.

NAVAN AREA D.Q.L.A., NORTH EASTERN HEALTH BOARD: MILLENNIUM CONFERENCE 'DRUGS QUESTIONS, LOCAL ANSWERS'.

RATOATH HERITAGE GROUP: PUBLISH HISTORY OF RATOATH AND FLOODLIGHT TOWER OF OLD PROTESTANT CHURCH.

ENFIELD GIRL GUIDES: 'FOUR CENTRES MILLENNIUM SERVICE GROUP'. THREE WOMEN FROM MEATH GIRL GUIDES WILL JOIN WITH SIX OTHERS FORM AROUND THE COUNTRY TO TRAVEL TO THE FOUR WORLD CENTRES OF GUIDING (INDIA, SWITZERLAND, MEXICO AND LONDON).

NAVAN TRAVELLERS WORKSHOP LTD: A CONFERENCE CELEBRATING TRAVELLER'S CULTURE AND LIFESTYLE.

MEATH YOUTH FEDERATION: SUMMER SOLSTICE MILLENNIUM STREET PAGEANT INVOLVING SEVENTY YOUNG PERSONS FROM AROUND THE COUNTY.

MAGGI NIC SHIOMOIN, RATH CAIRN: MILLENNIUM GARDEN ENTITLED 'TÍR NA NÓG', DEVELOPED AND MAINTAINED BY THE CHILDREN OF NAIONRA RATH CAIRN.

KILDALKEY ACTIVE RETIREMENT GROUP: MILLENNIUM PROJECT TO RESTORE ST. DYMPNA'S WELL ADJACENT TO KILDAKEY CEMETERY, STEPS TO WELL AND STONE WALL SURROUND.

ASHBOURNE AND DISTRICT CHAMBER OF COMMERCE: DEVELOP NEW MILLENNIUM PARK IN ASHBOURNE.

IRISH WHEELCHAIR ASSOCIATION: SPECIAL RECOGNITION AWARDS.

ASHBOURNE COMMUNITY SCHOOL: MILLENNIUM POD – A TIME CAPSULE BURIED IN A GRASS MOUND IN FRONT OF SCHOOL ON LAST DAY OF SCHOOL TERM.

DARK HORSE VENTURE PROGRAMME: MILLENNIUM PROGRAMME-AN AWARDS SCHEME FOR OLDER PERSONS TAKING PLACE IN MEATH, DUBLIN, KILDARE AND CORK.

GAELSCOIL NA CILLE, ASHBOURNE: MILLENNIUM ARTIST IN RESIDENCE PROGRAMME/MILLENNIUM SCULPTURE.

KELLS HERITAGE FESTIVAL: MILLENNIUM LECTURE PROGRAMME AS PART OF KELLS HERITAGE FESTIVAL 2000.

CO. MONAGHAN
MILLENNIUM OFFICER: SOMHAIRLE MACCONGHAIL

ARDAGHEY ICA GUILD: SENIOR CITIZENS MILLENNIUM PARTY.

CORCAGHAN COMMITTEE CENTRE: HERITAGE EVENTS CELEBRATING CORCAGHAN.

CREMARTIN DEVELOPMENT AND G.F.C. COMMITTEE: MILLENNIUM CELEBRATION FOR ALL AGES.

TYDAVNET COMMUNITY DEVELOPMENT, SCOTSTOWN: MASS AND DEVELOPMENT OF WILDLIFE PARK.

BALLYBAY CAILINÍ WOMEN'S GROUP: DESIGN MILLENNIUM CALENDAR.

LISDOONAN DEVELOPMENT ASSOCIATION: SENIOR CITIZENS NIGHT.

INNISKEEN COMMUNITY CENTRE: MILLENNIUM VIDEO OF EVENTS IN PARISH.

ANNO DOMINI MILLENNIUM COMMITTEE: ECUMENICAL EXHIBITION AND SERVICE.

BLADES MOVING ON, CASTLEBLANEY: CELEBRATION OF ACHIEVEMENTS OF YOUNG MOTHERS.

CAVAN/MONAGHAN MENTAL HEALTH SERVICES: MILLENNIUM PUBLICATION OF WORKS BY STAFF AND SERVICE USERS.

CASTLEBLANEY PLAYERS: COMMUNITY PLAY BASED ON LIFE OF CHRIST.

BALLYBAY CHAMBER OF COMMERCE: STREET PARTY.

ARDAGHEY HALL COMMITTEE: MILLENNIUM CONCERT.

MILLENNIUM CLUB FOR THE ELDERLY, AUGHERAKELTON, SCOTSTOWN: CLUB LAUNCH FOR THE ELDERLY.

ARDAGHEY MILLENNIUM CÉILÍ: A CÉILÍ FOR ALL AGES.

CASTLEBLANEY HERITAGE GROUP: PUBLICATION OF LOCAL HISTORY BOOK.

CASTLEBLANEY PEACE GARDEN COMMITTEE: MILLENNIUM PEACE GARDEN.

KNOCKATALLON DEVELOPMENT COMMITTEE: LAUNCH OF RURAL TOURISM CENTRE.

KNOCKATALLON DEVELOPMENT COMMITTEE: LAUNCH OF MILLENNIUM WALKS .

ARDAGHEY COMMUNITY DEVELOPMENT: MILLENNIUM CALENDAR.

ARDAGHEY FAROIGE CLUB: MILLENNIUM TABLE QUIZ.

THE GARAGE THEATRE: THREE PLAYS FOR THE MILLENNIUM.

FARNEY YOUTH GROUP: DESIGN A MILLENNIUM MOSAIC.

MONAGHAN FILM SOCIETY: SCREENING OF CULTURAL FILMS.

INNISKEEN ENTERPRISE GROUP: CELTIC SPIRITUALITY AT THE MILLENNIUM DURING KAVANAGH WEEKEND.

MONAGHAN FOROIGE DISTRICT COUNCIL: PRESENTATION ON A THEME AROUND THE MILLENNIUM.

CASTLEBLANEY COMMUNITY ENTERPRISE: ENCOURAGE PEOPLE TO CONTRIBUTE A NEW INVENTION.

MULLANDOY CONSERVATION GOUP, CSTLEBLANEY: PROTECT CELTIC MONASTIC SITE.

MONAGHAN YOUTH FEDERATION: MILLENNIUM CROSS-BORDER PROGRAMME.

CASTLEBLANEY DRAMA FESTIVAL: MILLENNIUM EVENTS IN FORM OF DRAMA.

THE DESIGN HOUSE: MONAGHAN THROUGH THE MILLENNIUM WEBSITE.

TARKA RICHARD KING, GLASLOUGH: WORKING FACILITY FOR ARTISTS.

MONAGHAN YOUTH THEATRE: MILLENNIUM MAYHEM CELEBRATION EVENT.

EILEEN FERGUSON/NEAL GREIG, GLASLOUGH: LARGE SCALE ART PROJECT.

CONVENT JUNIOR SCHOOL, CASTLEBLANEY: GALA CONCERT AND CHRISTMAS CARD DESIGN.

SCOIL MHUIRE, CASTLEBLANEY: BOYS SCHOOL MILLENNIUM BOOK.

GAELSCOIL ULTAIN: MILLENNIUM CONCERT AS GAEILGE.

ST. LOUIS SECONDARY SCHOOL, CARRICKMACROSS: SEVERAL EVENTS, INCLUDING PLANTING TREE AND SOUVENIR CANDLES.

LARGY COLLEGE, CLONES: CD OF COLLEGES CHOIR AND MUSICIANS.

MONAGHAN YOUTH FOOTBALL CLUB: INTERNATIONAL YOUTH FOOTBALL TOURNAMENT.

DOOHAMLET MILLENNIUM COMMITTEE, CSTLEBLANEY: CELEBRATION OF THE MILLENNIUM.

SLIABH BEAGH ASC.: OPEN SPORTS SEMINAR.

COSITE CHONTAE MHUINEACHÁIN CLG: HONOURING THOSE WHO CONTRIBUTED TO MONAGHAN GAA.

TYDAVNET GYMNASTICS CLUB, KILLYMARRON, BALLINODE: INTERNATIONAL GYMNASTICS SHOW.

HARVEST TIME BLUES, MONAGHAN: BLUES FESTIVAL CELEBRATING 10TH ANNIVERSARY.

LMB ENTERTAINMENT'S, CLONES: CLONES MILLENNIUM LAUGHTER FESTIVAL.

CARRICKMACROSS MILLENNIUM CHORAL FESTIVAL: YOUNG SINGER SOLO COMPETITION.

IRISH WHEELCHAR ASSOCIATION: SPECIAL RECOGNITION AWARDS.

CARRICKMACROSS, MAGHERACLOONE, DOOHAMLET, INNISKEEN AND IVER COLLEGE SOCIAL SERVICES GROUP: HONOURING UP TO 600 SENIOR CITIZENS.

HOLLYWOOD DEVELOPMENT COMMITTEE, BALLINODE: SESSIONS OF IRISH TRADITIONAL MUSIC AND DANCE.

EMYVALE COMMUNITY COUNCIL: SERIES OF MUSIC EVENTS.

NET-MUSIC, MONAGHAN: MILLENNIUM EXTRAVAGANZA BRINGING TOGETHER YOUNG BANS FROM NORTH AND SOUTH.

BARRATITOPPY CEILE BAND, SCOTSTOWN: TRADITIONAL IRISH NIGHT INVOLVING CROSS-BORDER ARTISTS.

CO. OFFALY
MILLENNIUM OFFICER: ANNE COUGHLAN

COISTE GAEILGE, BÓRD CHONTAE UIBH FHAILLI (CCE): IRISH LANGUAGE WRITING COMPETITION.

BIRR CHAMBER OF COMMERCE: MILLENNIUM PUPPET FESTIVAL.

EDENDERRY CANAL & HARBOUR DEVELOPMENT ASSOCIATION: TWO-DAY EVENT TO INCLUDE CONCERTS AND EXHIBITION OF HARBOUR AND CANAL MEMORABILIA.

TULLAMORE COMMUNITY MILLENNIUM GROUP LTD.: UNITED NATIONS MILLENNIUM FAMILY DAY.

BIRDWATCH IRELAND, MIDLAND'S BRANCH: MILLENNIUM FARMLAND BIRDS POSTER.

GEASHILL PASTORAL COUNCIL: DEVELOPMENT OF MILLENNIUM GARDEN ON SITE OF OLD HALL.

OFFALY COMMUNITY ARTS GROUP: R.T.É. MILLENNIUM CONCERT ORCHESTRA TO PERFORM IN TULLAMORE COURT HOTEL.

TULLAMORE TENNIS CLUB: MILLENNIUM TENNIS PROJECT – PROVISION OF FACILITY FOR INDIVIDUALS WITH SPECIAL NEEDS.

PULLOUGH GROTTO COMMITTEE: MONUMENT RECOGNISING CONTRIBUTION OF PULLOUGH BRICK AS A SIGNIFICANT LOCAL INDUSTRY IN AREA IN THE '30S & '40S.

TULLAMORE ASTRONOMICAL SOCIETY: COSMOS 2000 ASTRONOMICAL FESTIVAL. AN ALL-IRELAND FESTIVAL.

CRINKLE VILLAGE MILLENNIUM COMMITTEE: MILITARY WEEKEND FESTIVAL. PUBLICATION OF BOOKLET ON CRINKLE AND EXHIBITION ON CRINKLE BARRACKS.

TULLAMORE GRAMPAPHONE SOCIETY: A SERIES OF PUBLIC MUSIC APPRECIATION RECITALS.

ST. MARY'S YOUTH CENTRE, TULLAMORE: PRODUCTION OF THE MUSICAL FAME AND PROJECT TO ASSIST IN THE PROVISION OF CREATIVE STRUCTURED ACTIVITY FOR YOUNG PEOPLE.

CLAREEN MILLENNIUM CLUB: UNVEILING OF MONUMENT DEPICTING ST. KIERAN'S LIFE, INCLUDING THE BELL ASSOCIATED WITH THE SAINT.

CLARA MILLENNIUM COMMITTEE: COLLABORATIVE PROJECT INVOLVING ALL STRANDS OF COMMUNITY ENDEAVOUR TO MARK THE MILLENNIUM THROUGH ACTIVITIES AND EVENTS.

KEVIN CARROLL, A.L.S.M., BIRR: MILLENNIUM VOICES – A CHORAL SPECTACULAR WHICH WILL FEATURE 250-300 PRIMARY SCHOOL CHILDREN FROM OFFALY.

BANAGHER/CLOGHAN: TRADITIONAL MUSIC GROUP. TO RECORD LOCAL AND VISITING ARTISTS IN CELEBRATION OF IRISH TRADITIONAL MUSIC IN THE BANAGHER AND CLOGHRAN AREAS.

BALLINAHOWN MILLENNIUM COMMITTEE: PUBLICATION AND LAUNCH OF MILLENNIUM BOOK.

KILCLONFERT COMMUNITY CENTRE: RESTORATION OF OLD PUMP AND SURROUNDING WALL BESIDE THE COMMUNITY CENTRE.

KILMURRAY HALL COMMITTEE: TREE PLANTING AT KILMURRAY HALL TO INVOLVE CHILDREN, PARENTS AND THE WIDER COMMUNITY.

ST. BRIGID'S PIPE BAND, MOUNBOLUS, TULLAMORE: PERFORMANCES BY PIPE BAND AT MILLENNIUM FUNCTIONS.

CLOGHAN FOROIGE & HALL DEVELOPMENT COMMITTEE: PRESENTATIONS TO CLOGHAN VOLUNTARY ORGANISATIONS IN RECOGNITION OF OUTSTANDING CONTRIBUTION.

RAHAN COMHALTAS CEOLTÉOIRÍ EIREANN: THE MILLENNIUM ARCHIVAL EXHIBITION.

BIRR STAGE GUILD LTD.: INAUGURAL PRODUCTION TO COINCIDE WITH OPENING OF OXMANTOWN HALL THEATRE AND ARTS CENTRE.

THE FLOATING THEATRE COMPANY: MILLENNIUM VOYAGE AT EDENDERRY AND FERBANE.

BIRR FESTIVAL OF FLOWERS: CELEBRATION OF THE CHURCH THROUGHOUT THE AGES INCLUDING THE COMMISSIONING OF PIECE OF MUSIC IN HONOUR OF ST. BRENDAN.

OFFALY HOSPICE – BANAGHER BRANCH: THE CELTIC SOUL CONCERT "LEGENDS OF LIGHT" BY LIAM LAWTON TOGETHER WITH THE CHORAL GROUP "LUMINA" TO BE PERFORMED IN THE CHURCH OF THE ASSUMPTION, TULLAMORE.

TULLAMORE ONE WORLD GROUP: PAN AFRICAN CULTURAL AWARENESS EVENT ENCOURAGING A GREATER APPRECIATION AND RESPECT FOR AFRICAN ARTS, CULTURE AND PEOPLE.

CLOGHAN PASTORAL COUNCIL: PUBLICATION OF CLOGAN MILLENNIUM CALENDAR USING LOCAL PHOTOGRAPHS.

DAINGEAN MILLENNIUM COMMITTEE: TREE PLANTING PROJECT, CHILDREN'S MILLENNIUM CELEBRATION, PLANTING OF 2000 CROCUSES IN DAINGEAN SCHOOL GROUNDS AND SENIOR CITIZEN'S CELEBRATIONS.

KILLOUGHEY MILLENNIUM COMMITTEE: PUBLICATION OF A LOCAL HISTORY BOOK AND ACCOMPANYING VIDEO.

CADAMSTOWN TIDY TOWNS: ERECTION OF DOLMEN AT CADAMSTOWN AND AT FAIRYFIELD, NEAR RINGFORT SITE.

FIRST OFFALY SCOUT UNIT: CAMPFIRE AT SUNDOWN – TRADITIONAL SCOUT CAMPFIRE WITH MILLENNIUM FOCUS.

SHAMROCK G.A.A. CLUB: MILLENNIUM EVENT TO CELEBRATE THE CONTRIBUTION OF OLDER MEMBERS.

TULLAMORE MUSICAL SOCIETY: CONCERT FEATURING HIGHLIGHTS OF 45 YEARS OF MUSICAL THEATRE IN TULLAMORE.

BRACKNAGH FOROIGE CLUB: A CELEBRATION OF BRACKNAGH'S HERITAGE WITH CAROL SINGING AND TORCH LIGHT PROCESSION.

TULLAMORE CHAMBER OF COMMERCE: MILLENNIUM LIGHTING IN TULLAMORE AND IN PARTICULAR AT VENUE IN MARKET SQUARE TO FACILITATE FULL PARTICIPATION, PARTICULARLY OF THE ELDERLY.

NORTH OFFALY DEVELOPMENT COMPANY: PRESENTATION OF CERTIFICATES TO THE PARTICIPANTS IN THE COMMUNITY DEVELOPMENT TRAINING PROGRAMME.

IRISH WHEELCHAIR ASSOCIATION: SPECIAL RECOGNITION AWARDS .

MIDNET INTERNETR CAFÉ, TULLAMORE: INSTALLATION OF WEB CAM OVERLOOKING O'CONOR SQUARE, CENTRAL SQUARE AND MAIN STREET TULLAMORE. BROADCAST LIVE PICTURES OVER THE INTERNET OF TULLAMORE'S MILLENNIUM CELEBRATIONS.

OFFALY ROWING CLUB: DEVELOPMENT OF BOATING FACILITIES AND PROVISION OF BOAT TO PROMOTE PARTICIPATION IN ROWING IN THE COMMUNITY.

BALLYCOMMON ORGANISATION FOR LOCAL DEVELOPMENT: COMMUNITY GATHERING AT LAST LIGHT CEREMONY; TREE PLANTING AND PRESENTATION OF SPECIALLY COMMISSIONED MEDALLION.

TULLAMORE PARISH PASTORAL COUNCIL: CONFERENCE FOR LAITY AND CLERGY REPRESENTING 70 PARISHES AROUND THE COUNTY.

CLARA/BELARUS ORPHANAGE AID: VISIT TO TULLAMORE OF THE CHILDRENS'S BRASS BAND FROM THE ORPHANAGE OF BELARUS AND PERFORMANCES BY THE BAND IN SCHOOLS.

TRAVELLERS ARTS DEV. COM: ARTS & LIBRARIES SERVICES. AN ARTIST IN RESIDENCE PROJECT FOR THE CHILDREN AT THE HALTING SITE AT TULLAMORE TO DEVELOP AN EDUCATIONAL PROGRAMME.

ST. BRENDAN'S PRIMARY SCHOOL: PLANT 150 NATIVE DECIDUOUS TREES IN THE GROUNDS OF THE SCHOOL AND INVOLVE PARENTS, CHILDREN AND WIDER COMMUNITY.

ST. BRENDAN'S COMMUNITY SCHOOL, BIRR: STUDENTS AND STAFF TO REFLECT AND CELEBRATE ON THE LIFE OF CHRIST THROUGH LITURGIES, ASSEMBLIES, ART, MUSIC AND VIDEO.

ST. JOSEPH & SARAN'S SECONDARY SCHOOL, FERBANE: PRODUCTION OF MUSICAL ANNIE BY TRANSITION YEAR & SECOND YEAR STUDENTS.

LOUGH BOORA PARKLANDS GROUP: A SERIES OF EDUCATIONAL/RECREATIONAL PROGRAMMES FOCUSING ON THE UNIQUE ENVIRONMENT AND CULTURAL HERITAGE OF CUTAWAY BOGS.

FOCUS ON FERBANE ENVIRONMENTAL GROUP: ECUMENICAL SERVICE WITH EARLY CHRISTIANITY FOCUS, MILLENNIUM PARADE, ECCLESIASTICAL PAGEANT AND OPENING OF CRAFT/ART VISITOR CENTRE.

CLARA MUSICAL SOCIETY: PRODUCTION OF GEORGE GERSHWINS CRAZY FOR YOU.

BISHOR OF ARDAGH & CLONMACNOISE: GREAT JUBILEE PAGEANT, INCLUDING LIGHT & SOUND, FOR PATTERN DAY.

CO. ROSCOMMON
MILLENNIUM OFFICER: CAITLÍN NÍ FHLOINN

TULSK PARISH SERVICES: MILLENNIUM PARTY FOR SENIOR CITIZENS AND TRIPS TO LOURDES OR KNOCK FOR OTHERS.

LECARROW MILLENNIUM SOCIAL COMMITTEE: MILLENNIUM CELEBRATIONS FOR TWO CENTENARIANS.

MOYLURG WRITERS, BOYLE: BOOK COLLECTION OF CREATIVE WRITING WITH SPECIAL THEME OF 'THE MILLENNIUM'.

VITA HOUSE FAMILY CENTRE DEVELOPMENT TEAM: FAMILY AFTERNOON & OPEN FORUM ON THEME: THE FAMILY FACING THE NEW MILLENNIUM'.

BOYLE ARTS FESTIVAL COMMITTEE: RTE CONCERT ORCHESTRA FOR A MILLENNIUM CONCERT.

ROSCOMMON WOMEN'S COALITION: 'ROSCOMMON WOMEN MEETING THE NEW MILLENNIUM'.

ROSCOMMON PARISH C/O MONSIGNOR TRAVERS: SENIOR CITIZENS PARTY, ESPECIALLY FOR ELDERLY PEOPLE LIVING ALONE IN THE PARISH, TO CELEBRATE THE MILLENNIUM WITH FRIENDS.

COUNTY ROSCOMMON ACTIVE AGE GROUP: INFORMATION DAY WITH PROFESSIONALS. SOCIAL AFTERNOON OF CELEBRATION.

BALLAGHADERREEN SOCIAL SERVICES COUNCIL: MILLENNIUM PARTY FOR ELDERLY IN AREA.

BALLAGHADERREEN SOCIAL SERVICES COUNCIL: OFFICIAL OPENING OF DAY CENTRE FOR ELDERLY WITH ENTERTAINMENT.

BROTHERS OF CHARITY/ROSCARA SERVICES: MILLENNIUM PILGRIMAGE TO KNOCK FOLLOWED BY CELEBRATORY MEAL.

LOUGHGLYNN SENIOR CITIZEN'S MILLENNIUM COMMITTEE: MILLENNIUM PARTY FOR 100. PHOTOGRAPHS OF EACH PERSON PRESENT.

STROKESTOWN POETRY FESTIVAL COMMITTEE: STROKESTOWN INTERNATIONAL POETRY FESTIVAL.

CONAL KEARNEY – THE FLAOTING THEATRE COMPANY: FLOATING THEATRE MILLENNIUM VOYAGE – TWO DAYS ARTS/MUSIC WORKSHOPS IN SCHOOL ALONG THE RIVER SHANNON (LECARROW N.S).

JOSIE MCDERMOTT MEMORIAL FESTIVLA COMMITTEE: ANNUAL JOSIE MCDERMOTT MEMORIAL FESTIVAL. SPECIAL MILLENNIUM CATEGORIES AND PRIZES AWARDED.

BALLYFARNON COMMUNITY GROUP: LAUNCH 'MILLENNIUM CALENDAR', HISTORICAL INFORMATION & PHOTOGRAPHIC EXHIBITION; AND SENIOR CITIZENS MILLENNIUM PARTY.

ENTERPRISE KILTULLAGH LTD.: AWARDS FOR SENIOR CITIZENS AND OTHERS WHO HAVE CONTRIBUTED TO COMMUNITY.

CLOONBONNIFFE PARISH COUNCIL: MILLENNIUM PARISH BOOKLET DETAILING NAMES OF ALL WHO LIVED IN THE PARISH FORM 1990-1999.

GRANGE COMMUNITY ALERT: MILLENNIUM EVENT FOR ELDERLY IN AREA. INCORPORATING SKETCH BY BOYLE ACTIVE AGE GROUP WITH IRISH MUSIC AND DANCING.

LOUGH REE ENVIRONMENTAL SUMMER SCHOOL COMMITTEE: MILLENNIUM ENVIRONMENTAL AWARENESS EXPO, EXHIBITIONS & DISPLAYS ON ENVIRONMENT THROUGHOUT LAKESHORE-BALLYLEAGUE.

ROSCOMMON GAA SUPPORTERS CLUB (DUBLIN): COMPETITION FOR NOMINATIONS AND SELECTION OF ROSCOMMON GAELIC TEAM OF THE MILLENNIUM.

ORAN DEVELOPMENT COMMITTEE: REFURBISHMENT OF CLOVERHILL CHURCH BELL AND SPECIAL CELEBRATORY MASS AND BLESSING CEREMONY.

ARIGNA COMMUNITY DEVELOPMENT CO. LTD.: MILLENNIUM EXHIBITION IN LOCAL COMMUNITY CENTRE LINKED WITH MINING MUSEUM.

CONNAUGHT RURAL WOMEN'S GROUP LTD., DUN MAEVE, STROKESTOWN: MILLENNIUM CHILDREN'S BRICK WALL HANGING-EACH CHILD TO WRITE THEIR NAMES ON A MATERIAL 'BRICK' TO BECOME A BRICK WALL QUILT/HANGING.

DRUMBOYLAN DEVELOPMENT ASSOCIATION: INTERDENOMINATIONAL COMMUNITY EVENT TO RECOGNISE THOSE WHO HAVE CONTRIBUTED TO THE COMMUNITY.

DUN MAEVE PATCHWORK & QUILTING GUILD: MILLENNIUM COMPUTER WALLHANGING – 'SCENES FROM STROKESTOWN TODAY'.

TULSK ACTION GROUP: INVITATION TO ALL WHO HAVE LEFT TULSK TO RETURN FOR WEEKEND – DATABASE COMPILED.

CLOONCAGH N.S.: PLANTING OF MILLENNIUM FOREST. SCHOOL AND COMMUNITY TO PLANT A MILLENNIUM FOREST OF NATIVE TREES TOGETHER.

SLIABH BÁN 2000 COMMITTEE: COLLATING AND PRINTING THE HISTORY, FOLKLORE AND CULTURE OF THE AREA.

STROKESTOWN COMMUNITY PLAYSCHOOL: CHRISTMAS/MILLENNIUM CONCERT. FLOAT FOR EASTER PARADE WITH MILLENNIUM THEME.

BOYLE GALA MILLENNIUM FESTIVAL COMMITTEE: FAMILY ORIENTATED FESTIVAL AND MILLENNIUM FUN FAIR.

SHANE HOLOHAN, ELPHIN COMMUNITY COLLEGE: COMPETITION AND WORKSHOPS IN ROSCOMMON, LONGFORD, LEITRIM AND SLIGO. FOR SCHOOLS TO WRITE A 30-MINUTE PLAY (THEME - 'THE MILLENNIUM').

THE CRESCENT MILLENNIUM COMMITTEE, BOYLE: TRADITIONAL IRISH MUSIC FESTIVAL – MINI-FLEADH.

DRUMLION COMMUNITY COUNCIL: ERECT STONE PLACENAMES ON 15 TOWNLANDS IN PARISH, CHURCHES AND CEMETERIES.

ROSCOMMON TOWN ACTIVE AGE GROUP: PRODUCE AND STAGE PAGEANT ON THE PAST OF CO. ROSCOMMON.

THEATRE LABORATORY (SAM DOWLING): OUTDOOR/INDOOR THEATRICAL EVENT PERFORMED AT HISTORIC SITES THROUGHOUT THE COUNTY BETWEEN THE ANCIENT FESTIVALS AT SUMMER SOLSTICE AND AUTUMN EQUINOX.

ST.COMAN'S CHURCH OF IRELAND COMMITTEE/ROSCOMMON HERITAGE GROUP: RESTORATION OF CHURCH BELL AND CLOCK MECHANISM AT SITE OF CONSTANT CHRISTIAN WORSHIP SINCE THE SIXTH CENTURY.

BOYLE ACTIVE AGE GROUP: MILLENNIUM CELEBRATION GET-TOGETHER. REMINISCENCE MORNING WITH TUTOR FROM ACTIVE AGE IRELAND.

ST. ASICUS DAY CENTRE FOR THE ELDERLY: MILLENNIUM MASS AND AWARDS RECEPTION FOR SENIOR CITIZENS.

FRENCHPARK PARISH MILLENNIUM GROUP: MILLENNIUM MEMORIAL GARDEN AND GROTTO WITH OFFICIAL OPENING.

ELPHIN MILLENNIUM COMMITTEE: BURIAL OF TIME CAPSULE, FESTIVAL AND ENTERTAINMENT.

ABBEY WRITERS, ROSCOMMON: EVENING OF MILLENNIUM READINGS AND MUSIC WITH GUEST SPEAKER.

BALLINAHEGLISH COMMUNITY CENTRE COMMITTEE: MILLENNIUM FUN DAY FOR WHOLE PARISH INCLUDING SPORTS DAY WITH BOUNCING CASTLES AND PUPPET SHOWS.

CARRICK ROAD MILLENNIUM COMMITTEE, BOYLE: ECUMENICAL SERVICE, CANDLE LIGHTING – CANDLE TO BE LIT EVERY NIGHT THROUGH THE YEAR.

BOYLE NEIGHBOURHOOD YOUTH PROJECT: PHOTOGRAPHIC AND MOSAIC EXHIBITION – 'BOYLE – PAST, PRESENT & FUTURE.'

BALLINTUBBER FESTIVAL COMMITTEE: EILEEN ÓG MILLENNIUM FESTIVAL FEATURING ARTS AND CRAFTS EXHIBITION.

CLOONEYCOLGAN DEVELOPMENT ASSOCIATION: REDEVELOPMENT OF ST. PATRICK'S HOLY WELL, ORAN WITH NEW STATUE OF ST. PATRICK: PUBLISH PARISH BOOKLET.

BROTHERS OF CHARITY RESPITE CENTRE: MILLENNIUM SENSORY GARDEN FOR PEOPLE WITH LEARNING DISABILITIES.

SCOIL MHUIRE, STROKESTOWN: STUDENTS TAKE PHOTOGRAPHS OF ALL THE BUSINESSES IN STROKESTOWN; WRITE A BRIEF ACCOUNT OF EACH AND TALK TO EMPLOYEES. HOST EXHIBITION IN SCHOOL HALL.

KILBRIDE COMMUNITY CENTRE: PLANT BANK AT FRONT OF COMMUNITY CENTRE, PLANTING OF SPECIAL TREE AND SPECIAL LIGHTING.

ROSCOMMON CHAMBER OF COMMERCE/TOWN TWINNING COMMITTEE: MILLENNIUM EXHIBITION IN CHARTRETTES, FRANCE. ROSCOMMON'S TWINN TOWN. 25 MUSICIANS, DANCERS AND ARTISTS FROM ROSCOMMON VISIT CHARTRETTES.

BALLINGARE COMMUNITY CENTRE ASSOCIATION: MILLENNIUM BALL – CELEBRATIONS OF EMIGRANTS AND LOCALS; SENIOR CITIZENS EVENT AND PUBLICATION OF 'A MILLENNIUM IN BALLINAGARE'.

CONVENT OF MERCY, ROSCOMMON: UNVEILING SCULPTURE TO MARK EDUCATION PROVIDED BY SISTERS OF MERCY.

CONVENT OF MERCY, ROSCOMMON: BOOK OF THE MILLENNIUM – A SPECIAL HARD-BACKED EDITION OF SCHOOL MAGAZINE WITH MILLENNIUM THEME AND FOCUS.

BOYLE COUNTRY & WESTERN MILLENNIUM CARNIVAL COMMITTEE: MILLENNIUM CARNIVAL WITH OUTDOOR GIGS, FREE STREET ENTERTAINMENT, SPECIAL BANDS & LOCAL TALENT.

LOUGHGLYNN MILLENNIUM COMMITTEE: PAGEANT RE-ENACTING BATTLE OF THE WOODLANDS: PLACING OF TIME CAPSULE; PLANTING OF OAK TREE AND PLACING OF PLAQUE IN CHURCH GROUNDS.

ROSCOMMON INDUSTRIAL & AGRICULTURAL SHOW SOCIETY: 31ST AGRICULTURAL SHOW INCORPORATING SPECIAL MILLENNIUM CATALOGUE.

FRENCHPARK DRAMA GROUP: MILLENNIUM CONCERT WITH SKETCH AND ONE-ACT DRAMA.

BALLAGHADERREEN & DISTRICT DEVELOPMENT LTD.: EXHIBITION OF 2000 ITEMS TO CELEBRATE AND REFLECT LIFE IN THE AREA UNDER VARIOUS THEMES.

ST. MICHAEL'S SCHOOL, CASTLEREA: CONCERT INVOLVING MUSIC, MOVEMENT AND DANCE TO BUILD LINKS WITH LOCAL PEOPLE AND THE SCHOOL WHICH CATERS FOR CHILDREN WITH SPECIAL NEEDS.

DRINANE LAKE HERITAGE GROUP: RE-CONSTRUCT CRANNOG DWELLING AT THE LAKE.

ARDCARNE PARISH MILLENNIUM COMMITTEE: MILLENNIUM TALKS AND LECTURES ON THE HISTORY AND ARCHAEOLOGY OF THE PARISH.

DRUM HERITAGE GROUP: THE GREAT MILLENNIUM WALK FROM ARDKEENAN TO CLONMACNOISE ALONG THE ANCIENT FUNERAL ROUTE FOR RELIGIOUS CELEBRATIONS.

CAVETOWN RESIDENTS ASSOCIATION: MILLENNIUM AMENITY AREA. CONSTRUCT TWO STONE ARMCHAIRS AT AMENITY AREA AT LAKE AND TWO WOODEN SEATS AT DISABLED PERSONS' FISHING STAND.

KILMURRAY LADIES CLUB: BRINGING TOGETHER VARIOUS LOCAL GROUPS FOR MILLENNIUM CELEBRATION INCLUDING MASS, A CONCERT WITH LOCAL TALENT AND A PRESENTATION TO BOTH YOUNG AND OLD OF COMMUNITY.

IRISH WHEELCHAIR ASSOCIATION: SPECIAL RECOGNITION AWARDS.

CASTLEREA BRASS & REED BAND: SPECIAL CONCERT IN CASTLEREA AND OTHER LOCAL TOWNS.

BALLYFORAN PARISH COUNCIL: UNVEILING COMMEMORATIVE PLAQUE AT CENTRAL LOCATION; COLLECT LOCAL MATERIAL RELATING TO HISTORY OF PARIAHS, CATALOGUE ALL ITEMS AND MOUNT PERMANENT DISPLAY AREA.

LISACUL COMMUNITY COUNCIL: MILLENNIUM CELEBRATIONS INCLUDE TIME CAPSULE, WATER FEATURE AND SPECIAL MASS FOLLOWED BY PARTY FOR CHILDREN AND THE ELDERLY OF PARISH.

ROSCOMMON FESTIVAL COMMITTEE: ROSFEST 2000. STREET PAGEANT WITH MEDIEVAL THEME AND INCORPORATING LOCAL HISTORY OF TOWN.

CO. ROSCOMMON PERCY FRENCH SOCIETY: MILLENNIUM CROSS-BORDER CULTURAL WEEKEND. 80 PEOPLE FROM CO. DOWN PERCY FRENCH SOCIETY INVITED TO ROSCOMMON FOR A CULTURAL EXCHANGE WEEKEND.

ROBERT STEINKE, FRENCHPARK: EXHIBITION AND ILLUSTRATED TALK ON PHOTOGRAPHS AND ARTEFACTS DEPICTING 'THE CRAFT OF THE MASTER SADDLER' OVER THE LAST MILLENNIUM.

IRISH WHEELCHAIR ASSOCIATION - GALWAY: WESTERN REGION OF IWA MILLENNIUM/ ANNIVERSARY CELEBRATION. THEME OF

INCLUSIVENESS WITH PROGRAMME OF EVENTS FOR FAMILY AND FRIENDS.

ELPHIN DIOCESAN HERITAGE SOCIETY: PUBLISH AND LAUNCH A BIBLIOGRAPHY OF THE DIOCESE WITH DETAILED HISTORY AND TOWNLAND INDEXED MAPS.

GORTAGANNY MILLENNIUM COMMITTEE: RECEPTION TO HONOUR INDIVIDUALS' CONTRIBUTIONS TO LOCAL COMMUNITY.

ATHLEAGUE DEVELOPMENT ASSOCIATION: SCULPTURE TO COMMEMORATE MLLENNIUM AND PICTORIAL HISTORY EXHIBITION IN COMMUNITY CENTRE.

RUSKEY COMMUNITY AND VARIETY GROUP: A MILLENNIUM SHOW INVOLVING THREE GENERATIONS OF PERFORMERS.

MILLENNIUM EXILES RE-UNION & CASTLEREA INTERNATIONAL QUEEN OF ROSCOMMON: INTERNATIONAL FESTIVAL AND SPECIAL MILLENNIUM EXILES RE-UNION.

CO. ROSCOMMON ARTS & CRAFTS ASSOCIATION: MIXED MEDIA GROUP EXHIBITION WITH THE THEME 'CO. ROSCOMMON 2000'.

SOUTH ROSCOMMON CELTIC FESTIVAL COMMITTEE: RESIDENTIAL MUSIC WORKSHOPS THROUGHOUT SOUTH ROSCOMMON, OUTREACH MUSIC PROGRAMMES WITH BANDS/DANCE TROOPS FROM WALES, SCOTLAND, IRELAND, BRITTANY AND ISLE OF MAN.

KILRONAN PARISH: TORCHLIGHT PROCESSION FROM KEADUE VILLAGE TO KILRONAN ABBEY AT SUNSET.

C/O FRANK FEIGHAN OR MATT MCLOUGHLIN, BOYLE: MILLENNIUM BALL WITH THREE MAJOR BANDS.

BALLINAGARE DEVELOPMENT GROUP: BOOK COMPILATION OF HISTORY AND FOLKLORE OF THE PARISH.

CASTLEREA DEVELOPMENT CO-OPERATIVE: MILLENNIUM CONCERT INCORPORATING ALL ASPECTS OF ENTERTAINMENT & CULTURE.

SCOIL MHUIRE, STROKESTOWN: STAGING MUSICAL. CELEBRATION OF THE MILLENNIUM THROUGH SONG AND DANCE.

CASTLEREA GUIDE/SCOUT/YOUTH COMMITTEE: MILLENNIUM FUN DAY FOR PEOPLE AGED 7-15 YEARS FROM ALL AROUND THE COUNTY.

PÁDRAIG PEARSES GAA CLUB: FOOTBALL, HURLING & LADIES FOOTBALL TEAMS OF THE CENTURY.

ELPHIN VILLAGE RENEWAL GROUP: CELEBRATORY EVENT TO UNVEIL A MONUMENT AT THE MILLENNIUM PLAZA IN MAIN STREET.

COPERNICUS PROJECT, SUMMERHILL COLLEGE,

ATHLONE: FORUM FOR 16/17 YEAR OLDS FORM IRELAND, NORTHERN IRELAND, BRITAIN AND SIX CENTRAL EUROPEAN COUNTRIES WITH A SERIES OF WORKSHOPS 'HOPE FOR THE FUTURE'.

COUNTY LIBRARY, ROSCOMMON: BINDING OF ALL 'WRITE HERE, WRITE NOW' SUBMISSIONS FROM COUNTY ROSCOMMON.

COUNTY ROSCOMMON MILLENNIUM COMMITTEE: LAST LIGHTS CEREMONIES.

COUNTY ROSCOMMON MILLENNIUM COMMITTEE: FUNCTION TO HONOUR COUNTY'S CENTENARIANS AND NEW YEAR BABIES.

ROSCOMMON GARDENING CLUB: MILLENNIUM FLOWER FESTIVAL.

CO. SLIGO
MILLENNIUM OFFICER: KEVIN COLREAVY

TERSA GILIGAN: AGRICULTURAL MILLENNIUM BALL.

SLIGO CONCERT BAND: MILLENNIUM CONCERT.

ST. MARY'S PRESBYTERY: ALL SLIGO LITURGICAL CELEBRATIONS.

COMHARTAS CEOLTÓIRÍ ÉIREANN, R'TOWN: OUTDOOR SESSION AND CHURCH BELLS.

YEATS SOCIETY: MILLENNIUM YEATS SUMMER FESTIVAL.

SLIGO ORPHEUS CHOIR: PERFORMANCE OF HANDEL'S MESSIAH.

SLIGO TOWN TWINNING COMMITTEE: CELEBRATION OF 20TH ANNIVERSARY OF CROZON & KEMPTEN.

BUNNACRANNAGHS N.S.: MILLENNIUM REUNION OF PAST PUPILS.

FORTHILL HISTORY SOCIETY: HERITAGE PROJECT AT ST. EDWARD'S SCHOOL.

MARTIN SAVAGE: MILLENNIUM PROGRAMME OF EVENTS.

COOLERA DRAMA SOCIETY: MILLENNIUM BALL AT KILMACOWEN HALL.

CARTRON VIEWPOINT RES. AS: MILLENNIUM SPORTS PARTY.

CLOONACOOL FOROIGE CLUB: EXHIBITION OF PHOTOGRAPHS OF PARISH.

HILL PARK NATOINAL SCHOOL: POTTERY & WEAVING EXHIBITION.

HIGHWOOD COMMUNITY RESOURCES: RE PRINT "THE MOYTURA RECORD".

SKLEEN DROMARD MILL COMMITTEE: MILLENNIUM PUBLICATION HIGHLIGHTING LOCAL GROUPS.

MULLACH RUADH DEVELOPMENT GROUP: CELEBRATION OF IRISH SCIENTISTS.

SLIGO HERITAGE & GENEALOGY SOCIETY: MILLENNIUM CELEBRATIONS, 300 YEARS OF GENEALOGY IN SLIGO.

WOODBROOK HEIGHTS RESIDENTS ASSOCIATION: MILLENNIUM TREE PLANTING AND CONSERVATION EVENTS.

COUNTESS MARKIEVICZ MILLENNIUM COMMITTEE: MEMORIAL TO COUNTESS MARKIEVICZ.

SLIGO FIELD CLUB: PUBLICATION OF "A CELEBRATION OF SLIGO".

GURTEEN SENIOR CITIZENS' CLUB: MILLENNIUM CHRISTMAS & EASTER PARTY FOR ELDERLY.

GURTEEN PARISH COUNCIL: MILLENNIUM PROJECT TO ESTABLISH LINKS WITH EMIGRANTS.

SLIGO FAMILY GROUP: MILLENNIUM EXHIBITION THROUGH STORIES.

ROCKWOOD ROWING CLUB: MILLENNIUM REGATTA ON LOUGH GILL.

FORKHILL MEN'S GROUP: OPENING OF CHILDREN'S PARK WITH MILLENNIUM SHRINE.

SLIGO ARCH CLUB: A MILLENNIUM DISCO PARTY.

DOO DEVELOPMENT GROUP: MILLENNIUM SERVICE LECTURE.

POWELSBORO COMMEMORATION: MILLENNIUM CONCERT & EXHIBITION.

CURRY MOYLOUGH DEV. ASSOCIATION: MILLENNIUM PROGRAMME OF EVENTS.

MOYLOUGH N.S. DEVELOPMENT COMMITTEE: MILLENNIUM MAGAZINE LAUNCH & ECUMENICAL SERVICE.

HILLVIEW DRIVE, BALLYMOTE: GARDENING WORKSHOP FOR CHILDREN.

CURRY GAA CLUB: MILLENNIUM EVENTS WEEKEND.

TUBBERCURRY RESOURCE GROUP: DRAMA WORKSHOP AND GARDENING PROJECT.

TUBBERCURRY COMMITTEE: PLAYGORUP. MILLENNIUM CONCERT FOR PLAYGROUP CHILDREN.

BELLAGHY DEV. ASSOCIATION: CELEBRATION OF HERITAGE AND CULTURE IN BALLAGHY.

FRIENDS OF ROSSES POINT: MILLENNIUM PROJECT – SCULPTURE.

ACLARE SENIOR CITIZENS ASSOCIATION: RECEPTION FOR SENIOR CITIZENS.

RIVERSTOWN ENTERPRISE DEVELOPMENT: JULIAN MILLENNIUM CELEBRATION.

IRISH SOCIETY FOR MUCOPOLYSACCHARIDE: WEEKEND WORKSHOP.

MAUGHERABOY COMM: GAMES. MILLENNIUM CELEBRATIONS.

SLIGO INTERNATIONAL CHOIR FESTIVAL: FESTIVAL 2000.

ST. JOSEPH'S SENIOR CITIZENS CLUB: MILLENNIUM BREAKS FOR SENIOR CITIZENS.

CURRY WOMEN'S GROUP: MILLENNIUM COMMUNITY EVENT.

TEMPLEBOY JUBILEE 2000 MILL : LOCAL HISTORY.

FR. GERRY GILLESPIE, DRONORE: ECUMENICAL COMMUNITY CEREMONY.

BALLINLEG NATIONAL SCHOOL: LOCAL HISTORY.

DROMARD WEST COMMITTEE COUNCIL: COMMEMORATION OF RED HUGH O'DONNELL.

SKREEN DROMARD MILL COMMITTEE: LOCAL HISTORY.

SLIGO GOLF CLUB MALE VOICE CHOIR: MILLENNIUM CONCERT.

ACLARE DEVELOPMENT COUNCIL: COMMUNITY WEEKENDS FOR SENIOR CITIZENS.

YOUTH SPORT WEST: MILLENNIUM SPORTS JAMBOREE FOR YOUNG PEOPLE.

OX MOUNTAINS DEVELOPMENT CO. LTD.: MILLENNIUM WALKING FESTIVAL.

CLOONTIA DEVELOPMENT ASSOCIATION: CHRISTMAS PARTY FOR SENIOR CITIZENS & LOCAL HISTORY.

IRISH WHEELCHAIR ASSOCIATION: SPECIAL RECOGNITION AWARDS.

"CLASP" GLEANN COMMUNITY: TWO DAY CULTURAL FESTIVAL.

CARNEY DEVELOPMENT ASSOCIATION: FESTIVAL FOR OPENING OF MILLENNIUM PARK.

NORTHSIDE COMM: RESOURCE CENTRE. HISTORICAL FASHION SHOW.

BALLINTOGHER COMM. ENTERPRISE: FESTIVALS & WORKSHOPS.

IRISH GUIDE DOGS FOR BLIND: LAUNCH OF IRISH GUIDE DOGS ON WEB SITE.

SLIGO LOCAL AUTHORITIES: LAST LIGHTS CEREMONY.

W.K.O. IRELAND: MILLENNIUM KARATE CHAMPIONSHIP.

OMAGH/SLIGO STEERING GROUP: PUBLICATION OF MILLENNIUM COMMUNITY DIRECTORY.

INTO, SLIGO BRANCH: MILLENNIUM PUBLICATION – "NATIONAL SCHOOLS OF COUNTY SLIGO".

SKREEN DROMARD COMMUNITY COUNCIL: OPENING OF AMENITY PARK.

IRISH KIDNEY ASSOCIATION – SLIGO BRANCH: INFORMATION DAY.

BALLYMOTE YOUTH STEERING COMMITTEE: SCHOOL FOR YOUTHFUL ACTIVITIES.

BUNNINADDEN CENTENARY COMMITTEE: COMMEMORATION OF PRIMARY EDUCATION IN BUNNINADDEN.

BALYMOTE COMMUNITY ENTERPRISE: BALLYMOTE 700 MILLENNIUM CELEBRATIONS.

CRANMORE YOUTH CLUB: MILLENNIUM GARDEN PROJECT.

DRUMCLIFFE DEVLEOPMENT ASSOCIATION: MILLENNIUM COMMUNITY FEST & HISTORICAL EVENT.

ST. MICHAEL'S FAMILY LIFE CENT: MILLENNIUM SYMPOSIUM ON BEREAVEMENT.

SKREEN DROMARD COMMUNITY CARE GROUP: MILLENNIUM EVENTS FOR SENIOR CITIZENS.

CONNACHT VETERAN MOTOR CLUB: MILLENNIUM CAR RALLY.

SLIGO FEIS CEOIL: MILLENNIUM COMPETITIONS.

BALLYMOTE COMMUNITY CARE COUNCIL: OUTING FOR SENIOR CITIZENS.

CULLY ALLCOURT RESTORATION COMMITTEE: EMIGRANTS WEEKEND AND SPORTING EVENTS.

SILVER APPLES PRODUCTIONS: MILLENNIUM CELEBRATIONS OF SLIGO ABBEY IN FORM OF PLAY.

EASKEY COMMUNITY: MILLENNIUM EVENT FOR SENIOR CITIZENS

CLOONLOO DEVELOPMENT ASSOCIATION: MILLENNIUM MAGAZINE.

RANSBORO PARISH COUNCIL: SCHEDULE OF EVENTS INCL. MILL, HISTORIES.

RANSBORO DEVELOP. ASSOCIATION: MILLENNIUM PROGRAMME OF EVENTS FOR THE ELDERLY.

RATHLEE NATIONAL SCHOOL: MILLENNIUM HISTORY OF LOCAL SCHOOL.

PHOENIX PLAYERS, TUBBERCURRY: MILLENNIUM PAGEANT COSTS.

TIPPERARY NORTH
MILLENNIUM OFFICER: MELANIE SCOTT

LITTLETON VILLAGE CHURCH OF IRELAND & CATHOLIC CHURCH LEADERS: PRAYER STONE & LAST LIGHT CEREMONY.

BORRISOLEIGH COMMUNITY DEVELOPMENT ASSOC.: LECTURE SERIES AND SCHOOLS ART COMPETITION.

CARRIG N.S.: COLLECTION OF POEMS WRITTEN BY PEOPLE IN THE PARISH.

COMHALTAS CEOLTÉOIRÍ ÉIREANN COUNTY BOARD: MILLENNIUM CONCERT.

ROSCREA COMMUNITY DEVELOPMENT COUNCIL: MILLENNIUM SEMINAR SERIES

ROSREA COMMUNITY CRAFT GROUP: 'PRIDE IN OUR CRAFT CULTURE INTO THE NEW MILLENNIUM'.

KENNY BOELENS, ARTIST, KERRYGLASS: PARADE OF LIGHT BY LOCAL CHILDREN.

CLONEYBRIEN CIVIL DEFENCE: RESTORATION OF LOCAL HISTORICAL LANDMARK & PROVISION OF INFORMATION STONE.

PORTROE TIDY OWNS COMMITTEE: STONE CIRCLE, SUNDIAL & SHANNON PATHWAY.

BALLINACLOUGH MILLENNIUM COMMITTEE: EVENT TO RECOGNISE CONTRIBUTION OF A LOCAL MAN WHO DEVOTED HIS LIFE TO THE COMMUNITY, IN IRISH DRAMA AND DANCE.

NENAGH SINGERS CIRCLE: A NEW MILLENNIUM OF SINGING.

NENAGH & DISTRICT FLOWER AND GARDEN CLUB: PROJECT 2000 – GOLD & SILVER GARDEN IN GROUNDS OF LIBRARY.

ADULT EDUCATION OFFICE, NENAGH VEC: MILLENNIUM LECTURE SERIES.

R.L.W. RESIDENTS ASSOCIATION: ESTATE ENHANCEMENT WITH LOCAL CHILDREN INVOLVED IN PLANTING TREES, SHRUBS ETC. AND TAKING RESPONSIBILITY FOR THEIR CARE.

THURLES MILLENNIUM COMM: MILLENNIUM EVENTS.

TIPPERARY REGIONAL YOUTH SERVICE. YOUTH PROJECT: CROSS-BORDER INITIATIVE.

SLEODAR NA MILAOISE: "SLEODAR NA MILAOISE".

NENAGH UDC : MILLENNIUM COMMEMORATION OF THREE OLYMPIC CHAMPIONS IN BRONZE.

NENAGH TIDY TOWNS COMMITTEE: SCULPTURE FOR MILL REFLECTING THE CULTURE OF AONACH URMHUMHAN.

TIOBRAID ÁRANN AG LABHAIRT: TIPPERARY TALK 2000-GACH AON LÁ.

IRISH WHEELCHAIR ASSOCIATION: SPECIAL RECOGNITION AWARDS .

ROSCREA TIDY TOWNS COMMITTEE: MILLENNIUM LIGHTING PROJECT.

ASHBURY-GLENTARA RESIDENTS GROUP: MILLENNIUM MEMORY GARDEN.

TEMPLEMORE LYONS CLUB: MILLENNIUM PLAYGROUND AT TOWN PARK.

THE BRIDEWELL CENTRE: MILLENNIIUM PHOTOGRAPHY COMPETITION AND CALENDAR.

JOSEPH P. DELANEY P.P.: COMMISSION OF STAINED GLASS WINDOW CELEBRATING 2000 YEARS OF CHRISTIANITY.

MOYCARKEY RESIDENTS ASSOCIATION: MILLENNIUM MONUMENT WITH REFERENCE TO DERRYNAFLAN CROSS AND BIBLICAL GARDEN.

DUCHAS DAOINE: TO RECORD AND COLLECT MEMORIES AND RECOLLECTIONS OF OLDER PEOPLE.

TIPPERARY GAA MILLENNIUM COMMITTEE: COMPILE AND PUBLISH A COLLECTION OF GAELIC GAMES BALLADS FROM COUNTRY TIPPERARY.

KILBARON MILLENNIUM FESTIVAL COMMITTEE: NEW YEAR'S EVE EVENTS.

TIPPERARY (N.R) LOCAL AUTHORITIES: MILLENNIUM MUSIC COMMISSION.

TIPPERARY CENTRE FOR INDEPENDENT LIVING: THE MILLENNIUM BUS.

MARIAN QUINLAN CURTIN: BOOK OF POETRY INCLUDING A POEM ABOUT THE MILLENNIUM.

INCH TIDY VILLAGE ASSOC: MILLENNIUM CROSS IN VILLAGE OF BOULADUFF TO MARK ROLE OF RELIGION.

MILESTONE DEVELOPMENT ASSOCIATION: REJUVENATING THE MULTEEN RIVER ENVIRONMENT, INCLUDING MILLENNIUM FLOWERBEDS.

MOYNE-TEMPLETUOHY PARISH HISTORY COMMITTEE: MILLENNIUM MEMOIRS OF A TIPPERARY PARISH.

ROSCREA HERITAGE SOCIETY: MEDIEVAL MILLENNIUM PAGEANT.

CLONAKENNY TIDY VILLAGE: MILLENNIUM WELCOMING STONES TO VILLAGE.

KENNEDY PARK DEVELOPMENT GROUP: MILLENNIUM PICNIC GARDEN AND BASKETBALL STANDS.

HENRY MORGAN, NEWPORT: "MILLENNIUM MIX" EVENT INCLUDING MUSIC, SONG, CREATIVE DANCE ETC.

RATHCABBIN PLAYERS: "PASSION 2000" MILLENNIUM PAGEANT.

ROCHE WILLIAMS, CLOUGHJORDAN: LOCAL HISTORY TO CELEBRATE MILLENNIUM.

CLONEYBRIEN MILL. COMM & PARISH: STAINLESS STEEL CROSS ON CLONEYBRIEN HILL.

SILVERMINES GAA CLUB. MILLENNIIUM NEW YEAR'S CARD DESIGNED BY LOCAL CHILDREN AND SENT TO EVERY HOUSE

TIPPERARY LEADER GROUP: "THE GOLDEN MILE OF TIPPERARY".

AONACH PADDY O'BRIEN NENAGH: MAJOR MILLENNIUM CONCERT AS PART OF FESTIVAL 2000.

DIOCESE OF KILLALOE-JUBILEE 2000 COMMITTEE: ECUMENICAL MULTI-DENOMINATIONAL EVENTS INCLUDING AN ECUMENICAL BOAT TRIP ON THE SHANNON

VISITING SOME OF THE ANCIENT CHRISTIAN SITES.

NORTH TIPPERARY HOSPICE: SHINE A LIGHT FOR A LOVED ONE AND LAST LIGHT CEREMONY.

THURLES DRAMA GROUP & DONAL O'REGAN: PRODUCTION OF A NEW PLAY DURING THE MILLENNIUM.

THURLES MILLENNIUM COMMITTEE: VIDEO PRODUCTION WRITTEN TO THE THEME OF ' THURLES OF THE PAST AND THURLES OF THE FUTURE'.

SEAN TREACY'S GAA CLUB, KILCOMMON: HISTORY OF PARISH CLUB.

TWO-MILE-BORRIS ALL IRELAND MILLENNIUM COMMITTEE: MILLENNIUM MONUMENT TO COMMEMORATE AL IRELAND SENIOR HURLING VICTORY IN 1900.

MOYNRE VARIETY GROUP: MILLENNIUM MUSICAL DRAMA.

MOYNE I.C.A.: SENIOR CITIZENS TRIP FOR MILLENNIUM.

LITTLETON TIDY TOWNS AND RESIDENTS ASSOCIATION: MILLENNIUM RUN.

ST. CUALANS SENIOR CITIZENS CLUB: SENIOR CITIZENS MILLENNIUM OUTING.

REV. M.J. BARRY: "FROM BORRISOLEIGH TO LOURDES FOR THE MILLENNIUM".

CARRIG DRAMA GROUP: MILLENNIUM CONCERT.

LISMACKIN PARENTS ASSOCIATOIN, GORTNA-GOONA: MILLENNIUM OUTDOOR PLAYHOUSE.

ST. CRONANS NATIONAL SCHOOL, ROSCREA: MILLENNIUM CALENDAR & SCHOOL HISTORY.

CORAL SWAN, RATHURLAS: MILLENNIUM SCULPTURE RELATING TO GAA INCORPORATING MILLENNIUM CARVING.

BOHER DRAMA GROUP, BALLINA: MILLENNIUM STAGE UPGRADE.

SILVERMINES SENIOR CITIZENS COMMITTEE: MILLENNIUM FUNCTION TO HONOUR SENIOR CITIZENS.

CILL AN DAINGEAN GAA CLUB, MONSEÁ, NENAGH: HISTORY OF CLUB.

PUCKANE & DISTRICT TENNIS CLUB: MILLENNIUM TREASURE HUNT.

BALLINACLOUGH LADIES FOOTBALL CLUB: MILLENNIUM "CAILÍN GAELACH FESTIVAL".

LIONS CLUB - NENAGH: MILLENNIUM HOLIDAY FOR ELDERLY.

NENAGH ACTIVE RETIREMENT ASSOCIATION: MILLENNIUM OUTINGS.

ST. MARY'S SECONDARY SCHOOL,NENAGH: MILLENNIUM BOOK.

TIPPERARY – SOUTH RIDING
MILLENNIUM OFFICER: RONNIE FITZGERALD

NED KELLY MILLENNIUM COMMITTEE: PROMOTE LINKS BETWEEN MOYGLASS AND AUSTRALIA.

TIPPERARY TOWN COMMUNITY CENTRE: CREATION OF GARDEN FOR ELDERLY.

MICHAEL WALSH AND VIVIENNE CHALONER, GORMANSTOWN: RECORD WILDLIFE ON ISLAND IN RIVER SUIR AT ARDFINNAN.

CLOGHEEN COMMUNITY COUNCIL: ERECT TOWN CLOCK IN BELFRY OF COMMUNITY CENTRE.

IRISH WHEELCHAIR ASSOCIATION: SPECIAL RECOGNITION AWARDS.

TIPPERARY REGIONAL YOUTH SERVICE: MILLENNIUM ART WORKSHOP.

TIPPERARY PEACE CONVENTION: SONG CONTEST AND ANNUAL PEACE AWARD.

SOLOHEAD MILLENNIUM COMMITTEE: HOLIDAYS AT HOME AND LOURDES FOR SENIOR CITIZENS.

ST. MARY'S ART GROUP: ART EXHIBITION FEATURING WORK OF CHILDREN.

DYDX YOUTH THEATRE, CAHIR: THEATRICAL PERFORMANCES BY YOUNG ADULTS AND TEENAGERS.

ST. MICHAEL'S N.S. MULLINAHONE: MURAL DEPICTING C.J. KICKHAM.

GAILE N.S. HOLYCROSS: CENTENARY CELEBRATIONS OF SCHOOL.

PETER AHEARNE, RATHRONAN, CLONMEL: INSTALLATION OF STAINED GLASS WINDOWN IN LISRONAGH CHURCH.

BOHERLAHAN/DUALLA MILLENNIUM COMMITTEE: PARISH PAGEANT INVOLVING ALL HOUSEHOLDS.

FETHARD AND KILLUSTY COMMUNITY COUNCIL: LIGHTING UP OF FETHARD'S MEDIEVAL PAST.

JOHN KELLY, PHOTOGRAPHER, CLONMEL: END OF YEAR PHOTOGRAPHIC EXHIBITION.

CARRICK-ON-SUIR CHAMBER OF COMMERCE: FESTIVAL OF LIGHTS.

ARDMAYLE HERITAGE SOCIETY: PROGRAMME OF EVENTS TO CELEBRATE MILLENNIUM.

SUIR COMMUNITY DEVELOPMENT PROJECT: EXHIBITION ON CARRICK-ON-SUIR'S DIVERSITY AND WEALTH OF TALENT.

ANGLICAN DIOCESES OF CASHEL, OSSORY, WATERFORD, LEIGHLIN, LISMORE AND FERNS: "CELEBRATION OF THE FAITH".

NEWCASTLE COMMUNITY ALERT: CELEBRATION OF THE INTERNATIONAL YEAR OF THE ELDERLY.

BALLYPOREEN COMMUNITY COUNCIL: RECORD

OF NUMBER OF PEOPLE IN PARISH AND FLOODLIGHTING OF PAROCHIAL HOUSE.

BALLINGARRY MILLENNIUM COMMITTEE: FLOODLIGHTING OF PARISH CHURCH.

GALLOWGLASS THEATRE COMPANY, CLONMEL: SPECIAL PRODUCTION OF GULLIVER'S TRAVELS.

BOLTON LIBRARY MANAGEMENT COMMITTEE, CASHEL: MILLENNIUM BOOK FAIR AND LITERARY EVENT.

CLONMEL 350 COMMITTEE: DEVELOPING AND PROMOTING PROJECTS.

CASHEL CULTURAL FESTIVAL: FIELD DAY AND PEACE AND RECONCILIATION EVENT.

DUNEASLY MUSIC ASSOCIATION, CAHIR: MILLENNIUM CONCERT WITH GUEST ARTISTS.

ST. VINCENT DE PAUL SOCIETY, CLONMEL: PURCHASE OF MOBILE HOME FOR USE BY VULNERABLE FAMILIES.

SOUTH TIPPERARY ARTS CENTRE: ESTABLISH MUSIC TRUST FOR CHILDREN.

TIPPERARY UDC: NUMBER OF PROJECTS, INCLUDING ARTISTIC FEATURE, MILLENNIUM CARDS AND MILLENNIUM CLOCK.

SOUTH TIPPERARY ARTS CENTRE: CLONMEL CHRISTMAS STREET CARNIVAL.

SOUTH TIPPERARY ARTS CENTRE: "REEL EYES ON THE MILLENNIUM".

SOUTH TIPPERARY ARTS CENTRE: "REFLECTIONS"-A COMMUNITY CAPTURES ITS MILLENNIUM.

TOM KEITH, BALLINARD, DUNGARVAN: RESEARCH AND WRITE THE HISTORY OF ST. JOSEPH'S COLLEGE, CAHIR.

CO. WATERFORD
MILLENNIUM OFFICER: TOM KEITH

BALLINROAD SOCCER CLUB: MILLENNIUM COMMUNITY SPORTS DAY TO COINCIDE WITH NATIONAL CHILDREN'S DAY.

DUNGARVAN MILLENNIUM COMMITTEE: CELEBRATION OF NEW YEAR'S EVE- CEREMONY OF LAST LIGHT / STREET PARTY / BEAT ON THE STREET / BANDS / DISCO / RADIO LINK-UP / FACE PAINTING.

DUNGARVAN ALZHEIMER GROUP: SENSORY GARDEN AT ST. JOSEPH'S HOSPITAL.

CAPPOQUIN COMMUNITY DEVELOPMENT CO.: HISTORY OF CAPPOQUIN TO COMMEMORATE MILLENNIUM.

ARDMORE LADYBIRDS/BROWNIES/GUIDES: ERECT INFORMATION BOARDS AT CLIFF WALK, PUBLISH "A CHILDREN'S GUIDE TO CLIFF WALK".

SISTERS OF BON SAUVEUR: MILLENNIUM GARDEN FOR RESIDENTIAL AND VISITING TRAINEES WITH INTELLECTUAL DISABILITY.

SISTERS OF BON SAUVEUR: MILLENNIUM DISNEY DAY FOR RESIDENTS AND VISITING TRAINEES WITH INTELLECTUAL DISABILITY.

STRADBALLY COMMUNITY: ERECTION OF 12 FT LATIN CROSS MADE IN GRANITE TO CELEBRATE MILLENNIUM.

FLEADH NA MUMHAN 2000, LISMORE: ASSISTANCE IN RUNNING THE MUNSTER FLEADH CHEOIL.

IRISH WHEELCHAIR ASSOCIATION: SPECIAL RECOGNITION AWARDS.

LISMORE AND WATERFORD MILLENNIUM CHOIR: PRESENTATION OF "GERMAN REQUIEM" BY BRAHMS.

LISMORE CHOIR: THREE SPECIAL MILLENNIUM CHRISTMAS CONCERTS IN THE GREAT HALL, LISMORE CASTLE.

FINNISK COMHALTAS CEOLTÉOIRÍ ÉIREANN: CONCERT OF MUSIC, SONG AND DANCE AND SEAN-NÓS SCÉALAIOCHT.

KILBRIEN COMMUNITY GROUP: RENOVATION OF OLD SCHOOL AS COMMUNITY HALL.

BALLYDUFF UPPER COMMUNITY: COUNCIL. MILLENNIUM SCULPTURE AND NEW YEAR'S EVE CELEBRATIONS.

ST. OLIVER'S GAA, UNDER 11 SECTION: ATTENDANCE OF TEAM AT MILLENNIUM ALL-IRELAND GROUND HURLING TOURNAMENT.

BALLYSAGGART DEVELOPMENT COMMITTEE: NEW YEAR CELEBRATIONS IN VILLAGE, NEW LIGHTS AND COMMEMORATION STONE.

BALLYLANEEN COMMUNITY: CENTRE AND PARISH EVENT TO COMMEMORATE POET TADHG GAELACH Ó SUILLEABHAIN.

NEWTOWN AND GUILLAMENE SWIMMING CLUB, TRAMORE: PROVISION OF CHANGING FACILITIES AT OUTDOOR SWIMMING PLACE.

FÉILE NA NDÉISE, DUNGARVAN: WEEKEND OF IRISH MUSIC, SONG AND DANCE AND STREET ENTERTAINMENT.

ARDMORE TIDY TOWNS COMMITTEE: COMMEMORATIVE FLOWER-BED, LAID OUT IN FLOWERS AND SHRUBS TO SHOW 'MILLENNIUM'.

STRADBALLY TOURISM AND ENTERTAINMENT GROUP: MILLENNIUM BOOK COMMEMORATING 1000 YEARS OF STRADBALLY'S HISTORY.

WATERFORD CO. GAA BOARD: HONOURING MILLENNIUM TEAMS AND RECOGNITION OF LONG SERVICE.

ABBEYSIDE PATTERN COMMITTEE: SPECIAL DECORATIVE LIGHTING LINKING ABBEYSIDE TO DUNGARVAN.

DUNGARVAN CHAMBER OF COMMERCE: A BOOK TO CELEBRATE THE LAST CENTURY OF THE SECOND MILLENNIUM.

COISTE MÍLAOISE NA GAELTACHTA: COLLECTION OF MILLENNIUM POEMS IN IRISH BY SECONDARY SCHOOL STUDENTS.

BALLYDUFF/KILMEADAN MILL. GROUP: CONSTRUCTING OF PUBLIC GREEN AND PROVISION OF TREES, SHRUBS, SEATING AND MILLENNIUM STONE.

DUNGARVAN PIPE BAND COMMITTEE: PROVISION OF EXTRA BANKS FOR MILLENNIUM ST. PATRICK'S DAY PARADE.

ABBEYSIDE SOCCER CLUB, DUNGARVAN: RECEPTION TO UNVEIL MILLENNIUM COMMEMORATIVE MURAL.

DUNGARVAN CHAMBER OF COMMERCE: MARITIME SCULPTURE IN ALUMINIUM AT ROUNDABOUT IN DUNGARVAN.

ARDMORE GAA CLUB: ERECTION OF COVERED STAND AT GAA GROUNDS.

MODELIGO COMMUNITY CENTRE: MILLENNIUM CELEBRATION BANQUET AND AWARDS CEREMONY.

CAPPOQUIN BOYS NATIONAL SCHOOL: MILLENNIUM FRIENDSHIP SEAT AND SCHOOL GARDEN.

SCOIL MHUIRE, MODELIGO: MILLENNIUM COMMEMORATIVE STONE LINKING PAST, PRESENT AND FUTURE.

KNOCKANORE COMMUNITY: ERECTION OF MILLENNIUM CROSS IN GRAVEYARD.

GEALACH GORM THEATRE GROUP: "CINDERELLA AND THE MILLENNIUM BALL".

COISTE FORBARTHA AN TSCAN PHOBAIL: CONSTRUCTION OF TENNIS COURT TO COMMEMORATE MILLENNIUM YEAR.

SLIABH GCUA MILLENNIUM CELEBRATIONS : SOCIAL EVENING FOR COMMUNITY.

ARDMORE 2000 COMMITTEE: MILLENNIUM BOOK "TWENTIETH CENTURY ARDMORE".

ARDMORE 2000 COMMITTEE: CONCERT, STREET CARNIVAL AND RECEPTION.

CATHAL BRUGHA ESTTATE COMMITTEE: STREET PARTY AND CARNIVAL.

RATHGORMACK N.S. PARENTS ASSOCIATION: COMMEMORATIVE GARDENA AND ROCKERY.

CÁIRDE, PORT LAIRG: TREE DAY NON-RESIDENTIAL CAMP FOR SPECIAL CHILDREN.

COLÁISTE NA RINNE: EAGRÁN MILAOISE 2000 DEN LINN BHUI IRIS GAELTACHT NA NDÉISE.

ARDMORE N.S.: MILLENNIUM YEARBOOK OF PUPILS AND STAFF.

COMHAIRLE POBAIL NA RINNE: REFURBISH AND EXTEND HALLA PHOBAIL.

WATERFORD MUSIC CITY AND COUNTY: COMPETITION TO COMPOSE PIECE OF MUSIC TO MARK MILLENNIUM.

DUNGARVAN PARISH: MILL CHOIR AND VARIOUS COMMEMORATIVE EVENTS.

TRAMORE PARISH: MILLENNIUM CROSS.

TRAMORE PARISH: NON-DENOMINATIONAL MILLENNIUM CELEBRATION OF CHRISTIANITY.

CELEBRATION OF FAITH COMMITTEE: COMBINED DIOCESES CELEBRATION OF FAITH.

CONVENT OF MERCY, DUNGARVAN: MILLENNIUM STUDY GROUP OF CATHOLIC CATECHISM.

PARISH OF ABBEYSIDE: MILLENNIUM MEMORIAL STONE TABLETS AT EACH OF 3 CHURCHES.

DAY CARE CENTRE, CAPPOQUIN: MILLENNIUM CONCERT FOR ATTENDEES OF CENTRE.

COISTE BAILTE SLACHTMHARA NA RINNE: FLORAL DISPLAY IN VILLAGE FOR MILLENNIUM.

PINEWOOD RESIDENTS ASSOCIATION, DUNGARVAN: STREET PARTY / CARNIVAL ON NEW YEAR'S EVE.

LISMORE Y2K COMMITTEE: TOWN'S OFFICIAL CELEBRATIONS FOR ALL RESIDENTS.

MASTER MCGRATH COMMUNITY GROUP: COMMEMORATION STONE TO MARK THE MILLENNIUM AND CELEBRATION AT UNVEILING.

AGLISH DEVELOPMENT COMMITTEE: WELCOME SIGN FOR VILLAGE SET OUT IN SHAPED SHRUBS.

AGLISH TIDY TOWNS: TIDY AND IMPROVE 17TH CENTURY HISTORIC GRAVEYARD IN VILLAGE.

BALLINROAD MILLENNIUM COMMITTEE: NEW YEAR'S EVE PARTY.

COLÁISTE NA RINNE: SPECIAL GARDEN WITH IRISH TREES AND PLANTS FOR STUDENT EDUCATION.

RATHGORMACK RESIDENTS ASSOCIATION: MILLENNIUM TRADITIONAL LANTERN CAROL SERVICE FOR ALL RESIDENTS.

DUNGARVAN YOUTH CLUB: REFURBISH-MENT OF DUNGARVAN Y.C. PREMISES.

AGLISH PARENTS ASSOCIATION: MILLENNIUM REUNION OF PAST PUPILS OF AGLISH SCHOOL.

DUNGARVAN BOXING CLUB: MILLENNIUM TOURNAMENT.

DUNGARVAN AGRICULTURE SHOW: NEW DOG SHOW FOR MILLENNIUM.

DUNGARVAN PARISH COUNCIL: MILL YOUTH CAROL SERVICE.

ABBEYSIDE YOUTH CHOIR: CHOIR TO MAKE COMMEMORATIVE TAPE.

DUNGARVAN UTD. AFC: ASSIST WITH PROVISION OF ALL WEATHER PITCHES.

LIAM DESMOND: BOOK ON CONSTABULARY IN WATERFORD.

DUNGARVAN DRAMATIC SOCIETY: MILLENNIUM PLAY BY LOCAL AUTHOR.

VTOS ARTISTS: MILLENNIUM SCULPTURES FOR LOCAL PLACEMENT IN DUNGARVAN.

DUNGARVAN MUSEUM SOCIETY: 20 COMMEMORATIVE WALL PLAQUES TO MARK HISTORIC BUILDINGS.

ÁRD SCOIL NA NDÉISE, PARENTS COUNCIL: MILLENNIUM GARDEN AND COMMEMORATIVE STONE.

COMBINED SECONDARY SCHOOLS OF WEST WATERFORD: MILLENNIUM COMMEMORATIVE BOOK BY STUDENTS OF FIVE SECONDARY SCHOOLS.

AISTÓIRÍ AN TSEAN PHOBAIL: MILLENNIUM PERFORMANCE OF "THE COUNTRY BOY".

DUNGARVAN MOTOR SPORT: MILLENNIUM MOTOR SPORT WEEKEND.

PORTLAW COMMUNITY DEVELOPMENT LTD.: CELEBRATIONS INCLUDING PAGEANT.

WATERFORD AREA MUSEUM SOCIETY: TO COMMEMORATE THE 'COPPER COAST' AT BONMAHON AND DUNHILL/FENOR BOG WITH SCALE MODEL OF TRAMORE COASTLINE.

TALLOW PARISH: FLOODLIGHTING OF PARISH CHURCH.

A.M.P.S., KILMACTHOMAS: CONCERT FOR THE MILLENNIUM.

DUNGARVAN MILLENNIUM COMMEMORATIVE GROUP: PUBLISH COMMEMORATIVE BOOK OF PHOTOS REPRESENTING THE EVENTS WHICH TOOK PLACE UP TO 10 JANUARY 2000.

WATERFORD CITY
MILLENNIUM OFFICER: TOM HARTERY/LIAM QUINLAN

CENTRAL TECHNICAL INSTITUTE: MILLENNIUM CITY GARDEN PROJECT.

ATTACK 2000: "QUAY TO OUR FUTURE" COUNTDOWN CONCERT, DANCE PERFORMANCE EXTRAVAGANZA.

DE LA SALLE COLLEGE BRASS BAND: MILLENNIUM BRASS BAND TO DEVELOP THE MUSICAL ACTIVITIES ALREADY AVAILABLE IN SCHOOL.

DE LA SALLE HURLING AND FOOTBALL CLUB: MILLENNIUM YEAR BOOK - FEATURING GROWTH AND ACHIEVEMENTS OF CLUB FROM THE FOUNDATION IN 1927.

EDMUND RICE CHORAL AND MUSICAL SOCIETY: FULL SCALE PRODUCTION OF "MARITANA" WITH PROFESSIONAL DIRECTION.

FERNDALE RESIDENTS ASSOCIATION: THE LANDSCAPING OF UNUSED LAND AT ENTRANCE TO ESTATE.

INTER COM.COMPUTER TRAINING: "ACT LOCAL THINK GLOBAL" - MILLENNIUM PROJECT TO PUT 20 VOLUNTARY ORGANISATIONS ON THE INTERNET FOR THE YEAR 200.

IRISH WHEELCHAIR ASSOCIATION: SPECIAL RECOGNITION AWARDS.

FOCUS IRELAND: MILLENNIUM GOLF CLASSIC AS PART OF MAJOR FUND-RAISER.

GRANGE HEIGHTS RESIDENTS ASSOCIATION: LARGE DECORATIVE FEATURE INCLUDING ROCKERY AND SHRUB AREA.

VIEWMOUNT RESIDENTS ASSOCIATION: MILLENNIUM GARDEN WITH WOODEN SCULPTURE.

MOUNT SION SILVER BAND: "MILLENNIUM OUTDOOR GIG" IN ASSOCIATION WITH PULSE PERCUSSION.

"JIVEIRE" - CHERYL & TOM O'NEILL: MODERN JIVE PERFORMANCE - "GLEN MILLER" TYPE MUSIC FOR THE WORLD WAR II SECTION OF WATERFORD'S MILLENNIUM CLOCK.

EILEEN POWER: SPECIAL MILLENNIUM GARDEN FOR DIVERSIONAL THERAPY FOR PATIENTS IN ST. PATRICK'S HOSPITAL.

PRESENTATION SECONDARY SCHOOL: EXCHANGE PROGRAMME TO OMAGH.

PULSE PERCUSSION: MILLENNIUM OUTDOOR GIG IN ASSOCIATION WITH MOUNT SION SILVER BAND.

ST. JOSEPH'S CENTRE: CHILDCARE PROJECT.

SYMPHONY CLUB OF WATERFORD: MILLENNIUM FAMILY CONCERT BY E.U. CHAMBER ORCHESTRA.

WATERFORD CATHEDRAL YOUTH CHOIR: MUSICAL EVENT TO MARK LIFE AND DEATH OF JESUS.

WATERFORD CITY CHOIR: TWO PERFORMANCES OF GERMAN REQUIEM BY BRAHMS, IN ASSOCIATION WITH LISMORE CHOIR.

WATERFORD HEALING ARTS TRUST: ERECT WATER BASED, MOBILE, SCULPTURE ARTWORK AT THE ENTRANCE TO WATERFORD REGIONAL HOSPITAL.

WATERFORD LIONS CLUB: WORKSHOPS AND CULTURAL AND SOCIAL EVENTS.

WATERFORD MILLENNIUM CELEBRATIONS: DAY - STREET THEATRE, HUMAN MILLENNIUM CLOCK, DANCE, BRASS BANDS, SINGING. GALA CONCERT WITH LOCAL AND FAMOUS ARTISTS - COLOURFUL COUNTDOWN, DRAMATIC SETS AND STAGE, FIREWORKS, CHOIR OF 1000 VOICES, WLR BROADCAST.

WATERFORD REGIONAL YOUTH SERVICE: MILLENNIUM TWINNING PROJECT.

WATERFORD YOUTH DRAMA: SPECIAL YOUNG PEOPLES THEATRE PROJECT TO CELEBRATE THE MILLENNIUM.

WATERFORD AND SUIR VALLEY RAILWAY COMPANY: SETTING UP OF NARVION GAUGE RAILWAY ON DISUSED TRACK FROM KILMEADEN TO BILBERRY.

JANUS CHORAL GROUP: INVOLVEMENT IN LIVE BROADCAST OF GALA CONCERT AND LAST LIGHT CEREMONY ON NEW YEAR'S EVE.

STAGE FRIGHT MUSICAL THEATRE COMPANY: NATIONAL PERFORMANCES OF THE SHOW "PENTIMENTI".

WATERFORD TREASURES AT THE GRANARY: EXHIBITION CELEBRATING 2000 YEARS OF CHRISTIAN ART.

"MADRIGALLERY": ORCHESTRAL AND CHORAL PERFORMANCE OF FAURÉS REQUIEM WITH PROFESSIONAL MUSICIANS AND SOLOISTS.

ST. DECLAN'S NATIONAL SCHOOL: FLOOD LIGHTING OF SCHOOL, 165-YEAR-OLD LISTED BUILDING.

CO. WESTMEATH
MILLENNIUM OFFICER: CIARAN MCGRATH

BALLINAHOWN MILLENNIUM COMMITTEE: BOOK ON THE PARISH OF LEAMONAGHAN.

MULLINGAR ARTS CENTRE: CONCERT FOR OLDER PEOPLE; LAST LIGHTS CEREMONY AND CONCERT FOR CHILDREN. THREE LOCAL ARTISTS COMMISSIONED TO UNDERTAKE PAINTING 'THE GARDENS OF WESTMEATH'.

THE THATCH TAVERN, ATHLONE: ILLUMINATION OF A SECTION OF THE RIVER SHANNON USING FOUR LARGE PUMPS AND LIGHTS UNDER WATER.

MS. GERALDINE O'REILLY THOMASTOWN: PRODUCTION OF A SMALL COLOUR CATALOGUE AND SIX COLOUR POSTCARDS TO ACCOMPANY A VISUAL ARTS EXHIBITION.

MULLINGAR CHORAL SOCIETY: CONCERT IN CATHEDRAL OF CHRIST THE KING, MULLINGAR TO PERFORM HANDEL'S MESSIAH.

BALLINAHOWN LADIES GROUP: A 'TIME CAPSULE' TO BE OPENED IN THE YEAR 3000.

ATHLONE LITTLE THEATRE: FURTHER EXTENSION TO LITTLE THEATRE; PERFORMANCE OF SELECTED WORKS FROM MIRAGE OF MIRIAD MIDLAND ARTISTS.

CASTLEPOLLARD MILLENNIUM COMMITTEE: HISTORICAL MILLENNIUM TAPESTRY OF CASTLEPOLLARD AND MILLENNIUM STONE ON THE SQUARE.

DEVLIN FRIENDSHIP CLUB: MILLENNIUM CONCERT INVOLVEING SCHOOL CHILDREN AND CLUB MEMBERS.

KILBEGGAN MILLENNIUM COMMITTEE: LAUNCH OF "KILBEGGAN 2000-A MILLENNIUM BOOK OF PHOTOGRAPHS" AND MILLENNIUM LIGHTING OF KILBEGGAN.

TAUGHMON-TURIN SOCIAL SERVICES: SOCIAL EVENING FOR SENIOR CITIZENS.

FR. MICHAEL KILMARTIN, CATHEDRAL HOUSE, MULLINGAR: A FAMILY FUN DAY.

FR. SÉAN HENRY, CATHEDRAL PARISH, MULLINGAR: FLOODLIGHT THE CATHEDRAL IN MULLINGAR.

DELVIN COMMUNITY EDUCATION: REFURBISHMENT OF ROOM FOR WEEKLY MEETINGS AND PERMANENT STANDS FOR FLORAL DISPLAY ON MAIN STREET.

RATHCONNELL CEMETERY RESTORATION GROUP: CLEAN UP OF CEMETERY AND RSTORATION OF BOUNDARY WALL.

MOATE COMMUNITY DEVELOPMENT ASSOCIATION: MILLENNIUM BOOK RECORDING THE HISTORY OF THE LOCALITY.

IRISH WHEELCHAIR ASSOCIATION: SPECIAL RECOGNITION AWARDS.

ROSEMOUNT 2000 "MARKING THE MILLENNIUM" BALLINTOBER, MOATE: CONSTRUCTION OF MILLENNIUM MONUMENT ENTITLED "TRANQUILLITY - A NEW BEGINNING". AND A "WELCOME HOME" CELEBRATION.

MULLINGAR PARISH PILGRIMAGE COMMITTEE: DESIGNATION OF MASS PATHS IN THE VICINITY OF THE CATHEDRAL AND ST. PAUL'S CHURCH.

MULLINGAR PARISH PILGRIMAGE COMMITTEE: PILGRIMAGE TO PATROLMAN, CLEANING AND TIDYING OF FAMINE GRAVEYARD, GRAVEL FOR PATHS AND ERECTION OF AN ALTAR.

MOATE MUSEUM AND HISTORICAL SOCIETY: A "MOATE QUAKERS MILLENNIUM CELEBRATION", RESTORATION OF MOATE QUAKER CEMETERY AND MEETING HOUSE AREA.

MILLTOWNPASS COMMUNITY ACTION GROUP: MILLENNIUM CELEBRATION; EXHIBITION OF OLD PHOTOGRAPHS, VIDEOS, SLIDES AND OTHER ITEMS OF 20TH CENTURY.

ST. MICHAEL'S JUBILEE COMMITTEE, CASTLETOWN GEOGHAN: MILLENNIUM PATTERN DAY, TO ON THE SITE OF LOCAL MASS ROCK. MUSIC AND SPECIAL PAGEANT.

FR. JOE BRILLY, DRUMRANEY, ATHLONE: ERECTION OF STONE MONUMENT.

WESTMEATH V.E.C.: MILLENNIUM LECTURE ON "EDUCATIONAL CHALLENGES IN THE NEW MILLENNIUM" AND ITS PUBLICATION IN BOOK FORM.

BALLINAHOWN DEVELOPMENT ASSOCIATION: LAUNCH OF MILLENNIUM SCULPTURE WITH WATER FEATURE.

MULLINGAR FESTIVAL LTD.: FESTIVAL, "HOPE FOR THE MILLENNIUM". THE BELGIUM BRASS BAND AND THE MULLINGAR TOWN BAND WITH MUSIC FOR THE RELEASING OF WHITE BALLOONS AND FIREWORKS DISPLAY.

KILLUCAN/RATHWIRE MILLENNIUM PROJECT: STREET LIGHTING AND ECUMENICAL CAROL SERVICE.

SOROPTIMIST INTERNATIONAL MULLINGAR AND DISTRICT: SCULPTURE OF TWO FRIARS TO COMMEMORATE THE MILLENNIUM.

RAHARNEY TIDY TOWNS: RENOVATION OF RUN DOWN RAHARNEY MILK STAND.

KINNEGAD DISTRICT ACTION GROUP: CHRISTMAS LIGHTS ON MAIN STREET.

MR. MATT NOLAN, BALLAGH, MULLINGAR: BOOK ON THE HISTORY OF MULLINGAR; FORTY PROFILES OF MULLINGAR PERSONALITIES AND HISTORIC COLOUR PHOTOGRAPHS.

WESTMEATH COUNTY COUNCIL: PUBLIC PAGEANT AND COMMEMORATION EVENT TO COINCIDE WITH THE LAST LIGHT CEREMONY AND OTHER EVENTS. THIS WITH LIGHTING CEREMONY ON THE HILL OF UISNEACH.

MULLINGAR TOWN COMMISSIONERS: AN APPROPRIATE MILLENNIUM EVENT.

CO. WEXFORD
MILLENNIUM OFFICER: FIONNUALA HANRAHAN

THE COMMUNITY HOUSE WEXFORD: FESTIVAL OF MUSIC, DANCE, DRAMA AND ART.

BALDWINSTOWN COMMITTEE BRIDGETOWN: REOPENING OF OLD SCHOOL IN BALDWINSTOWN AS COMMUNITY CENTRE FOR LOCAL PEOPLE OLD SCHOOL BUILT IN 1848.

CO. WEXFORD CHILDREN'S CHOIR AND DEMON DRUMMERS: CHORAL AND PERCUSSION CONCERT ENTITLED "VOICES OF THE MILLENNIUM".

KILMORE QUAY COMMUNITY DEVELOPMENT ASSOCIATION: MEMORIAL TRAIL AND GARDEN LAUNCH LINKED TO MARITIME TRADITION AND CUSTOMS.

RATHANGAN NATIONAL SCHOOL DUMCORMICK: EVENT ENCOMPASSING DRAMA, DANCE AND MUSIC INVOLVING THE CHILDREN AND COMMUNITY CHOIR.

JUNIOR CHAMBER WEXFORD WEXFORD PERSONS OF THE MILLENNIUM EXHIBITION.

WESTGATE HERITAGE CENTRE GROUP: CHRISTMAS AND NEW YEAR CHILDREN'S FESTIVAL.

PAT KAVANAGH CRAANFORD, GOREY: MILLENNIUM PAGEANT EVENT TO FEATURE OLD AND MODERN MACHINERY AND PASTIMES OF LOCALITY.

EDDIE DOYLE: THE HYDRO, KILMUCKRIDGE, GOREY. KILMUCKRIDGE MARDI GRAS INVOLVING YOUNG VIBRANT COMMUNITY GROUP.

ST. PATRICK'S DAY COMMITTEE GOREY : PARADE WITH SPECIAL MILLENNIUM FLAVOUR.

ST. AIDAN'S DAY CARE CENTRE. GOREY: PHOTOGRAPHIC EXHIBITION "GOREY PAST AND PRESENT".

GOREY PHOTOGRAPHIC CLUB: PHOTOGRAPHIC RECORD OF EVERYDAY LIFE IN GOREY AND MAJOR EVENTS DURING 2000 RECORDED TO CULMINATE IN PUBLICATION OF A BOOK.

CASTLETOWN COMMUNITY ALERT CLONOUGH, ARKLOW: MILLENNIUM MASS AND CONCERT. ACKNOWLEDGEMENT OF CONTRIBUTION OF SENIOR CITIZENS TO THE LOCALITY.

DON KENNY. ASKAMORE PARISH: GOREY . PAGEANT INVOLVING THE WHOLE PARISH.

WHITTY CLAN GATHERING, WEXFORD: CLAN GATHERING WITH INTERNATIONAL GUESTS.

ANGLICAN DIOCESE OF FERNS, WEXFORD: CELEBRATION OF FAITH, WORKSHOPS, ENTERTAINMENT AND EXHIBITIONS.

ST. ANNE'S SUNSHINE CLUB: KNOCKTOWN, DUNCORMICK . MILLENNIUM COMMUNITY DAY FOR SENIOR CITIZENS.

BUÍ BOLG. SOUTH MAIN STREET, WEXFORD: MILLENNIUM PARADE, LOCAL STREET THEATRE, MUSICAL SOCIETIES AND MUSIC AND DRAMA.

WEXFORD ARTS CENTRE, CORNMARKET, WEXFORD: "MILLENNIUM WOMEN'S MONTH" FEATURING EXHIBITION, DEBATES, LECTURES, PLAYS, CONCERTS, READINGS AND WORKSHOPS.

CLEAMAIREACHTAÍ CONTAE, LOCH GORMAN: MUMMERS BALL REVIVING CUSTOM OF MUMMERS.

ROWE STREET CHURCH SUMMER FESTIVAL: NEWTOWN ROAD, WEXFORD. MILLENNIUM MUSICAL SUMMER FESTIVAL.

ROW STREET BELL RINGERS: ROWE STREET, WEXFORD. NEW YEAR BELL RINGING, INCLUDING INTRODUCTION OF NEW TENOR BELL.

CLONARD YOUTH CLUB, CLONARD, WEXFORD: JUBILEE BANNERS FOR CHURCH DESIGNED, PAINTED AND SEWN BY THE YOUTH CLUB.

TAGHMON HISTORICAL SOCIETY, PARK HOUSE, WEXFORD: MILLENNIUM CALENDAR BASED ON THE TAGHMON PARISH AREA WHICH DATES FROM 597 AD.

OUR LADY'S ISLAND SENIOR CITIZEN COMMITTEE: MILLENNIUM CHORAL CONCERT DEDICATED TO THE SENIOR CITIZENS OF THE COMMUNITY.

IRISH WHEELCHAIR ASSOCIATION, CO. WEXFORD: SPECIAL RECOGNITION AWARDS.

MUSIC FOR WEXFORD: SPRING FESTIVAL 2000 FEATURING CONCERTS, EXHIBITIONS AND CHILDREN'S WORKSHOPS.

ROSSLARE ACTIVE RETIREMENT ASSOCIATION: MILLENNIUM MUSIC AND SONG FESTIVAL.

SCOIL MHUIRE, WEXFORD: EXHIBITION OF PHOTOGRAPHS AND INVOLVEMENT OF PARENTS, CHILDREN AND TEACHERS IN CELEBRATION OF THE SCHOOL.

CLEARLSTOWN COMMUNITY SERVICES: HERITAGE AND HOPE EXHIBITION OF HISTORICALLY SIGNIFICANT MATERIALS.

BIRDWATCH IRELAND WEXFORD BRANCH: PREPARATION AND LAUNCH OF MILLENNIUM WETLANDS BIRDS POSTER.

WEXFORD HISTORICAL SOCIETY: LECTURERS AT A POPULAR LEVEL BASED IN LIBRARIES THROUGHOUT THE COUNTY ON THEMES SUCH AS RELIGION, EDUCATION, FOOD, MUSIC AND RURAL LIFE OVER LAST 2000 YEARS IN SOUTH EAST.

BREE MACRA NA FEIRME: A HISTORY OF BREE MACRA NA FEIRME AND ITS CONTRIBUTION TO COMMUNITY DEVELOPMENT.

ST. SENAN'S PARISH, ENNISCORTHY: 'ENNISCORTHY 2000' BOOK OF THE MILLENNIUM HISTORY AND DIRECTORY.

NEW ROSS WRITER'S GROUP: A CASUAL COLLECTION: MILLENNIUM EDITION.

POULPEASTY PARISH COMMUNITY: "ECHOES OF POULPEASTY" HISTORY OF AREA.

OUR LADY'S ISLAND COMMUNITY COUNCIL: HISTORY OF OUR LADY'S ISLAND.

BALLYMURN MILLENNIUM COMMITTEE: A CELEBRATION OF THE HISTORY AND CURRENT STRENGTHS OF THE DISTRICT.

MILLENNIUM PASSION PLAY, CAMROSS, FOLKSMILLS: MILLENNIUM PASSION PLAY WITH FULL COMMUNITY INVOLVEMENT.

RAMSGRANGE PARISH CHURCH: COMMUNITY ORGANISED EVENT FOR THE LOCALITY.

COCKLESHELL ARTS CENTRE: DUNCANNON . SAND SCULPTING EXHIBITION AND COMPETITION UTILISING MARITIME LINK.

COUNTY WEXFORD COMMUNITY WORKSHOP, NEW ROSS: MUSICAL VARIETY CONCERT PERFORMANCE BY PEOPLE WITH SPECIAL NEEDS.

NEW ROSS MILLENNIUM COMMITTEE: NEW YEARS EVE/DAY CELEBRATIONS.

CHILDCARE NETWORK NEW ROSS: EXHIBITION FEATURING MATERIAL CONTRIBUTED FROM ALL CHILDCARE FACILITIES IN THE COUNTY.

GUSSERAN CHURCH, GUSSERAN, NEW ROSS: COMMUNITY LAUNCH OF RENOVATED CHURCH HALL. FIRST PEAL OF REPAIRED CHURCH BELL.

RAHEEN YOUTH CLUB. RAHEEN, CLONROCH: YOUTH CLUB MEMBERS PHOTOGRAPHIC RECORD OF MIDSUMMER'S DAY 2000. FOR 'DAY IN THE LIFE OF RAHEEN' EXHIBITION.

HOOK PRODUCTIONS COMMITTEE:, CHRISTCHURCH PLACE, DUBLIN: LAUNCH OF FILM "POSTER'S GATE" WHICH TELLS OF THE ROLE OF HOOK LIGHTHOUSE WITHIN SOCIETY, FROM MANNED OPERATION TO AUTOMATED.

CHERNOBYL CHILDREN'S PROJECT. NEW ROSS: "BLACK WIND/WHITE LAND", A TRAVELLING EXHIBITION, IN WHICH ARTISTS EXPRESS THEIR RESPONSES TO NUCLEAR ENERGY.

NEW ROSS PARISH: MILLENNIUM CELEBRATION, INCLUDING CANDELABRA BLESSING AND MILLENNIUM MOSAIC YOUTH PROJECT.

RAHEEN PARISH: MILLENNIUM TIME TRAIL.

WEXFORD MILLENNIUM STORYTELLING FESTIVAL, BUNCLODY: MILLENNIUM STORYTELLING FESTIVAL.

ENNISCORTHY MILLENNIUM COMMITTEE: MILLENNIUM WELCOME CEREMONY.

BUNCLODY FLOWER FESTIVAL: ECUMENICAL FLOWER FESTIVAL BASED IN THE LOCAL CATHOLIC AND CHURCH OF IRELAND CHURCHES.

BUNCLODY PARISH COUNCIL: JUBILEE 2000 CELEBRATION; A YEAR OF EVENTS INCLUDING DEDICATION OF JUBILEE ROCKERY. WAY OF THE CROSS FOR ALL CHRISTIANS.

ACE - A CULTURAL EXPERIENCE ENNISCORTHY: STREET THEATRE FESTIVAL AND FIRE SCULPTURE.

COURTNACUDDY MILLENNIUM NATURE TRAIL PROJECT: OPENING OF MILLENNIUM NATURE TRAIL.

ST. SENAN'S PRIMARY SCHOOL, TEMPLESHANNON: ENNISCORTHY PRIMARY SCHOOLS MILLENNIUM DAY - A JOINT PROJECT INVOLVING FIVE TOWN PRIMARY SCHOOLS.

SCREEN PARENTS ASSOCIATION: SCREEN MILLENNIUM MURAL; COMMUNITY ARTIST WORKING WITH CHILDREN AND PARENTS IN PLANNING, DEVISING AND CREATING A MURAL.

FR. JIM FINN. YOUTH MINISTRY, COURTNACUDDY, ENNISCORTHY: CREATIVE CELTIC INITIATIVE IN

WHICH YOUNG PEOPLE RESTORE PLACES OF CELTIC SIGNIFICANCE AND THROUGH THIS WILL RESTORE A PERSONAL SENSE OF THEIR OWN HERITAGE.

ADAMSTOWN SHOW SOCIETY, ADAMSTOWN: ADAMSTOWN SHOW, A COMMEMORATION AND CELEBRATION OF RURAL TRADITIONS.

FR. WILLIAM COSGRAVE. MONAGEER PARISH COMMITTEE: MILLENNIUM PHOTOGRAPHIC EXHIBITIONS OF LOCAL ORGANISATIONS, FAMILIES, INDIVIDUALS, CLASSES AND GROUPS.

RATHNURE PANTOMIME SOCIETY. MASTERPIECE OF MILLENNIUM 2000, A COMMUNITY ORGANISED CELEBRATION OF MUSIC PAGEANTRY AND COMEDY.

BOOLAVOGUE COMMUNITY TAPESTRY GROUP: TAPESTRY EXHIBITION.

CO. WICKLOW
MILLENNIUM OFFICER: SEAMUS WALKER

MILLENNIUM FISHERY FOLK FESTIVAL, ARKLOW : A WEEKEND OF FESTIVITIES, HISTORICAL AND CULTURAL EVENTS FOR CHILDREN, YOUTHS AND ADULTS.

GREYSTONES TIDY TOWNS COMMITTEE: A WINTER GARDEN AND WALKWAY TO CELEBRATE THE MILLENNIUM IN AN INNOVATIVE AND ENVI-RONMENTALLY SUSTAINABLE WAY.

WICKLOW YOUTH THEATRE: EASTER COMMUNITY ARTS PROGRAMME, SERIES OF DRAMA AND MUSIC WORKSHOPS CULMINATING IN A FESTIVE STREET PAGEANT.

ARKLOW TOURIST AND HERITAGE ASSOCIATION: MILLENNIUM MARITIME NIGHT ACKNOWLEDGING THE MARITIME MUSEUM'S LONG STANDING IN THE COMMUNITY.

WICKLOW UILLEAN PIPES FESTIVAL: MEMORIAL WEEKEND TRIBUTE TO ONE OF THE BEST PIPERS OF THE CENTURY/ MILLENNIUM - JOHNNY DORAN.

AVONMORE MUSICAL SOCIETY, ARKLOW: LAUNCH OF BOOK TO CELEBRATE 21 YEARS OF THE AVONMORE MUSICAL SOCIETY, AND MILLENNIUM SUMMER SHOW.

ST. JOSEPH'S NATIONAL SCHOOL, GLENEALY : CLOS NA MÍLAOISÉ, A SEATING AREA, SUITABLY PLANTED FLORAL DISPLAY AND A MILLENNIUM CAPSULE.

THE LA TOUCHE LEGACY COMMITTEE, GREYSTONES: A 64 PAGE MAGAZINE TO CELEBRATE GREYSTONES IN 2000.

BRAY CHORAL SOCIETY: MAJOR CHORAL WORK - VERDI'S REQUIEM - PERFORMED BY CHORAL GROUPS FROM THROUGHOUT CO. WICKLOW.

WICKLOW RETAIL AND BUSINESS ASSOCIATION: A SPECIAL MILLENNIUM CHRISTMAS PARADE WITH FESTIVE LIGHTING, STREET PARTY AND FESTIVAL INCORPORATING THE WICKLOW YOUTH THEATRE.

LEINSTER MOTOR CLUB, WICKLOW: MILLENNIUM CELEBRATION SPRINT TO INCLUDE TWO SEPARATE SPRINT EVENTS FOR CARS.

WICKLOW REGATTA COMMITTEE: MILLENNIUM CONCERT AS PART OF THE REGATTA.

EDDIE FITZGERALD, ARKLOW: MILLENNIUM BOOKLET ON THE ARTWORK OF THE PEOPLE, BUILDINGS AND STREETS OF ARKLOW.

ST. COLMAN'S MILLENNIUM COMMITTEE, RATHDRUM: MILLENNIUM SENSORY GARDEN WITHIN THE HOSPITAL GROUNDS WHERE RESIDENTS CAN ACCESS IT FROM GROUND FLOOR ROOMS.

COMMUNITY OF DONARD: TWO MILLENNIUM COMMEMORATIVE SITES REMEMBERING THE FOUR PRIME ACTIVITIES IN THE AREA OVER THE LAST 100 YEARS – SHEEP FARMING, TIMBER INDUSTRY, HILL WALKING AND THE ARMY PRESENCE.

WICKLOW ST. PATRICK'S DAY PARADE COMMITTEE: SPECIAL MILLENNIUM PARADE WITH EMPHASIS ON THE MILLENNIUM CELEBRATIONS.

STRATFORD ON SLANEY MILLENNIUM PILGRIMAGE COMM.: PILGRIMAGE FROM SITE OF OLD R.C. CHURCH, STRATFORD ALONG 2KM ROUTE TO OLD CEMETERY AT RATHBRAN.

ARKLOW ROWING CLUB: THE ARKLOW MILLENNIUM WALL -A PERMANENT EXHIBITION OF ART PHOTOS.

BALTINGLASS GAA CLUB:TERRACING WITH PERMANENT FLORAL DISPLAY, AND MUSICAL RECITAL.

THE OSCAR WILDE AUTUMN SCHOOL: CREATIVE WRITING WORKSHOPS IN BRAY AND WICKLOW PRIMARY SCHOOLS.

ARKLOW TIDY TOWNS COMMITTEE: MILLENNIUM PEACE PARK WITH PLANTING TO REFLECT PEACE AND RECONCILIATION.

ROUNDWOOD AND DISTRICT HISTORICAL AND FOLKLORE SOC.: PUBLICATION OF THE 1838 ORDNANCE SURVEY LETTERS FOR WICKLOW RECORD AVAILABLE TO ARCHAEOLOGISTS, HISTORIANS AND THE GENERAL PUBLIC.

BRAY CHURCHES TOGETHER WEEK: A CALENDAR OF EVENTS, SPREAD THROUGHOUT THE YEAR, INVOLVING ALL THE CHURCHES IN BRAY.

EVENT WICKLOW 2000: A CALENDAR OF EVENTS FOR LOCAL SCHOOL CHILDREN INCLUDING

POETRY, ARTS, POSTER AND ESSAY COMPETITIONS.

ST. BENEDICT'S A.C., ARKLOW: MILLENNIUM STAR AWARDS TO ONE PERSON FROM EACH OF THE 32 COUNTIES UNDER 18 YEARS FOR ATHLETIC ACHIEVEMENTS.

GREYSTONES SUMMER ARTS FESTIVAL: INTERNATIONAL NIGHT WITH MUSICIANS, DANCERS AND PERFORMERS FROM DIFFERENT COUNTRIES.

SCULPTURE IN THE WOODLAND: A MAJOR MILLENNIUM CELEBRATION IN THE DEVIL'S GLEN TO MARK THE RESTORATION OF IRISH FORESTS.

ARKLOW AND DISTRICT MILLENNIUM AWARDS COMMITTEE: COMMUNITY EVENT AND AWARDS TO HONOUR THE CONTRIBUTIONS OF INDIVIDUALS AND GROUPS TO THE DEVELOPMENT OF ARKLOW AND ITS SURROUNDING AREA.

CHARABANC AND ENNISKERRY CARING RESOURCE: THE CHARABANC MINIBUS AND SOCIAL CLUB IDENTIFIED BY THE COMMUNITY AS THE FIRST MAJOR JOINT PARISHES MILLENNIUM PROJECT.

KNOCKANANNA TIDY TOWNS COMMITTEE: RELOCATE EXISTING CROSS, LANDSCAPE THE AREA AND PROVIDE A WATER FOUNTAIN.

GREYSTONES YOUTH ORCHESTRA: MILLENNIUM FESTIVAL OF NEW MUSIC AROUND THE COUNTY.

HALF MOON SWIMMING CLUB, BRAY: THE P.J. KILMARTIN MEMORIAL RACES FOM BRAY HARBOUR TO BRAY HEAD HOTEL.

SELECT VESTRY CHRIST CHURCH BRAY: CHURCHES TOGETHER SERVICE FOLLOWED BY A FULL EIGHT BELL PEAL. AT MIDNIGHT ILLUMINATION OF SPIRE.

BRAY TOASTMASTERS CLUB: MILLENNIUM CELEBRATION EVENING OF TEN SPEECHES, EACH FOCUSING ON ONE OF THE CENTURIES OF THE LAST MILLENNIUM.

SIAMSA FHÉILE PÁDRAIG, GREYSTONES: MILLENNIUM 2000, A CELEBRATION OF TRADITIONAL IRISH MUSIC, SONG AND DANCE.

RATHDOWN PARK RESIDENTS ASSOCIATION LTD.: MILLENNIUM BARBECUE, SPORTS AND FUN DAY.

GREYSTONES CANCER SUPPORT: MILLENNIUM REMEMBRANCE OF ALL THOSE WHO WERE MEMBERS OF THE GROUP SINCE IT WAS FORMED IN 1994 THAT HAVE PASSED AWAY.

BALTINGLASS TIDY TOWNS: A MILLENNIUM PARK FOR THE TOWN.

FOROIGE CLUB, NEWCASTLE: HISTORICAL TALK, PAGEANT AND CEREMONIAL LIGHTING OF

CANDLES AS PART OF LAST LIGHT OF THE MILLENNIUM.

EAST GLENDALOUGH SCHOOL MILLENNIUM PROJECT: MILLENNIUM LINK TO SCHOOL IN SOUTH AFRICA WITH £10,000 WORTH OF EQUIPMENT. EVENING OF WORLD MUSIC PERFORMED BY THE PUPILS.

CARNEW COMMUNITY CARE: RECEPTION TO RECOGNISE THE CONTRIBUTION OF SENIOR CITIZENS.

IRISH WHEELCHAIR ASSOCIATION, ARKLOW: SPECIAL RECOGNITION AWARDS.

ARKLOW BOXING CLUB: MILLENNIUM BOXING TOURNAMENT WITH CONTESTANTS FROM ENGLAND, WALES AND LOCAL CLUBS.

KILAVENEY MILLENNIUM COMMITTEE, TINAHEALY: MANUSCRIPT BASED ON THE DOOMSDAY BOOK WHICH WILL RECORD FOR FUTURE GENERATIONS WHO WE ARE, OUR BELIEFS AND HOW WE LIVE.

CINE ART 2000, BRAY: PROVIDE A PLATFORM FOR YOUNG FILMMAKERS TO MEET AND TRAIN WITH LEADING INDUSTRY PROFESSIONALS.

WICKLOW ARTS OFFICE: AN ARTISTIC FEATURE AT COUNTY BUILDINGS WICKLOW TO CELEBRATE THE MILLENNIUM AND THE CENTENARY OF WICKLOW CO. COUNCIL.